CITIZENSHIP AND T
SERIES

General Editor
ROBERT BLACKBURN
Professor of Constitutional Law
King's College, University of London

Other titles in this series

CROWN POWERS, SUBJECTS AND CITIZENS

CHRISTOPHER VINCENZI

PINTER
London and Washington

First published 1998 by
Pinter, A Cassell Imprint
Wellington House, 125 Strand, London WC2R 0BB
PO Box 605, Herndon, Virginia 20172–0605

© *Christopher Vincenzi 1998*

British Library Cataloguing in Publication Data

A catalogue record for this book is available from the British Library
ISBN 1–85567–454–8 *(hb)*   1–85567–539–0 *(pb)*

Library of Congress Cataloging-in-Publication Data

Vincenzi, Christopher.
   Crown powers subjects and citizens/Christopher Vincenzi.
       p.   cm.—(Citizenship and the law)
   Includes bibliographical references and index.
   ISBN 1–85567–454–8 *(hc)*
       1. Prerogative, Royal—Great Britain.   I. Title.   II. Series:
   Citizenship and the law series.
   KD4435.V56 1998
   342.41'083—dc21
                                                                97–20138
                                                                CIP

Typeset by BookEns Ltd, Royston, Herts.
Printed and bound in Great Britain by Bookcraft (Bath) Ltd.

Contents

Preface

The residual powers and immunities of the Crown remain one of the most obscure areas of English public law. No one, since Joseph Chitty in 1820, has attempted an exhaustive examination, and this book does not pretend to be one. Some of the more esoteric powers of the monarch and her ministers are, in any event, of interest only to the most dedicated legal historian or constitutional specialist. However, research in the area of immigration, nationality and citizenship, commencing with work for my doctoral thesis over twenty years ago, has convinced me that the royal prerogative and the immunities enjoyed by the Crown, as interpreted and reinterpreted in the jurisprudence of the courts, play an important and much underestimated role in the way that the rights and liberties of both citizens and non-citizens are exercised. Ministers draw on prerogative powers in a way that would surprise public lawyers working within the constraints of a written constitution. A discussion about the nature and scope of these powers and how they affect such basic rights and liberties as the right of free movement of people, access to public information, political expression, accountability and involvement in the political process seems particularly apposite in the context of a developing European citizenship and renewed consideration of fundamental rights in a reformed British constitution. Much the greatest part of this book was written before the General Election of May 1997. Details of the Human Rights Bill, incorporating the European Convention, were only available shortly before proof stage, so that the extent to which I have been able to take its likely effects into account has, necessarily, been limited.

I am indebted to the University of Huddersfield, the Institute of Advanced Legal Studies at the University of London, the Federal Trust for Education and Research and the Economic and Social Research Council for their support in research projects on the content of European citizenship rights and on their implementation in the United Kingdom. Some of the ideas considered in this book I have discussed with colleagues involved in a programme on the implementation of European Community Law sponsored by ESRC in 1992–94 and coordinated by Professor Terence Daintith of the Institute of Advanced Legal Studies. Most of the material used has, however, been written outside the context of those projects and any errors, of course, remain my own. I have not pursued some of the more technical points of English public law because I hope that the text will be accessible to non-lawyers. The reform of the constitution and the rights of all people who live and work in this country, or seek its shelter from persecution, are matters which are too important to be left to lawyers.

I am very grateful to Veronica Higgs of Cassell Academic and Robert Blackburn, the Series Editor, for their help and advice and for their comments on the text. Most of all I have benefited from the support of Ruth Vincenzi, with whom I have discussed much of the material in the book. Without the stimulus of those discussions and her unfailing encouragement, and that of Simon, Dominic and Rebecca, it would not have been completed.

Christopher Vincenzi
November 1997

1

Prerogative Powers and the Constitution

The power of King, Lords and Commons is not an arbitrary power. They are
the trustees, not the owners of the estate. The fee simple is in us.

Dedication, *Letters of Junius, 1767–1772*[1]

INTRODUCTION

Constitutions are about power and who has it. The unique feature of
the British constitution is that those who appear to have it do not.
The Queen, who is head of the executive, has very little executive
power, and Parliament, to which the executive is meant to be
accountable, is, in practice, controlled by it. The Cabinet, which is
the body that makes most of the important political decisions, does
not exist as far as constitutional law is concerned. Although the
Queen has little political power, her position and influence largely
derive from the fact that she is the head of state and that she and her
family have, traditionally, enjoyed the respect and affection of the
public.

The Queen's position was well described by Bagehot in 1867:

A *family* on the throne is an interesting idea ... It brings down
the pride of sovereignty to the level of petty life. No feeling
could seem more childish than the enthusiasm of the English at
the marriage of the Prince of Wales ... A princely marriage is a
brilliant edition of a universal fact, and as such it rivets
mankind.[2]

A princely divorce can, however, be as damaging to the family
concept of monarchy as a marriage can be beneficial, as George IV
found to his cost, and as the Queen has recently discovered. Much of
her traditional influence as the nominal source of authority remains,
however, and it confers a kind of legitimacy on those who exercise
power in her name.

A striking consequence of Britain's lack of a formal, written constitution is the extent to which government ministers are dependent on traditional powers which they have inherited from the time when Britain was an absolute monarchy. Those powers are collectively called 'the royal prerogative'. Despite their antiquity, they provide the legal authority for activities which are modern enough. In the name of the Crown, ministers appoint judges and civil servants, wage war and make peace, promote and dismiss members of the armed forces and civil service, prosecute and pardon offenders, negotiate treaties and approve European Union legislation in the Council of Ministers, issue (and deny) passports to British citizens, enjoy immunity from statutes (unless the Crown is expressly or impliedly referred to) and generally conduct all those processes of government for which Parliament has not provided by specific statutory authorization.

During a period in which, despite a public commitment to the rolling back of the frontiers of the state, government became increasingly powerful, these vague and ill-defined powers sat uncomfortably with modern notions of legal certainty, political accountability and the rule of law. They are, however, essential to the proper working of any government. The problem for liberal democracies is how to define them in such a way as to enable governments to have sufficient discretion to be able to govern effectively, while at the same time providing essential safeguards to prevent abuse. In written constitutions this is done, typically, in two ways: first, by defining as specifically as possible the powers of the primary institutional components of executive, legislature and judiciary; second, by providing a catalogue of basic rights which must be respected by the institutions of government. Neither of these systems of constitutional protection is fully reflected in Britain's unwritten constitution. The duties and powers of Britain's major institutions are largely undefined, and the concept of rights in the common law is so narrow that it affords little protection against many abuses of power.[3] The definition of the boundaries of institutional power and the protection of individual rights is left to custom, convention, ministerial accountability to Parliament and judicial review by the courts. There is now a widely held view that government by traditional prerogative powers, and the protection of basic rights by statutes which are vulnerable to change by the smallest majority in the House of Commons, or even to the inadvertence of a Parliamentary draughtsman, are not acceptable in a state that aspires to be an advanced democracy. The development of a modern concept of citizenship, with citizens playing an active part in the decision-making processes of the administration, is impossible 'if the

State is genetically programmed to view the business of governance as the exercise of sovereignty, and the duty of the governed to obey'.[4] That is, undoubtedly, the tradition of which we are the heirs and of which the prerogative powers, rights and immunities of the Crown form part. As Joseph Chitty, the author of the only authoritative text devoted solely to the subject, *The Law of the Prerogatives of the Crown*, published in 1820, observed,

> In every community, it is highly important that the greatest reverence towards the sovereign should be instilled into the minds of the governed, – unattended by respect, authority speedily diminishes; and without a due share of authority, it would be impossible for the King to enforce respect to the laws; on the observance of which depends the happiness and security of his subjects.[5]

An expectation of deference to be shown by subjects to their sovereign is hardly appropriate to the relationship between citizens and their elected government. It persists, however, in the belief of some senior civil servants and politicians that many of the processes of government are a mystery that should not be exposed to the public view. It is no coincidence that the areas of government policy which are most impervious to parliamentary questions and most resistant to effective judicial review are those in which the authority for ministerial action is derived from the royal prerogative.[6] Policies relating to defence and foreign affairs are sensitive matters in any country. But there are few industrialized Western societies in which there is so little openness and accountability in these areas. Both figured prominently in the Scott Inquiry, which condemned the secrecy and evasion about changes in policy relating to the sales of arms and defence-related equipment to Iraq:

> A denial of information to the public denies the public the ability to make an informed judgment on the Government's record. A failure by Ministers to meet the obligations of Ministerial accountability by providing information about the activities of their departments undermines, in my opinion, the democratic process.[7]

Suggestions for constitutional reform abound. Some are partial, such as those espoused by the Labour government and the Liberal Democrats. These involve such changes as the devolution of some legislative power to Scotland and Wales, or the reform of the composition of the House of Lords, the system of voting in general elections, the enactment of legislation to provide access to information or the incorporation of the European Convention on

Human Rights. Scottish and Welsh devolution and the incorporation of the Covention are already under way. Other proposals, like those of Tony Benn in *Common Sense: a New Constitution for Britain* and the Institute for Public Policy Research (IPPR) in *A Written Constitution for the United Kingdom*,[8] envisage a wholly reformed constitutional structure.

Before we embark on a course of major constitutional reform, however, it is important to be clear on the point from which we begin. This is especially the case in relation to the powers and immunities of the Crown. The last major statutory excursion into this area, the Crown Proceedings Act 1947, was intended to place the Crown (but not the monarch personally) on the same footing as ordinary individuals in civil proceedings in contract and tort. It did not attempt to define the powers of the Crown under the prerogative, or the extent to which the Crown was to remain immune from legislation. It simply declared that the prerogative powers were unaffected and 'retained' the statutory immunity of the Crown, even though the extent of that immunity was hotly disputed. It is likely, in fact, that this provision actually conferred *greater* immunity on the Crown than it had previously enjoyed.[9] A similar reservation in section 33(5) of the Immigration Act 1971, retaining the prerogatives of the Crown 'in relation to aliens', in all probability limited to *enemy* aliens, has now become, through a process of judicial misinterpretation, an overriding prerogative of immigration control exercisable by the Home Secretary over *all* foreign nationals and Commonwealth citizens, or at least all non-Commonwealth foreign nationals[10] (see Chapter 4). The IPPR constitution no longer relies on the prerogative as a source of executive power, although it is not expressly abolished. The Benn constitution, though more radical in purpose, repeats the errors of the Glorious Bloodless Revolution of 1688 by transferring all existing prerogative powers to a new republic.

A reluctance to confront such constitutional fundamentals is not, regrettably, a novel characteristic of the legislature or of common lawyers. During the impeachment of the Earl of Strafford in 1640 on a charge of subverting the fundamental laws of the United Kingdom,

> The Commons were just about to vote the charge when the witty and malicious Edmund Waller rose, and with seeming innocence, asked what the fundamental laws of the United Kingdom were. There was an uneasy silence. No-one dared to attempt a definition, which would certainly have divided the heterogeneous majority ... The situation was saved only by a lawyer who leapt to his feet to say that if Mr Waller did not

know what the fundamental laws of the kingdom were, he had no business to be sitting in the House.[11]

A similar reluctance is demonstrated by the Bill of Rights of 1688, which abolished two prerogative powers (the maintenance of a standing army and the power to suspend Acts of Parliament) and curtailed another (the power to dispense with laws or their execution 'as it hath been assumed and exercised of late'), but was otherwise simply declaratory of the limits of Crown powers in the most general terms. The constitutional settlement of 1688/9 was, essentially, a fudge. The joint monarchs, William and Mary, who had been invited to replace James II and his absolutist aspirations, inherited 'a panoply of legal powers as ample as that borne by their two immediate predecessors'.[12] The Whigs, who would have liked to grasp the opportunity of imposing new checks on royal authority, had to work with Tories who had no such object. The exercise of those powers had, however, passed to the political factions who had invited William and Mary to the throne. What the powers were, and how they could be used, remained to be tested in the courts by the Whigs, who took control of the machinery of government and retained it for the next sixty years. In this process the judges were guided partly by the traditional pragmatism of the common law and partly by the new political philosophy of John Locke, which exerted a powerful effect upon the thinking of Whig judges.[13] There was no comprehensive attempt to address the scope of the remaining prerogative powers in the eighteenth or nineteenth centuries, although the shape and extent of the major powers became clearer through judicial decision-making, limitations imposed by statute and the conventions that accreted around their use.

A reforming House of Commons in the late twentieth century will need more courage, not least because, at common law, prerogative powers do not fade away through non-use, and may revive when a statute removing or curtailing them is repealed. Any major constitutional changes will need to take account of that resilience and deal comprehensively with its consequences. The object of this book is to attempt to identify what remain of the traditional prerogative powers, rights, duties, privileges and immunities of the Crown, and to discuss the ways in which the courts have defined and, in some cases, reinterpreted them in a modern context. In this process, account will have to be taken of relevant legislation, and the rights enjoyed by individuals under the law of the European Union and under the European Convention on Human Rights. Before doing so, it is necessary to deal with the ambiguous terminology which our evolving constitution has bequeathed to us. At the centre of that ambiguity is 'the Crown'.

THE CROWN

'The Crown', the historian Maitland once famously declared, 'does nothing but lie in the Tower of London to be gazed at by sight-seers.'[14] The term has, however, provided a useful shorthand for 'central government' and will continue to be used it in that way. The courts have recently endeavoured to clear away some of the obfuscation which governments have sometimes thrown around their activities by the use of the term, often to protect them from proper accountability to Parliament or effective judicial review. In considering the powers of the Board under the original, non-statutory Criminal Injuries Compensation Scheme, the Court of Appeal in R. v. Criminal Injuries Compensation Board ex p. P in 1995 referred to the power of the Crown to grant 'pardons to condemned criminals . . . and bounty from money made available to the executive government by Parliament'.[15]

> The phrase 'distribution of bounty by the Crown', or by the government on behalf of the Crown, has an archaic flavour which prompts what Diplock LJ called 'nostalgic echoes of Maundy Thursday' (see R. v. Criminal Injuries Compensation Board ex p. Lain [1967] 2 QB 864 at 888). That particular ceremony must be regarded, however, as an act of the 'Crown as monarch' (see M v. Home Office [1994] 1 AC 377 at 395 per Lord Templeman). The present case is concerned with the 'Crown as executive', the royal prerogative of mercy being similar (see Ex p. Bentley [1994] QB 349 at 360, citing Lord Denning MR in Hanratty v. Butler (1971) 115 SJ 386).

Rather than refer to 'the Crown as monarch' or 'the Crown as executive' in this book, it will be simpler to use the expressions 'the monarch' in the first instance and 'the Crown' in the second. An examination will be made in Chapter 3 of the prerogative powers which remain with the monarch. The subsequent chapters will deal with the exercise by ministers of governmental functions based on the prerogative. There will be a more detailed examination of the nature and extent of the 'Crown as executive' in relation to its immunity from statute and its civil and criminal liability. It will, however, first be necessary to attempt a definition of 'the royal prerogative'.

PREROGATIVE OR PREROGATIVES?

Where there is no statutory provision, prerogative powers remain the legal basis for all executive action. Before examining specific aspects of their application, we need to consider the political philosophies which have shaped judicial decisions on the nature of prerogative powers. These are far from coherent, and some of those which appear to coexist are irreconcilable. The choice of the singular or plural in this context is not a mere semantic exercise but raises very important questions about the nature and origins of prerogative powers. Is there a residual executive power called 'the prerogative', of which the various recognized government activities which are based upon it are merely aspects, or are there a finite number of prerogative or related powers and immunities which, although subject to reinterpretation by the courts, cannot be extended or supplemented?

The question is not merely academic, as Croom-Johnston LJ suggested in the Court of Appeal in *R. v. Secretary of State for the Home Department ex parte Northumbria Police Authority*,[16] but fundamental, because under our common law constitution, every act of government must have its basis in a rule of law. This may be a provision of a statute or a custom which has been recognized by a decision of the courts. Any other act carried out by a minister or civil servant will be unlawful if it adversely affects individual rights or interests. If there is a general power to act for the public good, of which the recognized prerogatives are but part, then the scope for lawful action by the Crown will be immeasurably greater. The courts, in interpreting prerogative powers, have demonstrated a reluctance to accept new powers which adversely affect existing rights. The scope of the Crown to engage in other activities which do *not* affect individual rights and interests (as narrowly interpreted by the common law) emerges much less clearly from their decisions.

By the eighteenth century, it had become generally accepted that the nature and scope of prerogative powers and the immunities, rights and privileges of the Crown were to be determined by the ordinary courts. This remains the case today. The position with regard to the prerogative had been laid down by the Lord Chief Justice, Sir Edward Coke, at the beginning of the seventeenth century, when he had declared: 'The King hath no prerogative but that which the law of the land allows him.'[17] It took the abolition of the Star Chamber by Parliament in 1641, a civil war and a revolution for it to be unequivocally accepted by the Crown. There are two principal authoritative statements on prerogative powers which are frequently cited by the courts when their nature and extent is under discussion. Neither throws a great deal of light on what they attempt to define, but both say much about the essentially political nature of the exercise and of the values of the two proponents, William Blackstone and Albert Dicey.

Blackstone's definition is not the first, but it is the first which attempts a comprehensive description of the powers, immunities and duties of the Crown after the revolutionary changes of the preceding century.[18] Blackstone declares:

> By the word prerogative, we usually understand that special pre-eminence, which the King hath, over and above all other persons, and out of the ordinary course of the common law, in right of his regal dignity. And hence it follows, that it must be in its nature singular and eccentrical; that it can only be applied to those rights and capacities which the King enjoys alone, in contradistinction to others and not which he enjoys in common with any of his subjects; for once any one prerogative of the Crown could be held in common with the subject, it would cease to be prerogative any longer. And therefore Finch lays down as a maxim, that the prerogative is that law in the case of the King, which is law in no case of the subject.[19]

Besides the disparate, specific, prerogatives which custom and common law had conferred exclusively upon the king, Blackstone asserted that the king also had a power of a more general kind, described by Lord Denning in *Laker Airways Ltd* v. *Department of Trade* in 1977: 'The prerogative is a discretionary power exercisable by the executive government for the public good, in certain spheres of governmental activity for which the law has made no provision.'[20] The language used by Blackstone to describe this residual power is remarkably similar to that of Locke in his *Second Treatise on Government*.[21] 'Many things there are, which law can by no means provide for, and those must necessarily be left to the discretion of him, that has the Executive Power in his hands, to be ordered by him as the public good and advantage shall require.'

It is, however, clear that the prerogative envisaged by Locke is that which is necessary in an emergency when the legislature is not sitting, even to the extent of doing what the law has prohibited, as, for example, 'to pull down an innocent Man's House to stop the Fire, when the next to it is burning'. Locke does not appear to be contemplating a general executive discretion to act in any circumstances where the law supplies no authority, including, it would seem, no hitherto recognized prerogative power. This is what Blackstone (and, possibly, Lord Denning MR in the *Laker* case above) appeared to have had in mind, and it is not so far removed from the position claimed for the monarch by the absolutists of the seventeenth century. Writing during the reign of Charles I, Sir Henry Finch declared that 'the king hath a prerogative in all things that are not injurious to the subject, but the king's prerogative stretcheth not to the doing of any wrong'.[22]

In relation to the exercise of the prerogative powers, Blackstone added that 'the king is irresistable and absolute'. In relation to the treaty-making power of the king he asserted that 'no other power in the kingdom can legally delay, resist or annul' it.[23] Again, that overstates the case. As we shall see, it is always open to Parliament to abolish or limit a prerogative power, and for the courts to see whether the Crown has acted within its prerogative. In describing the use of prerogative powers in this way, Blackstone was, Lord Roskill declared in 1985 in the GCHQ case, 'harking back to what Lord Atkin once called ... the clanking of medieval chains of ghosts of the past'.[24] Dicey, too, rejected Blackstone's approach and accused him of 'applying old and inapplicable terms to new institutions, and especially of ascribing in words to a modern and constitutional King the whole, and perhaps more than the whole, of the powers actually possessed and exercised by William the Conqueror'.[25] Dicey's criticism is undoubtedly well founded. Blackstone's principal error was in describing the prerogative powers as though they remained exercisable by the king *personally*, and not through his ministers. He was a Tory and appears to have believed that the king *should* govern in this way. Hunt relates that the young George III was given a copy of Blackstone's *Commentaries* before they were first published in 1765 because they 'magnified ... the royal authority' and offered him an alternative to government by the Whig oligarchy.[26] George followed the advice of his mother to 'Be a King, George!', and to rule as well as to reign, with such enthusiasm, and with such disastrous results, that the American colonists who declared their independence in 1776 appear to have held him personally responsible for all the ills which they had suffered at the hands of the British.[27]

Blackstone's belief that the King had a general, residual prerogative of 'acting for the public good where the positive laws are silent' does not sit comfortably with *Entick* v. *Carrington*, one of the most important cases of British constitutional law, and decided in 1765, the same year as the first publication of Blackstone's *Commentaries*.[28] The defendants in this case were King's Messengers. They had forcibly entered the house of John Entick to conduct a search. Entick was the printer of a newspaper, *The Monitor or British Freeholder*, which had published a number of articles by John Wilkes that were both highly inflammatory and critical of the government. The search was conducted under a general warrant, in the hope that incriminating evidence of sedition or some such offence by Wilkes or Entick might be discovered. None was found, and Entick sued for trespass. The court held that such general warrants, which did not specify the suspected offence or the suspected offender, were illegal. The defendants tried to justify their actions on the basis that such warrants had long been used. Lord Camden dismissed the defence with some asperity. Having described the breadth of the power which was claimed, he said:

> Such is the power, and therefore one should naturally expect that the law to warrant it should be clear in proportion as the power is exorbitant. If it is law, it will be found in our books. If it is not to be found there, it is not law ... The great end, for which men entered into society was to secure their property. That right is preserved sacred and incommunicable in all instances, where it has not been taken away or abridged by some public law for the good of the whole ... By the laws of England, every invasion of private property, be it ever so minute, is a trespass. No man can set his foot upon my ground without my licence ... If he admits the fact, he is bound to show by way of justification, that some positive law has empowered or excused him.

The defendants also argued that they were justified in their action by 'State necessity'. That argument was dismissed even more forcefully by Lord Camden: 'And with respect to the argument of State necessity, or a distinction that has been aimed at between State offences and others, the common law does not understand that kind of reasoning, nor do our books take notice of any such distinctions.'

That refusal to recognize any general right of officers of state or police officers to enter a person's property without the specific authority of common law or statute has, until recently, at least, been maintained by the courts. In the absence of such authority, no directions from a minister to a departmental officer to enter could make such an entry lawful. The position is now less certain following *R v. Khan (Sultan)*.[29] In this case, police officers entered, without a warrant, on to private property to attach a bugging device. The object was to secure evidence against an alleged drug dealer. The case was primarily concerned with the admissibility of evidence obtained in this way, but the issue of the legality, or otherwise, of the officers' entry was a relevant consideration in the decision on admissibility. The Court was satisfied that the evidence could be admitted:

> We would emphasise, in particular, the fact that in proceeding as they did the police were, so far from acting in an arbitrary or uncontrolled manner, proceeding in accordance with the

relevant Home Office guidelines. True it is that these do not have statutory authority: but they have been publicized, at least to the extent of being placed in the library of the House of Commons, as the Parliamentary answer that we have cited shows, and plainly regulated and defined the conduct of the police officers.[30]

Although there has been a serious increase in drug-related crime, such a radical departure from the principles of the *Entick* case, which is regarded as one of the principal bases of the rule of law, is extraordinary. It has attracted some criticism.[31] Although the court does not go as far as accepting the entry as lawful, and refers to it as a 'trespass', the impression is conveyed of a 'permissible' trespass. Legal authority has never, hitherto, derived from an answer to a parliamentary question, still less from the deposit of 'guidelines' in the House of Commons Library. Indeed, it is nearly a century since Parliament was obliged to pass legislation to enable the resolution of the Commons approving the Chancellor's Budget speech to provide legal authority for the tax changes made by it.[32] It is true that it is the practice of the Home Office to announce changes in the application and interpretation of the Immigration Rules in response to questions in the House, but this is, ordinarily, in relation to the exercise of powers conferred on the Home Secretary and immigration officers by the Immigration Act 1971, and indicates how they will be used in specific cases. Such statements cannot *confer* legal authority on anyone to do anything. The *Khan* decision seems somewhat at odds with a recent decision of the Privy Council involving an appeal against conviction of a defendant accused of drug trafficking with another person, who turned out to be an undercover police officer.[33] The case turned on whether or not the undercover officer could be guilty of an offence which he had been 'authorized' to commit. The Privy Council held that he could, because the 'authorization' would not constitute a defence. Lord Griffith quoted with approval Gibbs CJ of the High Court of Australia in *A* v. *Hayden (No. 2)* (1984) 156 CLR 532: ' "It is fundamental to our legal system that the executive has no power to authorise a breach of the law and that it is no excuse for an offender to say that he acted under the orders of a superior officer." This statement of the law applies with the same force in England and Hong Kong as it does in Australia.'

Although that decision involved a purported authorization of a breach of the criminal law, the principle seems no less applicable to the authorization of a civil wrong. It would still, therefore, seem safe to say that governments have no general power to disregard the rights of individuals which are protected by the criminal or civil law. It

11

remained unclear following *Entick* v. *Carrington* whether acts of the government which were not specifically authorized by common law were only unlawful if they interfered directly with an existing personal or proprietorial right. Lord Camden evidently thought so, for the following year he advised the government that it could, without legislation, prohibit the export of wheat by proclamation. This advice was almost universally condemned, and the government was forced to secure the passage of an Act of Indemnity to protect officers who had taken steps to enforce it.[34] A similar view prevailed with regard to any general powers involving interference with the liberty of the person. Although there was seventeenth-century authority supporting the view that the Crown enjoyed a general power to detain individuals to prevent them from going abroad, by the eighteenth century it was thought that this could only be accomplished by Act of Parliament.[35]

The dominant opinion throughout the late eighteenth and nineteenth centuries was that there was a 'universally accepted principle that all administration was essentially the mere fulfilment of duties imposed by common or statute law'.[36] Dicey reflected this opinion when he described the prerogative as 'both historically and as a matter of actual fact nothing else than the residue of discretionary or arbitrary authority which at any given time is legally left in the hands of the Crown ... Every act which the executive government can lawfully do without the authority of the Act of Parliament is done in virtue of this prerogative.'[37]

His minimalist approach to the processes of government and administration can be appreciated by his near equation of discretionary and arbitrary powers. Such powers were a denial of the individualism in which he so passionately believed, and were incompatible with his perception of the rule of law. 'Individualism has meant hatred of the arbitrary prerogative of the Crown or ... the collective and autocratic authority of the State and has fostered the instinctive and strenuous effort to secure for the humblest Englishman the rule of law.' If powers had to be given to officials by statute, they should be as specific to their objects as possible. Although he was a Liberal Unionist, Dicey's dislike of government intervention is more typical of the Whigs of the early nineteenth century than of the Liberals of his time. 'The beneficial effect of state intervention, especially in the form of legislation, is direct, immediate, and, so to speak, visible, whilst its evil effects are gradual and indirect, and lie out of sight.'[38] His approach is best captured by the maxim coined by John O'Sullivan, an American who shared the Whig philosophy in business, law and politics. 'The best government is that which governs least.'[39] Dicey emphasizes the need for the lawfulness of

12

every government action: that is, its recognition by the common law in the decisions of the courts or by the grant of powers to take the necessary action by Act of Parliament. In his way, Dicey's adherence to a narrow, legalistic, common law constitution was as dated when he was writing in 1885 as Blackstone's monarchical constitution had been in the mid-eighteenth century. It was at the very time that the limited constitution of the Whig tradition was beginning to be challenged by a new collectivism and a new concept of administrative law that 'the culture of the ancient tradition came to be articulated through the language of analytical positivism'.[40] The success of the *Law of the Constitution* ensured that Dicey's positivism dominated legal thought well into the twentieth century. It is still reflected in the view of Hayek that all government action must be founded on specific legal authority, not just permitted because there is no law prohibiting such action.[41]

Prerogative powers were a necessary evil, to be defined by the courts and, ultimately, perhaps, to be replaced by statute, in so far as they were necessary to support essential state functions. Dicey's emphasis is on their *residual* nature, their *legality*, the requirement that they must have survived the attentions of Parliament and have been recognized by the courts. His definition has been called 'careless',[42] and it is not helpful in identifying which powers once belonged to the Crown and which remain, and at what date the legality, or illegality, of a presumed prerogative power is to be determined. Are they those powers which survived the Revolution of 1688 and have, since that date, received judicial recognition? Can older prerogatives now be recognized by the courts? How can the courts determine whether or not a prerogative is still extant, if it has not been specifically abolished or curtailed by statute? As we shall see, where the Crown insists that an act is done by virtue of the prerogative, it must 'make good its claim ... the mere plea of prerogative no longer ousts the jurisdiction of the court'.[43] The task will not be easy. As the historian Maitland once memorably declared, 'Our course is set about with difficulties, with prerogatives disused, with prerogatives of doubtful existence, with prerogatives which exist by sufferance, merely because no one has thought it worthwhile to abolish them.'[44]

One thing does, however, seem clear. Although there are numerous specific prerogatives, and some less specific aspects of those prerogatives, it would seem that, in the absence of a formal recognition by the courts (or Parliament), there is no general prerogative to act for the public good as envisaged by Blackstone. Lord Denning, following Blackstone, appeared to accept in the *Laker* case that such a general, residual power existed, but neither of the other two Appeal Court judges in the case (Roskill and Lawton LJJ) went so far. It would, therefore, seem correct to say that there is a finite, though as yet not fully defined, number of prerogative powers. For that reason 'public authorities cannot justify their acts merely by invoking public needs'.[45] This is certainly true where the action by the public authority would interfere with the common law or statutory rights of individuals. However, the extent to which the Crown is free to act in the same way as a private individual without infringing common law or statute is a much more difficult question. It is intimately connected with the extent to which the law of Britain recognizes a distinction between public and private powers.

'TRUE' AND SECONDARY PREROGATIVES

The criticism of Dicey most commonly made is that the powers he describes are not genuinely 'prerogative', in the sense described by Blackstone (above): that is, that they are not functions which belong (or should belong) exclusively to a head of state, and are, in fact, shared with others. To this is sometimes added the requirement that a 'true' prerogative should enable the Crown to do something which has a direct effect on the rights of others.[46] Very few powers and privileges are, however, exclusive to the Crown, in the sense that no similar powers are enjoyed by others. Professor Wade cites as 'real' prerogatives the power to make peers, to dissolve Parliament, and to establish corporations by royal charter. Foreign policy is not a 'real' prerogative because foreign policy decisions cannot, unlike all the above prerogative decisions, directly affect the rights of subjects. This is true, but while the ability to affect rights is a characteristic of a number of important prerogatives, it is certainly not a *sine qua non*. Prerogative powers whose exercise did not affect individual rights were recognized as such by the courts long before Dicey's *Law of the Constitution* ever saw the light of day.

Actions which fall to be considered within Dicey's definition do indeed include the most mundane activities of government officials, many of which might be performed by private citizens on their own behalf. However, this is equally true of many of the prerogative powers, rights and privileges which were extant when the powers of the Crown were exercised personally by monarchs, and were described long before Dicey (or Blackstone) was writing. Many of these could be called 'permissive', in that they do not enable the rights of individuals to be affected without their consent. Francis Bacon, for example, writing in the late sixteenth century, refers to the prerogative right of erecting beacons and lighthouses.[47] Any benevolent individual concerned about the welfare of seafarers might do likewise on his own land, although he could not (unlike under

14

the prerogative claimed by Bacon for the Crown) enter someone else's land to do it. Some prerogatives are relics of the position of the Crown as tenant in chief or the ultimate feudal lord. Into this category will fall the right to goods which have been abandoned, such as *bona vacantia* or treasure trove. Other rights and privileges, like forestry and hunting rights, were shared with other feudal chiefs but not with the ordinary individual. Many are of a quite ordinary kind, such as the right to own land or to exploit minerals. In some of these activities, the Crown has, or had, special privileges. Generally, however, the rights and powers are as numerous and diverse, and as incapable of definition, as they are in the case of a private person.

The legal basis for the general proposition that the Crown can act in the same way as a private person is that, in law, the Crown is a legal person (a corporation sole), having all the powers and rights of an ordinary person, including the right to own and manage all kinds of property.[48] Provided that neither Parliament nor the common law has prohibited them, the monarch, her ministers, civil servants and, indeed, anyone else may (in a legal sense, at least) do as they please, although there may be political or moral sanctions if they do so.[49] Whether this is a satisfactory state of affairs in terms of legal and political accountability, given that all the money and powers dealt with by the Crown are public rather than private in origin and may have very great political consequences for individuals, is a different matter. Activities of this kind, based upon the 'personal' nature of the Crown, are in modern times diverse, and may, for example, concern such matters as the payment of compensation to victims of war or crime or the distribution of information. Although these acts do not have the qualities ascribed to the prerogative by Professor Wade, the courts continue to describe them as being based on the prerogative.[50] Since they do not involve major incidents of state power, such as defence or foreign policy, or entitle the Crown to interfere with the security of the person or the enjoyment of property rights, these 'personal' powers exercised by the Crown might properly be called 'secondary prerogatives'. Secondary prerogatives of this kind are as much prerogatives as 'true' prerogatives, in that they derive from the powers of the Crown in its form as a feudal 'person'.[51] The main difference between secondary prerogatives and 'true' prerogatives is that the former are not definable because they are as diverse as the potential actions of private persons, while the latter are limited by the rule that they must be traditional incidents of state power which have been recognized by the courts. No new prerogatives of this kind can now be recognized by the courts.[52]

As we shall see, whether or not a power is described by the courts as a prerogative power may still significantly affect the way it is reviewed by the courts, although since the GCHQ case it is not the *source* but the *subject matter* of government or other official or semi-official action which decides whether or not it can be subject to judicial review.[53] There is now even a willingness by the courts to review decisions which do not involve the exercise of powers conferred by law at all, or which have not been made by legally constituted bodies but which have a public aspect, and which may have an adverse effect upon a business or an individual.[54] Powers which are seen to originate in 'true' prerogatives are still, however, more likely to be seen as 'unreviewable' because they raise non-justiciable issues such as defence or foreign policy. It is also useful to bear in mind that the word 'power' has a number of meanings. In this chapter it has been used in two senses: either in the sense of a common law or statutory authorization to do something which affects the legal rights of others, or in the sense of a permissive power to enter a legal relationship if the holder of the power desires it. There are, of course, other non-legal powers which may be equally effective in the hands of government. Terence Daintith has made the important point that, instead of legal compulsion (*imperium*), governments may use their economic and political strength to achieve policy goals (*dominium*).[55] The first option will involve the prerogative in the 'true' sense, and the second will rely, if at all, only on the secondary prerogatives of the Crown. The use of both, however, raises important issues of legal and political control and accountability. Essential to the application of both is also an understanding of how true and secondary prerogative powers are affected by statute.

PREROGATIVE AND STATUTE

Since the establishment of full parliamentary legislative supremacy at the turn of the seventeenth and eighteenth centuries, every prerogative power, whether a 'true' or secondary prerogative, must be looked at in the light of its compatibility with legislation. Dicey emphasized the *residual* nature of prerogatives for that very reason. Although some seventeenth-century judgments had emphasized that some major prerogative powers were inseparable from the Crown, that notion did not survive the revolution of 1688. There are, however, echoes of it in Blackstone's description, touched on above, of an 'irresistible' foreign policy prerogative.[56] After 1688 the Crown had become a political appointment, august and highly important in the constitutional structure though it was, but still an office, for which the qualifications and conduct had been set in the Bill of Rights 1688 and the Act of Settlement 1700. Thereafter, the principal prerogatives were exercised by the dominant party in the House of Commons through a process which has been called 'parliamentary monarchy'.[57] They continued largely in the hands of ministers, restricted partly by developing conventions of ministerial accountability to Parliament, partly by the extent to which they or their predecessors had chosen to abolish or limit such prerogatives by statute, and partly by decisions of the courts.

The limitations imposed by Parliament may not, necessarily, be directed at the particular prerogative in question, but may be sufficiently general to affect its exercise. It is important to recognize this in a historical context, because the development of limitations to the use of prerogative powers has taken place over more than three centuries. This is most evident in legislation intended to protect individuals against arbitrary arrest or detention, or to prevent the confiscation of property, such as Magna Carta and the Habeas Corpus Acts of 1679 and 1816. Other statutes may particularly address the powers or functions previously covered by the prerogative, and may expressly abolish them or impliedly limit their exercise. These limitations will be explored in more detail in subsequent chapters when we deal with specific prerogative powers, but there are some important general issues which need to be tackled here. As we have seen, 'true' prerogatives enable the Crown to take action which has legal consequences, sometimes affecting the powers and duties of institutions and, on other occasions, the rights of individuals. The limits of these powers were largely set in the seventeenth century, but they were not fully applied by the courts until the eighteenth century. The attempts of the eighteenth-century courts to ascertain the limits of executive power are not now merely matters of antiquarian interest. They remain relevant to decisions of the courts today when interpreting modern statutory provisions and administrative practices.[58]

During the seventeenth century, when the Stuarts were attempting to govern without Parliament, attempts were made by the Crown to raise money by special levies of taxation and by forced loans. The principle that taxation could only be levied with the consent of Parliament had been established by the end of the fifteenth century, so that resistance to such tax by the common lawyers of the House of Commons was assured. Those who refused to pay were, however, committed to prison. The king undoubtedly had a prerogative to take property for the defence of the realm, a relic of which is the modern power to requisition property. He also had a power to imprison unruly subjects, although this was generally carried out by the Court of the Star Chamber. In *Darnel's case* [59] the Court of King's Bench had to consider the imprisonment of an applicant for habeas corpus, Sir Thomas Darnel, who had refused to contribute to a forced loan. His imprisonment was supported simply by the bald return of the Warden of the Fleet Prison that it had been ordered 'by the special command of his majesty', without any other cause shown. The Court found in favour of the king. The Lord Chief Justice, Sir Nicholas Hyde, declared: 'if no cause of the commitment be expressed it is to be presumed to be for matters of state, which we cannot take notice of'.

The refusal of the court to question the grounds of imprisonment outraged the common lawyers in Parliament, and led directly to the drafting of the petition of Right of 1629 by Sir Edward Coke, the former Lord Chief Justice. Although the Petition did not follow the path of ordinary legislation, it received royal assent and has been accepted by the courts since as being declaratory of the common law and as having the force of statute.[60] The Petition of Right is, like Magna Carta and the Bill of Rights of 1688, not so much a charter of liberties, in the manner of the American Declaration of Independence of the Thirteen Colonies of 1776, but more a list of grievances, with a promise attached by the king not to offend again. It repeats the assurance of Magna Carta that no one henceforth should be deprived of his land or property, nor taken, nor imprisoned, nor disinherited or put to death, without being charged with anything or without due process of law (ss IV, V and X). It specifically repudiates the practice of detention on the order of the king alone (s. V). The Habeas Corpus Acts were, nominally, measures dealing with procedures for challenging supposedly unlawful detention, and the need to indicate a return showing a proper legal basis for that detention. Their application and interpretation by the courts, however, has been a valuable weapon in determining not only the legal basis, but the actual facts on which decisions were founded, in a whole range of executive detentions, including those of slaves, soldiers, immigrants and psychiatric patients.[61] As a consequence, any physical restraint imposed on an individual by officers of the Crown must be justified by the clearest authority of common law or statute.

Of equal significance, but only infrequently recognized as such, is the Act of 1641 abolishing the Star Chamber.[62] This Act abolished not only the Court of the Star Chamber itself, but the jurisdiction of the Court. It also prohibited the erection of any new court 'which shall have use or exercise the same or like jurisdiction as is, or hath been used practised or exercised in the said Court of the Star Chamber'. Since all modern courts have been set up since, and especially the new combined common law and equity courts established in 1875 by the Judicature Acts, this prohibition would appear to exclude from the jurisdiction of those modern courts the laws and practice of the Star Chamber other than those 'tried and determined in the ordinary courts of justice and by the ordinary course of the law'. Although the Star Chamber worked as an ordinary criminal court (and more efficiently than many of its contemporary courts), it was also a political court giving effect to policy decisions of the Privy Council. This was especially the case in the ten years preceding its abolition. During that time, the vast majority of cases which went as far as judgment concerned breaches of proclamations.[63] Twenty years previously the Court of King's Bench had ruled (Coke LCJ) in the *Case of Proclamations* that the king had no power to make new law, but could only, by proclamation, urge his subjects to abide by existing laws. Coke's report significantly concludes: 'if the offence be not punishable in the Star Chamber, the prohibition of it by proclamation cannot make it punishable there'.[64] In other words, the Star Chamber could only deal with offences which were already such by virtue of common law or statute. The Star Chamber could not, therefore, in the view of Coke LCJ, punish individuals for actions which breached proclamations, but not common law or statute. This dispute between the two courts continued until the Star Chamber was abolished in 1641.

Although the language of the Star Chamber is antiquated, some of its proceedings have an extraordinarily modern flavour. Prices were fixed by proclamation; houses were demolished and shops were shut in order that the cathedral of St Paul might appear to better advantage.[65] Proceedings against individuals in the court included those for unlawful residence in London, 'the making of irreligious and profane speeches to the disgrace of the State and his Majesty's Government', the building of tenements in the suburbs, against fraudulent manufacturers and the exporters of prohibited commodities, retailers who sold goods at prohibited times, hoarders of corn and those who breached monopolies which had been created by the Crown. Self-evidently, all these cases involved restraints imposed on individuals, both physically and upon their goods, and on the expression of their opinions, in cases where what they had done was not intrinsically unlawful either by statute or at common law. Often, they were no more than a political embarrassment to the government or an obstacle to the implementation of state policy. They are incidents of what today we would call an interventionist, even authoritarian, government. Later claims by governments to be able to control the movement of persons, to regulate trade, within the country and abroad, in relation both to imports and exports, to censor the press, and to impose planning controls, without the authority of either common law or statute, must take into account the abolition of this court and the jurisdiction which it exercised. It is not always easy to do this, because the Court of the Star Chamber administered both its own 'law' created by proclamation under the royal prerogative in the Privy Council, and ordinary statutory and common law rules.

The modern position on the relationship between prerogative and statute can be found in an important decision by the House of Lords in the aftermath of the First World War: *Attorney-General* v. *De Keysers Royal Hotel*.[66] In this case, the government purported to requisition a hotel during the war on the basis of the royal prerogative (under which it was thought that no compensation was payable) rather than under a statutory scheme under which compensation had to be paid to the owners. The House of Lords held that, once Parliament had enacted legislation which covered the same field as the prerogative, the use of the prerogative in that field was, effectively, prohibited, and the government could proceed only on the basis of the statutory scheme of compulsory acquisition. The same principle has recently been applied by the House of Lords in relation to the Criminal Injuries Compensation Scheme. This scheme was set up under the secondary prerogative in 1964, and continued on that basis until the enactment of the Criminal Justice Act 1988. The Act put the scheme on a statutory basis, but it had to be brought into operation by the Home Secretary. Instead, however, of bringing it into operation, the Home Secretary introduced another scheme under the royal prerogative, having announced in a White Paper that he had decided not to proceed with the new statutory scheme. A majority of the House of Lords held that he could not do so.

> It is for Parliament, not the executive, to repeal legislation. The constitutional history of this country is the history of the prerogative powers of the Crown being made subject to the overriding powers of the democratically elected legislature as the sovereign body. The prerogative powers of the Crown remain in existence to the extent to which Parliament has not expressly or by implication extinguished them. But, under the principle in *A-G* v. *De Keyser's Royal Hotel Ltd*, if Parliament has conferred on the executive statutory powers to do a particular act, that act can only thereafter be done under the statutory powers so conferred: any pre-existing prerogative power to do the same act is pro tanto excluded.[67]

The House held that the Home Secretary had a discretion as to when to bring the statutory scheme into effect. What he did not have, while the Act remained in force, was the power to decide *against* bringing the statutory scheme into effect and to proceed instead under the royal prerogative. 'The executive cannot exercise the prerogative power in a way which would derogate from the due fulfilment of a statutory duty. To that extent the exercise of the prerogative power is curtailed so long as the statutory duty continues to exist.'[68]

The principle of giving primacy to statutory provisions in relation to the exercise of prerogative powers is often easier to state than to apply. This is especially the case if the statute saves a primary or 'true' royal prerogative, or saves certain aspects of its exercise, affecting the personal liberty of individuals or their property. In these cases it is necessary to look at the extent to which the prerogative which has been saved by the statute may have already been affected by the general statutory provisions concerning the liberty of the person and rights to property enacted in the seventeenth century and outlined above. For example, s. 9 of the Emergency Powers (Defence) Act 1939 provided that 'The powers conferred by or under this Act shall be in addition to, and not in derogation of, the powers exercisable by virtue of the prerogative of the Crown.' That reservation declared, but did not enlarge, the Crown's defence (or war) prerogative. Indeed, the Crown's undoubted prerogative power to requisition property, and even to destroy it for defence purposes, although apparently carried out without payment of compensation in early times, was held by the House of Lords to be only exercisable in modern times if compensation is paid. Lord Reid warned against 'looking at the older authorities through modern spectacles. We ought not to ignore the many changes in constitutional law and theory which culminated in the revolutionary settlement of 1688–89.' On this basis the House of Lords decided, by a majority, that the prerogative of requisitioning property for defence purposes today carried with it an obligation to pay compensation. Lord Reid referred to the prohibitions in the Bill of Rights against the taking of property and money and the raising of taxation without authority of Parliament. All statutes enacted since the Revolution of 1688 authorizing the taking of property, invariably provided for the payment of compensation, and the common law powers under the prerogative should be approached in the same way.[69]

A similar approach needs to be adopted in relation to the saving in the Immigration Act 1971 of the Crown's powers with regard to aliens 'This Act shall not be taken to supersede or impair any power exercisable by Her Majesty in relation to aliens by virtue of Her prerogative.' The power retained is not that enjoyed by Queen Elizabeth I, who by proclamation in 1601 commanded all 'black-amoors' to depart from the kingdom, or the supposed power of Charles II to expel a German cloth merchant in 1674 for breaching a monopoly created by royal charter.[70] It is the more limited power which the Crown enjoys, apart from statute, of detaining individuals, following the enactment of the Habeas Corpus Acts and a number of decisions of the courts confirming that friendly aliens have equal rights in tort in this country to protect their persons and property as British subjects, even against senior officers of the Crown.[71] The powers of the Crown under the prerogative in relation to aliens saved by s. 33(5) of the Immigration Act is, therefore, in all probability no more than its power under the defence prerogative to detain and expel enemy aliens in wartime (see Chapter 5).

Where there is no saving section in a statute, the use of prerogative powers would appear to be excluded, at least if the statute covers the whole gamut of powers hitherto derived from the prerogative, as in the *De Keyser* case. It is sometimes a difficult matter of interpretation of the relevant statute by the courts to decide how much of the prerogative power has been superseded by the statute. In *Laker Airways Ltd* v. *Department of Trade*[72] the power of the minister to come to an agreement with the government of the United States about the landing rights of airlines in Britain and the USA was held to have been curtailed by the Civil Aviation Act 1971. The Act contained no saving of the royal prerogative, and the restriction it implicitly imposed affected only a small part of the Crown's foreign policy prerogative. That was, however, sufficient to prevent the Secretary of State for Trade from coming to an agreement with the United States which effectively barred the holder of a licence issued under the 1971 Act from using it. Similarly, the power of the Foreign Secretary to provide aid to Malaysia, which would normally be a matter of discretion under the foreign policy prerogative, was held to have been limited by the Overseas Development and Co-operation Act 1989, so that it could only be granted in accordance with the criteria laid down in the Act.[73]

Exceptionally, even where the prerogative has not been saved, and the statute appears to cover the relevant field in the most exhaustive fashion, the courts have been willing to accept that a prerogative power remains to supplement the statutory powers. The most striking example of this occurred in *R.* v. *Home Secretary ex p. Northumbria Police Authority*.[74] In this case the Authority challenged the power of the Home Secretary to supply CS gas to the police service for which it was responsible without its consent. The case is primarily about the extent to which chief constables have total autonomy in relation to day-to-day policing policy, and how far the Home Secretary has power to supply chief constables with equipment of which the elected police authority disapproves. In the event, the Court of Appeal decided that the Police Act 1964 entitled the Home Secretary to supply the chief constable without the authority's approval. None the less, the Court also held, *obiter*, that even if this was not the case, the Home Secretary had the power to supply CS gas under the royal prerogative. The decision is surprising for two reasons. The first, which need not concern us here, is the novelty of the recognition of a prerogative power of the Home Secretary to supply CS gas and other riot-control equipment. How far such a power could be said to exist will be considered in Chapter 8 in relation to the maintenance of public order. The second reason is the fact that the 1964 Act contains an apparently exhaustive statement of the legal rules governing the relationship between the Home Secretary, police authorities and chief constables.[75] It clearly binds the Home Secretary and contains no reservation of any prerogative power to maintain public order. In those circumstances, it is difficult to see how there is any room for such a prerogative to coexist with the statute. The Court of Appeal does not attempt to explain how this supposed prerogative has survived the legislation. Purchas LJ, however, puts a gloss on the *De Keyser* decision by holding that the restriction on prerogative powers by statute only applies 'to prevent executive action ... in violation of property or other rights of the individual ... Where the executive action is directed towards the benefit or protection of the individual, it is unlikely that its use will attract the intervention of the courts.'

There is not the least authority for holding that the Crown can ignore statutory provisions, even supposedly for the public good, or that the courts should be passive in the face of such action. To do so runs counter to the Bill of Rights, which forbids the Crown from suspending or dispensing with statute.[76] A recently developed practice of surrendering criminal suspects between states without going through the sometimes lengthy procedures laid down in extradition treaties and the Extradition Act of 1989 was roundly condemned by the House of Lords in *R. v. Horseferry Road Magistrates' Court ex p. Bennett* in 1994. Despite the obvious convenience of the practice for national police forces, and the fact that it ensured the arrival of suspects who might not otherwise be brought to trial, it was wholly unacceptable because 'the principle involved goes ... even beyond the rights of those victims who may or may not be innocent. It affects the proper administration of justice according to the rule of law and with respect to international law.'[77]

Crucial to determining whether or not a prerogative has been abolished, superseded by a statute covering the same ground or partially curtailed is the question of whether or not the statute actually binds the Crown. Not all statutes do. In principle, the Crown enjoys a privilege of immunity from statute. The basis of this privilege is that, when the Crown assents to a statute after its passage through Parliament 'he [the monarch] does not mean to prejudice himself or to bar himself of his liberty and his privilege, but he assents that it shall be law among his subjects ... Laws are made by rulers for subjects.'[78] The Crown 'is not bound by a statute which imposes obligations or restraints on persons or in respect of property unless the statute says so expressly or by necessary implication'. Given the breadth of government activity, this exemption has a wide application. The immunity from statute attaches to all government departments and their civil servants, members of the armed forces and other public bodies or persons. The test to be applied is whether the body or person is to be regarded as a servant or agent of the Crown and whether it is carrying out its functions at the direction of officers of the Crown.[79] A consequence of the doctrine was that the Public Health Acts were held not to apply to National Health hospitals. As a result, public officials escaped criminal liability when 19 patients died at Stanley Royd Hospital in Wakefield in 1984. It required a specific statutory amendment to give hospital patients the protection of the criminal law.[80]

The principle of Crown immunity from statutes seems hardly compatible with modern ideas of the rule of law. There is no reason, in principle, why the executive should start from a position of exemption, although there may well be individual cases where liability should not apply. The distinction between rulers and subjects is also repugnant to modern ideas of democratic control and accountability. There is a strong argument to be made for there to be a reverse presumption, that statutes *do bind* the Crown unless it is clearly excluded from their scope. The House of Lords has held, however, that where the Crown is bound by a statute in general terms, the prerogative cannot be used by the Crown to override the statute in specific cases.[81] The importance of Crown immunity to the position of prerogative powers and other Crown rights and privileges is that they cannot be abolished or curtailed except by the clearest language. As was demonstrated in the *Northumbria Police* case (above) the courts are reluctant to accept that a prerogative power has been abolished or curtailed by implication. Some statutes have, however, expressly abolished prerogatives and Crown privileges. For example, the Crown's right to receive various payments originally arising under the feudal system, including dues relating to wardship and marriage, purveyance and pre-emption, were all abolished by Parliament at the Restoration in 1660. By way of compensation, it voted the Crown various taxes on wines and spirits. In addition, the prerogative power of maintaining an army was limited, and such powers as remained were re-enacted annually in the Mutiny Acts.[82]

More modern statutes have limited the scope of, for example, the old prerogative of making a child a ward of court. Under the Children Act 1989, this cannot now be done while a child is in the care of a local authority.[83] Other statutes have regulated the way in which prerogative powers are exercised. Among the more significant are those regulating the grant of royal assent to statutes under the Assent Act 1967, the issue of public immunity certificates relating to the disclosure of sensitive material under the Crown Proceedings Act 1947 and the recognition of diplomatic status under the Diplomatic Privileges Act 1964.

The fact that old statutes referred to existing prerogative powers does not necessarily mean that such powers are still extant. It is a difficult question to answer whether, for example, the power to recruit young men into the navy or army under the old system of impressment still exists, and whether it survived the repeal of the National Service Acts. Forcible recruitment into the army under the royal prerogative was effectively discontinued after it had been limited by statute to times of foreign invasion.[84] Naval impressment, on the other hand, continued until the beginning of the nineteenth century and was recognized after the English Revolution by Parliament in the reign of Queen Anne. It gradually fell into disrepute and disuse, and in 1859 a Parliamentary Commission declared that 'it could not now be successfully enforced'.[85] Neither prerogative power relating to impressment for the land or naval forces has, however, ever been abolished by statute. Any attempt to improve army or naval recruitment figures at a time of national crisis by physical coercion in the streets of Plymouth or Aldershot would be politically unacceptable, but not clearly illegal.

Prerogative powers, unless they are abolished by statute, do not fade away. There is no doctrine of loss of such powers by long disuse. At the same time, as with the taking of land by the Crown without compensation, the forcible taking of the liberty of individuals even for the defence of the country, without Parliamentary authority, would seem a total anachronism. A prerogative of this kind could be described as 'grossly anomalous' and unrecognizable in modern conditions.[86] In *McKendrick* v. *Sinclair* in 1972 the House of Lords held that such prerogatives were incapable of revival, but until the accidents of litigation bring each prerogative before the court, or until each has been expressly abolished by Parliament, it is impossible to know which has survived. Some prerogatives, such as the power to requisition ships in time of war or emergency, which are regarded as essential state functions, certainly did survive the repeal of the Emergency Powers (Defence) Act 1939 and were used as recently as the Falklands emergency. The existence and scope of other minor prerogatives, not now used but never abolished, remain shrouded in uncertainty. Some of these will be examined in subsequent chapters. There is, however, a clear need for such powers to be scrutinized by the Law Commission with a view to the abolition of those which are now useless, anomalous or anachronistic, if they are not to be disposed of in a more sweeping programme of constitutional reform.

STATUTE AND EXTRA-STATUTORY CONCESSIONS BY THE CROWN

A great many statutes impose obligations on individuals in various capacities: to drive their motor vehicles with care, to travel with their passports to ensure exit from and return to the United Kingdom, to provide safe working conditions for employees and to sell goods which are safe. Some of these laws are enforced by private individuals in civil proceedings who may sue if they have suffered injury and are entitled to compensation under the law. Others which carry criminal sanctions fall to be dealt with in the courts by local authorities or the Crown Prosecution Service. The decision by, for example, a local environmental health inspector to deal with a particular defaulter by a warning rather than a prosecution after a breach of the law may be affected by a number of considerations: the seriousness and frequency of breaches, the prevalence of the offence, the resources available to the local authority and so forth. Similarly, HM Collector of Taxes may have to decide in individual cases of non-payment of tax how far to pursue defaulters. The amount and the difficulty of securing payment may outweigh the resources involved. The police, too, necessarily have discretion in deciding whether or not to arrest or charge individuals in relation to specific offences. The courts have, traditionally, been reluctant to interfere in the exercise of what are seen as wide discretionary powers given by common law or statute to the Crown or other authorities to take or to refrain from action.[87] The essential feature which distinguishes these different discretions is that each decision is taken on a case-by-case basis according to the merits and circumstances of each case. Once a decision-taker makes a decision not to enforce this or that law, serious constitutional issues are raised. If Parliament has determined that this type of activity shall be an offence, or that type of business will be subject to a particular rate of tax, it is not for the executive to decide to free one group or another from the obligations imposed upon them. As Lord Browne-Wilkinson declared in R. v. *Secretary of State for the Home Department ex p. Fire Brigades Union*, 'It is for Parliament and not the executive to repeal legislation.'[88]

In recent years it has become a practice of governments to issue guidance to civil servants, immigration officers and police officers, local authority housing departments as to how legislation is to be interpreted and applied. This should not give rise to legal difficulty, provided that such guidance is in accordance with the substantive provisions of law which the guidance concerns. If the guidance is in conflict with the law then the courts are, in principle, ready to strike it down.[89]

What the government cannot do is to issue instructions, or to state, that a statute will not be enforced. The reason why this cannot be done lies in Articles 1 and 2 of the Bill of Rights 1689:

1. That the pretended power of suspending of laws, or the execution of laws by regal authority, without consent of Parliament, is illegal.

2. That the pretended power of dispensing with laws, or the execution of laws, by regal authority, *as it hath been assumed and exercised of late*, is illegal. (Emphasis added.)

The Bill of Rights was passed, it will be recalled, with a view to the prevention of a repetition of the abuses which were seen to have arisen in the late seventeenth century during the reigns of Charles II and James II. In 1670, Parliament had passed the Conventicles Act. The Act was designed to reassert the supremacy of the Church of England and to suppress the growth of dissenting and non-conformist churches. Roman Catholicism continued to be suppressed too, and public posts were excluded to all except those who, under the Test Acts, took the sacraments of the established church. Charles II had made a public declaration in 1672, stating that such penal laws were 'immediately suspended'. In addition, he granted individual licences to dissenting meeting houses, which were coupled with directions to local magistrates not to enforce the legislation against the licensees.[90] Parliament angrily objected to what it described as 'interrupting the free course of the laws, and altering the legislative power', and Charles withdrew the Declaration in 1673. James II attempted a similar venture, when he, too, made a Declaration of Indulgence in 1687, similarly purporting to suspend all penal religious laws, their execution and the requirement that applicants for public office should have to take the oath of allegiance and the sacraments of the Church of England under the Test Acts. Individual applicants for Crown posts and commissions in the military and civil service were also individually excused the obligation to meet the requirements of the Test Acts.[91] The Declaration led directly to the Revolution of 1688 and to the passage of the Bill of Rights in 1689.

There is little to celebrate about the religious intolerance of late seventeenth-century England, but this final conflict between Crown and Parliament is important because it set the bounds between the legislative function of Parliament and the executive powers of the Crown. It is clear from Article 1 that the Crown no longer has the right, by making a general declaration that certain laws will not be enforced, either to alter the law by purporting to suspend it or to suspend the *execution* of the law by instructing its officers not to enforce it. The position with regard to dispensation is more complex. The Crown always had a power to dispense with the execution of laws in certain cases. Decisions not to prosecute, not to apply the full rigour of the law by, for example, remitting part of a sentence and to pardon convicted offenders are all examples of that power. Where, however, that dispensation is handed out on a large scale to whole categories of cases, irrespective of the merits of each case, and before any breach in the law may even have occurred, then dispensation becomes *suspension in the execution* of the law. It was to such wide dispensations 'as hath been exercised of late' in relation to the Test Acts that Parliament referred in Article 2 of the Bill of Rights.[92] In the light of these provisions two widely used modern practices are almost certainly illegal and are not saved by the traditional prerogative of dispensation. The first relates to extra-statutory tax concessions and the second to extra-statutory leave and amnesties granted to illegal immigrants outside the terms of the Immigration Acts.

Each year the Inland Revenue announces concessions which will be made in relation to taxes which, although in law they are due, the Revenue has resolved will not be collected. They are published in a booklet, with annual supplements. Similar concessions are published by the Commissioners of Customs and Excise in relation to value added tax.[93] Such concessions may be made because it is thought that the tax will weigh particularly heavily on certain groups, that it will be difficult to collect or for some other policy reason. In *IRC* v. *Bates* in 1968 Lord Upjohn declared that he was 'quite unable to understand on what principle they [the Commissioners] can properly do so'.[94] If concessions were thought appropriate they could be inserted in the Finance Bill which is approved every year by Parliament following the Budget. It has been suggested that tax concessions, while not having the force of law, exist 'in a legal limbo' and do not constitute the dispensation forbidden in the Bill of Rights because they do not purport to change the legal position of the taxpayer in a way which a court would recognize.[95] This view is almost certainly wrong, because Article 2 of the Bill of Rights prohibits not only the purported suspension of *laws*, but also suspension of their *execution*. In other words, it is aimed at both attempts to declare statutes to be of no effect, and attempts to render them ineffective by non-enforcement.

Tax concessions are of two kinds. There are, first, those that are published, affecting a whole category of taxpayers. Second, there are concessions made to small groups, or even individual taxpayers, on a case-by-case basis. The first type of concession is clearly unlawful and has been unequivocally condemned by the courts in a number of decisions as breaching the Bill of Rights.[96] Governments have shown little inclination to abandon this unlawful practice, and it has, unfortunately, been given some legitimacy by attempts by the courts to ensure that concessions are at least administered according to minimum standards of procedural fairness.[97] The second type of individual or group concessions may, in some cases, be defended, not as the grant of purported exemptions to the law, but as management decisions that, in certain circumstances, attempts to collect taxes due may not be cost-effective. This occurred where the Inland Revenue decided not to pursue self-employed print workers ('the Fleet Street casuals') for tax unpaid on earnings received under a host of fictitious names in R. v. IRC ex p. National Federation of Self-employed. The challenge was unsuccessful on the technical grounds of the lack of legal standing of the Federation, but the House of Lords expressed the view that a decision whether or not to pursue particular defaulting taxpayers was a matter of policy for which the Inland Revenue were accountable to Parliament and not to the courts.[98]

However, the fundamental flaw in the system of extra-statutory tax concessions remains. While they may be welcomed by the taxpayers affected, they are not authorized by Parliament in the Finance Acts or the statutes dealing with the collection of taxes, and their use is prohibited by the Bill of Rights. There is no prerogative power which justifies them, they have been condemned on a number of cases by judicial dicta, yet they continue. 'One should be taxed by law and not untaxed by concession.' 'No judicial countenance can or ought to be given in matters of taxation to any system of extra-legal concessions.'[99] Their continued use, outside the framework of the law, often in circumstances beyond effective Parliamentary control, can only be described as an abuse of power. Under our adversarial system no one, except the National Federation of Self-employed, has directly challenged the concessions in the courts. They are convenient for the Treasury and the government, because valuable parliamentary time does not have to be devoted to considering primary or secondary legislation aimed at fine-tuning the system, and individual taxpayers are more concerned about getting the concessions than questioning their validity. The loss is suffered by the general body of taxpayers, who may not be happy about carrying a heavier burden of tax because revenue is diminished by the concessions, or the community at large who may question the constitutionality of allowing unelected officials to determine what taxes will be paid by whom.

Not dissimilar problems arise in relation to leave given to enter outside the Immigration Rules. Under the system of control put in place by the Immigration Act 1971, leave to enter the United Kingdom must be given by immigration officers according to criteria laid down in the Rules. Under those Rules, a person who does not meet the criteria must be refused.[100] The process of control is examined in more detail in Chapter 4. For the purpose of this discussion of dispensation, however, it is relevant to note that it is an offence for anyone who requires leave to enter without being granted it. Once a person has been granted leave, any extensions of that leave must be granted by the Home Secretary.[101] The Home Secretary does not, however, have the power under the Act to grant *leave to enter*. He can only *vary* an existing leave. Every year the Home Secretary grants 'exceptional leave' to hundreds, possibly thousands, of entrants outside the Act and the Rules. Many of these are people who are the victims of war, but who cannot bring themselves within the terms of the Geneva Convention of 1951. Others are individuals or groups whom the Home Secretary may wish to favour for less obviously commendable reasons, such as the domestic servants of diplomats or business people. Some of these, outside the regime of work permits and supervision by the Department for Education and Employment, work in conditions of near slavery.[102] Other categories of entrant may also, from time to time, be given exceptional leave to enter and remain.

How can this be done? No power to grant leave to enter in exceptional circumstances outside the Rules is conferred on the Home Secretary by the Act. There is a suggestion that he may do so because he has a general power to control immigration under the royal prerogative. However, even if such a power existed with regard to aliens (which is highly unlikely), there was undoubtedly no such power with regard to British subjects and Commonwealth citizens before the Act, and none was preserved by it.[103] In any event, if there was one, it cannot, under the *De Keyser* (above) principle, coexist with the Act. The Home Secretary does, however, it is argued, have the power to 'under-enforce' the Act. Such an argument presupposes that the Home Secretary has a power which can be 'under-enforced'. This is certainly the case in relation to the variation of an existing leave, which comes within the Home Secretary's competence under s. 4(1) of the Act,[104] but it cannot be the case with regard to leave to enter. Although it may be that the Home Secretary might legitimately not take criminal proceedings against an individual who had entered without leave, he could not, without breaching Article 2 of the Bill of Rights, give leave to enter to a person or a category of persons. To do so would be to purport to 'dispense' with the need to obtain leave from an immigration officer under the Rules. There may well be a need for the Home Secretary to have such a power. At present he does not have it and any 'leave' which he grants should be treated as having no effect. That will not happen, of course. Those who have the 'leave' are not likely to challenge it. For the Home Secretary the ability to override the Rules whenever the circumstances appear appropriate, or to insist on them in other cases, enables him to have his cake and eat it! The only litigation will be about how he has *used* his supposed discretion, not whether or not he has it. Neither party will be so inept as to raise before the court the possibility that, in the case of entry at least, the Home Secretary has no discretion to exercise. Again, we are ill-served by our adversarial judicial process, in which the public interest in having an open system of immigration control with decisions taken in accordance with Rules approved by Parliament has no place. There is a danger that the public system of immigration control is being overlaid by a patchwork of concessions never debated in the House of Commons, and issued in a series of answers to Written Questions and replies to immigrant advisory bodies.

EUROPEAN COMMUNITY LAW AND THE EUROPEAN CONVENTION ON HUMAN RIGHTS

The primacy of European Community law in the United Kingdom means that provisions of statutes and rules of common law which are incompatible with Community law are unenforceable and must be repealed, abolished or amended. For this reason Member States are not permitted to meet their obligations by 'under-enforcing' national law, or by allowing Community rights to be given effect by the sort of administrative discretion used by the British government in tax and immigration cases. The rule applies with equal force to Crown powers and immunities.[105] Even before the Convention on Human Rights became part of the law of the United Kingdom, the principles of the Convention form part of the fundamental law of the Community, and will be relevant whenever they are applicable to the exercise or enforcement of rights conferred by Community law. The effect of this basic rule is that the Convention can be called upon to assist in interpreting Community law and in deciding how Community law should be implemented in Member States. To that extent, and as far as it comprises part of Community law, the

Convention has been legally enforceable in the courts of the United Kingdom since we joined the Community.[106]

Community law impinges on a number of primary prerogative powers. The way it operates in relation to specific prerogative powers will be considered in more detail in the ensuing chapters of this book. Most importantly, perhaps, it affects the way in which the foreign policy prerogative is exercised through the Council of Ministers. Although foreign policy itself is outside the scope of the Community's power to make legally binding rules, the workings of the Council of Ministers and its decision-making processes affecting such divers matters as agriculture, the environment, competition policy and health and safety at work are all made by British ministers or members of Britain's diplomatic mission in Brussels, and are subject to the Council's Rules of Procedure and the provisions of the Treaty. For example, unlike decisions made under prerogative, Council decisions having legal effect must always be supported by reasons. This is generally true of administrative decisions made by Member States affecting the rights of individuals derived from Community law.[107] Specific areas of government activity in foreign policy, affecting, for example, the imposition of restrictions on exports may be subject to Community law. In its evidence to the Scott Inquiry the government declared that 'export controls are a perfectly legitimate instrument of foreign policy'.[108] They are no longer, however, solely, the province of *national* policy, nor are they always a matter of foreign policy alone. Decisions may well be taken under the Community's Common Commercial Policy, as was the case in relation to sanctions against Argentina in the Falklands War and the prohibitions imposed upon the export of dual-use equipment to Iraq (i.e. defence or non-defence related). Such measures will bind Member States and exporters in those states.[109] Restrictions on the departure of British nationals, such as potentially disruptive football supporters travelling to a match in another Member State, arguably justifiable at common law under the prerogative, either through denial of a passport or a direct ban, are limited by the free movement rights enjoyed by Citizens of the European Union under the Treaty.[110] The common law power of the Crown to dismiss civil servants or members of the armed forces at will may be subject to Community rules prohibiting sexual discrimination in employment. Even the supposed prerogative power to maintain public order and the wide discretion of chief constables in that context may, for example, be affected by the overriding requirement to ensure that the right to export goods is not impeded. Thus a failure by a chief constable to ensure that sufficient police are available to protect vehicles carrying live animal exports against campaigners, although a matter entirely at the Chief Constable's discretion at common law, may constitute an unlawful restriction on exports.[111] All proceedings affecting the exercise or denial of Community rights will be subject to Community and European Convention rights of due process, fairness and the need for effective remedies.

Under the Human Rights Bill, all public authorities will have to act in a way which is compatible with the rights conferred by the Convention, and the courts of this country will have to apply decisions of the Court of Human Rights. As we will see in the next chapter, not all prerogative powers are subject to judicial review and control by the courts. Incorporation of the Convention will, however, mean that a wide range of decision-makers under the prerogative will have to take the Convention into account as a 'relevant consideration'. The Convention permits exceptions on the grounds, *inter alia*, of national security, public health and public safety, but it is probable that incorporation will mean that decisions of the courts supporting the dismissal of homosexuals from the armed forces, some decisions affecting the rights of asylum-seekers, and the restrictions imposed on the BBC under its royal charter with regards to broadcasts by terrorists, will not be repeated.[112]

CONCLUSIONS

Although it is not possible to define, with confidence, the full nature and scope of primary or 'true' prerogative powers, it is at least possible to come to some tentative conclusions about them. Those prerogative powers relating to the principal functions of government – defence, foreign policy, the administration of justice and the legislative process – and those powers of the Crown under which individual common law rights may be affected, such as the detention of enemy aliens in wartime, or the seizure of civilian property, are finite, have been judicially recognised and described, and cannot be extended further by those who exercise the powers or by decisions of the courts. Consequently, there is no general, residual prerogative power which ministers of the Crown or civil servants can call upon in circumstances where there is no relevant rule of common law or statute to enable them to override common law or statutory rights.

On the other hand, secondary prerogative powers, which derive partly from the traditional rights, privileges and immunities of the Crown and partly from the fact that the Crown is, in law, a legal person capable of doing anything which any other person with full legal status can do, are inherently incapable of exhaustive description. What the Crown might wish to do, for example, with property it owns, or with other rights which it enjoys, such as its power to make contracts, cannot be anticipated or defined, except by reason of the fact that its choice is limited by the type of rights and privileges which it has, and the extent to which their use has been curtailed by Parliament. Secondary prerogatives are also different from primary prerogatives in that, unlike some of the major prerogative powers, they are permissive. They enable the Crown to do various things, or to take advantage of various benefits, but they do not enable it to override the rights of others.

Both kinds of prerogative may be abolished or curtailed by statute or the rules of Community law, and the exercise of both will, to a greater or lesser extent, according to the type of power which is being exercised, be subject to control and review by the courts. The function of the courts is, in reality, more than one of control and review. The extent to which primary or secondary prerogatives are recognized as still surviving is a matter for the courts. The theory is that the Crown must make good its claim to a prerogative at common law. In practice, the reality is that the courts will, in some cases, through what is no more than judicial law-making, determine what ancient prerogatives are appropriate to the machinery of modern government.

NOTES AND REFERENCES

1. Carlton Classics (1915) p. 15.
2. Bagehot, W., *The English Constitution* (1963) p. 85.
3. A limited definition of the allocation of powers between Lords and Commons is provided by the Parliament Acts 1911, 1949. Interests protected by the common law are confined largely to personal security and the proprietorial. There is, for example, no common law right to be protected from telephone tapping: *Malone* v. *Metropolitan Police Commissioner* [1979] 2 WLR 200.
4. Hutton W., *The State We're In* (1995) p. 25.
5. Chitty J., *Prerogatives of the Crown* (1820) p. 4.
6. Some parliamentary questions about prerogative matters are never answered, others only partially. 'The supervision of prerogative powers does seem to be attended by greater than average difficulty ... [They are] imperfectly subject to parliamentary control, and in most cases removed from the Parliamentary Commissioner's purview.' Munro C.R., *Studies in Constitutional Law* (1987) pp. 173, 174.
7. Sir Richard Scott V-C, *Report of the Inquiry into the Export of Defence Equipment and Dual-use Goods to Iraq and Related Prosecutions* (1996) HC 115, Vol. IV para. K8.3.
8. Benn T. and Hood A., *Common Sense: A New Constitution for Britain* (1993); Cornford J. (ed.), Institute for Public Policy Research, *A Written Constitution for the United Kingdom* (1993).
9. S.11; see Harlow C., *Compensation and Government Torts* (1982) p. 27.
10. *R.* v. *Secretary of State for the Home Department ex p. Kaur and Others* [1987] Imm

AR 278, 291; compare *R. v. Immigration Appeal Tribunal ex p. Secretary of State* [1990] 1 WLR 1126, 1134.

11. Hill C., *The Intellectual Origins of the English Revolution* (1966) p. 65.

12. Keir D.L., *Constitutional History of Modern Britain 1485–1937* (1938) pp. 269, 271.

13. His *Second Treatise on Government* was published in 1689. Although started much earlier, it was substantially rewritten in the light of the events of the Revolution of 1688. Laslett P. (ed.), *J. Locke: Two Treatises on Government* (1994) pp. 48, 49. The most visible influence is in the judgment of Lord Camden in *Entick v. Carrington* (1765) 19 St Tr 1029; Keir, D.L., *op. cit.*, p 293.

14. Maitland F.W., *Constitutional History* (1909) p. 418.

15. Evans LJ [1995] 1 All ER 870, 875, quoting Lord Diplock in *Council of Civil Service Unions v. Minister for the Civil Service* [1985] AC 374, 410.

16. [1988] 1 All ER 556, 564; 2 WLR 290.

17. *Proclamations Case* (1611) 12 Co Rep 74, 76.

18. The Statute *De Prerogativa Regis* (of uncertain date, but probably late medieval: Keir and Lawson, *Cases in Constitutional Law* (1954) p. 44) is manifestly incomplete, and relates almost entirely to the King's rights and duties as a feudal lord.

19. *Blackstone's Commentaries*, Vol. I, p. 239.

20. *Ibid.*, Vol. I, p. 252; [1977] 2 WLR 249, 250.

21. Laslett, *op. cit.* (Of Prerogatives), p. 374.

22. *Stephens New Commentaries on the Laws of England* (13th edn, 1899) Vol. II, p. 413.

23. *Commentaries*, Vol. 1, c.7, para. 11; Maitland, *op. cit.*, p. 424, describes this statement as 'very untrue'.

24. *Council of Civil Service Unions v. Minister for the Civil Service* [1985] AC 374. Blackstone's absolutist language is, in many respects, identical to that of Dr Cowell in *Cowell's Interpreter*, published in 1607. The book was repudiated by an indignant House of Commons, and a more reluctant James I, in February 1610, and all copies were ordered to be called in and destroyed. Kenyon J. P., *The Stuart Constitution* (1969) p. 8; Taswell-Langmead T.P., *English Constitutional History* (9th edn, 1929) pp. 468–9; Prothero G.W., *Statutes and Constitutional Documents 1558–1625* (4th edn, 1913) pp. 409–11. Cowell, however, went much further than Blackstone, claiming that the king could quash Acts of Parliament, and was 'an absolute king'.

25. Dicey A.V., *Law of the Constitution* (1885) (9th edn, 1952) p. 8.

26. Hunt W., *History of England 1760–1801* (1905) pp. 5–6.

27. See the Preamble to the Declaration of Independence of 4 July 1776; Newton A.P., *Federal and Unified Constitutions* (1923) pp. 66–7.

28. (1765) 19 St. Tr. 1030.

29. [1994] 3 WLR 901, 909, CA.

30. At p. 909. The decision appears to imply that the publication of the instructions in some way legitimizes action taken under them. It falls short, however, of implying approval of the kind of unauthorized burglaries described by Peter Wright in *Spycatcher* (1987) pp. 54–5. See Chapter 5.

31. Marston J., 'Police surveillance', *New Law Journal*, 15 December 1995, p. 1862. See, now, Police Act 1997.

32. *Bowles* v. *Bank of England* [1913] Ch 57; see, now, the Provisional Collection of Taxes Act 1968.

33. *Yip Chiu-Cheung* v. *R.* [1994] 2 All ER 924, 928.

34. 7 Geo III, c.7. Heuston R.F.V., *Essays in Constitutional Law* (2nd edn, 1964) p. 75. It is now accepted that, without statutory authority, the Crown only has power to restrict imports and exports in wartime: *The Charlotta* (1814) 1 Dod. 387, 390 (per Lord Stowell); McNair Lord, and Watts A.D., *The Legal Effects of War* (1965) p. 357; *Scott Report*, Vol. I Cl. 4. See Chapter 6.

35. Chitty, *op. cit.*, p. 21; 22 Geo II, c.54 (An Act to restrain Sir Thomas Rumbold and Peter Perring from going out of the kingdom for a limited time); Holdsworth, W., *History of English Law* (1938) Vol. X, pp. 392, 393.

36. Keir D.L., *op. cit.*, p. 312.

37. Dicey A.V., *op. cit.*, pp. 424, 425.

38. Dicey A.V., *Law and Public Opinion in England* (1920) pp. 176, 257.

39. *The United States Magazine* (1837).

40. Loughlin M., *Courts and Governance*, SPTL Seminar, 23 January 1993, p. 5.

41. Hayek F.A., *The Road to Serfdom* (1946) p. 54.

42. Munro C., *Studies in Constitutional Law* (1987) p. 160.

43. Keir D.L. and Lawson F.H., *Cases in Constitutional Law* (1954) p. 70.

44. *Op. cit.*, p. 421.

45. *Op. cit.*, p. 169.

46. Wade H.W.R., *Constitutional Fundamentals* (1980) pp. 46, 47; Harris B.V., *The Third Source of Authority for Government Action* (1992) 109 LQR 626, 628.

47. Bacon F., *Abridgement*, Vol. 5, p. 510; Chitty, *op. cit.*, p. 175.

48. *M.* v. *Home Office* [1994] 1 AC 377, 424 HLL; *Town Investments Ltd* v. *Department of the Environment* [1978] AC 359; Daintith T.C., 'Regulation by contract: the new prerogative' [1979] *Current Legal Problems* 4.

49. *Malone* v. *Metropolitan Police Commissioner* [1979] 1 Ch 366; Harris, *op. cit.*, p. 633.

50. See, for example, *R.* v. *Secretary of State for the Home Department ex p. Fire Brigades Union and Others* [1995] 2 All ER 244, 247 (Lord Keith), 254 (Lord Browne-Wilkinson) HL; *R.* v. *Criminal Injuries Compensation Board ex p. P* [1995] 1 All ER 870, CA.

51. Holdsworth calls them 'ordinary' or 'incidental' prerogatives: Holdsworth W.S., (1929) CLXXVI LQR 162, 163. They have also been called 'third source' government powers: Harris B.V., *op. cit.*, pp. 633, 634.

52. 'It is 350 years and a Civil War too late for the courts to broaden the prerogative.' *BBC* v. *Johns* [1965] Ch 32, 79, per Diplock LJ.

53. *Council of Civil Service Unions* v. *Minister for the Civil Service* [1985] AC 374; *R.* v. *Secretary of State for the Home Department ex p. Bentley* [1993] 4 All ER 442 at 452, 453, QBD per Watkins LJ.

54. *R.* v. *Panel on Take-Overs and Mergers ex p. Datafin Plc* [1987] QB 815; *R.* v. *Panel on Take-Overs and Mergers ex p. Guinness Plc* [1990] 1 QB 146; *R.* v. *Advertising Standards Authority Ltd ex p. The Insurance Service Plc* [1990] C.O.D. 43.

55. Daintith T., 'The techniques of government', in *The Changing Constitution* (Jowell J. and Oliver D., eds, 1994) pp. 209–14.

56. In *R.* v. *Hampden (The Case of Ship-Money)* (1637) 3 St Tr 825, 1235, Finch

LCJ declared: 'No Act of Parliament can bar a king of his regality ... acts to take away his royal power are void.' Thomas Hobbes in *Leviathan* (1651) (Everyman Edition, 1914) Chapter 18, p. 95, describes such powers as 'incommunicable and inseparable'.

57. Keir and Lawson, *op. cit.*, Chapter V.

58. *Malone v. Metropolitan Police Commissioner* [1979] 2 WLR 700, *R. v. Secretary of State for the Home Department ex p. Ruddock* [1987] 1 WLR 1482 (telephone tapping and European Convention on Human Rights); *Morris v. Beardmore* [1981] AC 446 HL (privacy and property rights and police powers under Road Traffic Act 1972); *R. v. Khan (Sultan)* [1994] 3 WLR 901, CA (police powers and private property rights); *Vestey v. IRC (Nos 1 and 2)* [1979] 3 All ER 976 (tax concessions by Crown and Income Tax Act 1952); *R. v. Secretary of State for the Home Department ex p. Northumbria Police Authority* [1988] 1 All ER 556, CA (supply of CS gas under royal prerogative and powers under Police Act 1964).

59. *Darnel's or the Five Knights' Case* (1627) 3 St. Tr. 1.

60. *Marais v. General Officer Commanding* [1902] AC 109, 115; *R. v. Halliday ex p. Zadig* [1917] AC 160, 297. Maitland, *op. cit.*, p. 307, states that Charles I 'gave his assent to the Petition of Right, which turned it into a statute'. It was duly enrolled as 3 Car. I c.1.

61. See Sharpe R.J., *The Law of Habeas Corpus* (1976); *De Smith's Judicial Review of Administrative Action* (4th edn by Evans J.M., 1980) Appendix 2; *Somersett v. Stewart* (1772) 20 St. Tr. 1; *Eshugbayi Eleko v. Government of Nigeria* [1928] AC 459; *R. v. Board of Control ex p. Rutty* [1956] 2 QB 109.

62. 16 Car. I, c.10.

63. Kenyon, *op. cit.*, pp. 119, 120.

64. 12 Co. Rep. 74 (1611); Kenyon, *op. cit.*, pp. 117, 118.

65. Maitland F.W., *op. cit.*, p. 302.

66. [1920] AC 508.

67. Lord Browne-Wilkinson in *R. v. Secretary of State for the Home Department ex p. Fire Brigades Union and Others* [1995] 2 All ER 244, 254, HL.

68. *Ibid.* Lord Nicholls at p. 275.

69. *Burmah Oil Company v. Lord Advocate* [1965] AC 75, 111, 112, HL (S) (Lord Reid). The Defence Acts 1803, 1842 and the Army Act 1881 all provided for the payment of compensation. The War Damage Act 1965, reversing the *Burmah* decision, now stands as an exception to this pattern.

70. Kiernan W.G., 'Britons old and new', in *Immigrants and Minorities in British Society* (Colin Holmes, ed., 1978); *Case of Otto*, Lord Nottingham's Chancery Cases, Seldon Society (1957) p. 121.

71. *Mostyn v. Fabrigas* (1771) 1 Cowp. 160; *Johnstone v. Pedlar* [1921] 2 AC 262; *Kuchenmeister v. Home Office* [1958] 1 QB 496.

72. [1977] QB 643, CA.

73. *R. v. Secretary of State for Foreign Affairs ex p. World Development Movement Ltd. The Independent*, 11 January 1995; see also *R. v. Secretary of State for Foreign and Commonwealth Affairs ex p. Rees-Mogg* [1994] 2 QB 552, DC, on the application of the European Assembly Elections Act 1978.

74. [1988] 1 QB 26, CA; 1 All ER 556.

75. Lustgarten L., *The Governance of the Police* (1986) pp. 79–94; Marshall G. and

Loveday B., 'The police: independence and accountability' in *The Changing Constitution* (Jowell J. and Oliver D., eds, 1994), pp. 314–15.

76. Art. 1; *R.* v. *LCC* [1931] 2 QB 215. See further the discussion on extra-statutory concessions below.

77. [1994] 1 AC 42, 76, HL (Lord Lowry).

78. Plowden 240; *BBC* v. *Johns* [1965] Ch 32, 78 (Diplock LJ).

79. *BBC* v. *Johns*, above; *Tamlin* v. *Hannaford* [1950] 1 KB 18. Bennion F., *Statutory Interpretation* (1984) pp. 100, 101. *British Medical Association* v. *Greater Glasgow Health Board*, Times Law Report, 20 May 1988 (Scottish Inner House).

80. National Health Service (Amendment) Act 1986, ss 1 and 2.

81. *Lord Advocate* v. *Dumbarton District Council* [1990] 2 AC 580.

82. Maitland, *op. cit.*, pp. 443, 448–9.

83. Children Act 1989, s. 91 (4); Bromley P.M. and Lowe N.V., *Bromley's Family Law* (8th edn, 1992) pp. 478–9.

84. 16 Car. 1, c.28. It was temporarily revived by statute during the American War of Independence: 19 Geo. III, c.10. Taswell-Langmead, *op. cit.*, p. 359.

85. The last statutory reference is in 4 & 5 Anne, c.6; Erskine May, *Constitutional History of England 1760–1860*, (1861) Vol. II, p. 275.

86. *De Smith's Constitutional and Administrative Law* (Street H. and Brazier R., eds, 1985) pp. 143, 146; *McKendrick* v. *Sinclair* (1972) SLT (HL) 110, 116–117.

87. *R.* v. *Metropolitan Police Commissioner ex p. Blackburn* [1968] 2 QB 118; *Gouriet* v. *Union of Post Office Workers* [1978] AC 435; *R.* v. *Chief Constable of Devon and Cornwall ex p. CEGB* [1981] 3 WLR 961.

88. [1995] 2 All ER 244, HL, at p. 254.

89. *Gillick* v. *West Norfolk and Wisbech Area Health Authority* [1986] AC 112; *R.* v. *Secretary of State for the Environment ex p. Greenwich LBC, The Times*, 17 May 1989.

90. Declaration of Indulgence of 15 March 1672, Kenyon, *op. cit.*, p. 407; As to the licensing system, see, for example, a licence granted in relation to 'a roome or roomes in the house of John Hall, in Thornton in the Parish of Bradford, Yorkshire, to be a place for the use of such as do not conform to the Church of England'. Issued on 16 May 1672 (copy reproduced in *The Brontës* by William Scruton (1898)).

91. Kenyon, *op. cit.*, p. 410. Although a compliant judiciary upheld the Declaration and the exemptions granted to Crown officers in *Godden* v. *Hales* (1686) 11 St. Tr. 1165, the bishops who refused to order the reading of the Declaration from the pulpit on the grounds that it was illegal were acquitted of sedition in the *Trial of the Seven Bishops* (1688) 12 St. Tr. 183.

92. Maitland, *op. cit.*, pp. 302–6; Heuston R.F.V., *Essays in Constitutional Law* (2nd edn, 1964) pp. 66–72.

93. See, for example, a concession announced by HM Customs and Excess on 28 February 1996 to mitigate an unforeseen effect of the VAT (Buildings and Land) Order 1994 SI 1994/3013. The concession is to have retrospective effect to November 1994: *Simon's Weekly Tax Intelligence*, Issue 10 (409–44) 7 March 1996. Effectively, this amends the Order, without meeting the requirements for the making of a new Statutory Instrument!

94. [1968] AC 483, HL, at p. 516; See also *Absalom* v. *Talbot* [1943] 1 All ER 598,

CA, in which Scott LJ observed, 'No judicial countenance can or ought to be given in matters of taxation to any system of extra-legal concession'; *IRC* v. *Frere* [1965] AC 402, HL, at p. 429 (Lord Radcliffe). Lord Wilberforce criticised the practice as 'a radical departure from constitutional principle' in *Vestey* v. *IRC* [1979] 3 WLR 915, HL.

95. Ganz G., *Quasi-legislation: Recent Developments in Secondary Legislation* (1987) p. 21; Wade, *op. cit.*, p. 59.

96. *Vestey* v. *IRC (No. 2)* [1979] Ch 198, 203 (Walton J); *R.* v. *Board of Inland Revenue ex p. MFK Ltd* [1989] STC 873, 986 (Judge J).

97. *R.* v. *IRC ex p. Preston* [1985] AC 835, HL (concession construed as a representation not to levy tax). The Public Accounts Committee of the House of Commons has suggested that long-standing concessions could be included in a non-controversial Bill, or the more transient concessions could be included in a statutory instrument if there is insufficient time for them to be included in the Finance Bill. See 1981–1982, HC 339 para. 33; 1968–1969, HC 185-I, para. 1. Ganz, *op. cit.*, pp. 93–4.

98. [1982] AC 617 (Lord Diplock).

99. *Absalom* v. *Talbot* [1943] 1 All ER 589, (Scott LJ); *Vestey* v. *IRC (No. 2)* [1979] Ch 198, 203 (Walton J).

100. S. 3(1), s. 4(1) Immigration Act 1971. Para. 320(1) Immigration Rules, HC 395 (Statement of Changes in Immigration Rules, 23 May 1994). See also Vincenzi C., 'Extra-statutory ministerial discretion in immigration law', *Public Law*, Summer 1992, p. 300.

101. S. 24(1)(a); s. 4(1). The Secretary of State may give directions to immigration officers, but only in a manner which is 'not inconsistent with the immigration rules': schedule 2, para. 1(3).

102. *The Independent*, 14 November 1991.

103. *R.* v. *Secretary of State ex p. Rajinder Kaur* [1987] Imm AR 278; compare *R.* v. *Bhagwan* [1972] AC 60, 80, in which Lord Diplock confirmed that British subjects and Commonwealth citizens were free to enter the United Kingdom and were not subject to any control at common law.

104. *R.* v. *Immigration Appeal Adjudicator ex p. Bowen* (1982) Sol. J. 480; *R.* v. *Immigration Appeal Tribunal ex p. Bhaktaur Singh* [1986] 1 WLR 910.

105. Article 5 EC Treaty; Case 6/64 *Costa* v. *ENEL* [1964] ECR 585; ss 2 and 3 European Communities Act 1972; Case 167/73 *Commission* v. *France (Re French Merchant Seamen)* [1974] ECR 359; Case C-213/89 *R.* v. *Secretary of State for Transport ex p. Factortame* [1990] ECR I-2433.

106. Article F(2) EC Treaty; Case 36/75 *Rutili* v. *Minister of The Interior* [1975] ECR 1219 (Arts 8, 9, 19 and 11 ECHR); Case 222/84 *Johnston* v. *Chief Constable of the Royal Ulster Constabulary* [1986] ECR 1651 (Art. 6 ECHR).

107. Article 190 EC Treaty; Case 222/86 *Union Nationale des Entraineurs et Cadres Techniques Professionels du Football* v. *Heylens* [1987] ECR 4097. Compare *R.* v. *Secretary of State for Education ex p. Duggan* [1994] 3 All ER 277, 287 in which Rose LJ declared that there is 'no authority for the proposition that there is a general duty to give reasons for an administrative decision'.

108. *Scott Report* (1996) Vol. IV, para. K2.19.

109. Hartley T.C., *The Foundations of European Community Law* (1994) p. 24; *Scott*

Report, para. K2.8; EC Regulation 3381/94, made under Article 113 EC Treaty. Compare *R. v. Foreign Secretary ex p. Rees-Mogg* [1994] 2 WLR 115, 127 (Lloyd LJ), where the Divisional Court held that the non-legally binding provisions of Title V of the Treaty on European Union 1992 on a common foreign and security policy did not divest the Crown of its prerogative powers in those areas. See also Eaton M.R., 'Common foreign and security policy' in *Legal Issues of the Maastricht Treaty* (O'Keeffe D. and Twomey P., eds, 1994) pp. 215, 216.

110. It has been claimed that the Crown still has the power to prevent subjects going abroad under the old writ of ne exeat regno: see Bridge (1972) 88 LQR 83. The Crown undoubtedly has a wide power to refuse to issue passports: *Secretary of State* v. *Lakdawalla* [1972] Imm AR 26; *R. v. Secretary of State for Foreign and Commonwealth Affairs ex p. Everett* [1989] 2 WLR 224. Exit rights are enjoyed by EU citizens under Directives 68/360 and 73/148, together with the right to be issued with travel documents. These rights are, however, subject to the derogations on the grounds of public policy, public security and public health contained in the EC Treaty and Directive 64/221. See, generally, Chapter 4.

111. *R. v. Secretary of State for the Home Department ex p. Northumbria Police Authority* [1988] 1 QB 26; Arts 30, 34 and 36 EC Treaty; *R. v. Chief Constable of West Sussex ex p. International Trader's Ferry* [1995] 4 All ER 364.

112. *R. v. Ministry of Defence ex p. Smith* [1996] 1 All ER 257; *Bugdayacay* v. *Secretary of State for the Home Department* [1987] AC 514. The breadth of the Home Secretary's discretion as to conditions in foreign states is still very wide: *R. v. Secretary of State for the Home Department ex p. Canbolat, The Times*, 24 February 1997; *Brind* v. *Secretary of State for the Home Department* [1991] 1 AC 696.

2

The Judicial Review of Prerogative Powers

Until 1985 it was axiomatic that the way in which prerogative powers were exercised was beyond the reach of the courts. The judicial function was confined to deciding, first, whether or not a prerogative power under which a minister or civil servant claimed to be acting actually existed (including the extent to which it may have been limited by statute) and, second, if the power were extant, whether the action undertaken actually fell within it. Further than that the courts could not go. In *Chandler* v. *DPP*, for example, the defendants, who had been arrested for attempting to obstruct the taking-off of aircraft which they believed carried nuclear weapons, argued that the use of such weapons was against the interests of the United Kingdom. The House of Lords refused to consider the argument. 'If the methods of arming the defence forces and the disposition of those forces are at the decision of her Majesty's Ministers for the time being, it is not within the competence of a court of law to try the issue whether it would be better for the country that that armament or those dispositions should be different.'[1] There were two principal reasons for this reluctance to intervene. The first lay in the sensitive policy nature of the issues involved in the exercise of primary prerogative powers. In the early days of the common law, this reluctance was expressed in terms of a difference between adjudication and government. The first role was that of the courts and the second that of the executive government. The executive was concerned with matters of state over which the courts had no jurisdiction. The courts were, in many instances, obliged to accept the certificate of the appropriate minister that this or that foreign government was recognized, that territorial waters were to be defined in a certain way or that a state of war did or did not exist with another country. In a civil action, a foreign secretary's certificate on any of these things, or a claim that the matter was not justiciable by the courts because it was an 'act of state', might effectively terminate those proceedings.[2] Judicial reluctance has been most marked in time of war, and much of the vigour with which the courts were prepared to examine the acts of Crown servants both at home and in the colonies in the nineteenth century was lost in the two world wars. The maxim *salus populi suprema lex*, that government had the ultimate responsibility of deciding what was necessary for public safety, played an important part in both wars and lies behind much of the unwillingness of the courts to limit the sweeping use of powers of arrest and internment against both enemy and neutral aliens, and even British subjects.[3]

The second reason for judicial reluctance lay in a perceived lack of competence of the courts to rule upon essentially administrative matters in which there was a very high policy content about which the courts lacked the necessary skills to adjudicate. When courts explained that certain matters were not 'justiciable' this was, and is, what is most often intended to be conveyed. They also, undoubtedly, wanted to avoid opening the floodgates to everyone disappointed by an administrative decision. This principle of non-intervention in decisions taken, apparently, within the four-square bounds of a power given by Parliament or the common law was applied for some forty years in relation to powers which Parliament had conferred on ministers and other public officers, even when the decision affected the livelihood, or even the liberty, of the applicant. The applications for relief in these cases were, in many cases, directed at *the way in which the decisions had been taken*, rather than the substance of the decision. Since the mid-nineteenth century the courts have required that decisions affecting the livelihood, property or liberty of individuals be taken according to minimum standards of fairness and, in the case of decisions with more serious consequences, according to the principles of natural justice. These procedural standards were attracted by the limited rights which the common law recognizes. Foreign nationals, since they did not have a right to be in the United Kingdom, or individuals who might benefit from some official exercising a discretion to grant them a licence, had no rights to be protected.[4] These purely 'administrative' decisions did not entitle the person affected to be heard by the decision-maker before the decision affecting him or her was made. Decisions under the royal prerogative were supremely matters of high administrative/ policy content and, therefore, peculiarly unreviewable. It is significant that the powers which attracted the least judicial intervention were those which had their origin in actual or supposed prerogative powers, such as the review of detention under emergency powers, the deportation or exclusion of aliens and matters relating to the employment of civil servants.

The ground so often given in these cases for the lack of judicial intervention was, besides the desire of the judges not to intervene in what were essentially policy matters, the availability of the more appropriate forum of Parliament to deal with conflicting issues of policy. It took a long time for the ineffectiveness of Parliament as a method for the redress of individual grievances, especially those taken under prerogative powers and the subject of political controversy, to penetrate the collective consciousness of the judiciary. Those judges who had been reared on the works of Dicey and the doctrine of the separation of powers continued to intone that it was for Parliament to ensure that ministers and their civil servants were held to account for bad, or unjust, administrative decisions, while it was for the courts simply to ensure that decision-makers acted *intra vires*, within the law. Although MPs successfully deal with innumerable matters which concern disputes between their constituents and various departments of government, they become ineffective when the subject of concern becomes a matter of the political standing of a minister. Although, since 1967, some complaints can be successfully dealt with by the Parliamentary Commissioner for Adminstration (the Ombudsman), the most sensitive issues, such as defence, foreign policy, the civil service and the award of government contracts, are outside the Commissioner's jurisdiction.[5] The dominance of Parliament by the executive through the use of the party system has tended to make individual Members increasingly ineffective in this context. This was a problem which Dicey himself recognized in one of his last, and most perceptive, articles. Commenting on the decision of the House of Lords in *Local Government Board* v. *Arlidge*, he referred to the observation of the Lord Chancellor that the 'Minister at the head of the Board is directly responsible to Parliament ... and the only authority that can review what has been done is the Parliament to which the Minister in charge is responsible.'[6]

This reference to so-called ministerial responsibility is somewhat unfortunate. It is calculated to promote the belief that such ministerial responsibility is a real check upon the action of a Minister or a Cabinet when tempted to override the law of the land. But any man who will look plain facts in the face will see in a moment that ministerial liability to the censure not in fact by Parliament, nor even by the House of Commons, but by the party majority who keep the Government in office, is a very feeble guarantee indeed against action which evades the authority of the law courts. A Cabinet is rarely indeed tempted to defy the wishes of the majority of the House of Commons, since it is the majority which keeps the Cabinet in office.

If a Minister or the Government is tempted to evade in some form or other the authority of the law, the temptation must arise from the fact that his action is desired, or at lowest, will not be censured, by the majority of the House of Commons. It were an exaggeration to say that ministerial responsibility is an unmeaning term. It does mean the necessity of conforming to the wishes of the party which forms a majority of the House of Commons and keeps a ministry in power, but it is no security whatever that a Cabinet will scrupulously obey that rule of law which has been created, and must be enforced, if at all, by the power of the law courts.[7]

Although this passage was written more than eighty years ago it carries as much force today as when it was written. It had little impact on the judiciary at the time, however, and, in fact, it coincided with the start of a period of judicial quiescence in administrative law that only began to show signs of drawing to a close in 1962, with the landmark decision of the House of Lords in *Ridge* v. *Baldwin*. This was most marked in relation to the way in which decisions were taken by administrators. If a decision was taken clearly within the powers conferred by Parliament or the common law, and did not have the characteristics of an adjudication between parties to a dispute, the courts would describe it as 'purely administrative' and beyond the reach of judicial review. After 1962, the courts were more concerned to look at the impact which a decision had on an individual, rather than the kind of decision-making process, in determining whether or not minimum standards of natural justice or fairness applied. For a long time even after *Ridge* v. *Baldwin*[8] judges continued to refer litigants wishing to challenge the more sensitive administrative decisions to Parliament for a remedy. Some of these decisions were made under the prerogative, others were made under statutory powers which had either replaced prerogative powers or were thought to have done so.

The decision of the Court of Appeal in *R.* v. *Secretary of State ex p. Hosenball* in 1977 exemplifies a wholly ingenuous view of the efficacy of ministerial accountability. The case concerned the limits of the power of the courts to control the exercise of a power that was statutory, but had elements in it of the prerogative relating to defence and supposed prerogative powers relating to aliens. The proceedings resulted from the decision of the Home Secretary to deport an American journalist who had worked for a number of years in Britain. It appeared that articles which he had written, drawing upon published sources about military intelligence-gathering operations, had upset the authorities. The Home Secretary, Merlyn Rees, made a personal order for his deportation. Such an order was not subject to any right of appeal, but Hosenball was allowed to make representations to three Advisers. He was not told what he had done, or which of his publications had offended. Nor was he told the outcome of the hearing before the Advisers. He challenged the decision by way of judicial review. He was unsuccessful. The decision of the Court of Appeal seems to have been informed, at least in part, by the 'no rights' perception of the status of aliens and the wide powers the Crown was supposed to enjoy over them at common law. More significantly, the Court of Appeal seemed to believe that whether there was or was not a case against Mr Hosenball, and whether he should be told about it if there was, was not a matter for them, but for the Home Secretary. Lord Denning MR quoted a previous Home Secretary, Mr Reginald Maudling, who described the procedure and concluded:

> Whether an individual's presence in this country is a danger to this country is not a legal decision. It is not a justiciable issue or a matter of law; it is a matter of judgment. Judgment should be exercised by the Government, subject to the House of Commons, and not by a Tribunal not under the control of the House.

Lord Denning agreed:

> There is a conflict here between the interests of national security on the one hand and the freedom of the individual on the other. The balance between these two is not for a court of law. It is for the Home Secretary ... In this case we are assured that the Home Secretary himself gave it his personal consideration, and I have no reason whatever to doubt the care with which he considered the whole matter. He is answerable to Parliament as to the way in which he did it and not to the courts here.

He also offered as broad a blanket of judicial approval of past administrative action as has ever been made:

> Both during the wars and after them successive ministers have discharged their duties to the complete satisfaction of the

people at large ... They have never interfered with the liberty
or the freedom of movement of any individual except where it
is absolutely necessary for the safety of the state.[9]

On this basis the Court of Appeal held that the decision to deport
Hosenball and the processes of the Advisers were not justiciable. As
we shall see in Chapter 10, not only is the scope for a realistic
political challenge for such a decision extremely limited, but
ministers habitually refuse to answer questions involving matters of
national security, and, as we have noted above, such issues are also
outside the jurisdiction of the Parliamentary Commissioner for
Administration. In addition, under the Parliamentary Commissioner
Act 1967, any act which is within the competence of the
Ombudsman, but is also susceptible to judicial review, is excluded
from review by the Commissioner because complainants should first
exhaust any existing legal remedies.

There has been a growing judicial realization in the last three
decades of the twentieth century that Parliament is not an effective
forum for the adjudication of difficult issues affecting individuals.
Initially, this awareness was reflected in an increased willingness to
review hitherto 'unreviewable' statute-based decisions of ministers
and civil servants. That rising tide of judicial review eventually
reached decisions made under the royal prerogative. The law in the
area of judicial review of prerogative powers was radically altered by
the decision of the House of Lords in *Council of Civil Service Unions* v.
Minister for the Civil Service (the GCHQ case). The case concerned the
decision of the government to withdraw recognition of the trade
unions operating at the intelligence-gathering centre at Cheltenham.
Despite the fact that it concerned the terms and conditions of work
of civil servants, a matter undoubtedly within the prerogative powers
of the Crown, the majority of the House unequivocally rejected the
old doctrine limiting the scope of review of prerogative powers, and
declared that the decision was, in principle, reviewable:

> If the executive, instead of acting under a statutory power, acts
> under a prerogative power ... so as to affect the rights of the
> citizen, I am unable to see ... that there is any logical reason
> why the fact that the source of the power is the prerogative and
> not statute should today deprive the citizen of that right of
> challenge to the manner of its exercise which he would possess
> were the source of the power statutory. In either case the act in
> question is the act of the executive. To talk of that act as the act
> of the sovereign savours of the archaism of past centuries.[10]

The GCHQ case does not mean that the courts are now free to

look at the way every prerogative power is exercised. The House drew a distinction between those decisions which were concerned with 'high policy', such as the making of treaties, defence, the grant of pardons to convicted criminals, the award of honours, the dissolution of Parliament and the appointment of ministers, and others, like that before them, which concerned decisions affecting the rights of individuals. In the event, they refused to hold that the government had acted unlawfully, because the Prime Minister maintained that the decision had been taken on security grounds, and the House was not prepared to question the adequacy of those grounds. In this case, defence and national security once again prevailed over individual rights. Despite the unwillingness of the House to extend the principle of review into the more sensitive areas of policy, the Divisional Court and the Court of Appeal have shown less reluctance. The issue of a passport is an aspect of the foreign policy prerogative, since the document is, in essence, a request to foreign governments to give free passage to the holder. Traditionally, its issue, and denial, has been immune from review. However, in *R. v. Secretary of State for Foreign and Commonwealth Affairs ex p. Everett*, the Court of Appeal held that a decision by the minister to deny a passport to the applicant was, in principle, reviewable. The court distinguished between 'policy decisions of foreign affairs' and the issue of a passport:

> That seems common sense. It is a familiar document to all
> citizens who travel in the world and it would seem obvious to
> me that the exercise of the prerogative ... is an area where
> common sense tells one that, if for some reason a passport is
> wrongly refused for a bad reason, the court should be able to
> inquire into it.[11]

Taylor LJ, agreeing, said that he could see no more reason why a decision to refuse a passport should be any less reviewable than a decision in the field of immigration, and should be 'just as justiciable'.[12] Common sense and the common law have not always been synonymous, and it is not clear from the decision what would constitute a 'bad' reason. In this case the court approved the grounds for decision to withhold the passport from the applicant, who was resident in Spain and was subject to a warrant for his arrest. It did, however, criticize the way in which the decision to deny the passport was conveyed to the applicant, and suggested that it would have been appropriate to have given him a reason for the refusal at the time of its formal notification. The reference to immigration as if it were quintessentially a matter for review is ironical, because after the *Venicoff* decision in 1920 and until the creation of the immigration appeals process in 1969, it was regarded by the courts as essentially 'administrative' and the few reported challenges to immigration decisions failed, almost without exception, because they were held to import matters of high policy which could not be the subject of review.[13] Lord Justice Taylor's observation does, however, demonstrate the extent to which 'justiciability' is a flexible concept, reflecting as much judicial willingness to intervene as judicial competence to do so.

The House of Lords in the *GCHQ* case specifically excluded decisions affecting national defence from the scope of judicial review. In a recent decision, however, the Court of Appeal has confirmed that the dismissal of homosexuals from the armed forces was an appropriate matter for review.[14] The House indicated that the grant of pardons was also a process in which the policy content of decisions was so high that it was beyond the bounds of justiciability. The Divisional Court has not heeded the warning and has, quite recently, decided that the Home Secretary's refusal to consider a posthumous pardon for Derek Bentley was, exceptionally, subject to review.[15] There has been a greater willingness on the part of the courts to review another, related, prerogative function, that of mitigating a sentence. This may involve the commutation of a sentence to a lesser one, or the mitigation of the effect of a sentence, by the order of the release of a prisoner by the Home Secretary before the full period of a sentence, not infrequently before a mandatory life sentence is served. Other, hitherto unreviewable prerogative powers may yet come to the fore in litigation and be found to be susceptible to review in the more flexible judicial climate.

JUDICIAL REVIEW AS AN APPROPRIATE MECHANISM FOR THE CONTROL OF PREROGATIVE POWERS

The use of any of the prerogative powers will involve the making of a decision by the monarch, a minister or civil servant about how that power is to be used. It will, in the terms of administrative law, concern the exercise of a *discretion*. The scope for discretion may be very wide: where to deploy contingents of the armed forces, which branch of the civil service is to undertake a new function, on whom to confer a knighthood, on which association to confer a royal charter or on what grounds a person is to be refused a passport. Every individual of full age and responsibility has a wide discretion to take decisions affecting his or her own person and property. The powers of public bodies are more circumscribed by law. In *O'Reilly* v. *Mackman* in 1983, an important decision of the House of Lords, a distinction was drawn between public functions, which are the appropriate subject matter of public law and, potentially, subject to control and review by way of an application for judicial review, and private law rights, for which, for example, an ordinary action in tort or breach of contract would be appropriate.[16] The distinction, and where the boundaries should be drawn, is often difficult in practice, and is primarily designed to protect public bodies from excessive litigation. They are not, however, of such importance in the field of the prerogative. This is because the exercise of prerogative powers, particularly of the primary kind, is, *par excellence*, concerned with matters in the public sphere, although the use of secondary prerogatives (as, for example, a contract for the management of Crown lands) may be more difficult to classify in this way. Judicial control of the exercise of prerogative powers will, therefore, be principally a response to applications for judicial review, although the scope of prerogative powers may, on occasion, also arise in actions in tort against civil servants or other public servants purporting to exercise those powers, who have caused loss or damage.

Since the way in which prerogative powers were used remained effectively immune from judicial review until 1985, the principles for the review of discretionary powers have, almost exclusively, been developed in the context of the review of *statutory* discretions. In such cases, when a court is attempting to ascertain whether or not a minister or public official has made a decision which he is free to make, it will look, first, at whether or not the decision is *within the powers* which Parliament has granted the decision-maker, and, second, if the decision is within those powers, at whether it has been taken *in the way* the statute has specifically prescribed, or a way which can be inferred from the language of the statute. A breach of the first requirement will be classified as 'substantive *ultra vires*', and of the second as 'procedural *ultra vires*'. This is a simplification, but it will serve for present purposes.

Where Parliament has given a public officer a discretion the courts will, generally, not interfere with the exercise of that discretion unless he or she is perceived by the court to have used it 'unreasonably'. 'Reasonableness' in this context is used in both its ordinary sense and according to established legal criteria laid down in the *Wednesbury* case.[17] A decision may be struck down if it offends either or both concepts, although the courts are not always careful to make clear the sense in which 'unreasonableness' or 'irrationality' are being used. In either sense, reasonableness will be an indispensable criterion for assessing the way in which a statutory discretion has been exercised, because it will always be assumed by the court that Parliament intended any power given to be used reasonably. What this means in practice is not always easy to anticipate. The guidance offered by Lord Greene MR in the *Wednesbury* case still offers a useful starting point:

> It is true the discretion must be exercised reasonably. Now what does this mean? Lawyers familiar with the phraseology commonly used in relation to exercise of statutory discretions often use the word 'unreasonable' in a rather comprehensive sense. It has frequently been used as a general description of the thing which must not be done. For instance, a person entrusted with a discretion must, so to speak, direct himself properly in law. He must call his own attention to the matters which he is bound to consider. He must exclude from his consideration matters which are irrelevant to what he has to consider. If he does not obey those rules, he may truly be said, and is often said, to be acting 'unreasonably'. Similarly, there may be something so absurd that no sensible person could even dream that it lay within the powers of the authority. Warrington LJ in *Short* v. *Poole Corporation*[18] gave the example of the redheaded teacher, dismissed because she had red hair. That is unreasonable in one sense. In another sense it is taking into consideration extraneous matters. It is so unreasonable that it might almost be described as being done in bad faith; and, in fact, all these things run into one another.

In the GCHQ case, Lord Diplock added another heading of review to the *Wednesbury* criteria: 'illegality'. 'The decision-maker must understand correctly the law that regulates his decision-making power and must give effect to it.' This seems to add little to Lord Greene's formulation. Understanding the legal bounds in which he has to operate is but one of the matters to which a decision-maker must direct his mind. Perhaps the most important legal rule is the need to address the express or implicit purpose for which the legislation was passed. Thus the courts have held that a public authority empowered to acquire unfit houses and to use them to provide temporary accommodation pending their demolition cannot acquire them in order to render them fit for habitation to add to its permanent housing stock.[19]

In such cases, identifying the purpose of an Act may not present much difficulty. In other cases, problems may arise because the legislature has set out the purpose in such wide terms that it is not clear what its attainment may involve. In *Bromley London Borough Council* v. *Greater London Council* (the 'Fares Fair' Case) the GLC had power to make grants to the London Transport Executive (the LTE) 'for any purpose'. The GLC, which had a duty under the London Transport Act to promote integrated, efficient and economic

50

transport facilities in the GLC area, decided that all fares should be reduced by 25 per cent. It did so, because the ruling Labour group had fought and won an election on the basis of an integrated transport scheme that was intended to relieve traffic congestion by encouraging the use of public transport. It was anticipated that, although this would result in the LTE running at a deficit, the overall economic and social benefits to the capital would be of more importance. The GLC won the case at first instance, but the House of Lords decided that there were to be implied in the words 'efficient and economic' the obligation to run the system according to 'ordinary business principles'. An intention to run at a loss conflicted with those principles, even if it resulted in other benefits. The decision was much criticized because it was thought that the judiciary had added its own criteria to those of the legislature.[20]

Other statutory requirements may present fewer difficulties of interpretation. A minister or public authority may be empowered to act when a certain situation obtains. For example, an environmental health officer may be required to take certain steps where food is sold in a state in which it is unfit for human consumption or a danger to health, or a police officer may be able to arrest a person who is committing an arrestable offence. These are factual situations which may or may not exist. If they do not exist, then the action will be unlawful. If, on the other hand, the power is expressed in terms that the officer may act 'if he is satisfied' that a situation exists, then the court may have to decide if his conclusion was reasonably arrived at. Did the matters which he took into account lead, logically, to the decision which he reached? Clearly, he has a margin of error. His decision will be assessed according to the *Wednesbury* criteria. If he took into account all relevant criteria and excluded all irrelevant matters from his consideration, then his decision may be lawful, even if his conclusion was subsequently proved to be wrong. An officer who was, for example, motivated by a personal dislike of the person concerned, or by a favour which he had received from that person, would be taking irrelevant considerations into account, and would probably also be acting in bad faith.

The courts are not eager to find that an official or minister has acted beyond his powers. There is a common judicial belief that, 'whilst public officials enjoy no special fallibility common to the human species it is in general not for the judges to correct them. And judges should beware of unduly extending their principal weapon of control, the requirement of legality, so as to bring within their purview matters that should properly be let to lie elsewhere.'[21] For that reason, and since Parliament often authorizes action in the most general terms, the courts may be willing to construe action as within powers given to an official if it 'may fairly be regarded as incidental to or consequential upon those things which the legislature has authorised'. There is specific statutory authority for courts to adopt such an approach in relation to the acts of local authorities.[22]

Besides assessing whether or not an official has acted within his *substantive* powers, courts will often be called upon to decide whether or not a decision has followed the *procedure* which Parliament has prescribed. A minister may, for example, be required to consult certain bodies before he or she makes regulations, or he may have to publish notices or hold an inquiry before proceeding with a road construction project. Failure to comply with those requirements, unless the failure is insignificant, may result in a finding by the court that a decision is procedurally *ultra vires*. The decision-maker, if he still wants to proceed, will have to go through the proper process, taking all the new information acquired through it into account in his final decision. Even if the statute contains no specific procedural requirements, the decision-maker may have to observe certain minimal rules of fair procedure implied by the courts. Such rules may be applied where major rights of individuals, such as property or the security of the person, are in issue, and more recently, even where only 'reasonable expectations' are in jeopardy.[23] Substantive and procedural matters are not always separable. A requirement that a decision-maker should consult people or bodies affected by his decision can be viewed either as a relevant consideration under the *Wednesbury* criteria, or as a procedure to be followed as a matter of procedural *vires*.

Stated in this relatively simplistic way, the application of both the *Wednesbury* criteria and express or implicit procedural rules may seem almost a value-free exercise. This is far from being the case. The concept of a decision that is 'perverse' or one that 'no reasonable decision-maker could reach' is a highly subjective one. So, too, is the idea of a 'decision which is so outrageous in its defiance of logic or of accepted moral standards that no sensible person who had applied his mind to the question to be decided could have arrived at it'.[24] Nor are the interests or expectations which attract the procedural protection of fairness or natural justice clearly identifiable from the case law. They have varied from time to time. During the long period of relative judicial quiescence from the end of the First World War until the early 1960s, many administrative decisions attracted no procedural protection because they did not concern vested rights but involved only what are today called 'legitimate expectations'. In other words, individuals merely had a hope, based on published rules or statements, that a decision might be made in their favour. In these cases, everything will depend upon the 'right' or 'expectation' being recognized by the court. In the forty years preceding *Ridge* v. *Baldwin* in 1962, decisions affecting mere expectations were classified as 'purely administrative', not meriting any procedural protection. Since the early 1960s, procedural protection has been extended so far as to cover not only situations in which there was the merest expectation of a favourable decision, but even decisions taken outside the statutory framework, contrary to statutory provisions, such as those in the fields of extra-statutory tax concessions and immigration law described in Chapter 1.[25]

These changes took place incrementally because English administrative law lacks a coherent, underlying philosophy. There is no jurisprudence of public law. That is not to say that the unwritten constitution is politically or, as two writers have suggested, economically neutral.[26] It reflects the values of the senior judiciary. Lord Devlin, a member of that group for many years, remarked that 'most judges do not question the status quo' and are likely to adopt a view of the public interest common to 'any other body of elderly men who have lived on the whole unadventurous lives'. Writing of nineteenth-century judges, who established many of the principles still applied in public law, he said:

> They [the judges] looked for the philosophy behind the Act
> and what they found was a Victorian Bill of Rights, favouring
> (subject to the observance of the accepted standards of
> morality) the liberty of the individual, the freedom of contract
> and the sacredness of property, and which was highly
> suspicious of taxation. If the Act interfered with these notions,
> the judges tended either to assume that it could not mean what
> it said or to minimise the interference by giving the intrusive
> words the narrowest possible construction, even to the point of
> pedantry.[27]

These often subconscious values are important when the scope of statutory powers is under consideration. They will vary from time to time. The values of modern judges are not the same as those of Victorian judges, but nineteenth-century decisions will have left their imprint on the modern common law. In determining the limits of the powers of the GLC in 1981 to subsidize public transport, the House of Lords referred to its decision in *Roberts* v. *Hopwood* in 1925.[28] In that case the House of Lords was called upon to decide whether or not a local authority, which had the power to pay 'such wages as [it] thinks fit', was entitled to fix a minimum wage above the market rate and to pay the same wage to both men and women. The idea was rejected by Lord Atkinson with indignation:

The vanity of appearing as model employers of labour had not then, apparently, taken possession of the council, nor had the council become such ardent feminists as to bring about, at the expense of the ratepayers whose money they administered, sex equality in the labour market ... The council would, in my view, fail in their duty if, in administering funds which did not belong to their members alone, they put aside all these aims to the ascertainment of what was just and reasonable remuneration to give for the services rendered to them, and allowed themselves to be guided in preference by some eccentric principles of socialist philanthropy, or by a feminist ambition to secure equality of the sexes in the matter of wages in the world of labour.

Although the payment of above-market wages and equal pay to men and women is, in the first case, often today thought desirable, and in the case of equal pay is now so far from being 'eccentric' as to be mandatory by law, the decision was cited as demonstrating an abiding economic principle, which, even in changing times, remains true: public bodies must run public services according to market principles. This is, undoubtedly, an arguable political philosophy which has many adherents, but is no more 'true' than any other political philosophy. The relevance of political and moral philosophies with regard to judicial review is that, among the heads of review on the grounds of 'irrationality' identified by Lord Diplock in the GCHQ case, is that relating to a decision 'which is so outrageous in its defiance of ... accepted moral standards that no sensible person who applied his mind to the question to be decided could have arrived at it'. Feminism and equal pay clearly outraged Lord Atkinson's economic and moral sensibilities, but that would not be the case with all judges today. In *Van Gorkem* v. *Attorney-General*, a New Zealand case decided in 1978, Woodhouse J in the Court of Appeal cited with approval the following passage from Cooke J in the court below relating to the interpretation of teachers' pay and conditions: 'In modern times discrimination on the ground of sex alone is so controversial, and so widely regarded as wrong, that I would not be prepared to infer authority to introduce it from such general language as is to be found in regulation 16(9).'[29]

Despite the abolition of the Star Chamber and the Church Courts, the ordinary common law courts still regard themselves as having a residual role as guardians of public morality. On this basis the House of Lords has held that the publication of a directory of prostitutes constituted the hitherto unknown criminal offence of a conspiracy to corrupt public morals. Lord Simonds quoted with approval the dictum of Lord Mansfield in the eighteenth century that the Court of King's Bench was *custos morum* of the people and had the superintendency of offences *contra bonos mores* [and] ... there is in that court a residual power, where no statute has intervened to supersede the common law, to superintend those offences which are prejudicial to the public welfare'.[30] The courts continue to make moral as well as legal judgments in the interpretation of the criminal law. In *R. v. Brown* in 1994 the House of Lords held the defendants guilty of assault, although their victims had consented to private acts of sado-masochism which resulted in varying degrees of injury. The House held that it was not in the public interest that a person should wound or cause actual bodily harm to another for no good reason.[31] The decision has been criticized, and it is difficult to distinguish the unattractive practice of sado-masochism from what is to some the equally unattractive sport of boxing. In boxing the participants also seek to injure one another for the gratification of each other and the onlookers. The court in both cases is making a moral choice which, even in our unwritten constitution, is one for legislators and not judges.

The role of the courts in applying judicial concepts of public morality as a long-stop to administrative decisions in the public sphere may not be wholly inappropriate if Parliament has indicated some moral parameters for a body with statutory powers, such as those laid down for commercial broadcasters.[32] In relation to other statutory powers, the objects of the legislation may supply some guidance on the sort of criteria that are to be applied in determining whether a decision-maker has gone so far as to be completely outside the discretion conferred upon him. In relation to prerogative powers, the whole process of review is much more difficult. There are no 'objectives' such as those which might have impelled the passage of legislation, and which might supply the relevant and irrelevant considerations to which the decision-maker must, or must not, have regard. Prerogative powers confer immense discretionary powers, but have only the most unspecific applications. Nevertheless, Lord Diplock, in the GCHQ case, declared that their exercise could be subject to a degree of judicial review, although, in his judgment, this was likely to be confined to procedural matters:

> While I see no a priori reason to rule out 'irrationality' as a ground for judicial review of a ministerial decision taken in the exercise of 'prerogative' powers, I find it difficult to envisage in any of the various fields in which the prerogative remains the only source of the relevant decision-making power a decision of a kind that would be open to attack through the judicial process

upon this ground. Such decisions will generally involve the application of government policy. The reason for the decision-maker taking one course rather than another do not normally involve questions to which, if disputed, the judicial process is adapted to provide the right answer, by which I mean that the kind of evidence that is admissible under judicial procedures and the way in which it has to be adduced tend to exclude from the attention of the court competing policy considerations which, if the executive discretion is to be widely exercised, need to be weighed against one another – a balancing exercise which judges by their upbringing and experience are ill-qualified to perform.[33]

While relevant considerations are hard to identify in relation to the use of prerogative powers, decision-makers, especially when making decisions which affect the rights or expectations of individuals, are accustomed to make those decisions according to certain declared policies. These may often be used in relation to statutory discretions, but they may equally apply in relation to prerogative decisions. The courts have long accepted that such statements of policy, although incapable of binding decision-makers in the long term, can hold them to the making of decisions according to the policy which has been announced, at least until the policy has been formally changed. Thus, assurances given to illegal immigrants in Hong Kong as to the procedure which would be followed in relation to those who gave themselves up, practices relating to the admission of adopted children to be admitted outside the immigration rules and procedures to be adopted in relation to planning applications within a development plan were all held to bind the decision-maker to the policies adopted while they remained in force.[34] The first of these decisions was made under the prerogative, but the second and third were in relation to statutory powers. All these decisions concerned procedural matters. As we have seen, Lord Diplock seemed inclined in the GCHQ case to limit the scope of judicial review to the way in which prerogative powers were exercised, and to exclude, on the basis of non-justiciability, consideration of whether or not a decision was 'irrational'. The courts have not followed his lead. In *Everett, Bentley* and *Ex p. P*,[35] the substantive grounds for the decision were considered as well as the procedure.

But the most significant change in approach was marked by the decisions of the Divisional Court and the Court of Appeal in *R. v. Ministry of Defence ex p. Smith and others*.[36] The applicants challenged a ban imposed on service personnel who had a homosexual orientation. The rule had led to their dismissal. On the face of it, the rule was unreviewable. It was concerned with the organization of the defence forces and clearly fell within the prerogative. It involved a challenge, unlike the GCHQ decision itself, not to the procedure by which the policy had been arrived at or implemented, but to the policy itself. The applicants argued that the policy was irrational and that it infringed their human right to privacy under the European Convention. In the Divisional Court, Simon Brown LJ had no hesitation in holding that the policy was justiciable. He went further, adding that 'only the rarest cases [involving the prerogative] today will be ruled strictly beyond the court's purview – only cases involving national security properly so-called and where the courts really do lack the expertise or material to form a judgment on the point at issue'.[37] If the policy could be subject to review, by what standards was it to be judged? The declared object of the policy was to ensure the delivery of an operationally efficient and effective fighting force. 'The real question becomes: is it reasonable for the minister to take the view that allowing homosexuals into the force would imperil that interest? Is that, in short, a coherent view, right or wrong?'

Simon Brown LJ decided that it was 'a wrong view, a view that rests too firmly upon the supposition of prejudice in others and which insufficiently recognises the damage to human rights inflicted'. He concluded, however, that it was not for him to decide whether the policy was right or wrong. He could only do this if the policy 'outrageously defies logic or accepted moral standards', and he was not prepared to hold that it fell into that category. Curtis J agreed, although he was not even prepared to go so far as to say that he disagreed with the policy. The Court of Appeal upheld the decision of the Divisional Court on the basis that, although there was now greater tolerance of homosexuality, it was not yet clear from the experience of other foreign services what effect a removal of a ban on individuals with a homosexual orientation (as opposed to conduct, which would always be inappropriate in the armed services) would have. Henry LJ acknowledged that there was no evidence before the court as to what effect toleration of servicemen and servicewomen with a homosexual orientation would have, but he was not prepared to conclude that the policy was 'irrational'. In the Court of Appeal, Sir Thomas Bingham MR agreed with Brown LJ in the Divisional Court that the policy was reviewable, but, he said, 'the threshold of irrationality is a high one ... The greater the policy content of a decision, and the more remote the subject-matter of a decision from ordinary judicial experience, the more hesitant the court must necessarily be in holding a decision to be irrational. That is good law, and like most good law, common sense.' Thorpe LJ agreed, holding that the policy 'clearly commands a wide measure of public support'.

The decisions of the two courts are confusing. It is not clear whether the judicial assessment of the policy is being made according to moral criteria or on the basis of logical coherence. Human rights are thrown in on the side of the applicants, although it is clear, since the European Convention was not, at the time, incorporated into English law, that they were only a factor which had to be weighed along with many others. On morality, both Simon Brown LJ in the Divisional Court and Thorpe LJ in the Court of Appeal have abandoned the earlier position of the courts as arbiters of moral behaviour and now adopt a more relativist, detached view, speaking of 'accepted moral standards' and 'evolving ... social attitudes'.[38] There was, however, no recognition in the case of the now widespread codes of practice in many spheres of employment, including the Bar, prohibiting discrimination on the grounds of sexual orientation. Although there is much discussion as to whether or not the acceptance of those who have a homosexual orientation (but whose behaviour is exemplary in military terms) is irrational in the light of new policies accepting homosexuals in foreign armed forces, the courts both agree in deciding that such comparisons are not for them. Both courts agree that no evidence from the experience of the British services had been tendered to support the refusal to accept homosexuals, and the evidence of the American forces which was offered in support of services policy was described by an American judge in *Able* v. *US*, to which the Court of Appeal was referred, as 'based on irrational prejudices'.[39] Despite the apparent lack of logical coherence in basing a policy either on irrational prejudice or, at least, on speculation rather than evidence, the courts were not prepared to hold the policy unreasonable. While decision-makers are not precluded from making intuitive decisions, where the statute, or the stated policy, is predicated upon the existence of certain facts, courts normally expect, as a matter of logic, that there is some evidence before the decision-maker that the relevant facts obtain.[40] The court's decision makes it clear that, in attempting to review the exercise of prerogative powers on substantive, rather than procedural, grounds, the lack of statutory objectives or constitutional safeguards laying down minimum standards means that the courts are operating in a context in which 'irrationality' in the *Wednesbury* sense has little meaning. The courts are reduced to 'common sense' and a subjective view of what is appropriate.

The current limits of judicial review of prerogative powers emerge most strikingly from the decision in *R.* v. *Secretary of State for Defence ex p. Sancto* in 1992.[41] The parents of a soldier who died in an accident in the Falkland Islands were, in this case, held not to be entitled to judicial review of a decision by the Secretary of State to refuse to disclose the report of the board of inquiry into his death. The judge, Rose J, said he was satisfied that the decision not to disclose was 'outrageous in the sense used by Lord Diplock' in the GCHQ case. However, that would only assist the applicants if they had legal rights to protect or there was a legal duty to enforce.

> In the absence of a freedom of information Act, there is no public right to know ... There is no legal duty on the Secretary of State, statutory or otherwise, to disclose or to exercise a discretion in relation to a board of inquiry report. The parents have no right to know how their son died in so far as that could be ascertained from the report. Although that last sentence might cause a gasp of astonishment from members of the public and perhaps some ministers, it accurately reflects the state of the law ... The situation is for Parliament to remedy, not the judge.

The decision illustrates both the limited nature of rights which are recognized by the common law and sufficient to found an application for judicial review, and the limited scope for review outside a statutory context. The court did, perhaps, adopt a narrower approach to the necessary legal standing to make an application for judicial review than was strictly required, bearing in mind that, five years previously, the Divisional Court had recognized the right of a journalist to challenge the policy of the chair of local justices not to reveal the names of magistrates in certain cases for security reasons.[42] Although journalists have a professional interest in obtaining information, there seems to be no sound basis on which to deny ordinary citizens the opportunity to seek to protect the public interest in freedom of information. A right to challenge the decision is, however, one thing. A right to have the information is another. As Rose J observed, there was no duty imposed on the minister, or any corresponding right of the parents. Within the prerogative, ministers are free to give or withhold information to the public as they please, provided that any information they give does not misrepresent the legal position.[43]

CONCLUSIONS

Judicial review provides an important means of ensuring that ministers and public bodies act within the law, especially in those cases where ministerial accountability to Parliament provides no effective remedy. Its use has grown enormously in the past fifteen years, with applications increasing fourfold between 1980 and 1992.[44] Part of that expansion has been in the field of hitherto unreviewable prerogative decisions. In the context of maintaining the rule of law, that must be welcomed. There must, however, be serious doubts about the extent to which the rules developed by the courts for the review of statutory powers are equal to the task. Prerogative powers, by their very nature, confer the most general discretions on ministers. Decisions which they make frequently involve both stated and unstated competing policy options. Judicial review 'often involves values and policy interests which must be balanced against and may transcend the individual interest'.[45]

In relation to decisions made under powers conferred by statute, the policy objects are usually expressed, or the intention of Parliament may be gathered from the legislation. In the case of prerogative powers, there are no such objectives. The reasons for decisions may have to be gleaned from policy statements, circulars, answers to written questions in Parliament or other evidence before the court. These may suffice to ensure that decisions are taken in accordance with that policy, or according to the principles of natural justice and fairness which the courts have developed in relation to all administrative decisions, but they are of little assistance where there is no clear policy. It is more than two hundred years since Lord Camden objected to the courts being called upon to determine the scope of a minister's powers from the practice of his office. 'Who ever conceived a notion, that any part of the public law could be buried in the obscure practice of a private office?'[46] That is, unfortunately, the case today in immigration, tax and, to an extent, planning law. A modern writer has remarked that it is 'difficult to imagine a more haphazard system for publishing or not publishing rules which may have legal force directly or indirectly or interpret legal provisions or structure the exercise of official discretion'.[47]

The lack of any concept in the common law of how competing principles of public and private interest should be balanced, or the recognition of any rights or duties as fundamental or overriding, has left our courts singularly ill-equipped to adjudicate effectively on the use of prerogative powers. Our courts have, in these cases, been acting as constitutional courts, but they have not been guided by any clear constitutional principles. The Court of Justice of the European Union is in a very different position. Although it has to adjudicate on the exercise by the Community institutions of powers of equal breadth to those enjoyed by ministers under the prerogative (often with little more than policy statements or programmes to guide it), it does so in the context of the objects of the Community which are set out in the preliminary articles of the Treaties and in the light of the fundamental rights created by the Treaties and developed by the Court. The Human Rights Bill may go some way to meeting the current deficiency faced by the courts of this country. The Bill will make it unlawful for a public authority to act in a way which is incompatible with one or more of the Convention rights (clause 6 (1)). Although the Bill limits direct challenges to public bodies to the victims of acts breaching the Convention, the rights enshrined in the Convention will now become 'relevant considerations' to which all public decision-makers (including the courts) will have to have regard. They will not, however, override any statutory provisions which are clearly in conflict with them, and incompatible provisions will remain in effect until the necessary amendments have received Parliamentary approval (clause 12). How far the newly incorporated Convention principles will persuade the courts to enter the sensitive space of executive policy-making, is yet to be seen. In some cases, where the impact on individual rights is clear, and the policy considerations are not well defined, as in the case of homosexuals in the armed forces, it may well be that incorporation will tell decisively in favour of individual rights. In other cases, where policy considerations are more compelling, it is likely that the wide exceptions allowed by the Convention will enable the courts to follow recent practice in cases involving the use of prerogative powers of expressing a willingness, in principle, to intervene, followed by a refusal, in the case in hand, to do so.

NOTES AND REFERENCES

1. *Chandler and Others* v. *DPP* [1964] AC 763 (Lord Radcliffe); *The Case of Proclamations* (1611) 12 Co Rep 74; *Duff Development* v. *Kelantan Government* [1924] AC 797, 824 (Lord Sumner).
2. *Buron* v. *Denman* (1848) 2 Exch 167. Compare *Madrazo* v. *Willes* (1820) 3 Barn & Ald 353, where the plaintiff succeeded on very similar facts and no act of state was claimed by the Crown (see Chapter 6).
3. *Ex parte Weber* [1916] 1 AC 227; *R.* v. *Vine Street Police Station Superintendent ex parte Liebmann* [1916] 1 KB 268; *R.* v. *Halliday ex parte Zadig* [1917] AC 260; *Liversidge* v. *Anderson* [1942] AC 206.
4. *R.* v. *Leman Street Police Station Inspector ex p. Venicoff* [1920] 3 KB 72. This was a case 'in which the courts refused to apply the rule at all in a situation in which it clearly ought to have been applied'. *De Smith's Judicial Review of Administrative Action* (Evans J.M., ed., 1980) p. 164; *R.* v. *Metropolitan Police Commissioner ex p. Parker* [1953] 1 WLR 1150.
5. Third Schedule, Parliamentary Commissioner Act 1967. Even within his or her jurisdiction, the Commissioner can only act in relation to the way in which a decision is taken, not with regard to its merits.
6. [1915] AC 120.

7. Dicey A.V., 'The development of administrative law in England' (1915) 31 LQR 148, 152.

8. [1964] AC 40.

9. *R.* v. *Secretary of State for the Home Department ex p. Hosenball* [1977] 1 WLR 766, 783. For the views of observers not sharing Lord Denning's total satisfaction, see, for example LXXX HC Debates (5th series) Cols 1234–1237 (2 March 1916), 364 HC Debates (5s) Cols 1540–1544 (22 August 1940); Lafitte F., *The Internment of Aliens* (1940); Gilman P. and Gilman L., *Collar the Lot!* (1980); Tolstoy N., *Victims of Yalta* (1977) (see Chapter 5).

10. [1985] AC 374 (Lord Roskill).

11. [1989] 1 QB 811, 817 (O'Connor LJ).

12. Ibid., p. 120.

13. *R.* v. *Leman Street Police Station Inspector ex p. Venicoff* [1920] 3 KB 72; *R.* v. *Brixton Prison Governor ex p. Soblen* [1963] 2 QB 43; *Hosenball* case (above, note 6). *Kuchenmeister* v. *Home Office* [1958] 1 QB 496 (a successful action for false imprisonment against immigration officers) stands as one of the few exceptions.

14. *R.* v. *Ministry of Defence ex p. Smith* [1996] 1 All ER 257.

15. *R.* v. *Secretary of State for the Home Department ex p. Bentley* [1994] QB 349. Note also *Reckley* v. *Ministry of Public Safety (No. 2)* [1996] 1 All ER 562, 572 in which the Privy Council considered the *Bentley* decision, but distinguished it. The Board (Lord Goff) quoted with approval the dictum of Lord Diplock, delivered before the GCHQ decision, in *de Fretas* v. *Benny* [1976] AC 239, 247: 'Mercy is not the subject of legal rights. It begins where legal rights end.'

16. [1983] 2 AC 237. The scope of the rule laid down in this case has been limited by the decision of the House in *Roy* v. *Kensington, Chelsea and Westminster FPC* [1992] 1 AC 624. See also the Law Commission Report, *Administrative Law: Judicial Review and Statutory Appeals*, Law Com No. 226 HC 669 (1994) pp. 22, 23.

17. *Associated Provincial Picture Houses* v. *Wednesbury Corporation* [1948] 1 KB 223.

18. [1926] Ch 66.

19. *Victoria Square Property Co. Ltd* v. *Southwark LBC* [1978] 1 WLR 463.

20. [1983] 1 AC 768. Loughlin M., 'Local government, the law and the constitution', Local Government Legal Society Trust (1983) pp. 45–7; Griffith J., 'Judicial decision-making' [1985] PL 564. Simon Lee, however, comments that 'the Left has rushed in to criticize without pausing to examine the detail, drawing simplistic, misleading analogies between cases'. Lee S., *Judging Judges* (1988) p. 61.

21. *de Smith's Judicial Review of Administrative Action* (Evans J.M., 4th edn, 1980) p. 34.

22. *A-G* v. *Great Eastern Railway Company Co.* (1880) 5 App Cas 473, at 478 (Lord Selbourne); s.111 Local Government Act 1972.

23. *Cooper* v. *Wandsworth Board of Works* (1863) 14 CB (NS) 180; *Attorney-General of Hong-Kong* v. *Ng Yuen Shiu* [1983] 2 AC 629.

24. *Council of Civil Service Unions* v. *Minister for the Civil Service* [1985] AC 374 (Lord Diplock).

25. *Preston* v. *IRC* [1985] 2 All ER 327; *R.* v. *Secretary of State for the Home Dept ex p. Asif Khan* [1984] 1 WLR 1337.

26. Daintith T. and Sah M., 'Privatisation and the economic neutrality of the constitution' [1994] PL 465.

27. (1976) 39 MLR 1.
28. [1925] AC 578.
29. [1978] 2 NZLR 387, 395; Walker P., 'What's wrong with irrationality?' [1995] PL 556.
30. *Shaw* v. *DPP* [1961] 2 WLR 897. See Griffith J.A.G., *The Politics of the Judiciary* (3rd edn, 1985) pp. 152–6; Lee S., *op. cit.*, pp. 197, 198.
31. [1994] 1 AC 212. Compare *R.* v. *Wilson, Times Law Report*, 5 March 1996, where the Court of Appeal held that a wife's consent to the burning of the defendant's initials on her skin could constitute a defence. Nash S., 'Consent: public policy or legal moralism?' *New Law Journal*, 15 March 1996, p. 382.
32. *Attorney-General (ex. rel. McWhirter)* v. *Independent Broadcasting Authority* [1973] QB 629.
33. [1985] AC 374, 410–411.
34. *Attorney-General of Hong Kong* v. *Ng Yuen Shiu* [1983] 2 AC 629; *R.* v. *Secretary of State for the Home Dept ex p. Asif Khan* [1984] 1 WLR 1337; *Niarchos (London) Ltd* v. *Secretary of State for the Environment* (1977) 35 P & CR 259.
35. *R.* v. *Secretary of State for Foreign and Commonwealth Affairs ex p. Everett* [1989] QB 811, [1989] 2 WLR 224, CA; *R.* v. *Secretary of State for Home Affairs ex p. Bentley* [1994] QB 349, DC; *R.* v. *Criminal Injuries Compensation Board ex p. P.* [1995] 1 WLR 845, CA.
36. *R.* v. *Ministry of Defence ex p. Smith* [1995] 4 All ER 427, DC; [1996] 1 All ER 257, CA.
37. [1995] 4 All ER 427, 446.
38. [1995] 4 All ER 427, 447, DC; [1996] 1 All ER 257, 274, CA. More recent decisions indicate a strong shift in judicial opinion against discrimination on grounds of sexual orientation, following the decision of the European Court of Justice in *P. V. S. and Cornwall County Council* (case c-13/94) *New Law Journal*, 14th June 1996: Bowley, M., 'More power to their elbows', *New Law Journal*, 14th September 1997, p. 1320.
39. (1995) 880 F Supp 968, US District Court, East NY District.
40. Walker P., 'What's wrong with irrationality?' [1995] PL 556, 557.
41. *Times Law Report*, 9 September 1992, QBD, 5 Admin LR 673.
42. *R.* v. *Felixstowe JJ, ex p. Leigh* [1987] QB 582. Cane P., 'Standing up for the public' [1995] PL 276, 277, 278. After the *Sancto* case the Ministry changed its policy in favour of disclosing such reports: Cane P., *An Introduction to Administrative Law* (1996) p. 297, note 23.
43. *Jenkins* v. *Attorney-General* (1971) 115 SJ 386; *Gillick* v. *DHSS* [1986] AC 112.
44. *Administrative Law: Judicial Review and Statutory Appeals*, Law Commission Consultation Paper No. 126 (1993) para. 2.14.
45. *Ibid.*, para. 2.1.
46. *Entick* v. *Carrington* (1765) 19 St. Tr. 1030.
47. Ganz G., *Quasi-legislation: Recent Developments in Secondary Legislation* (1987) pp. 40, 41. Another area in which police and prerogative powers exercised by the security services have been guided by the content of statements made to Parliament, rather than by any clear rule of law, is in relation to the placing of bugging devices on property: *R.* v. *Khan (Sultan)* [1994] 4 All ER 426. See, now, Police Act 1997.

3

The Monarchy

HEAD OF STATE AND NATIONAL SYMBOL

The Queen's Government was the title chosen by Sir Ivor Jennings for his popular introductory book on the British constitution published in 1954. Jennings was, perhaps, one of the best known writers on the constitution of this century and his book was described by one reviewer as 'an admirable short account of the machinery of British democracy'. To anyone coming to examine the British constitution completely afresh, and learning that it is a representative democracy, with government ministers drawn from the largest party in a representative Parliament, Jennings's description of that representative government as the *Queen's* government might seem a little strange. The government of the *people* of Britain, or of the United Kingdom, would seem more apt. Jennings, however, recognized the continuing important symbolic role of the monarchy in the constitutional structure, and also, perhaps, the very great personal popularity of the newly crowned Queen. He described the Queen's four principal functions as follows: first, 'appearing in an impersonal fashion as "the Crown", the Queen's name is the cement that binds the Constitution. Secondly, the Queen's name similarly binds the Commonwealth. Thirdly, there are constitutional duties which the Queen performs personally. Fourthly, the Queen is a social figure exercising important functions outside the social sphere.'[1]

As we have seen, 'the Crown' has come to mean 'the government', rather than the monarch in her personal or official capacity. 'The monarch' or 'the sovereign' have come to indicate the office of head of state, although the terms are often used to describe the office-holder in relation to a particular function, while the term 'the Queen' is normally used to indicate that flesh-and-blood person who, if she were a commoner, would be called 'Elizabeth Windsor'. None of these terms is wholly exact, but their relationship can be roughly compared to that of a Russian doll, with 'the Crown' as the outer skin, the monarch or sovereign as the inner one, and the Queen, the human individual, at its heart. Both Bagehot, writing in the mid-nineteenth century, and Jennings, writing in the middle years of the twentieth century, were keenly aware that it is the *person*, the Queen and her family, that provides the real focal point of the constitution.

Symbolism plays an important part in any constitution. The natural attachment which most people have to the country of their birth is reinforced by such things as flags, national symbols, national anthems and national monuments. These have long played an important role in Britain. The more concrete the symbol, the more effective it is. The monarch is the most prominent and the most easily identifiable part of what Bagehot called 'the dignified part' of the constitution. 'Royalty', he said, 'is a Government in which the attention of the nation is concentrated on one person doing interesting things. A republic is a Government in which attention is divided between many, who are all doing uninteresting things.' The national anthem has, since the eighteenth century, celebrated not the country in which the British live, nor the people themselves, but the monarch who presides over them. The personification of the state in the monarch, although not new when Queen Victoria came to the throne, was, on the size and scale we have it today, almost entirely a Victorian creation. It needed an active monarchy, obviously engaged in worthy projects and good works to which all subjects could aspire, and, as Bagehot would have it, a focus of their interest. For that reason Gladstone complained about Queen Victoria's retirement from public life after the death of Prince Albert. That absence coincided with the high point of Victorian republicanism. The fall of the Empire in France and the proclamation of the Third Republic gave a new impetus to republicanism in England. The rise was short-lived, however. Disraeli brought the Queen out of retirement and proclaimed her Empress of India. In a brilliant coup, he identified imperialism with Conservatism, and associated both with the monarch. Although allegiance to the monarch had always been a central feature of the constitution, it had been possible, in the latter days of George III, and in those of his inadequate son and brother, to mock the monarchy but still espouse loyalty to the nation. Shortly before the battle of Waterloo, the Duke of Wellington wrote to a friend, 'What dreadful times we live in! The King is mad and the Regent is a horrible man.'[2]

Disraeli's great achievement was to make the monarchy the

symbol of nationhood and empire. It became a popular symbol. The 'little old lady of Windsor' caught the popular imagination just when the extension of the franchise required the popular imagination to be stimulated.[3] The symbolism of monarchy has continued to pervade everyday life. Writing in 1954, Jennings took, as a simple example of the pervasiveness of that symbolism, an Irishman posting a letter in London to his girlfriend in Ireland before the First World War. He went, first, to a post office provided by the Crown, and controlled remotely by the King's Postmaster-General, and paid for the stamp with a penny with the King's head on it. The value of the penny had been fixed by the King in Council; so had the twelve pennies which made a shilling, and the twenty which made a sovereign. Next, he bought his stamp, also with the King's head on it, and placed it in a box marked with the King's initials. It was collected from the box by a servant of the King called a postman, and was ultimately delivered to the letter box of his girlfriend by another servant of the King, an Irish postman. King George V knew nothing about the letter, yet the whole transaction was carried out in his name.

The Queen's head is still on postage stamps, but so much else has changed that it is clear that the symbolism of monarchy has been diminished by events. Post offices are still provided by the Crown (just) after a failed attempt to privatize them, but neither the Postmaster-General nor the Post Office controls a body called 'Post Office Counters', which takes payment for the stamp. The penny, although it still bears the Queen's head, is now one unit in a metricated pound, which may shortly be called a 'Euro', or a 'Europound', its value fixed by a European Central Bank. The letter may be delivered by a postman, but a larger packet may well be transmitted by a firm of private carriers. The Republic of Ireland is no longer British territory, nor even part of the Commonwealth, nor was it even when Jennings wrote. Much symbolism, however, remains.

Justice is delivered by the Queen's judges and prosecutions are undertaken by the Crown Prosecution Service in her name. Her Majesty's Prisons confine the offenders, although a growing part of the process of confinement is undertaken by private security firms. Officers of the armed forces are commissioned and impose discipline in her name. Successful industrialists receive the Queen's Award for Industry. None of this is necessary from an administrative point of view, and the Queen is, of course, not involved in any way in the multiplicity of activities conducted in her name. The use of the monarchy in this way was originally only a consequence of the evolution of a traditional, absolute monarch into a constitutional head of state, retaining the trappings of monarchical power, but stripped of their substance. It has been seen to be a virtue in its own right. Bagehot called it 'the dignified' part of the constitution, feeding the child-like imagination of the public, while the serious business of government was carried on by those who really exercised power. It was symbolism, but it was, and remains, potent.

The state is reinforced by the traditional splendour and spectacle of the monarchy. Coronations, royal weddings and funerals, the investiture of the Prince of Wales and so on are great national occasions, bringing the past into the present amid splendid pageantry and ancient ritual.[4] The coronation of the Queen in 1952 was the occasion of high excitement, with talk of a new 'Elizabethan age' and a revival of national greatness. Referring to the recent coronation in 1952, the Archbishop of Canterbury declared, 'This country and the Commonwealth last Tuesday were not far from the Kingdom of Heaven.'[5] The Queen's role as head of the established church tended to strengthen the natural deference felt by many to the head of state with the respect shown by religious people to their spiritual ruler. The prayers of faithful Anglicans for the Queen and the Royal Family emphasized the link between the monarchy and the national church, and echoed the medieval doctrine of the monarch as ordained by God. At its height, this deference to the symbolic monarchy bordered on deification. Kingsley Martin described the prevailing mood in the late 1950s:

> A glorified, religious view of royalty is the vogue. The Queen is not allowed to wear a crown; nothing less than a halo will suffice. But the halo is neon-lighted – a combination which seems to make the worst of both worlds, the divine and the secular. This unreal light is reflected on all members of the royal family. Writers speak and change gear every time they mention royalty; their reverent phraseology makes the innumerable books about foreign personages astonishing to foreign readers who do not share our novel habit of simultaneously staring and genuflecting.[6]

Another contemporary account of the work of the Queen concluded:

> The Queen is filled with a sense of duty so deep it is a feeling of vocation ... She knows that if she works incessantly, cheerfully, and entirely without taking offence, she will do incalculable good ... When we are adding the pros and cons of life today, it is well to give thanks that in a position of such leadership and responsibility the people of the Commonwealth have as their Head Queen Elizabeth, our Queen.[7]

The spirit of those times has been much diminished by royal affairs, royal quarrels and royal divorces, but it has not quite gone. Sir John Stokes, a Conservative MP from 1974 to 1992, recently observed, 'We remember the Queen was anointed and crowned at her coronation and therefore is a quasi-religious person.'[8] Today, the more common view of the monarchy, while generally accepting its symbolic role, is much more practical and detached and less deferential. To an extent, the great attachment to the monarchy in the 1950s and 1960s reflected an attempt by those most closely wedded to Britain's imperial past to elevate and enlarge the monarchy, which had played a central role in the imperial enterprise, to fill the emotional gap left by loss of empire. Support for the monarchy as head of state is no longer as widespread or as unqualified as when the Queen came to the throne more than forty years ago. Surveys of public opinion show a much higher percentage of the population able to contemplate the future of this country without it.[9] Many more envisage a much reduced role for it. Perhaps the most striking example of the extent of public dissatisfaction with the Palace was provided by the response of the public to the death of Diana, Princess of Wales, and the extraordinary reaction to the critical funeral oration of the Princess' brother.

HEAD OF COMMONWEALTH

We have seen how the naming of Queen Victoria as 'Empress of India' was a defining moment in the development of both the monarchy and a kind of imperial patriotism, originally rejected by liberal radicals, but later embraced by them, and elevated as Britain's 'civilizing role in the world'. Queen Victoria, her son, grandson and great-grandson became the symbolic head not only of a United Kingdom of Great Britain and (Northern) Ireland but also of an empire covering more than a quarter of the surface of the globe. Anyone born in the imperial territory became a 'British subject'. Like St Paul in the Roman Empire he or she could claim '*civis Britannicus sum*' and move and live in any other territory ruled by the British Crown. Any alien becoming a subject by registration or naturalization swore an oath of allegiance, not to the Britain which ruled the colony, but to the monarch who was its titular head. All were 'subjects' of the King or Queen. They were subject to her control and authority, but they could also, within the imperial territory, look to her for protection.

That sense of a common subject status under one King-Emperor was eroded by the emergence of the new dominions. By 1926 most of the self-governing dominions were, in effect, independent states, equal in status to the United Kingdom. The surrender of the power of the Westminster Parliament to legislate for the dominions in 1931 was followed by a belated recognition of separate dominion citizenships in the British Nationality Act 1948. The dominions had long exercised their own immigration controls, and the Act recognized that British subjects of one Commonwealth country no longer had the right of entry and residence to another. The formal recognition of the transformation of the relationship between Crown and Empire to that of the King as head of a free association of Commonwealth states was made at a meeting of the Commonwealth prime ministers in 1949.[10] Citizens of Commonwealth states were still British subjects, and as such, continued to enjoy freedom of movement into what many persisted in calling 'the mother country'. That link was only finally broken in 1962, when all citizens of Commonwealth and colonial territories became subject to immigration control in the United Kingdom.[11]

Under the new arrangement King George VI, and then the present Queen, became head of a free association of Commonwealth states. Some also continued to maintain the Queen as head of state. Others followed the lead of India, and became republics within the Commonwealth. This was regarded as a special arrangement, but, inevitably, it became a precedent to be followed by the majority of new states, which wanted to retain their Commonwealth links but also to become republics. The British monarch continued to be a symbol of Commonwealth unity, and of certain shared values and beliefs. Some recognition of those values was demonstrated by the withdrawal of South Africa from the Commonwealth in 1961. The occasion was its conversion to the status of a republic, but it is likely that its departure anticipated expulsion for its *apartheid* policies. Many of the Commonwealth states have abandoned the Westminster model of democracy but all seem to continue to value their status as Commonwealth members.

The Queen takes her role as head of the Commonwealth very seriously. She remains the focus of Commonwealth unity. The Commonwealth is, however, no more than a loose association of states, and it is clear that the concept of the Commonwealth as an economic, political or legal entity is an illusion.[12] It is not now an organization which the Queen's father would recognize. When Jennings wrote in 1954 he was able to declare, 'The Queen is Queen of all the territories that admit allegiance to her ... She has a score or more governments governing in her name ... Everywhere in the Commonwealth the mails are the Royal Mails, engaged in Her Majesty's Service. The relationship of the Commonwealth governments are everywhere closer because they are all Her Majesty's

Governments.' Much of that closeness to Britain has gone. A number of factors have contributed to a gradual fragmentation. Among the most important are British membership of the European Union and the abolition of Commonwealth trade preferences, and the growing pressure in some Commonwealth states, particularly Australia, for a republican constitution. In others, there have been demands for the severing of the remaining formal links to Britain and ultimate control over their constitutional and judicial processes, including the abolition of appeals to the Judicial Committee of the Privy Council. Another important factor has been the manifest lack of enthusiasm shown for the Commonwealth by the British government during the years in which Margaret Thatcher was Prime Minister.

CONSTITUTIONAL FUNCTIONS

The monarch has, Bagehot said, 'three rights – the right to be consulted, the right to encourage and the right to warn'.[13] Like so much in the relationship between the monarch, the Prime Minister and the Cabinet, these functions are governed by convention. The most important convention is that the monarch should not become involved in party politics. The consultation with the Cabinet is undertaken through a process of keeping the Queen informed of developments and projected changes in policy in a very substantial flow of state papers and briefing documents. She does not read all the documents sent to her, but relies, to a large extent, on her Private Secretary to draw the most important issues to her attention and on weekly consultations with the Prime Minister. Like any permanent secretary in a government department, she has seen many prime ministers come and go, and has acquired a considerable depth of knowledge and experience. How they are deployed in her weekly audiences with the Prime Minster, and the extent of her influence, we have no idea. Successive prime ministers have been extremely discreet in their memoirs. It is unlikely, however, that she favours radical political or constitutional change:

> The person who becomes the sovereign is likely, because of birth and upbringing, to be on the right in political opinion. Moreover, she is surrounded by people of like persuasion. The sovereign is also a person of considerable wealth, apart from the income which she draws from the State ... The royal family have a personal and social magnetism and their recognition is much sought after by many men and women (including those in positions of political and economic power). The influence of

the Queen's court is not to be underrated, especially in a country where the chances of political success in the Conservative Party, and to some extent in the Liberal and even the Labour parties, are enhanced by social acceptability.[14]

The behaviour of earlier monarchs throws some light on their relationships with elected politicians, on the extent to which they took their political duties seriously and were able to influence the course of events. Dicey probably exaggerated the influence which the monarch had on policy when he declared, 'The fact that all important acts of State are done in the name of the King and in most cases with the cognisance of the King ... gives the reigning monarch an opportunity for exercising great influence on the conduct of affairs.'[15]

Queen Victoria never undervalued her constitutional function. When she disagreed with the Prime Minister, she would call a meeting of the Cabinet, to act as a kind of court of appeal against him. Between 1859 and 1861 almost weekly Cabinet meetings were held at the request of the Queen.[16] She carried on a voluminous correspondence with her prime ministers and cabinet ministers about ecclesiastical appointments, insisted on being involved in the making of diplomatic appointments and preoccupied herself with such matters as the style of army uniforms and the wearing of beards by naval officers. She was convinced that she was entitled to be consulted before new policies were announced or undertaken, particularly in the area of foreign policy. Bagehot referred to the 'control' which the Queen exercised 'over particular Ministers, and especially over the Foreign Minister', together with 'a certain control over the Cabinet'. She rewarded the unfailing, if long-winded, courtesy of Gladstone by persistent obstruction. After the Liberals had won a large majority in 1880 she wrote to Disraeli that 'she would take no notice of Mr Gladstone, who has done so much mischief. It is most essential that that should be known.' Fortunately, through the discretion and loyalty of both Disraeli and Gladstone, it was not.[17]

Edward VII was more circumspect and aware of his constitutional limitations. His reign spanned a crucial decade in the development of British government and politics. It saw a major split in the Conservative Party, the landslide victory of the Liberals in 1905 and a far-reaching programme of social reform which produced a bitter conflict between Lords and Commons in which the King played a crucial part.[18] Edward found himself able to work with Prime Minister Asquith, but was hostile to Lloyd George and his radical colleague Winston Churchill, whose policies would, he was sure, damage the harmony of society and weaken national security. During the budget crisis of 1909, when the House of Lords rejected a budget instituting a system of national old age pensions, the King refused to create sufficient life peers to ensure passage of the Bill. After his death in May 1910, George V, his son, the new King, was launched into the ongoing constitutional crisis. He agreed, reluctantly, to create the necessary number of peers if, after a general election, the government secured a majority. The necessary majorities, after two general elections, were secured, and the budget was ultimately passed, as was the Parliament Act 1911, which limited the power of the House of Lords to block legislation and deprived it of any further role in the approval of finance bills.[19] The impression left by these events is of two monarchs accepting political change, but with extreme reluctance. Their natural inclinations were to support the continuing veto of the House of Lords. An attack on the hereditary chamber might, after all, be ultimately extended to the hereditary monarchy. However, any stand with the Lords against the electorate would pit the King against the mass of the British people and bring with it the early demise of the monarchy.

George V was more conscientious about his constitutional duties than his father. He believed, as did his advisors, that the King had the right to intervene in political matters. Intervention was, however, now more discreet. Unlike his grandmother, he would never have considered the summoning of a Cabinet meeting. Like his father, he was keenly interested in the organization of the army and navy. There is evidence that his unstinting support for Field-Marshall Haig resulted in both Haig's advancement before the war of 1914–1918 and his retention in office as Chief of the General Staff, when his strategy, which was increasingly opposed by both Lloyd George and Churchill, had so manifestly failed and had led to the most appalling casualties. Haig, however, felt secure, and noted in his diary that, 'The King ... stated that he would "support me through thick and thin", but I must be careful not to resign, because Lloyd George would then appeal to the country for support and would probably come back with a great majority ... The King's position would then be very difficult.'[20]

King George VI and the present Queen have had a much less overt political involvement. Although both may well have shared the opinions of the courtiers and the large country land-owners and aristocrats with whom they spent much of their leisure time, the late King and the present Queen were, and are, very discreet in expressing their views. The King is credited with having cautioned Winston Churchill against putting to sea in a cruiser to watch the D-Day landings. He was less successful over India. He bitterly opposed

Lord Wavell's plan, as Viceroy, to release Gandhi and Nehru from prison, and was resolutely opposed to Indian independence, although this had been accepted as inevitable even by Winston Churchill.[21] He did, however, maintain an easy informal contact with Attlee and his ministers in the post-war government. Contacts between the Queen, the prime ministers and with other ministers are now, however, more formal. Clement Attlee described the sort of conversations which he had with King George VI in a newspaper interview in 1959: 'It would have been quite natural for George VI to say to me: "How is Mannie hitting it off with the French generals?" or, "Well, Nye, seems to be getting the doctors in line".'[22] The King believed that he was successful in securing the appointment of Ernest Bevin at the Foreign Office, rather than Hugh Dalton, whom Attlee had favoured. Attlee, however, always denied that he was influenced by the King in choosing Bevin.[23]

Tony Benn describes, in his *Diaries*, the resistance in the Palace to his policy, while Post-Master General in the 1964–6 Labour government, for the redesign of postage stamps, which, on some stamps, involved the removal of the Queen's head. It seems clear, however, that the opposition came not from the Queen herself, but from her Private Secretary, Sir Michael Adeane. Subsequently, when Benn was Minister for Technology, she expressed her strong opposition to him to the cancellation of the Concorde project. Benn describes her as 'not clever, but she is reasonably intelligent and she is experienced.'[24] Ironically, the Concorde project was one of the few that survived Benn's term of office, despite the verdict of the then Chancellor, Dennis Healy, that it was a 'disaster for economic common sense'.[25] It is recorded that her most heated confrontation with a minister was when she released a furious tirade against Geoffrey Rippon, who, as Minister of Housing, had dared to allow the new London Hilton to overlook Buckingham Palace.[26] In recent years, the breakdown of the marriage of the Prince of Wales and the death of Diana, Princess of Wales, the fire at Windsor Castle and the cost of its refurbishment, the replacement of the royal yacht and the payment of tax by the Queen have all become matters of political controversy, and the Palace has become active in the promotion of the cause of monarchy, which it has perceived to be under attack by the press, particularly by that section owned by Rupert Murdoch. How far this more direct involvement by the monarchy, albeit discreetly, in matters of controversy affecting itself, in which it appears to be taking sides, has affected its relationship with governments, and will affect the national view of the Queen and the long-term status of the monarchy is, as yet, unclear.

THE APPOINTMENT OF THE PRIME MINISTER

All prime ministers are, formally, appointed by the Queen. The decision is, in nearly every case, determined by the outcome of a general election. The Queen summons to Buckingham Palace the leader of the party that has secured a majority in the House of Commons. There is a potential difficulty for the monarch in two cases. The first is where the prime minster dies or retires from office while the government of which he or she is head remains in power. The second is where, following a general election, no one party has an overall majority in the House.

The retirement from office of a prime minister between general elections always risked drawing the monarch into internal party conflicts. The Parliamentary Labour Party elected its leader from the beginning, but in the earlier part of this century it was often not clear which Conservative or Liberal minister would attract enough support to form a stable government. In the case of retiring prime ministers, the practice in the 1930s, 1940s and 1950s was for the outgoing prime minister to advise, and the Palace and senior members of the party and the whips would take 'soundings'. That was not always the case. Queen Victoria did not seek Gladstone's advice in 1894. She had already decided to send for Lord Rosebery. Nor is it certain that Edward VII asked Lord Salisbury's advice in 1902, or Campbell-Bannerman's in 1908.[27] The practice of wide consultation began in 1923, with the appointment of Bonar Law, and ended in 1965, when the Conservative Party adopted the Labour Party practice, and replaced Lord Home by its first elected leader, Edward Heath. The replacement of Margaret Thatcher in 1990 by John Major was accomplished with only the most formal involvement of the Queen. Following her effective defeat, and withdrawal, from the leadership contest, Margaret Thatcher went to the Palace to surrender her seals of office, and John Major went shortly afterwards to 'kiss hands' on his appointment. The Queen was spared the political embarrassment which she suffered in both 1957, when Harold Macmillan 'emerged' as the preferred leader of the Conservative Party, to the evident disappointment of the supporters of Rab Butler, and again, in 1963, when the choice of the Earl of Home was made extremely rapidly, despite attempts by several ministers to lobby Sir Michael Adeane in order to delay the appointment.[28]

The greatest difficulty for the monarch is when there is a 'hung' Parliament, and no one party has an overall majority. In these circumstances the Queen would, it would seem, be expected to call upon the leader of the largest party to attempt to form a government, and to achieve an arrangement for a working majority in the House of Commons. If the leader of the largest party is unable to secure the support of one or more of the minority parties, the threat to the retention by the Queen of her perceived impartiality could become acute. It was rumoured that, in 1974, when the government of Edward Heath had been defeated after the first miners' strike, he attempted to secure the support of the Liberals to maintain him in office, even though he was no longer the leader of the largest party in Parliament. Whether or not this is true, if the Queen had called upon him to form a government, it would undoubtedly have embroiled the monarchy in a controversy that would have been deeply damaging.

Another situation fraught with risk for the monarchy is the decision whether to accept a request by a prime minister for a dissolution of Parliament. Generally, a request is made after a government has been in office for some time, and the prime minister believes that he or she has a good chance of winning an election. Such calculated self-interest is regarded as a proper exercise of political power and is never refused. A dissolution would never be refused if a prime minister had lost a vote of confidence in the House of Commons, and the Queen might even insist on a dissolution if the prime minister attempted to cling to office. If, however, a prime minister has a working majority, and it is not long since the last general election, some writers maintain that the Queen could refuse a dissolution. George VI was so advised by his Private Secretary in 1950, after the Labour government was returned with a majority of less than a dozen. He did not, in fact, refuse it when Attlee requested a dissolution a mere 18 months after the previous election.[29] Nor did the Queen refuse one when Harold Wilson made the same request in very similar circumstances in 1966.

It was for a time unclear whether or not the Queen had the power to dissolve Parliament against the prime minster's wishes, and, in effect, to dismiss the prime minister. In 1975, the Governor General of Australia, exercising the prerogative power of the monarch, did precisely that, dissolving the Federal Parliament and dismissing Prime Minister Gough Whitlam, although he still had a majority in the House of Representatives. Whitlam himself was only prepared to advise an election for the Senate alone.[30] For the Queen to take such a decision in the UK would be very damaging for the monarchy and would certainly breach the now well established convention that places it above party politics. To avoid that sort of situation, especially if a system of proportional representation is adopted which would make the achievement by any party of an overall majority inherently less likely, it has been suggested that the power to appoint the prime minister be removed from the sovereign and either put out to a commission of the great and the good, or delegated to the Speaker of the House of Commons. Peter Riddell, the political correspondent of *The Times*, has observed that the monarch's role as umpire only works if she remains above controversy. That position becomes progressively more difficult to hold in an era of intense and intrusive media attention. If there is a constitutional stalemate, it will be much harder than in the past to prevent the Crown being in the spotlight, particularly if the monarchy itself has become more controversial as a result of the private frailties of members of the royal family.[31]

FORMAL FUNCTIONS

Besides the regular contact which the Queen has with the Prime Minister, and less frequently with other members of the Cabinet, she has a number of formal duties as head of state. These include the State Opening of Parliament and the reading of the Speech. The Queen's Speech is not, of course, her speech at all. It is usually written by the Prime Minister and includes a review of the government's policies and its legislative programme for the session.[32] The monarch is also expected to give formal assent to parliamentary bills, after they have passed the appropriate stages. Royal assent has not been refused since Queen Anne refused her assent to a Militia Bill at the beginning of the eighteenth century. George V believed that he had the right of veto, and actively contemplated refusing assent to the Irish Home Rule Bill, although he finally assented to it. Jennings, writing in 1959, insisted that the monarch still had the power of refusal of assent, and argued that the Queen would be justified in 'refusing assent to a policy which subverted the democratic basis of the Constitution, by unnecessary or indefinite prolongations of the life of Parliament, by a gerrymandering of the constituencies in the interests of one party, or by fundamental modification of the electoral system to the same end.'[33] The better view would seem to be, however, that these are matters of political judgement best left to the people of this country and not to a hereditary monarch and her advisors, and that the assent to bills by the monarch is now only a formality. The Queen also undertakes state visits to foreign and Commonwealth countries and receives heads of state from overseas. She presides in person at meetings of the Privy Council, receives letters of credence from newly appointed foreign ambassadors, receives homage from the new bishops appointed by her on the recommendation of the prime minister, hands out the Maundy Money on Maundy Thursday and holds scores of audiences and receptions every year.[34]

THE HONOURS SYSTEM

The monarch is the 'fountain of honour'. Thousands of major and minor awards are made biennially at the New Year, on the Queen's birthday and on the resignation of a prime minister. Honours are awarded on the basis of a list of recommendations prepared in the office of the Prime Minister. They range from the Order of the Garter (founded in 1348), of which there are fewer than fifty holders, to the Order of the British Empire (invented by Lloyd George in 1917), of which there are scores of thousands. A cynic might observe that the honours system has the merit of being a cheap way for those exercising power to reward the immense number of people who spend their spare time doing valuable voluntary work. It also provides the means of repaying those who have rendered financial and other assistance to the party in power. What makes the system valuable to those who receive such honours is that, as Jennings observed, 'the person who receives the OBE is shown by the world to be a person who has been thanked by the Queen for his services to the community'.[35]

Monarchs are expected to accept the recommendations made for these awards, which are now the subject of independent vetting by a Political Honours Scrutiny Committee. They seem, in recent years, almost invariably to have done so. The only award which is exclusively within the power of the monarch's personal discretion is the Royal Victorian Order, which is given for personal services to the sovereign.

The system of awards has been the subject of some abuse in the twentieth century. Edward VII is reputed to have said that 'the monarchy is the fountain of honours, but it is not a pump!' George V strenuously objected to the award of peerages to both Rothermere and Beaverbrook, but backed down in the face of Lloyd George's insistence.[36] The editors of newspapers offering unqualified support to the government in the 1980s were more modestly rewarded by Margaret Thatcher with knighthoods. Newspaper hostility may, paradoxically, on occasions be equally productive. The former BBC political correspondent, John Cole, records that Marcia Williams, later Lady Falkender, Harold Wilson's Personal and Political Secretary, was recommended for a life peerage in 1974 because, the Prime Minister told the Queen, he wanted 'to raise two fingers to the press, which had been critical of his political secretary over land deals involving her family'. Cole does not note her response, but Marcia Williams got her peerage.[37] Lloyd George was undoubtedly the Prime Minster who was the most bare-faced in his abuse of the Honours List. He operated a system under which titles were exchanged according to a fixed rate of contributions to party funds. A donation of £10 000 would secure a knighthood. A baronetcy came dearer, at £40 000, and a peerage cost even more.[38] The scandal that erupted in 1922 led to the appointment of a Royal Commission and to the Honours (Prevention of Abuses) Act of 1925, and contributed in large measure to Lloyd George's fall from office in 1924. The Act effectively prevented the soliciting of funds with offers of honours. It does not, however, prevent governments rewarding those who have given political and other services to the nation, without, it must be assumed, any hope of reward.

The award of honours continues to cause controversy. In both 1970 and 1976 Harold Wilson's resignation honours list excited criticism. The second list was the notorious 'lavender list' reputedly written out by Lady Falkender. In 1970, George Weidenfeld, the publisher of Wilson's books, received a knighthood, as did Joseph Kagan, whose Gannex raincoats Wilson often wore, and Rudy Sternberg, who helped to finance Wilson's private office in opposition. All received peerages in 1976. John Brayley, the owner of the Canning Town Glass Company, who donated a large part of the shares in the company to the Labour Party, received a knighthood in 1970. He became a minister in the 1974 government but resigned when the Fraud Squad started investigating the company.[39] Most recently, the attention of newspapers has been attracted by the donation in 1995 of four million pounds to the Conservative Party, reputed to be the biggest ever single donation to the party, which was followed by the award to the donor of a knighthood in 1996. The deputy leader of the Labour Party, John Prescott, is reported to have described the gift as 'the crudest example yet, of honours being given for financial services to the Tory party'.[40]

Writing in 1965 in his *Anatomy of Britain*, Anthony Sampson observed that 'Most politicians, and some palace officials, would agree that honours have got out of hand ... but neither party dare suggest abolition.'[41] The intervening thirty years have seen little improvement. The honours system has, if anything, become more entrenched. It remains of crucial importance to the Conservative Party because 'the New Right has enlisted not just the British state structures but the deep-seated conservatism embodied in Britain's economic and political institutions and wider value systems to support its cause. The cachet of knighthoods and honours once bestowed on builders of empire has been exploited to reward loyal back-benchers, contributors to party funds or industrial tycoons.'[42]

Bagehot included the honours system in the 'dignified' part of the constitution, behind which the 'efficient' part operated to the benefit of all. Unfortunately, the danger is not that the 'dignified part' will be lost to the 'functional' part, but that those who operate the parts that are really meant to work become beguiled and are co-opted into the decorative, but ultimately debilitating, historic structures. Peerages, knighthoods and awards are an essential part of this process. 'What gives the British Monarchy its unique strength is the fact that the court, the aristocracy and the church – not to mention the middle classes – are just as credulous worshippers of [the magic power of the monarchy] as the masses.'[43]

There are no indications that New Labour, like old Labour in office, is any more committed to the abolition or restriction of the honours system than the New Right, although its history this century has shown it to be a corrupting influence, damaging both to the monarchy and to the credibility and good name of the British constitution. Arthur Henderson's minority report to the Report of the Royal Commission on Recommendations for Honours, published in December 1922, is still much to the point on the question of political honours:

> In a democratic country it is a distinguishing mark of the good citizen that he interests himself according to his opportunity in the well-being of the community. It is indisputable that public service of great value has been rendered by men and women whose thoughts have never dwelt upon titled reward, and in view of the difficulty of keeping the honours list pure, I do not believe that the abolition of political honours would in any way diminish either the volume or quality of services given to the community by its citizens.[44]

Although the award of honours is in effect in the hands of the Prime Minister, the Queen, who is supposed to be above politics, is made to appear to be closely involved in the process of the reward of political favours. A *Times* leading article in 1992 attacked the system as 'a parody of honour and an insult to those members of the community who truly merit national recognition', but cynically concluded that 'party funds need replenishing other than from taxes, and the de facto sale of honours achieves this'.[45] If awards of honours are to continue, there is a very strong case to be made for taking the whole system away from the Prime Minister altogether, and for putting it in the hands of a commission which could make awards on the basis of merit alone.[46]

THE ROYAL ESTATES AND THE ROYAL HOUSEHOLD

The only appointments over which the Queen retains exclusive control are those to the royal household. Among the offices in the royal household over which the Queen still retains a power of appointment are her Personal Secretary, the Lord Chamberlain, the Lords and Grooms in Waiting, the Ecclesiastical and Medical Households, the Gentlemen at Arms, the Yeomen of the Guard, the Royal Company of Archers, the Marshall of the Diplomatic Corps and the Lady of the Bedchamber. The royal household in 1959 consisted of 311 people in England and Wales, with a further 67 in Scotland.[47] The Queen's estates, her income and the property and income of members of the royal family fall into two categories. There is, first of all, the Crown Estate, over which George III surrendered control on his accession in exchange for an annual income, subsequently called 'the Civil List'. Second, there are the lands and properties which successive sovereigns have purchased out of their income for their own use. In addition, there are a number of additional benefits to which the Sovereign is entitled and which are mainly relics of the feudal system. These are considered in Chapter 9. The Crown Estate, which belongs to the Sovereign – that is, to the Queen in her official capacity, and not to her personally – yielded in 1993 an annual income of £78.9 million which is paid into the Consolidated Fund, the money allocated by Parliament for public spending.[48]

Under the Civil List Acts she received, in 1993, £7,900,000. The Duchy of Lancaster received a further £2,100,000. Some £359,000 was paid to the Duke of Edinburgh, £643,000 to the Queen Mother and £3,000,000 to the Prince of Wales. The Duke of York, Prince Edward, the Princess Royal, Princess Margaret, Princess Alice, the Duke and Duchess of Gloucester, the Duke and Duchess of Kent and Princess Alexandra all receive substantial annuities from Parliament, ranging from £87,000 for Princess Alice to £249,000 for the Duke of York. The Queen, however, reimburses Parliament for all the annuities. The Duchess of York now receives no income, although she is believed to have received a settlement of approximately £2 million on her divorce. The Princess of Wales received no income, either, although she too received a substantial settlement on her divorce. This is believed to have been in the region of £17 million. The Queen pays tax on her private income from the Sandringham and Balmoral Estates and council tax on a voluntary basis.[49]

All the royal palaces, except the Castle of Moy, which belongs to the Queen Mother, and Balmoral and Sandringham, which are the Queen's personal property, belong to the Crown Estate. The Estate consists of some eighty rural and urban estates, including Osborne on the Isle of Wight and extensive areas of the West End of London. In addition, the Sovereign owns the Duchy of Lancaster, comprising some 33,000 acres, and the Prince of Wales owns another 130,000 acres scattered across southern England, Cornwall and Wales, including Highgrove House and 70,000 acres of Dartmoor. As the Palace has pointed out, 'Estimates of the Queen's wealth have often been greatly exaggerated.' The vast majority of these properties, including art treasures from the Royal Collection and the Crown Jewels, are 'held by the Queen as sovereign rather than as an individual. They may not be disposed of ... and must be passed on in due course to Her Majesty's successor as Sovereign.'[50] Besides these land holdings, the Sovereign is entitled to half of the foreshore and the whole of the seabed to a distance of twelve miles from high water mark. Some of this yields valuable income in fishing, mineral and other rights. The Sovereign is also entitled to a miscellany of medieval relics, including the right to sturgeon, and certain swans and whales. As the head of the old feudal system of land tenure, the sovereign is entitled to *bona vacantia*, i.e. goods and other property to which no one else can establish a claim, and to treasure trove. Treasure trove is 'gold or silver in coin, plate or bullion hidden in ancient times' to which no one can establish a right (see Chapter 9). A number of feudal dues associated with forestry and husbandry were abolished by the Wild Creatures and Forest Laws Act 1971. Although the vast bulk of the wealth of the monarchy is not now owned by the Queen personally, and is either part the Crown Estate or is part of the assets held on trust for successive monarchs, she does have a considerable private fortune of her own, for which there is no reliable estimate.

PERSONAL, FAMILY AND SOCIAL INFLUENCE

Bagehot referred to the unique aspect of the monarchy: a 'family on the throne, bringing down the pride of sovereignty to the level of petty life'.[51] The Queen, and other members of the royal family, like their parents and grandparents before them, are active in their involvement in good works, opening major public and private projects and participating as spectators in great sporting events such as Ascot, Wimbledon and the FA Cup Final, major events in the world of entertainment, such as the Royal Variety Command Performance, and first nights of important theatrical and musical productions. The Queen is Commander in Chief of all her armed forces, and takes the salute at great military events. She leads the mourning at the Cenotaph on Remembrance Sunday, and takes the salute at the Trooping of the Colour. She also entertains other heads of state at Buckingham Palace, Windsor and Balmoral. Although the Palace is much less the centre of social life of wealthy people since the abandonment of presentation parties for young debutantes in 1958, attendance by any member of the royal family at a social function is still regarded as a great attraction.[52] The effect on otherwise rational people of the attendance of a royal person can be quite striking, as John Naughton has noted:

> I remember once seeing the Fellows of an Oxbridge college reduced to a state of gibbering idiocy when faced with the prospect of hosting a lunch for the Queen. While the bursar spent a fortune having the toilets painted, they devoured briefing documents explaining how the monarch should be addressed, reminding them that they should under no circumstances speak until spoken to, their wives scratched one another's eyes out for places in the receiving line.[53]

Most of these events are remote from the ordinary people of this country. If they participate at all, it is as spectators at parades or ceremonies, or as television viewers. Members of the royal family wave from cars or coaches, or smile out from pictures in the tabloid press. In the late 1960s, a serious attempt was made to bring the royal family closer to the public. The venture ran counter to Bagehot's grave admonition: 'Above all our royalty is to be reverenced, and if you begin to poke about it, you cannot reverence it. Its mystery is its life. We must not let in daylight upon magic.'[54] In the early years of her reign, the Queen stayed firmly with Bagehot. Television played a major role in bringing her coronation to the public, but for many years its function in relation to the royal family was limited to the royal round of public and social engagements. Daylight was first admitted to the royal family in 1969, when the Queen's Press Secretary, Sir William Heseltine, persuaded her to take part in a film about their daily lives. It was an immensely popular programme, and seemed to have, if anything, enhanced the standing of the royal family in the eyes of the public. In retrospect, however, twenty years later, Sir William wondered whether the original decision 'may have devalued the currency of monarchy by encouraging the unremitting small change of media interest'.[55]

The exposure of the Queen and the royal family worked very much to their advantage when their lives were seen to be happy and fulfilled. They served as a model to the rest of society. Bagehot had, however, also noted that 'we have come to regard the Crown as head of our morality', but cautioned that to expect that those on the constitutional throne will always be possessed of domestic virtues 'is to expect grapes from thorns and figs from thistles'. The divorces of Princess Margaret, Princess Anne, the Duke of York and, most importantly, the Prince of Wales have combined to dull the image of happy domesticity. Worse still, the affairs and mutual recriminations between the Prince and Princess of Wales, so thoroughly covered by both the newspapers and television, damaged the reputation and standing of the heir to the throne, to the extent that serious discussion again became possible about the throne missing a generation and passing direct to Prince William, or even the termination of the monarchy on the death of the present Queen.

ALLEGIANCE

The personal nature of the relationship that, at least nominally, subsists between monarch and subject is reflected in a network of oaths which judges, Privy Councillors, bishops, Members of Parliament, coroners, and members of the armed services all take on appointment. The oaths commit the office-holders to loyalty to *the Queen*, not, as would be the case in any other country, to *the constitution*. The Queen herself, at her coronation, takes an oath 'to govern the peoples of the United Kingdom according to their respective laws and customs'.[56] It is significant that in the draft constitution of the Institute for Public Policy Research, 'every person holding British nationality owes a duty of allegiance to this Constitution'. Under the old common law, the King was styled 'liege lord', and his 'liege subjects' were bound as such to serve and obey him. Under the Treason Act 1495, allegiance is due to the Sovereign, whether the rightful heir to the Crown or not, and the subjects are bound to serve in war against every rebellion, power and might reared against the Sovereign. The duty of allegiance is applicable to the Sovereign in both capacities; that is to say, in the natural as well as the regal capacity. This means that the subject is bound, whatever the person who is king or queen may do, and even if he or she is dispossessed. The obligation of loyalty to the monarch exists quite independently of the oath, but the oath both reinforces and, in some cases, enlarges the scope of that obligation.

Although the oath may be largely symbolic, in one important instance, at least, it has been held to have been legally significant. Privy Councillors accept an oath which pledges them that they will to their 'Uttermost bear Faith and Allegiance unto the Queen's Majesty; and will assist and defend all Jurisdictions, Preeminences, and Authorities, granted to her Majesty ... And generally in all things [they] will do as a faithful and true Servant ought to do Her Majesty.'[57] The effect of the oath, it was held in the Radcliffe Report on Ministerial Memoirs in 1976, and Tony Benn has argued, was to place 'retiring cabinet ministers under an obligation to protect official information entrusted to them, even from the people by whom they were elected and to whom they are accountable'. The other members of Cabinet cannot release ministers from their duty of confidentiality because, Lord Widgery CJ made it clear in the

Crossman Diaries Case, since the duty of confidence 'is imposed to enable the efficient conduct of the Queen's business, the confidence is owed to the Queen'.[58]

The shift in power that has taken place since the Treason Act from the Crown to Parliament, and the development of principles of democracy and accountability, is not recognized in the network of personal relationships of loyalty to the Sovereign. Although Parliament has the ultimate legislative sovereignty, the supremacy that it enjoys is not simply as the legislature, but to a curious amalgam of head of state and Parliament called the Queen-in-Parliament. This formula recognizes the completely nominal involvement of the monarch in assenting to legislation. The supremacy of Parliament is not, however, recognized in the oath of allegiance of judges, who are bound to the Queen alone. The Queen is, of course, bound by her coronation oath to uphold the laws, as are, indeed, the judges in their oath. But a commitment to the Queen may, as was the case in the former Southern Rhodesia, not prevent the judges from abrogating their commitment to fundamental rights and liberties implied in their oath to uphold the law, and from accepting an entirely new role in what was, under United Kingdom law, an illegal regime.[59] No oath could, of course, have prevented such a transfer of allegiance to a new constitutional arrangement, but an oath of loyalty to the constitution would have made their default more obvious. As it was, they continued to protest their loyalty to the Queen, while sanctioning the clearest breaches of the law they were supposed to uphold.

There is still a degree of reciprocity between Crown and subject. The subject must remain loyal, wherever he or she may be in the world, and when in the UK is protected by the law of the land against unlawful seizure. While, however, he may be guilty of treason wherever he is, he has no right to protection abroad.[60]

The absence of a right of protection means that the subject cannot compel the extension of protection in a court of law. The Crown has a discretion on whether or not to offer it. However, the absence of a right to claim protection under the common law does not mean that the persons and property of the subject abroad are not safe from the action of officers of the Crown themselves. They are under a duty not to cause accidental or intentional injury or damage to the persons and properties of subjects. Freedom from intentional or negligent injury or damage abroad in exchange for absolute and unqualified criminal liability under the law of treason seems a poor bargain for the subject.

Whatever the content of the contractual or quasi-contractual relationship of allegiance between the Sovereign and subject, Sovereign and officer of the judiciary, Sovereign and officer of the administration or Sovereign and officer of the armed services, it seems an inappropriate vehicle for representing the relationship between officers of the state, citizens and the head of state in the early twenty-first century, even in the constitution as it stands at present. It originated in a small society which could not yet be called a state, and was based on a complex of personal relationships. The size of the modern state, and the remoteness of citizens and even of important officials from the Sovereign, makes the concept of a personal relationship of allegiance largely meaningless. Experience in other states suggests that the perception of a personal relationship to the head of state is not necessary for securing the loyalty of either citizens or officers of state, although it has been argued that the arrangement is desirable to secure the loyalty of the armed forces and to keep them out of politics.[61]

CONCLUSIONS

The antiquity of the British constitution gives this country an immense advantage in terms of stability and continuity. The price we pay for that benefit is, however, a heavy one. The monarchy provides a symbol of the state, and in the Queen a person on whom the loyalty and patriotism of those who serve the state can be focused. But the monarchy operates within a conceptual framework that is wholly alien to modern ideas of representative government. The language of 'master and servant' is long gone from our books on employment law. The symbolism of oaths of fealty, submission and subjecthood is quite inapt for the modern state, creating a culture of deference and secrecy not found in any other West European state. The experience of Europe this century, and Germany in particular, has been that blind obedience and loyalty to a leader are not total virtues, but the language of the British constitution continues to celebrate them. We have had a government dedicated to a classless society, but have an honours system that reinforces both class and privilege, and the Queen as the fount of a system of honours that is polluted by abuse for party advantage. The royal family was the symbol of domestic virtue, but the adoption of the dangerous course of conscripting television to present the monarchy in this way has meant that the inevitable failings of the family, like any other, have received immense and damaging publicity.

Bagehot's belief that Britain enjoyed the efficiency of republican government behind an attractive, dignified show of monarchy was never wholly true. Governments were rarely efficient and were in no sense ever republican. But the images of royalty and aristocracy enjoying power seemed to acquire a life of their own, and permeated those parts of government that were intended to be both rational and democratic. As a result, institutions like Parliament and the courts, which are supposed to be open and accessible, often seem to the people they serve to be surrounded by a kind of mysterious aura of tradition and deference. The current discussion on constitutional reform will need to concentrate on the role of the head of state and to consider whether a hereditary 'family on the throne' remains an appropriate symbol for government in a representative democracy.

NOTES AND REFERENCES

1. Jennings I., *The Queen's Government* (1954) p. 30.
2. *Letters of the Duke of Wellington*, quoted by Stokes J., in *Power and the Throne: the Monarchy Debate* (Barnett A., ed., 1994) p. 83.
3. Martin K., *The Crown and the Establishment* (1962) pp. 50, 51; Jennings I., *The British Constitution* (1941), Chapter V.
4. Street H. and Brazier R., *de Smith's Constitutional Law* (1985) p. 123.
5. Martin, *op. cit.*, p. 11.
6. *Ibid.*, p. 12.
7. Laird D., *How the Queen Reigns* (1959) p. 352.
8. Sir John Stokes, 'Keep the Queen', in *Power and the Throne: The Monarchy Debate* (Barnett A., ed., 1994) p. 81. At her coronation, the Queen was anointed in the form of the cross on the palms of both hands, the breast and the crown of the head: Halsbury's Laws, *Constitutional Law* (1985) Vol. 8, para. 854.
9. Greenslade R., 'Royal ratpack scents the bluest blood', *The Observer*, 28 July 1996.
10. Communiqués of the Commonwealth Prime Ministers Meetings on 27 April 1949 and 11 September 1962; Roberts-Wray K., *Commonwealth and Colonial Law* (1966) p. 91; Halsbury's Laws of England, *Commonwealth and Dependencies* (1974) Vol. 8, para. 801.
11. Commonwealth Immigrants Act 1962. Commonwealth citizens continued to enjoy some advantages over other immigrants under the Immigration Act 1971 s. 1(5), but these were removed by the Immigration Act 1988.
12. de Smith, *op. cit.*, p. 672.
13. Bagehot W., *The English Constitution* (1963 edn) p. 111.
14. Hartley T.C. and Griffiths J.A.G., *Government and Law* (2nd edn, 1981) p. 52.
15. Dicey A.V., *Introduction to the Law of the Constitution* (9th edn, 1950) p. 464.
16. Gordon Walker P., *The Cabinet* (1970) p. 72.
17. Martin, *op. cit.*, p. 56. Bagehot, *op. cit.*, p. 111. The Queen told her Private Secretary, Sir Herbert Ponsonby, that she 'will sooner abdicate than send for or have any communication with that half-mad firebrand who would soon ruin everything and be a dictator!' Blake R., *Disraeli* (1966) p. 717.
18. Middlemas K., *Edward VII* (1975) p. 62.
19. Martin, *op. cit.*, pp. 67–70; Middlemas, *op. cit.*, pp. 74–9.
20. Martin, *op. cit.*, p. 97; Blake R. (ed.), *The Private Papers of Douglas Haig, 1914–*

1919 (1952); Clark A., *The Donkeys* (1961). The King may have felt able to offer such overt support to Haig because of the example set by his father in giving almost total and unqualified support to Sir John Fisher in the reorganization of the navy in 1904–7 against constant attacks by the media: Middlemas, *op. cit.*, p. 71.

21. Heuston R.F.V., *Essays in Constitutional Law* (1964) p. 77; Martin, *op. cit.*, p. 117.

22. *The Observer*, 23 August 1959; Sampson A., *Anatomy of Britain Today* (1965) p. 33.

23. Wheeler-Bennett J., *King George VI*, p. 638; Sampson, *op. cit.*, p. 33.

24. Benn T., *Out of the Wilderness, Diaries 1963–67* (1987) p. 335; Vol. II (1968–72) p. 190. Benn concludes, after an audience with the Queen following the defeat of the Labour Government in 1970: 'The courtiers could scarcely conceal their delight – Sir Michael Adeane, the equerries, the lady-in-waiting were obviously delighted at what had happened.' The Queen was very courteous, but 'I am sure that the idea that the Queen's Ministers are simply advisers, and that she really is the Government, in a position to thank them before they go, is deeply entrenched at the Palace.' *Ibid.*, p. 297.

25. Healey D., *The Time of My Life* (1989) p. 408.

26. Hoggart S., 'Mother of all our misfortunes', *The Guardian*, 20 April 1996.

27. Jennings I., *The British Constitution* (1941) p. 105.

28. Sampson, *op. cit.*, p. 34.

29. Heuston, *op. cit.*, p. 79; Jennings, *The British Constitution*, n. 27, p. 109; Jennings maintained that the monarch had the right to dismiss ministers and to refuse a dissolution in his *Cabinet Government* in 1959 (pp. 411–12); compare Gordon Walker *op. cit.*, p. 77.

30. de Smith, *op. cit.*, p. 128; Kerr J., *Matters of Judgment* (1978); Whitlam G., *The Truth of the Matter* (1979).

31. Riddell P., 'Her Majesty's controversy', *The Times*, 20 November 1995; see also Hennessy P., *The Hidden Wiring* (1995); compare Bogdanor V., *The Monarchy and the Constitution* (1995), who feels that 'alone in the state, the Sovereign enjoys a total freedom from party ties and the complete absence of party history'.

32. One of the few recorded instances of the speech reflecting the monarch's wishes is of the inclusion, at his insistence, of a reference to his successful tour of Ireland in his speech of 1904. Middlemas, *op. cit.*, p. 65.

33. Jennings I., *Cabinet Government* (1959) pp. 411–12. Gordon Walker argues that such matters are to be judged by public opinion, and the sanctions are political and not procedural or legal. The right to veto legislation is dead: *op. cit.*, p. 78.

34. de Smith, *op. cit.*, p. 134.

35. Quoted by Laird D., *How the Queen Reigns* (1959) p. 174.

36. Martin, *op. cit.*, pp. 80, 81; Macmillan G., *Honours for Sale: the Strange Story of Maundy Gregory* (1954) p. 25.

37. Cole J., *As It Seemed to Me* (1995) p. 155.

38. Macmillan, *op. cit.*, pp. 47 and 91. The figures emerged at Gregory's trial on charges under the Honours (Prevention of Abuses) Act 1925 in 1933.

39. Ponting C., *Breach of Promise: Labour in Power 1964–70* (1989) p. 263.

40. Blackhurst C., 'Yorkshire businessman gave £4m to Tory Party', *The Independent*, 11 July 1996.

41. Sampson, *op. cit.*, p. 343.

42. Hutton W., *The State We're In* (1995) p. 32.

43. Crossman R., Introduction to Bagehot, *op. cit.*, p. 33; Barnett A., 'The empire state', in *Power and the Throne: the Monarchy Debate* (1994) pp. 28, 29.

44. Macmillan, *op. cit.*, p. 81; In January 1924, Ramsay MacDonald became the first Labour Prime Minister. He was reminded, in the House of Commons, of Henderson's minority report and asked when he was going to act upon it. He said he was 'considering' it, but reminded the questioner of the crowded state of the House's business. *Ibid.*, p. 88.

45. *The Times*, 13 June 1992.

46. Blackburn R., 'Citizenship and the honours system', in *Rights of Citizenship* (Blackburn R., ed., 1993).

47. Laird, *op. cit.*, p. 77.

48. For a full account of the sources of royal revenue see Halsbury's Laws of England, *Constitutional Law* (6th edn, 1996) Vol. 8(2), paras 701, 702, 707.

49. Hencke D., 'Royal finance: the bottom line', *The Guardian*, 10 January 1995; 'Report of the Royal Trustees 1993, Royal Finances Report, Buckingham Palace', *The Times*, 13 July 1996.

50. Statement issued by Buckingham Palace on the royal finances in February 1993, *The Guardian*, 10 January 1995.

51. Bagehot, *op. cit.*, p. 85.

52. For the regulations drawn up by the Lord Chamberlain on eligibility for ladies, married and unmarried, to attend, see Laird D., 'The Queen, our hostess', in Laird, *op. cit.*, p. 265.

53. Naughton J., 'Defence of the realm', *The Observer*, 28 April 1996.

54. Bagehot, *op. cit.*, p. 101.

55. Morton A., 'Prospects for the family', in *Power and the Throne: the Monarchy Debate* (1994) p. 110.

56. S. 2 Act of Settlement 1700, Halsbury's Laws, *op. cit.*, para. 861.

57. The oath is reproduced, in part, by Benn T. and Hood A. in *Common Sense* (1993) p. 44.

58. *Ibid.*, p. 44; *Attorney;General* v. *Jonathan Cape Ltd* [1976] QB 752.

59. *Madzimbamuto* v. *Lardner-Burke* (1968) (2) SA 284; [1969] I AC 645.

60. *Calvin's Case* (1608) 7 Co Rep 1a at 5b; *China Navigation Co. Ltd* v. *A-G* [1932] 2 KB 197, CA. In *Joyce* v. *DPP* [1946] AC 337, the House of Lords went to so far as to say that an alien unlawfully possessed of a British passport could be guilty of treason, because he owed allegiance by virtue of the protection which he could expect to be provided simply on the basis of its possession. It is difficult to see how there can be an expectation of protection conferred by a document improperly issued to an alien outside the United Kingdom, or a reciprocal duty of allegiance. The decision is really only explicable on the basis of the court's determination to condemn the Nazi collaborator Joyce ('Lord Haw-Haw'), irrespective of the relevant legal rules (see Glanville Williams in (1948) 10 CLJ 54).

61. Fairhall D., 'Could the army be trusted?', *The Guardian*, 10 January 1996.

4

Freedom of Movement

THE ORIGINS OF IMMIGRATION CONTROL IN THE UNITED KINGDOM

The right of a state in international law to control the entry and residence of individuals within its borders is, as the French Conseil d'Etat recently declared, 'part of the essential condition of its sovereignty'.[1] Although the rights of states to refuse entry or to order expulsion may be limited by treaty, as, for example, the commitment under the Geneva Convention on the rights of refugees, or, for Member States, by the law of the European Union, the legal machinery which each state chooses to employ when exercising its powers is still very much a matter of national law. States retain the right to determine who holds and who does not hold their nationality, and how entry to and departure from their territories is controlled. In the United Kingdom, the position of both British subjects and the subjects of other monarchs, 'aliens', depended, for British subjects, to a large extent on their relationship with the Crown and, in the case of aliens, on the relationship between the Crown and the sovereign to whom the alien owed allegiance.

Under the feudal system, this was seen as a personal relationship between subject and sovereign. British subjects might be prevented from leaving the Kingdom, because they might, by so doing, avoid some obligation or service which they owed to the monarch. Aliens might be denied entry, or might even have to forfeit their property if their monarch was at war with the British Crown. How far the power of the Crown to control the entry and exit of individuals to and from the United Kingdom in the absence of parliamentary authority survived the Revolution of 1688 remains a matter of dispute. Although the free movement of persons is now largely covered by the Immigration and Extradition Acts and the relevant provisions of Community law, the powers of the Crown remain important where there is no legislation. A significant number of immigration decisions are still made by the Home Secretary outside the statutory framework of the Immigration Acts and Rules.[2] The Divisional Court, in seeking to find authority for such decisions, has quite recently described the scope of the powers of the Crown before the enactment of legislation in the most sweeping terms:

> Immigration was formerly covered by the royal prerogative and it was a matter which lay entirely within the exercise of that prerogative. Much of the prerogative powers vested in the Crown in this field have now been superseded by a statute but there remains – and this is what the royal prerogative is – a residual power in the Crown, through Her Majesty's Secretary of State for Home Affairs, to exercise such residual power as is necessary for the proper control of immigration.[3]

It is highly unlikely that the Crown ever had 'a residual power for the control of immigration' of this kind. Immigration control, as it is understood today, is a modern concept and its arrival coincides with that of nationality and citizenship and the evolution of the nation state. In the United Kingdom, it goes back no further than the Aliens Act of 1905. There was a statutory system of control set up during the Napoleonic Wars, but this was largely directed at French nationals who were *enemy* aliens, and it was established because the government was extremely doubtful about whether it had the power, without the authority of Parliament, to restrict even the free movement of non–combatant *enemy* aliens. It was removed after conclusion of hostilities.[4] The spirit of the age was against it. 'Any country which has made a single step in the road to freedom and civilization, will make liberty of locomotion the general rule, liable only to such exceptions as public policy may occasionally introduce.'[5] The Crown's powers to control entry and departure from the United Kingdom have to be understood in relation to the legality, or otherwise, of the physical controls which are required for enforcement against those subjected to control. The extent of the Crown's powers differs according to whether the person concerned is (a) a British subject, (b) a friendly alien or (c) an enemy alien.

CROWN POWERS OVER BRITISH SUBJECTS

Since the coming into effect of the British Nationality Act 1981, the term 'British subject' has a much narrower meaning than hitherto. Its application is now largely confined to those who retain some kind of subject-status in relation to the British Crown but who do not fall into the new classifications of 'British Citizen', 'British Dependent Territories Citizen', 'British Overseas Citizen' or 'Commonwealth Citizen'.[6] Before the Act, all citizens of the United Kingdom and Colonies were Commonwealth citizens and British subjects and Commonwealth citizens were also British subjects. Earlier still, all those born within the 'allegiance of the Crown' — that is, within territory controlled by the Crown — were British subjects.[7] It was stated unequivocally by Lord Diplock in *DPP* v. *Bhagwan* in 1972 that a British subject had 'the right at common law to enter the United Kingdom, without let or hindrance when and where he pleased and to remain here as long as he liked'.[8] This statement is not supported by any authority, which is surprising given the fundamental principle which it appears to declare. One would expect to find old cases in which the 'right' of British subjects to enter British territory was discussed, but there are none in which the issue is dealt with in this way.

The word 'right' is not capable of a comprehensive and exact definition in English law, its meaning depending upon the circumstances in which it is used. A useful definition, in this context at least, is that of Hohfeld: those rights and duties which the law recognizes and which it is willing to enforce and for violation of which it will provide remedies and sanctions.[9] A right of entry of this kind could be said to exist in current immigration law for British citizens under the Immigration Act 1971 or for European Union citizens under the Immigration (European Economic Area) Order 1994. Outside statute law, however, there are few rights of this kind in English common law. Most are, in fact, no more than basic rights to security of the person, property and reputation, protected by the appropriate remedies. It is trite law that most of the so-called 'civil rights' possessed by individuals in England and Wales are no more than 'liberties' in the Hohfeldian sense. English law has been meagre in its recognition of directly enforceable nominate rights, as the law of privacy, or lack of it, so amply demonstrates. The position was made clear by the Vice-Chancellor in *Malone* v. *Commissioner of Police of the Metropolis (No. 2)* in 1979: 'England ... is a country where everything is permitted except what is expressly forbidden.'[10] On this basis he held that, in the absence of legislation, or the infringement of recognized personal or propriety rights, the police, or indeed, anyone else, were free to listen to telephone conversations in the same way that one neighbour was free to overhear another. They did not have to establish a 'right' to do so but could do so because no law had been made to prohibit it and to do so infringed no right recognized by the common law.

91

The proper formulation of the question about the position of British subjects and their free movement rights is not, as suggested by Lord Diplock, 'Did the applicant have a right of entry?', but 'Did the respondent/defendant have the legal authority to *prevent* his or her entry?' The assumption at common law since the landmark case of *Entick* v. *Carrington* has been that an official must be able to point to a rule of law that enables him to impose some kind of physical restraint on another. The detention of a passenger in the absence of such authority will mean that the official has committed a trespass to the person and will be liable in damages.[11]

We have seen that the power of the Crown to order the detention of individuals simply at the royal pleasure, which the judges had supported in *Darnel's Case*, had effectively, been abolished by the Petition of Right in 1629.[12] There were examples of the arrest and detention of British subjects who had breached the government's trading agreements with foreign states during the reign of James II, which the courts upheld. These carry little authority, and can be dismissed as excesses in the use of prerogative powers, upheld by a subservient judiciary which did not acquire security of office until the Act of Settlement of 1700.[13] Sixty years later the position was very different. We have seen in Chapter 1 how attempts to prevent British traders from exporting corn by proclamation during an economic crisis was so generally regarded as unlawful that those who participated in its enforcement had to be protected against civil liability by a subsequent Act of Indemnity. The legal basis of attempts to force the gentry by proclamation to return to manage their country estates, or to prevent builders from building contrary to royal concepts of town planning, perished with the Star Chamber in the seventeenth century. The power of the Crown to detain British subjects who had not offended against the law was largely confined to those under military law or liable to impressment into the navy. As we have seen in Chapter 1, the enforcement of the Petition of Right by the courts after the Revolution of 1688, the growing effectiveness of the writ of habeas corpus and the awards of substantial damages by juries against officers of the Crown who unlawfully detained subjects or invaded property rights all combined to limit the inclination to abuse the use of prerogative powers.[14]

Agreements were from time to time made to surrender British subjects to foreign states, or to prevent British subjects from going abroad to serve in foreign armies as mercenaries. These agreements were never, however, simply enforced on the sole authority of any supposedly inherent Crown power. Although the power to conclude such agreements clearly belonged to the Crown under the prerogative of foreign policy, authority was invariably obtained from

Parliament to create the necessary legal authority to enable Crown officers to arrest and detain the individuals concerned. Maitland was quite clear on this. 'The king has no power to send men out of the country, and cannot give himself the power by making a treaty.'[15] The courts have, on many occasions since the Extradition Act of 1870, affirmed that any attempt to give effect to such arrangements without following the procedure laid down will be unlawful.[16] Many prisoners were also sent abroad following a sentence of the court. In some cases this was provided for in the statute which created the offence.[17] In others, defendants agreed to go 'voluntarily' in exchange for the commutation of the sentence. This was the case for the Tolpuddle martyrs, who were convicted of illegal trade union membership. Such was also the basis of the transportations to Australia suffered by so many convicts in the first half of the nineteenth century.

The Crown has never had a prerogative power to prevent its own subjects from entering the kingdom, or to expel them from it.[18] The only possibly surviving prerogative power in relation to the movement of subjects was that provided by the use of the writ *ne exeat regno*. By this writ medieval kings secured the residence of those who owed personal and other services under the feudal system. The power of the Crown to do this was limited by Chapter 42 of Magna Carta, which provides that 'In future anyone may leave the kingdom and return at will, unless at time of war, when he may be restrained for some short space of time for the common good.'[19] It has, however, quite recently been argued that the writ might be used by the Crown in other than a war or a national emergency situation, although an attempt by a member of the public to use it in New Zealand to restrain the New Zealand rugby football team from going to South Africa during the *apartheid* period was unsuccessful. Its current use is, however, almost certainly confined to private proceedings to prevent debtors from leaving the country to avoid their creditors.[20] Although subjects in the country were entitled to the protection of the Crown, the obligation of protection was confined to the realm, and they could not, and still cannot, insist on protection outside it. They are, however, protected from intentional or negligent action by Crown forces abroad and can, it would seem, sue for injury or damage caused by them.[21]

Any attempt today by the Crown to prevent a citizen entering the country must be seen in the light of the right of entry conferred on British Citizens by the Immigration Act 1971. Only citizens subject to exclusion orders under the Prevention of Terrorism (Temporary Provisions) Act 1989 can be excluded from any part of the United Kingdom. Individuals made the subject of an order by a civil or criminal court can be prevented from leaving the country. The right to leave the country is one of the fundamental rights conferred by European Community law. Any person holding European Union citizenship (a status enjoyed by anyone holding British citizenship) has a right of free movement in the Community. That right includes the right to leave their country of origin to receive a service in any other member state. This will include, as the Court of Appeal has recently made clear, the right to receive fertility treatment in another Member State, even where this might contravene UK law.[22] Such a service could also include a flight to any part of the world, so that the apparent restriction of the right to the area of the European Union is, in effect, not a real barrier. Community law now, in any event, since the creation of Union citizenship in the Treaty on European Union in 1992, contemplates rights of European Union citizens outside the Union, because the new citizenship confers a right of protection from the embassies and consulates of other Member States in countries anywhere in the world.[23]

PASSPORTS AND FREE MOVEMENT RIGHTS[24]

The passport is now an essential document for the exercise of free movement rights. Under the Immigration Act 1971, although British citizens have a right of entry to this country, that right is only exercisable on production of a valid passport showing the holder to be a British citizen with a right of abode in the United Kingdom. Carriers will refuse to accept a passenger wishing to enter or return to this country claiming citizenship, because there are heavy financial penalties for bringing passengers who do not have a right of entry or proof of leave.[25]

Although lack of a passport can effectively prevent a citizen exercising his or her rights of exit from and entry to this country, there is no right to a passport. It is issued by the Passport Office under the royal prerogative at the absolute discretion of the Foreign Secretary, although the processing of passport applications is dealt with by the Passport Office, a sub-department of the Home Office. The passport originated as a letter from the Foreign Secretary addressed to foreign governments and requesting them to allow the bearer to pass without let or hindrance. Words to that effect still appear in modern passports. Although there is no right to be issued with a passport, Taylor LJ has quite recently declared that 'The ready issue of a passport is a normal expectation of every citizen, unless there is a good reason for making him an exception.'[26] A 'normal expectation' falls far short of a right, and it is in striking contrast to the position of American citizens who do enjoy such a right, and to

Irish citizens who have a constitutional right to travel.[27] The right to leave this country to go to other Member States enjoyed by British Citizens as European Union citizens includes the right to be issued with 'an identity card or passport ... [which shall be] ... valid at least for all Member States and for countries through which the holder must pass when travelling between Member States' (Art. 2 Directive 68/360). It cannot be doubted that the rights enjoyed by British citizens under EC law override the power of the Crown to deny individuals a passport on any ground whatever, and must now be seen as subject only to restrictions on grounds of public policy, public security or public health permitted by Community law.

CROWN POWERS OVER ALIEN FRIENDS

Any national of a country with which this country is not at war, and who is not a Commonwealth or Irish citizen, will be classed as a 'friendly alien'. Science fiction has borrowed the term, but, strictly speaking, an alien is someone who is bound by a bond of allegiance to another sovereign. Under English common law, friendly aliens in this country were under the protection of the English Crown. They owed 'local' allegiance to the English Crown while they were here; that is, they had to obey the law and, most importantly, could be guilty of treason. By a process of reciprocity, they were also entitled to the protection of the law, although they did not enjoy anything like full equality before it until the British Nationality and Status of Aliens Act 1914.[28]

The process of acquisition of legal rights and status was gradual. By the end of the seventeenth century the courts had recognized the right of alien friends to maintain actions in tort to protect their persons and property, and to enforce contracts, although their property rights did not extend to the ownership of freehold land. As far as personal security was concerned, therefore, they could maintain an action in tort against an officer of the Crown who detained them with a view to exclusion or expulsion from the country, in the absence of any common law or statutory authority. Only briefly during the late eighteenth century, during the Napoleonic Wars, and in the nineteenth century during other periods of war or revolution did the Crown have a general statutory power of exclusion or expulsion over friendly aliens, although specific powers were conferred to secure the return of merchant seamen deserters and fugitive criminals.[29] Where there were no such statutory powers, the detention of friendly aliens by officers of the Crown for the purposes of either exclusion or expulsion was unlawful.

In *Mostyn* v. *Fabrigas* (1774), for example, the Governor of

Minorca, then a British colony, deported an inhabitant to Spain. The plaintiff sued for damages in trespass. Lord Mansfield rejected any suggestion that, as an alien, his position was any different from that of a British-born subject in Minorca, or that the Governor, as the Sovereign's representative on the island, was free to take whatever action he thought fit: 'To lay down in an English Court of Justice such a monstrous proposition as that a governor ... is accountable only to God and his own conscience; that he is absolutely despotic, and can spoil, plunder and affect His Majesty's subjects, both in their liberty and property, with impunity, is a doctrine which cannot be maintained.' Having found that there were no circumstances justifying the action under either English or Minorcan law, the court awarded substantial damages to the plaintiff. An action was even successful, in *Madrazo* v. *Willes* (1820), when brought by aliens against an officer of the Crown for trespass to the person and to property where the tort occurred *outside* British territory.[30] The absence of any common law power in the Crown to control the entry of friendly aliens led the Foreign Secretary, Earl Grenville, to declare in 1852:

> By the existing laws of Great Britain, all foreigners have the unrestricted right of entrance and residence in this country, and while they remain in it, are, equally with British subjects, under the protection of the law ... No foreigner as such can be sent out of the country by the Executive Government, except persons removed by treaties with other States, confirmed by Act of Parliament, for the mutual surrender of criminal offenders.'[31]

Like Lord Diplock in *Bhagwan*, in relation to British subjects, Earl Grenville goes too far in relation to aliens. Like British subjects, they benefit from the fact that the Crown has no general power at common law to detain them, but that cannot be called a *right of entry* or a *right of residence*. The common law is not expressed in such terms. As we have noted, statutes or Community law may recognize such rights. The common law does not do so, and it is not helpful to speak in terms of such rights or the absence of them. Much of the modern confusion about the Crown's common law powers over friendly aliens can be traced to two Privy Council cases, *Musgrove* v. *Chun Teeong Toy* (1891) and *Attorney-General for Canada* v. *Cain, Gilhula* (1906).[32] They are taken by many modern textbook writers as authority for the Crown to exclude aliens from the United Kingdom, in the first case, and to expel them, in the second. Neither case is authority for such action. *Musgrove* arose out of legislation passed by the Australian State of Victoria limiting the entry of Chinese contract labourers. Most of the case is devoted to interpretation of the Chinese Act 1881, but Lord Halsbury, delivering the opinion of the Privy Council, added the following observation:

> This is sufficient to determine the appeal against the plaintiff, but their Lordships would observe that the facts appearing on the record raise, quite apart from the statutes referred to, a grave question as to the plaintiff's right to maintain the action. He can only do so if he can establish that an alien has a legal right, enforceable by action, to enter British territory. No authority exists for the proposition that an alien has any such right.[33]

Lord Halsbury's observation is open to criticism on at least two counts. In the first place, the plaintiff was already within British territorial waters when the application for entry was made. It was already well established that an alien in territorial waters could secure his release from detention by an application for habeas corpus, as in *Somersett* v. *Stewart*,[34] where Lord Mansfield ordered the release of an African-born negro slave detained on board a ship bound for the American colonies. It was undoubtedly open to the defendant in *Musgrove* to *apply* to the court for his release, although it was clear in this case that there were statutory grounds for his detention. Second, the implication that, to obtain entry to the territory, the alien required a nominate right is, as suggested above, plainly wrong. An alien no more needs such a specific right than say, a subject requires a specific right to take tea on a Sunday or, for that matter, to listen to his neighbour talking in his garden.

It is likely that Lord Halsbury's *obiter* remarks have more to do with the political situation in the United Kingdom than the legal context of the Australian legislation. During the final decade of the nineteenth century immigration to the United Kingdom, largely from Russia and Poland, had increased very considerably. The bulk of the immigrants were Jews fleeing the pogroms that had followed the assassination of Czar Alexander II in 1881, and continued, sporadically, well into the twentieth century. It is estimated that a million fled Russia by the turn of the century, the majority going to the United States, but a substantial minority coming to the UK. The Conservative government, in which Lord Halsbury was Lord Chancellor, had been under growing pressure from within the party to take action about the volume of immigration and was seeking the means to restrict entry.[35] There was a widely held view in liberal circles, reflected in Earl Grenville's sweeping observation in 1852, quoted above, that aliens had a *right* to enter the country. This view is, as we have suggested, untenable, but Lord Halsbury seems to have been concerned to rebut it by deploying an argument of even less substance.

The second case on which much reliance is placed to found a power for the Crown to expel aliens in the absence of statutory authority is *Attorney-General for Canada* v. *Cain, Gilhula* (1906).[36] The case concerned the expulsion of two US citizens from Canada. The expulsion had involved not only their removal from Canada, but also their entry on to American territory under restriction by officers of the Crown. It was not contested that the Alien Labour Act conferred on the officers the power to effect the expulsion, but it was argued that they had no power to continue to effect that expulsion beyond the frontiers of Canada. The Crown argued that, irrespective of the legislation, which was limited to the territory of Canada, it had a power to effect such an expulsion under the prerogative, and any limitations in the scope of the statute could be supplemented by the prerogative power. Lord Atkinson, a former Conservative Attorney-General in Ireland, delivering the Opinion of the whole Judicial Committee of the Privy Council, accepted that the Crown had a power of expulsion and was not limited by the territorial scope of the statute. Lord Atkinson based his decision, first, on the fact that, at international law, all states have the power to exclude and expel aliens and to do all that is necessary to accomplish this, including their detention beyond the bounds of the territory; second, that it had already been established in *Re Adam* (1837) that the Crown had a power of expulsion in relation to the Crown colony of Mauritius, which was applicable in this case; and, third, that the Crown had a general power over the movement of aliens, relying on dicta in the case of *The Hoop* (1799).[37] None of these grounds provides a sound basis for a general power in the Crown to expel friendly aliens. The power of the state to expel aliens under international law, although it unquestionably exists, does not assist in determining by whom that power is exercisable within each state under its own law. As Strange CJ observed in *R.* v. *Symons* in 1814, 'When an international jurist talked of the State or government having authority to do a particular thing, *they must be taken always to mean the supreme power, which with us is the legislature.*'[38]

Under the old French *code civile*, which was applicable in both Mauritius and Lower Canada, from whence the expulsion was effected in *Cain*, the Crown had inherited the absolute powers over aliens under the *droit d'aubaine* enjoyed by French monarchs in pre-revolutionary France. These powers included expulsion at will. It was on the basis of these 'peculiar provisions of French law' that the Privy Council supported the expulsion in *Re Adam*, and which same provisions could have justified the actions of the Crown in *Cain*.[39] In no sense, however, could such powers be applicable in the United Kingdom or, indeed, in any colony in which the British Crown had not inherited the powers enjoyed by the monarch under the old *code civile*. The case of *The Hoop* was of no relevance, because it concerned the powers of the Crown over *enemy* aliens and their property following a declaration of war. The decision in *Cain* is, therefore, of very limited application. It is, at most, authority for the proposition that the Crown has a power of expulsion of aliens, in the absence of statutory authority, in former French colonies in which the old *code civile* still applies. It certainly does not support the existence of any general Crown power of expulsion of aliens from the United Kingdom. Despite these obvious limitations, Lord Atkinson, fifteen years later in *Johnston* v. *Pedlar*, now felt able to assert that: 'Aliens, whether friendly or enemy, can be lawfully prevented from entering this country and can be expelled from it: I Blackstone 259, and *Attorney-General* v. *Cain*, and at any time the Crown may revoke his [*sic*] licence, express or implied, to reside: *The Hoop*.'[40]

There is clearly value in asserting such principles as often as possible, however wrong, as though they were well established. The speeches of Lord Atkinson's colleague's in the same case bear witness to a growing confusion. Lord Cave thought that the Crown could prevent an alien from landing, but could only expel him if empowered by a statute. So did Lords Phillimore and Sumner, while Lord Dunedin in *Ertel Bieber & Co* v. *Rio Tinto Co.* cited with approval the view of Lord Reading LCJ in *Porter* v. *Freudenberg* in 1914 that,

> In ascertaining the rights of aliens, the first point for consideration is whether they are alien friends or alien enemies. Alien friends have long since been and are at the present day, treated in reference to civil rights as if they were British subjects, and are entitled to the enjoyment of all personal rights of a citizen, including the right to sue in the King's courts. Alien enemies have no civil rights or privileges *unless they are here under the protection and by the permission of the Crown.*[41] (Emphasis added.)

Despite a number of observations in cases since, largely based upon the *Musgrove* or *Cain* cases, it would still seem that Lord Reading's view is the correct one. In the absence of statutory authority the friendly alien is as secure from arrest and detention within the jurisdiction as a British subject. Alien enemies, however, are protected to the extent, and only to the extent, that they are here with the consent or licence of the Crown. There is a world of difference in their respective circumstances. It means that restrictions can only be imposed on friendly aliens in the process of immigration control to the extent to which they are specifically authorized by statute.

ALIEN ENEMIES

The position of alien enemies will be considered in more detail in Chapter 5 on the defence prerogative. In connection with immigration control, once war has broken out between the UK and another state, the nationals of that state become alien enemies. Until the case of *Liebmann* in 1916, it was thought that only subjects of that state who engaged in hostile activity could be detained either when attempting to enter the United Kingdom or when found elsewhere in the country.[42] The court in *Liebmann*, however, decided that conditions of modern warfare made every enemy alien a threat, and this was particularly the case with Germans, a people 'who consider that the acceptance of hospitality connotes no obligation and that no blow can be foul ... [since] spying has become the hall-mark of German "kultur"'.[43] Although the Aliens Restriction Act 1914 enabled all aliens to be detained on entry for examination, alien friends were released either after admission, or to return abroad after refusal of entry. Alien enemies were detained, unless they were given licence by the Crown, under the Defence of the Realm Regulations, to live at liberty in an area where they were thought not to constitute a threat to security.[44] Similar restrictions were imposed in the Second World War under the Defence Regulations.[45] Detention of an enemy alien is an act of state, the reasons for which cannot be questioned by a court of law. However, once the war is over, the enemy alien becomes an alien friend, and can no longer be detained without statutory authority.[46]

THE PREROGATIVE AND THE IMMIGRATION ACT 1971

How do these prerogative powers relate to the complex structure of immigration control given to the Home Secretary and to immigration officers under the Immigration Act 1971 and the subsequent legislation? The Immigration Act 1971, section 33(5), simply states: 'This Act shall not be taken to supersede or impair any power exercisable by Her Majesty in relation to aliens by virtue of Her prerogative.' In the first place it seems clear that, whatever general powers the Crown may have had (if any) over British subjects in relation to immigration control, the section only preserves those powers relating to *aliens*. The current definition of 'alien' excludes all

British Citizens, British Overseas Citizens, British Citizens of Dependent Territories, British Protected Persons and Commonwealth Citizens, so the scope for the use of the prerogative is nothing like as wide as Glidewell LJ suggested in *Kaur* in 1988 in the extract set out at the beginning of this chapter. In *R. v. IAT ex parte Home Secretary*, in the Court of Appeal, Stuart-Smith LJ observed that 'the Act *abrogates* the prerogative power, save to the limited extent provided by section 33(5)' (emphasis added). Glidewell LJ agreed with this view.[47] Given the very doubtful authority of both *Musgrove* and *Cain*, it would seem that the Crown's powers outside the structure of the Immigration Act 1971 are limited by section 33(5) to control of enemy aliens in time of war. For this reason, on the basis of the 'covering the field' doctrine propounded by the House of Lords in *De Keyser's Royal Hotel*, and described in Chapter 2,[48] attempts to prevent the free movement of anyone, except enemy aliens, into or from the country without statutory authority, by, for example, the issue of a writ *ne exeat regno* for purposes unrelated to personal debt liability, would be precluded.

Although a careful examination of the cases makes it clear that the Crown's powers over friendly aliens, in terms of arrest and detention, are no more than those over subjects, repeated and careless conflation of the law about enemy aliens and that of alien friends, sweeping pronouncements about the rights (or lack of them) of aliens, most recently by Lord Denning, and the subsequent incorporation of statutory provisions introduced to control both friendly and enemy aliens in the emergency of 1914 into the main body of immigration law in 1971, have all combined to infuse immigration control with a prerogative basis which it never had in modern times and which is quite inappropriate.[49] Thus, a Government Minister declared in 1976: 'The exercise of immigration control is the exercise of a prerogative under the discretion of [the Home Secretary]. The Rules are guidance to the officials and the tribunal about how they should operate, but there is still a reserve discretion which all Governments use.'[50]

The effect of this perception of immigration control as a 'prerogative power clothed in statute', besides giving rise to the use of the so-called 'residual prerogative power', has also had a very significant effect on the willingness of courts to review immigration decisions. Between the cases of *R. v. Inspector of Leman Street Police Station Inspector, ex parte Venicoff* in 1920 and *R. v. Secretary of State ex parte Khawaja* in 1984, it was accepted that, because an alien had no right to enter or any right of residence under statute or common law, decisions affecting his entry or residence were 'purely administrative' and did not require to be taken according to minimum standards of natural justice or fairness.[51] It has also been noted that 'the reluctance of the courts to challenge the Executive's exercise of statutory powers on matters touching national security may also have been influenced by the Crown's claim that the exclusion and expulsion of aliens were within its prerogative, the scope of which was never definitely established, but which still maintains a shadowy existence alongside contemporary statutory controls.'[52]

THE ADMINISTRATION OF IMMIGRATION CONTROL

The Immigration Act 1971 created an exhaustive regime of immigration control. For the first time, it combined the regulation of aliens with that of Commonwealth citizens. Legislative provisions which had first seen the light of day in the First World War, and which were directed at enemy aliens, became part of the currency of everyday immigration control. Subsequent legislation has modified the scope of the Act and the appeal process, but the overall regime remains the same. We are here concerned with non-statutory powers of the Crown, so that only a few major aspects of the process are important. The person with prime responsibility for the process of immigration control is the Home Secretary. The Act provides for a structure under which everyone wishing to enter the United Kingdom who is not a British citizen, or who is otherwise exempt from control, requires leave to enter. Leave may or may not be granted, according to the criteria laid down in the Immigration Rules. The Immigration Rules are laid before Parliament, and require its approval, but they are not rules of law. However, instructions issued by the Home Secretary to immigration officers must accord with them, and a deviation from the criteria for admission, or for variation of leave after entry, laid down in the Rules may result in a successful appeal to either an adjudicator or the Immigration Appeals Tribunal, whose decision is binding on the Home Secretary. The grant of leave and the variation of leave are different functions. The first is the responsibility of the immigration officer, who must act in accordance with the Rules. Variation of leave, once leave of entry has been granted, is the responsibility of the Home Secretary. Difficulties have arisen in recent years because individuals who do not qualify for entry under the Rules, and who should therefore be refused admission under the Rules, have been granted leave of entry by the Home Secretary. This has been done not merely in relation to individual cases on specific grounds, but for broad categories of entrant for whom the Rules make no provision. The Home Office has attempted to justify these departures from the Rules on the basis of the prerogative.

Two prerogative powers are offered to support the Home

Secretary's action. The first is the Home Secretary's supposed power to 'under-enforce' or dispense with the effect of legislation in specific cases. The effect of the Bill of Rights on this course of action has already been discussed in Chapter 2. At most, any remaining dispensing power would allow the Home Secretary to dispense with the effect of the legislation in single, very specific, cases, but not by the publication of broad, policy exceptions to the application of the Rules, as is the current practice.

The second prerogative power is the so-called 'residual power' to control immigration. As we have just seen, this 'residual power' is very limited and is almost certainly confined to alien enemies. Despite these limitations the practice has grown over the past twenty years of the Home Secretary granting 'leave' to an increasing number of categories of applicants. While it is arguable that the Home Secretary may vary an existing leave in a way not contemplated by the Rules, since he is given a power under the 1971 Act to *vary* leave in the most general terms by section 4(1) of the Act, he has no power under the same Act to grant leave.[53] This is within the exclusive power of the immigration officer. The Home Secretary may instruct immigration officers as to the manner in which they carry out their duties, but the Second Schedule to the Act makes it clear that such instructions must not be inconsistent with the Rules.[54] Even if there were a general, residual power over immigration, which seems highly unlikely, its use as a kind of alternative to the statutory structure seems highly inappropriate. As Lord Keith said in *Lord Advocate* v. *Dumbarton District Council*, 'It is no longer a feasible view that the Crown is in terms bound by the general words of a statute but that the prerogative enables it to override the statute.'[55]

The third prerogative power that is important in the process of immigration control is that relating to the internal control of the Civil Service. Immigration control has been the responsibility of the Home Civil Service since the passage of the Aliens Act 1905.[56] Except in those cases where the Act specifies that certain decisions are either the special responsibility of immigration officers or of the Home Secretary himself, decisions can be, and usually are, delegated to other officers. The interviewing of applicants in the home country when entry clearance is sought, originally intended as the responsibility of immigration officers at the port of entry, is now, almost exclusively, the responsibility of entry clearance officers. Most decisions made on a day-to-day basis on variation of an existing leave in the United Kingdom are made, under the *Carltona* doctrine, by civil servants in the Home Office.[57] Such a prerogative power is of a secondary kind. It does not enable the Home Secretary to takes steps which would affect the common law or statutory rights of individuals.

The use of the prerogative may seem an appropriate way to mitigate some of the harsher effects of immigration control, but its use has a number of serious defects. Besides the clear breach of the Bill of Rights that the prerogative used in this way involves, as discussed in Chapter 2, decisions made outside the statutory process, and outside the criteria laid down in the Rules, are not subject to a proper appeal under the Act.[58] They may be the subject of recommendations by adjudicators and the Immigration Appeal Tribunal, but recommendations, unlike formal determination, are not binding on the Home Secretary. The only possible avenue to challenge an extra-statutory decision is through an application for judicial review, on the basis that the Home Secretary is not operating his own policy fairly, or within its own terms. Such policies may change frequently, be unknown to any but a small group of immigration practitioners and be beyond the effective scrutiny of Parliament. Unlike the Immigration Rules, concessions made by the Home Secretary are not subject to the affirmative vote procedure under the Act, and often emerge in correspondence with immigration practitioners, or in answers to written Parliamentary Questions.

PERMISSIBLE RESTRICTIONS UNDER EUROPEAN COMMUNITY LAW

European citizens – that is, anyone holding the nationality of any Member State of the European Union, or of a Member State of the European Free Trade Area (currently Iceland and Norway) – have rights of free movement throughout the United Kingdom (as do members of their families), provided that they are engaged in activities of an economic kind, such as working as employed or self-employed people, or are recipients of services, or are retired or self-sufficient people.[59] These are all directly effective rights, and do not need national law to make them effective. In fact, the United Kingdom has recognized the rights conferred by Community law in the Immigration (European Economic Area) Order 1994. Although the Order falls short, in a number of important respects, of full implementation of Community law, it provides a useful framework within which Community rights can be claimed.[60] Community free movement rights are not absolute, and are subject to restriction by the Member States on grounds of public policy, public security and public health. The extent of the right of Member States to use these exceptions to limit free movement rights is limited by Directive 64/221 and a number of important decisions of the European Court of Justice.

The full extent of the Community rules cannot be considered here, but their main features can be summarized. Although Member States have a considerable degree of latitude in determining what constitutes a threat to public policy or public security, decisions must be based on the conduct of individuals and cannot be taken simply on the basis of one incident or one criminal conviction. The individual concerned must represent a 'continuing threat'. Decisions cannot be taken to achieve a deterrent effect, and must be proportionate to the threat to public security and public policy in each case. Exclusion or expulsion must be used without discrimination, so that such action is impermissible where no restrictive or repressive measures are deployed against citizens of the home state engaged in the same conduct.[61] All such decisions must be subject to effective appeal or review, or at least must be referred to a 'competent authority' for an independent 'opinion' before a decision to expel is put into effect.[62]

Except for Irish nationals, EU citizens, although they enjoy extensive rights under Community law, are aliens under British nationality law. As such, they are excluded from the Civil Service and the armed forces. They do, however, have access to certain Civil Service posts which fall outside the derogation permitted in relation to Article 48(4) EC Treaty.[63] They are, potentially, subject to detention and exhaustive examination on entry under the EEA Order and the Immigration Act 1971, although such examinations are prohibited by Community law unless there are grounds for suspecting a threat to public policy, public security or public health in a specific case.

The Act and the 1994 EEA Order retain the right of the Home Secretary to exclude or expel EU and EEA Citizens on, *inter alia*, political and 'conducive grounds', although these grounds are far wider than those permitted by Community law.[64] Those areas of statutory discretion, derived from powers to deal with enemy aliens in time of war, and subsequently extended to all aliens, are most likely to fall foul of Community law. Although Community law allows a wide measure of discretion to each Member State, expulsion for, say engaging in political activity which embarrasses the government would offend both Community law and the European Convention on Human Rights, which informs the interpretation of Community law in the European Court of Justice. Such an expulsion would be most unlikely to be supported by the Court.[65]

CONCLUSIONS

Although the prerogative is not central to immigration control, it plays an important part at the edges of the decision-making process. With little authority, it has been seen by successive Home Secretaries since the First World War as underpinning the statutory means of control, and is used by them, together with a misuse of the dispensing power in a way which almost certainly contravenes the Bill of Rights, to supplement the statutory provisions and the Immigration Rules where they are seen to be wanting. The view of immigration control as 'a prerogative in statutory clothing' caused the courts to deal less than fairly with aliens subject to exclusion and deportation. Since the alien could be excluded or deported at will by the Crown, it was inferred that any decision made to exclude or expel him under statutory powers could not be the subject of an application for review, because no 'rights' were at issue.[66] The position was partially retrieved by a powerful speech in *Khawaja* by Lord Scarman:

> There is no distinction between British nationals and others. He who is subject to English law is entitled .to its protection. This principle has been the law at least since Lord Mansfield freed 'the black' in *Somersett's Case* (1772) ... There is nothing here to encourage, in the case of aliens or non-patrials the implication of words excluding the judicial review our law normally accords to those whose liberty is infringed.[67]

Aliens can now, at least, expect the application of the rules of natural justice to decisions made about their exclusion or expulsion, unless that exclusion or expulsion is based on security grounds.[68] In the latter case, where representations to a panel of 'advisors' to the Home Secretary, in a procedure based on the hearing of war-time objections to detention under the notorious Regulation 18B of the Defence (General) Regulations 1939, have been substituted for a right of appeal, the process falls far short of what would ordinarily be regarded as fair.[69] The perception of an underlying prerogative has undoubtedly militated against effective judicial review where the immigration decision was taken in the context of defence or national security.

Many cases concerning applications for asylum have a high foreign policy content, involving an assessment by the Foreign Office of whether, for example, a nominally 'safe' third country will, in fact, breach its obligations under the 1952 Convention, and return the applicant to the country of persecution. Since the *GCHQ* case the courts have demonstrated a greater willingness to assess the reasonableness, in *Wednesbury* terms, of such decisions, made, of course, under the foreign policy prerogative.[70] Since the Asylum and Immigration Appeals Act 1993 came into effect, decisions to refuse admission on the basis of the existence of a 'safe' third country through which the asylum-seeker has passed have been appealable in the United Kingdom. Such appeals consider substantively whether or not such countries are, in fact, safe. A surprisingly high number in 1995 were found by special adjudicators, contrary to the view of the Foreign Office, not to be.[71] Under the Asylum and Immigration Appeals Act 1996, the right to appeal against removal to such 'safe' third countries from within the United Kingdom, under a policy agreed with other Member States in the European Union, was removed, and the only remedy available to individuals is, once more, an application to challenge such an assessment of a 'safe' country in judicial review proceedings. The Court of Appeal has recently demonstrated a willingness to strike down income support regulations which effectively frustrated asylum-seekers' rights to apply for asylum in this country in accordance with the Convention and the 1993 Act.[72]

It was remarkable that, in the *Everett* case, the Court of Appeal, when considering whether or not the decision to issue or withhold a passport, although carried out under the foreign policy prerogative, was reviewable, identified the decision as analagous to an immigration decision and thus pre-eminently one that should be subject to judicial review.[73] The effect of European Community law is, undoubtedly, that the issue of passports and the right to travel is subject both to Community limits on public policy and public security grounds and to the need, under Community law, for an effective remedy. Although Community law permits some limitation on procedural rights in the case of national security, some proof of the threat posed to security will be needed. The mere assertion will not be enough. This was the view of Lord Atkin in his celebrated dissenting judgment on Regulation 18B in *Liversidge* v. *Anderson* in 1940.[74] One could, perhaps, hope that the new judicial flexibility demonstrated by the House of Lords and the Court of Appeal in the *GCHQ* and *Everett* cases, and the growing influence of Community law on both substantive law and procedural rights in the English courts, will stimulate in both legislature and judiciary a desire for a similar transparency in the control and review of all immigration decisions, including those taken under powers perceived to derive, in their origin, from the royal prerogative. The current growth in concessionary decision-making outside the framework of the Rules and the appeals process is not compatible with open government or the rule of law.

NOTES AND REFERENCES

1. *Re Ratification of the European Union Treaty* [1993] 3 CMLR 45 at para. 49.
2. Vincenzi C., 'Extra-statutory ministerial discretion in immigration law', [1992] Public Law 300.

3. *R. v. Secretary of State for the Home Department ex p. Rajinder Kaur and Others* [1987] Imm AR 278,291 (per Glidwell LJ).

4. Aliens Act 1793. A special Act of Parliament had to be passed to authorize the continuing detention of Napoleon Bonaparte after the conclusion of hostilities.

5. Henry Brougham (later Lord Chancellor) writing under the pseudonym of 'An Alien', 'Alien law of England', *Edinburgh Review*, April 1825, 99 at p. 112.

6. Part IV and schedule 2, British Nationality Act 1981.

7. *Calvin's Case* (1608) 7 Rep. 1a, 4b; see Dummett A. and Nicol A., *Subjects, Citizens, Aliens and Others* (1990); British Nationality and Status of Aliens Act 1914; British Nationality Act 1948.

8. [1972] AC 60 at p. 74.

9. Hohfeld W.N., *Fundamental Legal Conceptions* (1923) p. 43.

10. Sir Robert Megarry VC [1979] Ch. 344, 366; compare the decision of the European Court of Human Rights in the same case which found a breach of Art. 8 of the Convention (1985) 7 EHRR 14. Following incorporation of the Convention, Art. 8 may become the cornerstone of a judicially created law of privacy in the UK; and see also Harlow C., *Compensation and Government Torts* (1982) pp. 40–5.

11. *Entick v. Carrington* (1765) 19 St. Tr. 1029. *Somersett v. Stewart* [1772] 20 St. Tr. 1; *R. v. Lesley* [1860] Bell CC 20; *Kuchenmeister v. Home Office* [1958] QB 496.

12. (1627) 3 St. Tr. 1; see Chapter 2.

13. *Sandys v. East India Company* 10 St. Tr. 461 (Jefferies CJ).

14. *Mostyn v. Fabrigas* (1774) 1 Sm LC 662; *R. v. Picton* (1806) in *Public Conscience, State Trials* (Thomas D., ed., 1972) p. 158; *Phillips v. Eyre* (1870) LR 6 QB 1.

15. See, for example, the Foreign Deserters Act 1852, the Extradition Act 1870 and the Foreign Enlistment Act 1870. May T.E., *The Constitutional History of England 1760–1860* (1861), p. 425.

16. *Brown v. Lizars* [1905] 2 CLR 837; *Diamond v. Minter and Others* [1941] 1 All ER 391 and *R. v. Horseferry Road Magistrates Court ex p. Bennett* [1994] 1AC 42.

17. Banishment was made a punishment in 1597 by 39 Elizabeth I, c.4. Transportation took place under Orders in Council made in 1614, 1615 and 1616 but became statutory in the eighteenth century by statutes of 4 Geo I, c.2; 6 Geo I, c.23. see Erskine May, *Constitutional History of England 1760–1860* (1860) p. 565.

18. Holdsworth W., *A History of English Law* (1938) Vol. X, p. 393.

19. The Great Charter of Liberties (1215) in Stubbs W., *Select Charters of English Constitutional History* (1870) pp. 296, 301; Taswell-Langmead T.P., *English Constitutional History* (9th edn, 1929) p. 102.

20. *Felton v. Callis* [1969] 1 QB 220; *Parsons v. Burke* [1971] NZLR 244, 248. Bridge J.W. (1972) 88 LQR 83, 85 argues that the writ may even be used in the absence of an emergency. However, de Smith, *Judicial Review of Administrative Action* (4th edn, by Evans J.M., 1980) p. 585 refers to its possible use only in 'war or serious national emergency'. Even that is doubtful. Blackstone, who was never one to underestimate the extent of a prerogative power, declared that 'everybody has, or at least assumes, the liberty of going abroad when he pleases'; and the practice of the Crown issuing writs to command a subject to return had long been disused; Blackstone's *Commentaries*,

I, p. 266. In the eighteenth century the practice was for Parliament to legislate: See 22 Geo III, c.54, an Act to restrain Sir Thomas Rumbold and Peter Perring from going out of the Kingdom for a limited time; 22 Geo III, c.69, an Act for compelling John Whitehill to return to this Kingdom. See further Holdsworth W., *A History of English Law* (1938) Vol. X, pp. 392, 393.

21. *China Navigation* v. *Attorney-General* [1932] 2 KB 197; *Nissan* v. *Attorney-General* [1970] AC 979; see Collier J.G., *Act of State as a Defence against British Subjects* [1968] CLJ 102. Paradoxically, although British citizens have no enforceable right to protection against their own government, as EU citizens, if there is no available British mission in third states outside the Union, they have a right under *Community* law to assistance and protection under the Treaty from the missions of other Member States under Art. 8c.

22. Arts 8a, 59, 60 EC Treaty, Council Directive 73/148. Medical treatment was held by the Court of Appeal in *R.* v. *Human Fertilisation and Embryology Authority, ex p. Blood,* Law report. *The Times,* 7 February 1997 to include artificial insemination in circumstances which might infringe national law.

23. Arts 8a, 8c EC Treaty; Art. 1 Directive 73/148. Restrictions on departure could only be imposed if the conditions limiting action on public policy/public security in Directive 64/221 and the jurisprudence of the European Court of Justice are satisfied.

24. See Justice, *Going Abroad: a Report on Passports* (1975); Jaconelli (1975) 38 MLR 314.

25. British citizens have a right 'to live in, and to come and go into and from the United Kingdom without let or hindrance except such as may be required under and in accordance with this Act to enable their right to be established': ss 1 and 2 Immigration Act 1971. Under para. 4(2)(a) of Schedule 2 of the Act, passengers are required to produce a passport or document establishing their identity and nationality. Penalties may be imposed by the Home Secretary on carriers under s. 1 of the Immigration (Carriers Liability) Act 1987.

26. *R.* v. *Secretary of State for Foreign and Commonwealth Affairs ex p. Everett* [1989] 1 QB 811, 820.

27. *Kent* v. *Dulles* 357 US 116 (1958); *Attorney-General* v. *X* [1992] 2 CMLR 277, 303 (Finlay CJ). The circumstances in which a passport will be denied or withdrawn were set out in a Foreign Office statement in 1974: 881 HC Deb. Nov. 15 1974 col. 265 (written answers).

28. *Calvin's Case* (1608) 7 Rep. 1a, 4b; *Wells* v. *Williams* (1684) Co. Litt. 1296, 91 ER 1086.

29. Aliens Acts 1793, 1844 and 1848, Foreign Deserters Act 1852 and Extradition Act 1870. All these statutes 'enabled' the Crown to take the necessary measures of detention, exclusion, expulsion, etc. None recognized or reserved to the Crown any prerogative power to do so. Craies W.F., 'The right of aliens to enter British territory' (1890) 6 LQR 27; Haycraft T.W., 'Aliens legislation and the prerogative of the Crown' (1897) 13 LQR 165; Holdsworth W., 'The Crown's powers over the movement of aliens', *History of English Law* (1938) Vol. X, p. 393 (and Vol IX, pp. 92–9); Thornberry C., 'Dr Soblen and the alien law of the United Kingdom' (1963) 12 ICLQ 414; Vincenzi C., 'Aliens and the judicial review of immigration law' (1985) PL 93.

30. 3 Barn. & Ald. 353. Compare *Buron* v. *Denman* (1848) 2 Ex. 167; 12 Jur. 82, a case also involving the slave trade, in which the action of the defendant was adopted by the Crown as an act of state. Such a plea by the Crown, if accepted by the court as appropriate to the act in question and if undertaken outside British territory, will constitute a complete bar to an action in tort. For a further discussion of act of state, see Chapter 6.

31. State Papers, Vol. 42 (1852–53) p. 421.

32. *Musgrove* v. *Chun Teeong Toy* [1891] AC 272; *Attorney-General for Canada* v. *Cain, Gilhula* [1906] AC 542.

33. [1989] AC 272, 282, PC.

34. (1772) 20 St. Tr. 1. See also *R.* v. *Lesley* (1860) Bell CC 20; *Ex parte Lo Pak* (1888) IX NSWR 221 (application for habeas corpus, prerogative raised by the Crown but rejected by the High Court of New South Wales as a bad return); *Ex parte Leong Kum* (1888) IX NSWR 250.

35. Gainer B., *The Alien Invasion* (1972) p. 62. Lord Halsbury does not appear to have believed that the Crown had the power to expel aliens once here, because he spoke, in the debate on the failed Aliens Bill of 1894, in favour of the government being *given* the power of expulsion: HL Parl. Debates Vol XXVII (4th series) Col. 155 (17 July 1894).

36. [1906] AC 542.

37. *Re Adam* (1837) Moore 470; *The Hoop* (1799) 1 C. Robb. 196.

38. (1814) 2 Stra. Madras Reports 93 (emphasis added).

39. *Donegani* v. *Donegani* (1834) III Knapp. 62. In this case the Privy Council held that 'the prerogative of the Crown with regard to aliens must be determined by the laws of the particular colonies in which the question arises and not by the law of England, which is only to be looked at to determine who are and who are not, aliens (III Knapp. 88). Lord Brougham, in delivering the Opinion of the Privy Council supporting the expulsion by the Crown in *Re Adam*, emphasized that he did so 'with regret' on account of 'the peculiar provisions of the French law'. 1 Moore PC 470, 477.

40. [1921] 2 AC 262, at p. 283.

41. *Ertel Bieber & Co.* v. *Rio Tinto Co.* [1918] AC 260, at p. 268; *Porter* v. *Freudenberg* [1915] 1 KB 857.

42. *R.* v. *Schiever* (1759) 2 Burr. 765; *The Three Spanish Sailors* (1779) 2 W. Bl. 1324; *R.* v. *Superintendent of Vine Street Police Station ex parte Liebmann* [1916] 1 KB 268.

43. [1916] 1 KB 268, at pp. 270, 274 (Bailhache J) 277 (Lowe J).

44. Aliens Restriction Act 1914, Aliens Restriction (Consolidation) Orders 1914 and 1916, Defence of the Realm (Consolidation) Act 1914, Defence of the Realm Regulation 14(b).

45. Emergency Powers (Defence) Act 1939, Defence (General) Regulations 1939 and Defence (General) Regulations 1940 (SR & O 1939 No. 927, as amended by SR & O 1939 Nos 978 and 1681, 1940 Nos 681, 770 and 942).

46. *R.* v. *Bottrill ex parte Küchenmeister* [1947] 1 KB 47; On the conclusion of the Napoleonic War special legislation was passed to authorize the continuing detention of Napoleon on St Helena: 'An Act for the more effectually detaining in custody of Napoleon Bonaparte'. See Bellot H., 'The detention of

Napoleon Bonaparte' (1923) LQR 170. After the First World War, detention was authorized by s. 9(1) of the Aliens Restriction (Amendment) Act 1919.

47. [1990] 1 WLR 1127, 1133–1134 (Stuart-Smith LJ) and 1138 (Glidewell LJ). The decision appears to overrule the earlier one of *R* v. *Secretary of State ex parte Kaur and Others* [1987] Imm AR 278, 291, in which Glidewell LJ referred to the minister's 'residual prerogative power' over Commonwealth citizens. 'Abrogate' means 'to repeal, cancel or annul': *Osborne's Concise Law Dictionary* (8th edn, 1993).

48. [1920] AC 508.

49. War-time confusion can be seen in: *R.* v. *Secretary of State ex parte Chateau-Thierry* [1917] 1 KB 922, 935; *Netz* v. *Ede* [1946] 1 All ER 628, 634; *R.* v. *Bottrill, ex parte Küchenmeister* [1947] 1 KB 41, 51. Lord Denning declared in *Schmidt* v. *Secretary of State for Home Affairs* [1969] 2 Ch 149, 168: 'I have always held the view that at common law no alien has any right to enter this country except by leave of the Crown; and the Crown can refuse leave without giving any reason.' And in *R.* v. *Brixton Prison Governor, ex parte Soblen* [1963] 2 QB 243, 300 (CA) he said: 'I always understood that the Crown had a royal prerogative to expel an alien and send him home, whenever it considered that his presence here was not conducive to the public good.' The last phrase, 'conducive to the public good', which first appeared in the Aliens Restriction (Consolidated) Regulations of 1916, illustrates how war-time, statutory powers, closely associated with the use of the defence prerogative and the control of *enemy* aliens, were initially transferred, by careless judicial language, to *friendly* aliens in peace-time. Any person, other than a British Citizen, may now be deported from the United Kingdom where the Home Secretary 'deems his deportation to be conducive to the public good'. S. 3(5)(b) IA 1971.

50. H C Deb. Vol. 905, col. 599 (12 February 1976).

51. [1920] 3 KB 72; [1984] AC 74, 110–111 (Lord Scarman); Wade H.W.R., *Administrative Law* (1982) p. 507.

52. Evans J.M., *Immigration Law* (2nd edn, 1983) pp. 422–3.

53. It was held in *R.* v. *Immigration Appeal Adjudicator ex parte Bowen* (1982) Sol J 489 that, in relation to the operation of his post-entry powers, the Home Secretary could 'under-enforce' those powers. The House of Lords, in *R.* v. *Immigration Appeal Tribunal ex parte Bakhtaur Singh*, held that, in exercising his powers, the Home Secretary was entitled to relax the rules or to apply them less restrictively. [1986] 1 WLR 910. He had, however, to be exercising *his* powers and could not exercise powers given to someone else under the Act.

54. Para. 1(3), Schedule 2, IA 1971.

55. [1990] 2 AC 580, 598.

56. Troup E., *The Home Office* (1925) pp. 143–8.

57. *Carltona* v. *Commissioner of Works* [1943] 2 All ER 560. The practice of such delegation received specific endorsement by the House of Lords in *Oladehinde* v. *Secretary of State for the Home Department* [1990] 3 WLR 797 (HL). See Vincenzi C., 'Extra-statutory ministerial discretion in immigration law' [1992] PL 300.

58. S. 19(2), IA 1971; *Wirdestedt* [1990] Imm AR 20; *Somasundaram* [1990] Imm AR 16, 19.

59. Art. 8a EC Treaty (as amended by the Treaty on European Union 1992; Arts 48, 52, 59, 60 EC; *Procureur du Roi* v. *Royer* (Case 48/75) [1976] ECR 497; *R.* v. *Pieck* (case 157/79) [1980] ECR 2171.

60. See Vincenzi C., 'European citizenship and free movement rights in the United Kingdom' [1995] PL 259.

61. Art. 3 Directive 64/221; *Bonsignore* v. *Oberstadtdirektor Koln* (Case 67/74) [1975] ECR 297; *R.* v. *Bouchereau* (Case 30/77) [1977] ECR 1999; *Adoui and Cornuaille* v. *Belgian State* (Cases 15 & 116/81) [1982] ECR 1665. Vincenzi C., 'Deportation in disarray' [1994] CLR 163.

62. Arts 8 and 9 Directive 64/221; *R.* v. *Secretary of State for the Home Department ex parte Santillo* (Case 131/79) [1980] ECR 1585; *R.* v. *Secretary of State for the Home Department ex parte Gallagher* [1996] 1 CMLR 557; White R.C.A., 'Procedural guarantees and expulsion' (1996) 21 E L Rev 241.

63. Aliens Employment Act 1955; European Communities (Employment in the Civil Service) Order 1991 (SI 1991 No. 1221); Handoll J., 'Article 48 (4) EEC Treaty and non-national access to public employment' (1988) 13 E L Rev 22.

64. Art. 20(2) Immigration (European Economic Area) Order 1994, SI 1994 No. 1895, which specifically retains all the powers of examination in Schedule 2 IA 1971, and s. 13(5) (exclusion conducive to the public good) and s. 15(3) (deportation conducive to the public good). The ECJ held in *Commission* v. *Belgium* (Case C-321/87) [1989] ECR 1997 that systematic questioning and examination at frontiers would breach Art. 3, Directive 68/360.

65. See, for example, *Rutili* v. *Minister for the Interior* (Case 36/75) [1975] ECR 1219, where the Court held that restrictions imposed on an Italian trade unionist in France infringed his rights as a worker and his right to freedom of expression under the Convention.

66. *R.* v. *Leman Street Police Station Inspector, ex parte Venicoff* [1920] 3 KB 72; *R.* v. *Brixton Prison Governor, ex parte Soblen* [1963] 2 QB 243. *Schmidt* v. *Home Secretary* [1969] 2 Ch 149.171; *de Smith's Judicial Review of Administrative Action* (4th edn, by Evans J.M., 1980) pp. 164–6.

67. [1984] AC 74, 111–112.

68. *Attorney-General for Hong Kong* v. *Ng Yuen Shiu* [1983] 2 AC 629.

69. *R.* v. *Secretary of State for the Home Department, ex parte Hosenball* [1977] 1 WLR 766, CA; *R.* v. *Secretary of State for the Home Department, ex parte Cheblak* [1991] 2 All ER 319, CA.

70. See, for example, *Bugdaycay* v. *Secretary of State for the Home Department* [1987] AC 514, HL.

71. Immigration Law Practitioners' Association, *Summary of Special Adjudicator Decisions*, No. 2, November 1995; Out of a total of 515 decisions on 'safe' third countries, 215 were found by special adjudicators to result in the return of asylum-seekers in circumstances which, for them, were unsafe.

72. *R.* v. *Secretary of State for Social Security, ex parte Joint Council for the Welfare of Immigrants, The Times*, 27 June 1996.

73. [1989] 1 QB 811, 820, CA (Taylor LJ).

74. [1942] AC 206, HL.

5

National Defence and the Security Services

The defence prerogative is essential to the process of government, in the sense that, without a system of defence against attack upon the inhabitants, the territory or the machinery of government the whole administrative process could become impossible. As Viscount Radcliffe put it when considering the nature of this prerogative power in *Burmah Oil Company* v. *Lord Advocate*:

> The essence of a prerogative power, if one follows out Locke's thought, is not merely to administer the existing law – there is no need for any prerogative to administer the existing law – but to act for the public good, where there is no law, or even to dispense with or override the law where the ultimate preservation of society is in question.[1]

In this sense, the prerogative power of national defence, when operated on national territory, is no more than the common law defence of necessity writ large. Property rights and other rights may have to be overridden in the interest of the immediate protection of life or property. Like that defence, however, its use has, ultimately, to be justified by the law. It cannot, in a state governed by the rule of law, operate outside the law. All democratic societies have to grapple with the difficult problem of preventing the system of defence that is intended to guarantee their form of government from *becoming* the form of government. The history of the United Kingdom, especially the period of the Commonwealth when the country was governed regionally by Major-Generals, and that of most modern states demonstrates how difficult this is to achieve and how unpleasant are the consequences of failure to achieve it. The common law has attempted, with only modest success, to draw a line between the control, disposition and administration of the armed forces, which is undoubtedly a matter for the Crown under the prerogative (although limited by numerous statutory provisions), and the use of the forces in the civil sphere. The scope for the use of armed force in war-time is obviously immeasurably greater than in peace-time, but the courts continue to define the parameters for its use in the civil context. While there undoubtedly exists, at both common law and statute, a species of law called *military* law, there is nothing under our existing constitution which can properly called *martial* law. As we shall see, martial law is a state of affairs in which, for the time being, the ordinary law cannot operate, rather than a system of law itself.

This chapter will explore the scope of the defence prerogative, the extent to which members of the armed forces and the intelligence services are able to undertake tasks in relation to the civil population and how far their activities are regulated by statute and are subject to control and review by the courts. These are crucial matters affecting the liberty of individuals and citizens and their ability to express themselves and to participate in the process of government where that process is seen to be under threat.

DECLARATION OF WAR

The scope for the use of the defence prerogative is enormously enlarged when a state of war exists between the UK and another state. Whether or not such a state of affairs exists is entirely a matter for the Crown to determine. It is also the Crown's exclusive decision whether or not to declare war. Once war has been declared, the Crown has power to regulate relations not only between this country and the state with whom we are at war, but also with neutrals. It can maintain an embargo on trade with other states where it believes that the trade will assist the enemy, and can license trade where it is believed that this would be beneficial to the war effort.

The effect of the declaration of war, said Willes J in *Esposito* v. *Bowden* in 1856, 'is equal to that of an Act of Parliament, prohibiting intercourse with the enemy except by the Queen's licence. As an Act of State, done by virtue of the Prerogative exclusively belonging to the Crown, such a declaration carries with it all the force of law.'[2] In the *Kuchenmeister* case in 1946 the Court of Appeal accepted, in effect, that a Foreign Office statement that a state of war existed could not be challenged in a court. It was, however, suggested by the Vice-Chancellor Sir Richard Scott, in his *Report on the Arms to Iraq* affair, that the existence or not of a 'state of emergency' (on which the relevant legislation, the Export and Customs Powers (Defence) Act 1939 was predicated) was a matter on which a court could adjudicate. This was the case even when, under the Act, the power to determine when the cessation of the emergency had occurred lay with the government.[3]

THE CROWN AND THE ARMED FORCES

The Queen is supreme commander of all the United Kingdom's defence forces, and has been formally recognized as such by statute since the Restoration of Charles II.[4] It is, however, more than three hundred years since a sovereign rode at the head of his army into battle. The disposition of the armed forces, like the exercise of other prerogative powers, is now a matter for the Secretary of State for Defence and the two Ministers of State, and the Chiefs of Staff of the three services. There is also a Cabinet committee, the Defence and Overseas Policy Committee, which is responsible for broader, strategic defence planning. Since the eighteenth century, the internal regulation of the army and navy has largely been under legislative provisions. These have been enacted, for the army and the air force, on an annual basis, since the Bill of Rights 1688 prohibited the maintenance of a standing army without the consent of Parliament. No such requirement was made for the navy, which had never been regarded as a threat to the civil population. Naval discipline is regulated by the Naval Discipline Acts, but the existence of the navy and its operation depends, still, upon the royal prerogative. In addition, the navy still retains the power of recruitment by impressment – that is, by force – because this prerogative power, although its use has long since been abandoned, and would be politically wholly unacceptable, has never been abolished.

SERVICE PERSONNEL AS CITIZENS

Although discipline is now on a statutory basis, in the form of Queen's Regulations, the terms and conditions of service of service personnel contained in regulations made under the Armed Forces Act 1966, the commissioning of officers and the general policy adopted towards recruitment and the general administration of the armed forces are matters still falling within the prerogative. Following the GCHQ case, and the challenge to the service policy of excluding homosexuals from the services, it is now clear that decisions made in this context are subject to judicial review. Only those whose rights or interests are directly affected will, however, be able to challenge decisions. There seems to be no public interest in the proper administration of the armed forces, or duty of disclosure of even routine, non-security information. The degree of irrationality will have to be high to attract judicial intervention, unless the life or liberty of the applicant is at issue.[5]

Service personnel, although subject to a special body of rules relating to conduct and discipline, are not outside the law. 'A soldier' (and the principle holds good for anyone in the services), as Dicey maintained, 'remains while in the ranks, as he was when out of them, subject to all the liabilities of an ordinary citizen.' He added the more general observation that 'No one can plead the command of a superior, were it the order of the Crown itself, in defence of conduct otherwise not justified by law.'[6] Like many constitutional principles, however, it has been modified by both statute and convention. The liability of soldiers may, in practice, be harder to establish than that of the citizen out of uniform. As we shall see in Chapter 6, although the Crown cannot authorize a wrong, the actions of Crown employees may be adopted as 'acts of state', which will effectively bar any claim in tort. Information on which a claim might be based can be excluded in discovery proceedings, before the case even comes before an open court, on the grounds of public interest immunity. Statutory liability may be avoided because the Crown is not specifically named in the legislation. Even where a claim in negligence is not precluded by statute, the courts may, as a matter of policy, hold that no duty of care is owed, in some circumstances, by service personnel.[7]

Criminal liability cannot, however, be avoided, because not even officers of the Crown can authorize the commission of a criminal act. Although superior orders may be a defence to a criminal charge where the act is not manifestly illegal, they cannot be a defence where the act ordered is in clear breach of the criminal law.[8] The twentieth edition of *Banning on Military Law*, issued in 1940, quoted with approval an observation made more than a half century earlier: 'So long as the orders of a superior are not obviously and decidedly in opposition to the well-known and established customs of the Army, or the laws of the land, or if in opposition to such laws, do not tend to an irreparable result – so long must the orders of a superior meet with prompt, immediate and unhesitating obedience.'[9] The experience of the holocaust, the revival of natural law concepts following the Nuremberg trials in 1945 and the development of international rules of criminal law have all given rise to a situation in which citizens and service personnel may be under an obligation to question even apparently legal orders. It must not be forgotten that the wholesale extermination of the Jewish people was accomplished by a Nazi government that had emerged as the largest political party in democratic elections in 1933. Its programme of suppression of the Jews was clear in its manifesto, and in Hitler's *Mein Kampf*. Its policies were translated into laws which were recognized and enforced by the German courts. The trial of Serbian soldiers at The Hague on charges relating to the massacre of prisoners following the fall of Srbnicza in Eastern Bosnia, and the issue of international arrest warrants in relation to Karadicz and Mladicz, the President and Commander in Chief respectively of the unrecognized Republica Srbszka, would seem to indicate a determination by the international community to continue to uphold the Nuremberg principles.

The position of service men and women as citizens, within the political process, is evident by their right to vote, and their right to equal treatment before the law. Citizenship, however, implies duties as well as rights. A soldier has the duty, like all subjects, of allegiance to the Crown, but he has also the duty to uphold the law. The difficulty in this context for service personnel is most acute in relation to the use of certain weapons. For example, the use of dum–dum bullets (that flatten on impact with the human body) and poisonous chemical and biochemical weapons are all forbidden by international law. The International Court has also recently declared that the threat or use of nuclear weapons would be 'contrary to the rules of international law applicable in armed conflict'. Although a minority of the Court thought that the use of such weapons might be justified as a last resort to secure national survival, the Court was unanimous in condemning their strategic use or threat of use.[10] International law is not, as we shall see, part of the law of the United Kingdom, unless and until it has been incorporated by Act of Parliament, but it is used as an aid to interpretation. Would a member of the armed services be justified in arguing that an order to prepare for use, to load or to fire a dum–dum bullet, or a chemical or a nuclear weapon, was a 'manifestly illegal' order? The House of Lords, in *Chandler* v. *DPP*[11] in 1964, held that the type of defence adopted could not be challenged in a court of law. The jury were not permitted to hear argument that the immobilization of nuclear weapons might safeguard rather than prejudice the interests of the nation. It has, however, been argued with some force by one of the defendants in the *Chandler* case that, even in a democracy, citizens have a duty to resist the application of laws which manifestly defy accepted international norms, and where there is an imminent threat and no prospect of a change in law through the ordinary political process, it may well be that a British jury might recognize that duty where a judge did not.[12] The right of a civilian to deploy such a defence is at least arguable. Service men and women are constrained by the rules of military law, and may be dealt with for its breach by courts martial.

COURTS MARTIAL

Soldiers can be brought to trial for both breaches of military law in military courts (courts martial) and offences which are crimes in the ordinary criminal courts, but they cannot be punished for the same offence in both courts. The system of courts martial is an ancient one set up under the prerogative in 'articles of war' to ensure the enforcement of military discipline.[13] It has jurisdiction only over military personnel. The Governor of Gibraltar was, in the early years of the eighteenth century, adjudged to pay a large sum in damages for trespass to a carpenter flogged after an act of alleged indiscipline because the court was satisfied that 'tradesmen who followed the train [of artillery] were not liable to martial [military] law'.[14] The system of justice in military courts, although now on a statutory basis, is a peculiar one. Defendants are often represented by officers with little or no legal training and there is inadequate supervision by the civil courts. The main offences tried by courts martial are not, rather surprisingly, breaches of the service disciplinary code, but offences against the 'civil' criminal law. In proceedings before the Divisional Court in December 1995, counsel for the Crown informed the judges that the army courts martial system imposed more severe sentences for any particular offence than would be imposed by a civilian court trying the equivalent offence. Their Lordships expressed some surprise.[15]

In the case of *Findlay*, in December 1995, the Commissioners of the Human Rights Commission, in a preliminary ruling, declared unanimously that the UK government was in breach of Art. 6(1), which guarantees a 'fair and public hearing before an independent and impartial tribunal'. The deficiencies of the pre-trial and trial procedures that emerged in the case were serious. The regime for keeping a soldier in close arrest is set out in the Army Act 1955, the Army (Rules of Procedure (Army) 1976) and Queen's Regulations. The decision to keep a soldier in close arrest in the guardroom is made by the commanding officer of the unit, the officer who is the investigator and the prosecutor of the soldier and, if the soldier is tried summarily, who tries and sentences him. There was some recognition of the conflicts of interest that arose under the system condemned by the Human Rights Commission in the *Findlay* case by amendments to the existing law by the Armed Forces Act 1996. The officer who convenes the court martial will no longer be responsible for confirming the decision of the court; that is, acting as the first level of the appeal. The amendments made by the Act fall far short of creating an objective, impartial and effective system of military justice. Although soldiers necessarily give up a part of their liberty as citizens by becoming members of the armed forces, they are, as the Court of Appeal acknowledged in *R. v. MOD ex p. Smith and Others*, still entitled to be protected by the Convention. Neither the statutory provisions which continue to regulate military discipline, as they emerged in the *Findlay* case, nor the very broad discretions under the prerogative appear to provide effective structures for protecting the human rights intended to be secured by the Convention.

Although soldiers are entitled to vote, their right to participate in the democratic process is limited. A serving soldier cannot be a candidate in a parliamentary election, and serving members of the armed services can be prevented from engaging in political activity. A distinction has, however, to be drawn between the actions of civilians in relation to the military and the actions of service men and women in relation to each other. Any attempt by one soldier at persuading another soldier that a particular activity in which they are engaged is wrong, or an attempt to persuade another not to carry out his duty, will be a mutiny under military law. In war-time, such conduct may even attract the death penalty.[16] In peace or war, civilians may be prosecuted for attempting to dissuade members of the armed services from undertaking any particular form of action, although pacifists are much more likely to be selected for prosecution than politicians who encourage mutiny and treason. The failure to prosecute Sir Edward Carson and F.E. Smith (later Lord Birkenhead) for inciting the Curragh Mutiny against Home Rule is, perhaps, the most notorious example.[17] It is an offence, under the Incitement to Disaffection Act 1934, 'maliciously and advisedly [to] endeavour to seduce any member of His Majesty's forces from his duty and allegiance'. This legislation effectively isolates the forces from participating in debate about the moral and legal rectitude of policies which they are ordered to put into effect, although a civilian charged under the Act who can show that an order may have resulted in illegal or criminal behaviour by members of the armed forces would undoubtedly be able to argue that it was their duty *not* to obey it.

THE USE OF THE ARMED SERVICES IN AID OF THE CIVIL POWER

During periods of national emergency, such as war, disorder, national strikes and strikes threatening essential services or supplies, the armed forces may be called upon to assist. Troops may be deployed to quell riots or armed insurrection, or they may be used to provide essential transport, policing, fire and other services.[18] In states with a written constitution the circumstances in which emergency powers of this kind may be used are usually clearly defined, because their use will normally involve interference with fundamental rights guaranteed by the constitution. In the United Kingdom, the basis for government action may be highly uncertain. It may be found in prerogative powers or in specific statutory powers created to deal with national emergencies, such as the Defence of the Realm Act 1914 and the Emergency Powers (Defence) Act 1939 in wartime, or, for example, in the Emergency Powers Acts of 1920 and 1964, or a combination of these.

There is a long-held historic concern that troops may be used to suppress opposition to the government of the day, or to quell legitimate political activity. That concern resulted in the prohibition of the use of martial law against the civilian population in time of peace by the Petition of Right in 1628, and the abolition of the standing army, at the Restoration in 1660. Although the belief lingered into the late eighteenth century that the Crown possessed a power to declare 'martial law', and thereafter to deal with both members of the armed forces and the civil population according to a special 'law' emanating from the Commander in Chief and entitled 'Articles of War', by the middle of the nineteenth century this view was no longer tenable.[19] It was clear from the argument which ultimately prevailed following the *Ship Money Case* in 1637 that the Crown could not make use of martial law in a case of merely apprehended danger when the ordinary courts were sitting.[20] If this were the case, the Crown, which claimed to be the sole judge of whether or not a state of war or a state of rebellion existed, could deal with its adversaries in a way that put them beyond the reach of the ordinary courts. Cockburn CJ declared the position in *R. v. Nelson and Brand* in 1867: 'Martial law when applied to the civilian is no law at all, but a shadowy, uncertain, precarious something, depending entirely on the conscience, or rather on the despotic and arbitrary will of those who administer it.' He concluded that martial law as a distinct code of rules does not exist. It is merely the application of the common law principle that 'life may be protected and crime prevented by the immediate application of any amount of force which, under the circumstances, may be necessary'.[21] Public officers must judge the amount of force necessary. The greater the disorder, the greater their discretion. Any person who uses more force than the necessity of the case requires can be made criminally or civilly liable. The principle is the same for soldiers or civilians, magistrates or police officers.

The position would, therefore, seem to be that, short of specific statutory authority, service personnel or government officers are in no better or worse position than the ordinary citizen. Short of a war or rebellion, where the scope for official action, at least for the duration of the crisis, may be greater at common law than that of the ordinary citizen, those ordering the disposition of troops to suppress disorder, or to assist the civil power, can do no more or less than an ordinary citizen. Ordinary citizens are under a duty to ensure that the peace is maintained. There is a difference, according to Lord Diplock in *Albert* v. *Lavin*, between the duty of the citizen and the duty of the official in relation to breaches of the peace. The duty of the citizen is one of 'imperfect obligation'; that is, it cannot legally be enforced. The duty of a police officer, however, is a matter of law. He is liable if he fails to meet his obligation, and the citizen is liable for obstructing an officer in the exercise of his duty if he prevents the officer from taking the necessary action to avoid a breach of the peace. Ordinary citizens are under no such legal liability. Lord Diplock's statement is, however, not borne out by earlier case law.[22] The obligation to maintain the peace appears to be a general one imposed by the common law on everyone.

In this context, the decision by the Court of Appeal in *R.* v. *Home Secretary ex p. Northumbria Police Authority* that there is an ancient prerogative power to maintain the peace, which has devolved on to the Home Secretary, is surprising, and probably wrong, although it is a view held by some writers.[23] The Home Secretary wished to arm the local police force with CS gas. The relevant police authority did not want it. Since the Police Act 1964 appeared to give the exclusive power to make decisions on the equipment of the local police force to the local police authority, the Home Secretary argued that he had the right to override the police authority and supply the gas under his general prerogative power to maintain the peace. The Divisional Court and the Court of Appeal agreed. The essence of a 'true' prerogative power (under which the rights of other persons or bodies may be set aside) as Blackstone noted (see Chapter 1), is that it is a power peculiar to the monarch and is not shared with any of his or her subjects. The defence or war prerogative derives from the position of the Crown as Commander in Chief of the armed forces and its role in maintaining the national defence. The maintenance of public order has no such exclusive quality and is, as we have seen, the obligation of every citizen. The Court of Appeal seems to have based its decision on an obscure nineteenth century judgment relating to the immunity of a building housing both courts and the police from taxation, since both were used for the maintenance of 'the peace'. Even if one accepts the existence of a prerogative to keep the peace (for which, Nourse LJ conceded, there was scant authority), it is not clear that it involved anything more than a power to respond to, and to take measures to repress, a situation of disorder. By their very nature, as residual powers of the Crown, prerogatives must be of ancient origin. They preceded, by many centuries, both the county police forces and, most obviously, CS gas and other crowd-control measures. Even if such a prerogative existed in relation to the police, it was not 'saved' by the 1964 Act, and it is unclear why the Court of Appeal believed that the Home Secretary remained free to use the power, when, according to the De Keyser doctrine, its use was quite incompatible with the statute which superseded it.[24] In any event, since the Court concluded that the Home Secretary did, in fact, have statutory authority under the 1964 Act to arm the local force with CS gas, despite the wishes of the police authority, its observations on the public order prerogative are obiter, and do not, therefore, have to be followed.

PRISONERS OF WAR

In war-time, during the course of combat combatants are wounded, killed or taken prisoner. At common law, under the defence prerogative, members of the armed forces have, in effect, a free hand in dealing with enemy aliens. It has long been established that alien combatants have no right to claim in tort for wrongful imprisonment in relation to their detention after capture or for injuries suffered, since both claims can be defeated by the plea of act of state, wherever the action took place.[25] Thus, there is no difference, in law, in the rights of an enemy pilot shot down over the UK or of one injured in combat abroad. The position of alien civilian non-combatants in this country is less clear.[26] Their situation was only seriously considered for the first time at the start of the First World War. The decision to imprison enemy aliens in time of war was, Prime Minister Asquith declared in November 1914, a 'military measure': 'The detention in custody of the subjects of an enemy state is a power which is exercisable by all states in case of war, the right of the military authorities to hold them as prisoners of war. It does not depend on statute at all. It is a prerogative ... When interned they remain in military custody.'[27]

Asquith explained that the decision to intern would be made in relation to 'all persons whose presence or conduct appears dangerous to the safety of the country'. The statement indicated that something more than the mere nationality of the individual would be required to constitute grounds for detention. He or she would have to constitute a threat of some kind. The statement was consonant with the practice which had prevailed in time of war, at least since the end of the eighteenth century. Enemy civilians were left at large during hostilities. Indeed, one of the justifications offered for the Aliens Act

1793 by the government was the need to control and, if necessary, detain *all* French nationals as they entered the country.[28] During the course of 1915 military and political events, and a relentless propaganda in the press, began to change public perceptions. The change can be seen first in political statements, and ultimately in judicial pronouncements. It concerned the nature of Germans, who were, it became widely accepted, not as other human beings. Lord David Cecil explained the transformation in a parliamentary debate in May 1915:

> I for one was prepared to regard the ordinary pre-suppositions about men as being applicable to Germans. I think, after poisonous gas, after the Lusitania, and the terrible Blue Book now published, it is really absurd to suppose that we have any right to think that the Germans are not capable of any crime. We have no right to assume that they will act as ordinary human beings, and we are, therefore, bound to take all possible precautions to protect ourselves and the people of this country against the most dastardly, treacherous and cruel attacks that the mind of man can conceive.[29]

The change was rapidly translated into 'fact', of which the judiciary felt bound to take note. The issue of civilian detention came before the Divisional Court in 1916, when a civilian detainee, Liebmann, challenged his detention in habeas corpus proceedings. It seems to have been accepted by the Crown that the applicant had been living quietly in the United Kingdom for a great many years, running a small business. No evidence was offered that Liebmann personally constituted a threat in any way. He was a German and he was a prisoner of war. Counsel for the Crown candidly admitted that there was no authority in the books for the proposition that the Crown had the power to control the liberty of aliens in these circumstances, 'the reason being that the need for controlling them has never arisen'. Once, however, the applicant had been made a prisoner of war, his detention could not be challenged. The court agreed. It accepted the need for indiscriminate detention of Germans. Bailhache J noted that 'methods of communication with the enemy have been entirely altered and largely used. I need only refer to wireless telegraphy, signalling by lights, and the employment, on a scale hitherto unknown, of carrier pigeons. Spying has become the hall-mark of German kultur!'[30] Having determined that anyone holding German nationality was liable to detention under the prerogative, the Courts were subsequently even prepared to accept similar treatment of those who had lost their German nationality and become British subjects, or who were of no nationality.[31]

The attitude of the government to internment throughout the war was ambivalent. It variously attempted to justify mass internment by the supposed threat posed by the internees, as a reprisal against German atrocities and as a means of protecting the internees themselves against the hostility of an enraged population. All or any one of these grounds would have justified detention in international law, but only the first would have justified action under the defence prerogative. In the atmosphere prevailing at the time it would not have been difficult to secure the rapid passage of legislation authorizing detention of enemy aliens *en masse*, incorporating, perhaps, some statutory system of appeal or review. The compliance of the judiciary rendered that unnecessary. A readiness by the courts to accept the widest interpretation of executive powers was paralleled in the leading case on the scope for emergency detention of British subjects, in *Ex parte Zadig*.[32] Reassuringly, however, for those whose fears were raised by what came to be regarded as 'the socialization of Great Britain' during the war, the courts showed more solicitude in the interpretation of both statutory and prerogative powers which invaded the rights of property owners in war-time, and showed no reluctance to strike down decisions which were not strictly authorized by statute or were seen not to be justified under the prerogative.[33]

The decision in both *Liebmann* and *Zadig* could perhaps be said to have been tainted by what Lord Denning subsequently described as a 'wartime submissiveness to the executive'. Probably, it also reflected a general and widespread suspicion of foreigners that went far beyond the bounds of reason, and continued well into the post-war period, merging with a general paranoia about Bolshevism, Irish nationalism and a growing anti-semitism. The mood was nicely captured by MI5's New Year's card for 1920, depicting an Irish rebel, a bloated German officer in a spiked helmet and a Bolshevik in a fur hat, with the type of features familiar in anti-Jewish caricatures, all together ranged against a symbolic female figure on a pedestal labelled 'Liberty and Security'.[34]

The history of the internment of enemy aliens in the First World War was to set the stage for its use in the Second World War and subsequently. The government embarked on the war in 1939 resolved not to engage in the 'excesses' of the First World War or to be moved again by outbreaks of 'spy fever'. For a while it maintained that policy. Until June 1940, most aliens of German or Austrian nationality remained at large, but following the fall of the Netherlands, a policy of mass internment was pursued. By July 1940, 30,000 enemy aliens had been interned. As in the First World War, the vast majority of enemy aliens were interned under the prerogative. All attempts to argue that the internment was undertaken for some military reason were abandoned. Symbolically, the procedures for internment were transferred from the War Office to the Home Office, although the internees were still guarded by soldiers, and their physical confinement remained a War Office responsibility. It was now frankly acknowledged by the Home Office that there was nothing against the great mass of the internees, the majority of whom were harmless. They had been interned 'for reasons for which they were not responsible'.[35] During the four or five years preceding the war, large numbers of Jewish refugees had arrived in the United Kingdom as refugees from Nazism. By July 1940, the majority were behind bars, many for the second time. Germans who had fled persecution because they were communists, social democrats or Jews were interned on the Isle of Man with Nazi sympathizers, and there were some ugly incidents. Others were shipped off to Canada or Australia. Many hundreds more perished when the *Arandora Star* was torpedoed in that same July. Although many of these detainees, especially those who were able to satisfy the authorities that they were 'victims of Nazi oppression', were released by 1942, Nazi-sympathizing Germans and those who had been politically inactive in opposing the Nazis in Germany remained interned until well into 1946.[36]

As long as the war lasted, there was little prospect of a successful challenge to internment in the courts. The decision in *Liebmann* had effectively established that once the court accepted that a person was a prisoner of war, no further examination of his or her detention in habeas corpus proceedings was permitted. The detention was analogous to an act of state.

In the latter stages of the war, after the liberation of France, several thousand Russians, many of whom had been forcibly conscripted by the Germans into slave battalions to work on the Normandy defences, were brought to the UK as prisoners of war. Most, including women and children, had never been in the German Army or the Soviet Army, but they were assembled under the supervision of the Home Office and guarded by the War Office as detachments of Soviet 'forces' under the Allied Forces Act 1940. They were then handed over to the Russians under the Yalta Agreement. Most subsequently perished in the gulags. Their detention was almost certainly illegal. Correspondence between the Foreign Office legal section and the Home Office indicates acute anxiety lest any of the detainees escape and challenge their detention in the courts.[37] Notwithstanding *Liebmann*, it appeared at least open to a detainee to argue that the status of 'prisoner of war' presupposed a condition of war. Although there was no formal conclusion of the war until 9 July 1961, actual hostilities were informally terminated in June 1945.

Küchenmeister, a German internee, applied for habeas corpus to secure his release in 1946. Goddard LCJ, in the Divisional Court, denied that he had even the right to apply for habeas corpus. The Court of Appeal upheld the decision, but did not accept that the applicant had no right to apply. It refused, however, to question the Foreign Office certificate that a state of war existed with Germany. The certificate also referred to an Allied declaration of 5 June 1945 affirming the discontuance of Germany as an independent state and the establishment of the Allied Powers as the responsible government. Under common law and statute an alien enemy is a person who is a national whose government is at war with the United Kingdom. The court did not begin to come to grips with the curious situation which the Foreign Office affidavit envisaged. Since June 1945, the government to which Küchenmeister now, nominally at least, owed allegiance was that of the Allied Powers. That government comprised representatives of the United States, France, the Soviet Union and the United Kingdom. 'A state of war' between Küchenmeister's government and the UK appears to contemplate a situation of some absurdity: a condition of war between the UK and the UK government of Germany. Courts have, in the past, questioned the circumstances in which an act of state was claimed. They did not do so on this occasion in relation to the termination of the Second World War, or subsequently.[38]

More recent detentions of civilian prisoners in the United Kingdom in time of war have been carried out under powers conferred by immigration law, but the taking of prisoners in the Falklands War in 1982 and in the Gulf fell clearly within the defence prerogative. Iraqis in the United Kingdom, or Iraqi sympathizers, were, however, detained under the Immigration Act with a view to their deportation. Although there were complaints about the criteria applied for their arrest and detention, the only major challenge to the process, the case of *Cheblak*, failed, largely on the grounds that the sufficiency of the security grounds for the applicant's detention were simply not open to review.[39]

THE SECURITY SERVICES

The gathering of intelligence, both at home and abroad, has long been a major preoccupation of government and military. After the Reformation, Thomas Cromwell, Robert Cecil and Robert Harley were prominent in devoting considerable public resources to training a network of spies and informers at home, who reported to individual ministers or to the Council of State.

Spies abroad worked in conjunction with the diplomatic service.

In those early days, outside the military and the diplomatic service, intelligence-gathering was essentially an *ad hoc*, freelance affair, with informants operating in much the same way as criminal informants operate in conjunction with the police today. Modern intelligence-gathering dates from the creation of the posts of Director of Military Intelligence and Director of Naval Intelligence in 1887. The Directorate of Military Intelligence did not last long. After the setbacks of the Boer War, military intelligence came under direct civilian control, through the committee of Imperial Defence. The direct successor to that committee is the Ministerial Committee on the Intelligence Services, which is a Cabinet committee chaired by the Prime Minister and including the Chancellor of the Duchy of Lancaster, and the Foreign, Defence and Home Secretaries.

In 1909, the Secretary to the Committee of Imperial Defence, Sir Charles Ottley, recommended to the Cabinet, with the backing of the Committee, that a Secret Service Bureau be created to take charge of all matters relating to intelligence gathering. The bureau was divided into two parts with quite separate areas of interest, home and foreign. The home section subsequently became MI5 and the foreign became the Secret Intelligence Service or MI6.

MI5 was given the responsibility of preventing the theft of secret information and the gathering of domestic intelligence on home-grown subversion 'from those political extremists bent on undermining the established system of government', both activities involving potential breaches of the criminal law. MI5 is the most important of the two intelligence services, because its activities most frequently impact on the exercise of liberties by citizens which are widely assumed to be protected by the laws of the United Kingdom. MI5 remained, nominally at least, within the fold of the War Office, consequently operating legally on the basis of the defence prerogative. Initially, at least, it had a close relationship with the Special Branch of the Metropolitan Police, which had been set up as a response to the Fenian bombings in 1883. Information was exchanged, and Special Branch officers would normally undertake any arrests which were necessary. Vernon Kell, a Captain in the Staffordshire Regiment, the first head of what became MI5, remained in post for more than thirty years. Members of the service were recruited from among serving officers of the army. These were generally those with a private income because intelligence work was so poorly paid. Most were known personally to Kell or were members of his social circle. Their sympathies were, not unnaturally, with the political right and Kell made a practice of cultivating newspaper proprietors to publicize the dangers of Bolshevism, primarily to engage support for greater funding for the service.[40]

There was a large expansion of MI5 in 1914–15, and the service was given the responsibility of coordinating the mass round-up of enemy aliens in 1915. As we have seen, there was in many of these cases little or no military justification. The government appeared to succumb to a kind of collective hysteria that gripped a large part of the population. A general hostility to and suspicion of aliens persisted after the War. The visa regime, instituted in 1914, was continued: 'One of the chief functions of the controls after the War would be to exclude Bolshevik agents from the United Kingdom ... At home, this would be achieved by Immigration Officers, while abroad ... officers would be attached to the consulates in the guise of Vice-Consuls ... These officers work within and receive their instructions from MI5.'[41] Even visiting seamen, who had hitherto been exempt from control, were now to be subject to the visa regime, in order, said Haldane Porter, 'to defeat Bolshevik propaganda'. In 1919, Sir Walter Long had begged the Prime Minister to pay attention to a report he had received from an unnamed secret agent, which said 'I now find myself convinced that in England Bolshevism must be faced and grappled with, the efforts of the International Jews of Russia combated and their agents eliminated.'[42]

Unlike in the years preceding 1914, little attention was paid by Britain's intelligence services during the 1930s to extreme right wing or German-sympathizing groups, although, on an individual level, Sir Barry Domvile, who had been Director of Naval Intelligence between 1927 and 1930, took a keen interest and was an active member of the British Union of Fascists (BUF). He was later interned with Sir Oswald Mosley.[43] Prominent members of society, such as the Dukes of Bedford and Westminster, Lord Nuffield and politicians from all the main political parties, joined together in the Link organization, chaired by Sir Barry Domvile, to promote Anglo-German friendship and to publicize, through newspapers printed in Germany by Joseph Goebbels, the achievements of the new Nazi government in Germany. The celebrated writer, Wyndham Lewis, wrote in praise of the 'personal neatness, the clear blue eyes', of those 'straightforward young pillars of the law': Nazi stormtroopers.[44] Anti-semitism was widely prevalent in both right wing and left wing circles, and permeated Home Office policy on naturalization.[45] Throughout the 1920s and 1930s, the energies of MI5 were directed at communists, socialists, pacifists and trade unionists, because the main threat to state security was seen to come from the East. It was only in 1938 that the Director of MI5, the long-enduring General Kell, turned his attention to the Germans and the BUF.

At the commencement of the war, only a few suspected spies and couriers were detained, but the fear of a real or imaginary 'fifth column' brought, as we have seen, a massive response, in the shape of wholesale internment of enemy aliens in June and July 1940. The arrests were in the hands of Special Branch, who detained large numbers more or less indiscriminately, carting off German and Austrian nationals they happened upon in the public library and the streets of Hampstead, and in towns and cities throughout the country. The process of classification of the detainees once arrested was in the hands of MI5, who advised the tribunals set up to review the classifications. Although Nigel West, in his history of MI5, describes MI5's system of internment and screening as 'remarkably efficient and successful', this view was not shared by many contemporary commentators, and is almost wholly at odds with the assessment made by historians who have examined the process.[46]

It was natural that, in the atmosphere of crisis, fear and imminent invasion that prevailed in the summer and autumn of 1940, mistakes in the process of classification should be made, and many were. Even Kell accepted that the tribunal system was far from perfect, and that certain regions seemed to act with perverse severity, while others seemed content to leave all but the most committed pro-Nazis at large. There was, and remains, a strong argument that such decisions should, as far as is compatible with genuine risks to national security, be subject to appeal, or effective control or review by the courts. Lord Denning's sweeping claim in the *Hosenball* case in 1977 that war-time decisions on internment 'have never interfered with the liberty of the freedom of movement of any individual except where it is absolutely necessary for the safety of the state' is simply untrue, but has provided an argument to convince successive governments that the quality of information supplied by the security services is of such a high order that an effective process of review of detentions and deportations is unnecessary. A distinguished judge has, however, recently remarked of the observation of Lord Denning that his 'sanguine view of the executive ... is not one likely to be adopted by the courts today in the light of recent experience'.[47]

After the war, MI5 was largely involved in combating Soviet and Eastern European espionage and subversion, and, since 1969, has been heavily involved in work against the IRA and other Northern Ireland terrorist organizations, and in monitoring the British Communist Party and any other organizations which were perceived as a threat to the existing political order. MI5 still had, until 1989, no statutory basis, but it gathered information, it must be assumed, on the basis of the defence prerogative. The connection was tenuous, however, and it was the Home Secretary, not the Secretary of State for Defence, who, on the basis of the prerogative (the branch is not specified), according to Taylor J in *R. v. Secretary of State for the Home*

Department ex p. Ruddock in 1987, apparently authorized the tapping of the telephones of officers of the Campaign for Nuclear Disarmament.[48]

During the 1950s and 1960s, some of the intelligence-gathering appears to have been accomplished by unlawful means, and, on occasion, the information was put to unlawful purposes. Reliable accounts of the actions of the secret services are, by the very nature of the service, almost impossible to obtain and equally impossible to verify, especially as most published accounts from within the services come from disaffected members. Peter Wright describes how he and a colleague, as the 'stormtroopers' of MI5's A2 section, set out to 'have fun. For five years we bugged and burgled our way across London at the State's behest, while pompous, bowler-hatted civil servants in Whitehall pretended to look the other way.'[49] The service seems not to have drawn the line at bugging and burglary. According to Wright, there were officers in MI5 in 1968 who were prepared to leak information to Cecil King, the then owner of the *Daily Mirror*, to smear the Prime Minister, Harold Wilson, and identify him as a Soviet agent, although there was no evidence to support such an allegation. According to Wright, King was a long-time agent of MI5, and was prepared to publish anything detrimental to Wilson. The plan did not proceed, but in 1974, a much more concerted effort was made 'by up to thirty officers [in MI5] who had given their approval to the scheme' to leak damaging material to sympathetic journalists. According to Wright, the scheme was only thwarted by his refusal to give access to the relevant files. By his own account, the refusal was motivated more by a desire not to lose his pension than by any loyalty to the service or to his country. 'The country seemed on the brink of catastrophe. Why not give it a little push?'[50] There is little independent verification of this account, but Harold Wilson himself seems to have been convinced that there were members of MI5 in 1974/5 who were bent on driving him from office.

The intelligence services have, since their inception, claimed many military and other successes. The most successful campaign, however, was that waged by Stella Rimmington, the first publicly recognized Head of MI5, to wrest control of anti-terrorism from the Special Branch. The use of new surveillance techniques and the penetration of terrorist organizations by MI5 has led to some spectacular breakthroughs.[51] But in the aftermath of the Cold War and during the Ulster ceasefire, there was an increasing public and government recognition that the intelligence services have operated in an environment in which they were, in their own jargon, 'self tasking', and in which the legal basis for their operations was inadequately defined. Despite the decisive role they were often able to take in relation to the liberties of individuals, and despite their access to very considerable public funds, they were beyond the scope of effective parliamentary control or judicial review.

Although there was no evidence of widespread wrong-doing by the British intelligence services, experience in the United States, now public knowledge under the Freedom of Information Act, has provided proof of serious breaches of the criminal law in the past by both the CIA and the FBI, including the organization of conspiracies to kill foreign heads of state and the use of information gathered in intelligence operations to blackmail senior members of the US government.[52] By 1989 it was accepted, largely on the basis of the American experience, that public accountability was not incompatible with the maintenance of an effective intelligence service.

The Security Service Act 1989 and the Intelligence Service Act 1994 placed MI5, MI6 and the Government Communications Headquarters at Cheltenham for the first time on a statutory footing. The 1989 Act laid down the functions of the Security Service (MI5) as 'the protection of national security' and 'to safeguard the economic well-being of the United Kingdom'. The Security Services Act 1996 added a further function: 'to act in support of the activities of police forces and other law enforcement agencies in the prevention and detection of serious crime'. 'Serious crime' is not as serious as a lay person might expect. It includes an offence involving violence, the acquisition of substantial financial gain or the involvement of a large number of persons in pursuit of a common purpose. Much concern was expressed at the time the Act was passed, not least by the police, that the Security Service had no experience of dealing with the public under the limits laid down in the Police and Criminal Evidence Act 1984.[53] Although the 1989 Act provides for supervision by a Security Service Commissioner of the issue of warrants to the service, accountable to the Prime Minister, the Commissioner's annual reports are subject to the removal of 'prejudicial' material before being placed before Parliament. There is also a Security Service Tribunal, to which individual complaints can be made, but it deliberates in secret, there is no right of access to information and no reasons for the Tribunal's decisions are given. Decisions of the Tribunal are also immune from review by the courts. To date, no complaints to the Tribunal have been upheld.[54] There is no reference in the legislation to the royal prerogative and, presumably, neither service may be used for tasks outside the functions allocated to it by statute, on the basis of the prerogative. Such action would appear to be precluded by the *De Keyser* principle. However, whereas MI6 can undertake its function of obtaining information 'only' if related to the prescribed purposes (S. 1(2) Intelligence Services Act

1994), there is no such express limitation in the 1989 Act in relation to MI5.

CONCLUSIONS

The use of armed force is rarely unaccompanied by political controversy. Wars and military expeditions may be opposed by a section of the population. On occasions, such as major national emergencies involving the loss of essential supplies, service men and women may be used against their fellow citizens. The security services may be employed in both war and peacetime to spy on groups of private citizens using terrorism or violence to achieve their ends, or possibly even on those holding radical views who use exclusively peaceful and non-violent means to further their aims. Most people accept, as Scrutton LJ declared in *Ronnfeld* v. *Phillips* in 1918, that 'in time of war there must be some modification in the interests of the State ... A war could not be carried on in accordance with the principles of Magna Carta.'[55] In wartime, the normal assumptions about freedom of expression must give way to the need to avoid supplying the enemy with useful information or support. Industrial disputes may have to be curtailed to protect the supply of war materials to the front; individuals who constitute an actual or potential threat to the security of the state may have to be detained. How far that process should be carried without the interference of the courts in the interpretation and application of emergency legislation and prerogative powers was one of the most difficult legal issues of both world wars.

With the notable exceptions of dissenting judgments by Lord Shaw in *R.* v. *Halliday* and Lord Atkin in *Liversidge* v. *Anderson* and of the unanimous judgment of the Divisional Court in the *Chateau Thierry* case (reversed by the Court of Appeal), cases involving the liberty of subjects or aliens were resolved by the judiciary in favour of the executive.[56] In relation to cases involving the requisitioning or confiscation of property, however, the courts took a much tougher stand to protect property rights. It was made clear in both *In Re a Petition of Right* in 1915 and *The Zamora* in 1916 that the Crown, in exercising a prerogative power, even in time of war, was obliged to make out at least a prima facie case justifying the requisitioning of property, while in *Liebmann* in 1916 the court was prepared to dispense with such a requirement, and to rely upon certain 'facts' about Germans, related in a highly partisan press.[57]

Problems of adjustment came with the arrival of peace. Habits acquired in wartime died hard. The change in political and judicial attitudes in 1914–18 was of seismic proportions and largely endures to this day. For more than two centuries it had been the received opinion that executive detention of subject or alien without express statutory authority was unlawful, with the very limited exceptions discussed in Chapter 4. Coke CJ had even gone as far as to state in 1611 in *The Case of Proclamations* that a *statute* authorizing the detention and expulsion of the Irish (then regarded as aliens) in time of war was 'absolutely *in terrorem* and was utterly against the law'.[58] The concept of a statute offending the *law* is an odd one to lawyers long familiar with the idea of parliamentary sovereignty, but in this case it indicates a belief by one of the greatest common lawyers of the seventeenth century in a fundamental common law right to liberty, and right to due process, transcending both legislative and executive power.

Breach of the principles contained in the Petition of Right, under which both person and property were protected from arbitrary executive action, whether by a secretary of state or the Governor of a colony, attracted exemplary damages. Both detention and the requisitioning of property were only accepted in time of war *in extremis* as a measure of defence. Whether or not such action was justified would have to be established before a court, in the absence of an Act of Indemnity.[59]

It is necessary to restate such well established principles to emphasize the extraordinary nature of the change that took place in 1914–18. The atmosphere of war fever in which the change became possible already existed to some extent before the commencement of hostilities and had given birth to the all-embracing and much criticized provisions of the Official Secrets Act 1911. It enabled the government, within the space of a few hours in August 1914, to introduce both the first of several Defence of the Realm Acts and the Aliens Restriction Act 1914, with virtually no debate. Under the former, thousands of British subjects were detained under Regulation 14B of the Defence of the Realm Regulations. Thousands more friendly and other aliens were detained and deported under the latter. McKenna, the Home Secretary, emphasized the emergency nature of both Bills: the Aliens Act, he said 'applies only to a state of war existing between this country and a foreign power when a grave national danger or a national emergency has arisen'. Five years later, another Home Secretary, Shortt, was, without apology, introducing legislation to put these 'emergency' powers on a permanent basis. The wartime power of the Home Secretary to expel aliens at will, without cause shown, was continued, and is now substantially reproduced in s. 3(5) of the Immigration Act 1971.

Prerogative powers to prevent trading with the enemy were supplemented in the war with legislation to control arms exports.

Additional powers were conferred by Parliament in the Export and Customs Powers (Defence) Act 1939, 'until such date as His Majesty may by Order in Council declare to be the date on which the emergency that was the occasion of the passing of this Act came to an end' (s. 9(3)). Like the Aliens Restrictions Acts, which so usefully supplemented the limited powers of control allowed under the prerogative, subsequent governments, from 1945 onwards, never came to accept that the emergency which had occasioned the passing of the 1939 Act had come to an end. This collective failure was described by the Vice-Chancellor, Sir Richard Scott, in his report on the sale of arms to Iraq, 'as a reprehensible abuse of executive power by successive administrations'.[60] It also serves as an example of how sweeping emergency powers, devoid of any objective criteria for the making of decisions, and, consequently, almost impervious to judicial review, can survive in peacetime when they remain useful to government. The atmosphere of emergency engendered by war affected not only the content of war-time legislation but also, as we have seen, the approach to that kind of legislation by the courts.

The words 'security of the state' or 'national security', so commonplace today, seem to have made their first public appearance in the Official Secrets Act. There appears to have been no discussion about what 'security of the state' actually meant during the brief debate in August 1911, although the terms became widely used in the Defence of the Realm Acts. When the scope of the 1911 Act was enlarged in 1920, there was a complaint by a Liberal member in the House of Commons that 'it was another attempt to clamp the powers of war on the liberties of the citizen in peace',[61] but his words went unheeded. War hysteria had been replaced, in a large section of the press, by a sense of near panic about the Bolshevik revolution. Long after the conclusion of the Second World War, too, the Cold War persisted. There continued to be a need for vigilance by the executive. As Lord Denning warned in the *Hosenball* case, 'Times of peace hold their dangers too. Spies, subverters and saboteurs may be mingling amongst us, putting on a most innocent exterior. They may be endangering the lives of our secret service, as Mr Hosenball is said to do.'

In the post-Cold War world, change is slow. Claims by governments that they had made decisions on the grounds of national security were, and still largely are, accepted without question, although some judges are beginning to show some unease about such an uncritical approach. Lord Devlin made the point in the *Chandler* case as long ago as 1964: 'Men can exaggerate the extent of their interests and so can the Crown. The servants of the Crown, like other men animated by the highest motives, are capable of formulating a policy ad hoc so as to prevent the citizen from doing something the Crown does not want him to do. It is the duty of the courts to be as alert now as they have always been to prevent abuse of the prerogative.' More recently, in the *McQuillan* case, Sedley J quoted with approval a statement by Simon Brown LJ, in which he said: 'The very words "national security" have acquired an almost mystical significance ... [which] instantly discourages the court from satisfactorily fulfilling its normal role of deciding where the balance of public interest lies.'

There is an inevitable danger that the plea of 'national security' may be used by governments as a means of concealing administrative mistakes or more serious errors in matters relating to defence and the security services. As we shall see, there is no effective accountability in these matters in Parliament, because questions in this area are routinely not answered. As the *Belgrano affair* demonstrated, in the aftermath of the Falklands War, only the most persistent questioning by an MP can elicit anything close to a truthful description of events, when governments, for political rather than military reasons, decide not to supply the necessary information. Parliament and the press may have to rely on the willingness of civil servants to jeopardize their careers to ensure that politically important, but militarily insignificant, information becomes available.[62]

These issues are too large to be addressed by the courts alone, and need to be evaluated and enacted in a Freedom of Information Act. However, until that happens, recent world developments, and the collapse of communism in particular, are surely events of which the courts can take judicial notice. The excessive secrecy of all aspects of government could be diminished by a willingness by the courts to look more deeply into claims by the executive that information on which deportations or exclusions are based, or which forms the basis of other administrative decisions, cannot be disclosed because to do so would adversely affect national security. In 1968, in *Conway* v. *Rimmer*, the court, for the first time, decided to look at material for which Crown privilege was claimed in civil proceedings. There had been a suspicion that such claims had been made in some cases simply to deny plaintiffs the necessary evidence to succeed in what were otherwise morally and legally justifiable claims.[63] The consequences of the *Conway* v. *Rimmer* decision in relation to the position of the Crown in proceedings are dealt with more fully in Chapter 8. But the new practice adopted by the courts following *Conway* v. *Rimmer*, in which the material for which privilege from disclosure was claimed was examined by the bench before a decision was made on whether or not it could be allowed in the trial, was not extended to evidence for which the protection of national security was claimed. An invitation to establish a new approach to claims of immunity on the grounds of national security in the new world climate was actually tendered to the court quite recently in *Balfour* v. *The Commonwealth Office* in 1994 and rejected by the Court of Appeal. Russell LC observed:

> In this case [counsel] for the applicant boldly invites this court [to accept that] the time is ripe for what he described as a more open approach when issues of national security are raised by appropriate ministers. Even if not constrained by authority we firmly decline to accept the invitation, for it seems to us to be contrary to principle and to good sense. In this case, the court has not abdicated its responsibility, but it has recognized the constraints placed upon it by the terms of the certificate issued by the executive.[64]

The decision is disappointing. There is no explanation of what principle and what good sense underlie a refusal to require the executive to provide evidence to justify its action, in closed court if need be. More generally, too, the exercise of the defence prerogative needs to be subject to more effective review. Non-operational decisions made by military officers affecting individuals in peacetime should at least be subject to the same principles of lawfulness and rationality as those made by civil servants. The old common law principle that soldiers, despite the necessary limitations imposed by military life, are citizens in uniform, and are legally and morally responsible for their actions, and are subject to and are protected by the law, needs to be properly acknowledged. The most effective way to achieve this would be to give it formal statutory recognition.

NOTES AND REFERENCES

1. [1965] AC 75, 118. HL (Sc.).
2. (1855) 4 El. & Bl. 963; (1857) 7 El. & Bl. 763; *The Hoop* (1799) 1 C. Rob. 196; Lord McNair and Watts A.D., *The Legal Effects of War* (1966) pp. 122, 123.
3. *R.* v. *Bottrill ex p. Kuchenmeister* [1947] KB 41; *Report of the Inquiry into the Export of Defence Equipment and Dual-Use Goods to Iraq and Related Prosecutions*, Cmd 115, Vol. I, para. C.1.68.
4. 13 Car. II, c.6. Maitland F.W., *Constitutional History* (1909) p. 326.
5. In *R.* v. *Secretary of State for Defence ex p. Sancto*, *Times* Law Report, 9 September 1992, Rose J held that 'in the absence of a freedom of information Act, there is no public right to know'. The parents of a soldier killed in an accident were, therefore, not entitled to a sight of the board of enquiry report into the circumstances leading to his death, since they had no other recognized legal

right and were not engaged in litigation with the ministry. The government's stated policy on the admission of homosexuals to the forces was reviewed in *R. v. Ministry of Defence ex p. Smith and Others* [1996] 1 All ER 257, 264, CA (Sir Thomas Bingham MR).

6. Dicey, A.V., *Law of the Constitution* (1952) p. 286.
7. *Mulcahy v. Ministry of Defence*, Times Law Report, 27 February 1996; *Lord Advocate v. Dumbarton District Council* [1990] 2 AC 580; *Air Canada v. Secretary of State* [1983] 2 AC 394; *Nissan v. Attorney-General* [1970] AC 179.
8. Dicey, *op. cit.*, p. 286; *R. v. Smith* (1900) Cape of Good Hope SC 561; *Yip Chiu-Cheung v. R.* [1994] 2 All ER 924, 928, PC (Lord Griffiths).
9. *Military Law (Banning)* (1940) p. 47, quoting Simmons T.F., *The Constitution and Practice of Courts-Martial* (1875) p. 255.
10. *The Independent*, 9 July 1996.
11. [1964] AC 763.
12. *Chandler v. DPP and Others* [1964] AC 763; Lord Devlin would not, however, accept that there is any 'rule of common law that whenever questions of national security are being considered by any court for any purposes, it is what the Crown thinks to be necessary or expedient that counts, and not what is necessary or expedient in fact.' The acquittal of the defendants charged with criminal damage to Hawk aircraft in July 1996, apparently to be used by the Indonesian government to implement a policy of genocide in East Timor, may indicate that some juries are prepared to take a broad view of acts taken to prevent a crime. For a general discussion by one of the defendants in the *Chandler* case of civil resistance to the disposition of weapons perceived to be being prepared for use for unlawful purposes, see Randle M., *Civil Resistance* (1994) pp. 184, 185.
13. See Holdsworth W.S., 'Martial law historically considered', in *Essays in Law and History* (1946) p. 8: 'Military law is a special code of rules administered by courts martial, to which the persons defined by the Army Act are subjected.'
14. The circumstances (but not the name) of the case are described by Lord Mansfield in *Mostyn v. Fabrigas* (1774) 1 Cowp. 160, 164. Babington A., *For the Sake of Example: Capital Courts Martial 1914–1918* (1985) recounts that of the 18 men shot between the Armistice in 1918 and the end of April 1920, 'Only three of the condemned were British soldiers, the remainder being members of Chinese, Egyptian, Cape Coloured or Black Sea Labour Companies and muleteers from the Macedonian Mule Corps' (p. 256).
15. Mackenzie J., 'Courts martial and human rights', *New Law Journal*, 19 January 1996, p. 48.
16. Complaints by soldiers about conditions at Etaples in September 1917 which led to a mutiny at the base resulted in the execution of at least one of the participants: Babington, *op. cit.*, pp. 167, 168.
17. Fourteen months after the Curragh Mutiny, Carson was appointed Attorney-General in Asquith's Coalition Cabinet. See Young T. and Kettle M., *Incitement to Disaffection* (1976) pp. 18, 19.
18. For a useful discussion, see Bonner D., *Emergency Powers in Peacetime* (1985) Chapter 1.
19. *Wolfe Tone's Case* (1798) 27 S.T. 613.

20. *R.* v. *Hampden* (1637) 3 St. Tr. 825.

21. *R.* v. *Hampden* (the Case of Ship-Money), the court had determined that the Crown was the sole determinant of whether or not there existed a threat giving rise to the use of its emergency powers. The decision was reversed by special Act. Keir D.L. and Lawson F.H., *Cases in Constitutional Law* (1954) p. 65; Holdsworth W.S., 'Martial law historically considered', in Goodhart A.L. and Hanbury H.G., *Essays in Law and History* (1946) p. 11.

22. In *R.* v. *Dytham* [1979] QB 722 it was held that a police officer who stood by when a vicious assault was made against a member of the public could be guilty of a common law offence of misfeasance in office. See Marston J. and Ward J., *Cases and Commentary on Constitutional and Administrative Law* (1991) p. 271. Despite the clear dictum of Lord Diplock to the contrary in *Albert* v. *Lavin* [1982] AC 546, 565, some early cases appear to indicate that private individuals who refuse to assist in suppressing a breach of the peace may also be criminally liable: *The Case of Arms* (1597) Popham's Rep. 121; *Burdett* v. *Abbott* (1812) 4 Taunt. 401, 449; *R.* v. *Brown* (1841) Car & M 314. Holdsworth, *op. cit.*, p. 17.

23. Stephen J., *History of the Criminal Law*, Vol. I, p. 185 states that the Keeping of the King's Peace is 'a Royal Prerogative as old as the monarchy itself'. Troup E., *The Home Office* (1925) p. 41 notes that 'while a primary responsibility for peace and order in each district rests with the Magistrates and the Police authorities, the ultimate responsibility falls on the King's Ministers and particularly on the Home Secretary who in this matter exercises a general controlling and co-ordinating authority over the whole country.'

24. *Coomber (Surveyor of Taxes)* v. *Berks Justices* (1883) 9 App Cas 61. For the *De Keyser* principle, see Chapter 2.

25. *Furly* v. *Newnham* (1780) 2 Doug 419. *R.* v. *Bottrill ex p. Küchenmeister* [1947] 1 KB 41.

26. McNair A.D., (Lord), *The Procedural Status of Enemy Aliens* (1915) 34 LQR 134; Hale-Bellot H., *The Detention of Napoleon Bonaparte* (1923) 39 LQR 170; Lafitte F., *The Internment of Aliens* (1940); Allen C.K., *Law and Orders* (1945); Cotter P., 'Emergency detention in wartime: the British experience' (1954) 6 Stanford LR 238; Stammers N., *Civil Liberties in Britain during the Second World War* (1983).

27. H C Debates, Vol. LXVII (5th series) cols 1841–1842 (12 November 1914).

28. Hall, *International Law* (1924) p. 467.

29. H C Debates Vol. LXXI (5th series) cols 1986–1987 (13 May 1915).

30. *R.* v. *Vine Street Police Station Superintendent ex p. Liebmann* [1916] KB 268, 270, 274, 277.

31. *Re Weber* [1916] 1 KB 280.

32. *R.* v. *Halliday ex p. Zadig* [1917] AC 260.

33. 'The socialization of Great Britain', in Wilson H.W. (ed.), *The Great War*, Part 134 (10 March 1917). *Chester* v. *Bateson* [1920] 1 KB 928; *Central Control Board* v. *Cannon Brewery Ltd* [1919] AC 744; *Attorney-General* v. *De Keyser's Royal Hotel* [1920] AC 563.

34. In *Secretary of State for Education and Science* v. *Tameside Metropolitan Borough Council* [1976] 3 WLR 641, referring to *Robinson* v. *Minister of Town and Country Planning* [1947] KB 702. The MI5 card is described in Dummett, A.

and Nicol, A., *Subjects, Citizens, Aliens and Others* (1990) p. 153. The Harmsworth history part-work, *The Great War*, describes the atrocities perpetrated by the Bolsheviks, led by Trotsky, 'a Jew of versatile talents', Zinoviev, 'a Jew who became virtual dictator of Petrograd', and Karl Radek, 'the Austrian Jew whose real name was Sobelsohn [and who] ... was Assistant Commissary for Foreign Affairs' (Part 262 (23 August 1919), pp. 384, 385).

35. Stent R., The internment of Her Majesty's loyal enemy aliens, *Oral History*, Vol. 9 (1981); Gillman P. and Gillman L., *Collar the Lot! How Britain Interned and Expelled Its Wartime Refugees* (1980); Lafitte, *op. cit.*, p. 76; H C Debates (5th series) Vol. 363, col. 587 (23 July 1940).

36. Gillman and Gillman, *op. cit.*, pp. 7, 8, 286.

37. Public Records Office, WO.32.11119, 52D; Tolstoy N., *Victims of Yalta* (1977) pp. 118, 448. Patrick Dean, the Foreign Office legal advisor, urged immediate repatriation of the women and children to 'avoid the legal and political difficulties which are likely to arise if these people are detained as civilians much longer in the UK'.

38. *R. v. Bottrill ex p. Kuchenmeister* [1946] 1 KB 635, 637 (Lord Goddard LCJ, KBD); [1947] 1 KB 41, 50, 53; *Hirsch v. Morrison* [1946] 2 All ER 27. Details of the formal termination of the War are discussed in *Oppenheimer v. Cattermole* [1972] 2 All ER 529, 536.

39. *R. v. Secretary of State for the Home Department ex p. Cheblak* [1991] 1 WLR 890; Leigh I., 'The Gulf War deportations and the courts' [1991] Public Law 331. The then Home Secretary, Kenneth Baker, ordered an inquiry in September 1991 into the Gulf War detentions of over fifty individuals of Middle Eastern origin on the recommendation of MI5 and the review process by three 'wise men' (the same process as used in the *Hosenball* case, see note 47). The review process is now to be placed on a statutory basis, but grounds for a decision can still be denied to an appellant: Immigration Appeals Commission Bill (HL 5th June 1997) Clause 4; Norton-Taylor N., 'MI5 faces investigation into Gulf War detentions', *The Guardian*, 9 September 1991.

40. West N., *MI5* (1983) pp. 38–48.

41. W Haldane Porter CB (Home Office), Aliens Committee Minutes, 27 December 1919 (Home Office Library).

42. Andrew, C., *Secret Service* (1986) p. 232, quoted by Dummett, A. and Nicol, A., *Subjects, Citizens and Others* (1990) at p. 153.

43. Gillman and Gillman, *op. cit.*, p. 128. Domevile was also a founder-member and chairman of the Link organization, an Anglo-German friendship association set up in 1936, active in the distribution of English-language publications by Dr Goebbels.

44. Wyndham Lewis, *Hitler* (1931) p. 65, quoted by Carey J., *The Intellectuals and the Masses* (1992) p. 197.

45. Dummett and Nicol, op. cit., p. 154, quoting Sir John Pedder, a senior civil servant in the Home Office who chaired the interdepartmental Aliens Committee. The statutory period for qualification was five years, and this was applied for 'Latin, Teuton and Scandinavian races' who had 'a certain kinship with British races'. For Jews, who 'do not want to be assimilated', the period was fifteen years.

46. The most detailed contemporary account is contained in Lafitte, *op. cit.* See also Gillman and Gillman, *op. cit.*; Stent R., *A Bespattered Page* (1980); Stammers N., *Civil Liberties in Britain during the Second World War* (1983).

47. *R.* v. *Secretary of State for the Home Department, ex p. Hosenball* [1977] 1 WLR 766, CA. Lord Denning cited in support of the proposition that Home Secretaries should enjoy the widest discretion in ordering detention on security grounds: *R.* v. *Halliday* (a decision described in Hartley T.C. and Griffith J.A.G., *Government and Law* (1981) p. 363 as 'almost incredible' even in war-time; and see Sharpe R.J., *The Law of Habeas Corpus* (1976) p. 95, and *Liversidge* v. *Anderson* [1942] AC 206 (disapproved in *Rossminster* v. *IRC* [1980] AC 952, 1011, as 'expediently wrong'). The rejection of Lord Denning's observation was by Sedley J in *R.* v. *Secretary of State for The Home Department ex p. McQuillan* [1995] 4 All ER 400, 414.

48. [1987] 1 WLR 1482. Whether or not telephone intercepts had actually carried out was unclear. The issue of warrants to tap phones is now on a statutory basis under the Interception of Communications Act 1985.

49. Wright P., *Spycatcher* (1987) pp 54, 55.

50. *Ibid.*, p. 370.

51. Rose, D., 'MI5', *The Observer*, 18 September 1994; Norton-Taylor R. and Davies N. 'On Her Majesty's Secret Service', *The Guardian*, 29 January 1996; Leach P., 'The Security Service Bill', *New Law Journal*, 16 February 1996.

52. Summers A., *The Secret Life of J Edgar Hoover* (1993) pp. 312, 313, 413.

53. Allason R., MP, 'I spy spooks' (extracts from Hansard on observations made in the debate on the Security Services Bill by the Conservative Member for Torbay), *The Guardian*, 15 January 1996.

54. Ss 1 and 2 Security Services Act 1996. Concern was expressed about extending the service's function to the criminal field by the Intelligence and Security Committee, set up under s. 10 of the Intelligence Services Act 1994; Leach, *op. cit.*, p. 224.

55. (1918) 35 TLR 46.

56. *R.* v. *Halliday ex p. Zadig* [1916] KB 738 HL; *R.* v. *Home Secretary ex p. Chateau-Thierry* [1917] 1 KB 922 (CA); *Liversidge* v. *Anderson* [1942] AC 206, HL. Note also the successful action for wrongful dismissal (the dismissal had been based on the 'disloyalty' of the plaintiff, as evidenced by his internment) brought in *Knight* v. *Borough of Guildford* (1942) Allen C.K., *Law and Orders* (1945) Appendix 6. In this case, 'All the facts were brought out, and a disturbing lack of substance to the charges against the internee, upon which the Home Secretary had acted, was shown.' Sharpe R.J., *The Law of Habeas Corpus* (1976) p. 102.

57. *In Re a Petition of Right* [1915] 3 KB 649; *The Zamora* [1916] 2 AC 77; *Re Liebmann* [1916] 1 KB 268.

58. (1611) 12 Co. Rep. 74.

59. *Leach* v. *Money* (1765) 3 Burr 1692, 1742; *Mostyn* v. *Fabrigas* (1774) 1 SM LC 662; *Phillips* v. *Eyre* (1871) LR 6 QB 16; *R.* v. *Allen* [1921] 2 IR 241.

60. *Report of the Inquiry into the Export of Defence Equipment and Dual-use Goods to Iraq and Related Prosecutions* by Sir Richard Scott, Cm 115, 15 February 1996, Vol. I, para. C.1.64. The 1939 Act has been placed on a permanent footing by the Import and Export Control Act 1990.

61. Sir Donald Maclean MP, quoted by Ponting C., *The Right to Know* (1985) p. 21.

62. See, generally, Ponting, *op. cit.* Following disclosure to the *Guardian* of information about how the press was to be handled in relation to the siting of cruise missiles in the UK, the *Guardian* was compelled, on national security grounds, to supply information to identify the source. The informant, Sarah Tisdall, was subsequently dismissed from the Civil Service, and successfully prosecuted. It was acknowledged in *Secretary of State for Defence* v. *Guardian Newspapers* [1985] AC 339 that no security interest was directly affected by the disclosure.

63. *Conway* v. *Rimmer* [1968] AC 910; *Ellis* v. *Home Office* [1953] 2 QB 135. The original, restrictive rules on Crown privilege from disclosure were formulated by the House of Lords in the war-time case of *Duncan* v. *Cammel Laird* [1942] AC 624.

64. [1994] 2 All Er 452 at 461; [1994] 1 WLR 681 at 688.

6

Foreign Policy

In medieval times and before the establishment of the constitutional monarchy, relations with foreign states were no more, or less, than the personal relationship of the English king or queen and the foreign sovereign. A personal quarrel could become a *casus belli*, a reconciliation a treaty of peace. However, a century or more before foreign policy became a matter of concern for Parliament, it had become distanced from the personal relationships of monarchs and developed into a major activity of government, closely linked to defence, foreign trade, commercial policy and the collection of the royal revenues. Even after the Revolution of 1688, the advantage to the executive of being able to make major decisions concerning peace and war, foreign trade and commercial policy, speedily, and without the need for prior consultation with Parliament, was felt to be so great that it was never taken away by legislation. Control was, however, exercised after the event through the mechanism of parliamentary accountability of ministers and the need for Parliament to vote the funds for major military or political adventures. Chitty described the foreign policy prerogative in the widest terms in 1820:

> Strength and dispatch are politically necessary throughout the whole machine of government, and more especially in that part of it which relates to foreign transactions ... Experience has shown that the rapidity and secrecy which are generally necessary to the due execution of public measures will never be found in large assemblies of people ... When the rights in question are concentrated in one department of the state, and the power of the realm is wielded by one hand, the execution of public measures will inspire the people with confidence, and strike into the enemies of the country that awe, that dread of its

activity and power, which it is the constant endeavour of good policy to create. For these reasons the constitution has made the King the delegate or representative of the people with regard to foreign affairs, and has invested his Majesty with the supreme exclusive power of managing them.[1]

Blackstone, too, believed that the King had exclusive control over foreign policy, both with regard to the making of treaties and alliances and in relation to giving effect to them in the United Kingdom. Since it is 'the Sovereign's prerogative to make treaties, leagues and alliances with foreign princes ... whatever contracts therefore he engages in, no other power in the kingdom can legally delay, resist or annul'.[2] This approach wholly misrepresents the role of the Crown under the prerogative. Ministers can, and do, make treaties with foreign states, but, in the absence of legislation, such treaties have absolutely no effect in English law. Blackstone's statement is, as Maitland said, 'very untrue'.[3] Unlike in certain foreign jurisdictions, in English law treaties are not 'self-executing'. They need legislation to give them effect, for the simple and obvious reason that, if treaties were to have immediate effect upon signature within the United Kingdom, the Crown could legislate for subjects without the participation of Parliament. Such an option has not been available to the Crown at least since the *Case of Proclamations* in 1611, and probably well before then.[4] The principle for this limitation on the scope of the treaty-making power of the Crown was recognized by Phillimore J in *The Parlement Belge* (1879), who held that it was not possible for the Crown, acting alone, to make decisions affecting the rights of subjects or in relation to the imposition of taxation. In the case in question the Crown had purported to decide which foreign ships were 'public' and thus immune from action in British courts on the basis of the doctrine of sovereign immunity (discussed below), and which were liable to seizure in the United Kingdom. Although his decision was reversed on appeal, the Court of Appeal did not dispute his conclusion that the extension of immunity required legislation by the United Kingdom Parliament.[5] In addition to the legislative requirement to make treaties effective against the rights of subjects, Parliament may also legislate in such a way as to restrict the scope of the treaty-making power. This is also discussed below.

Although some monarchs, notably George III and Queen Victoria, seem to have believed that the *personal power* to conduct foreign policy was still extant, it seems certain that, by the end of the nineteenth century at least, it was acknowledged that the power of the monarch was limited to the right to be informed by the minister of proposed changes in policy, and that by convention, decisions on foreign policy were entirely matters for the government of the day. The monarch clearly did not have a right of veto, as was amply demonstrated by the acceptance by George VI of the grant of independence to India in 1947, despite his strong personal misgivings.[6]

SCOPE OF TREATY-MAKING POWERS

At international law, states may enter into all kinds of agreements, treaties, conventions, pacts, acts, declarations and exchanges of letters. International law has no technical rules for the formation of treaties, but many of the basic principles relevant to contracts apply. It has been traditional that, after the terms have been negotiated by plenipotentiaries – that is, ministers or diplomats with the fullest authority to negotiate – the agreement or treaty will be signed, but will not come into force until it is ratified by all parties. This principle used to be based on the need to ensure that the sovereign was able to be sure that his delegate had not exceeded his authority before any agreement received formal approval. In democratic states it has come to provide an opportunity for a debate on the treaty to take place, and a vote to be held in the national Parliament. Although such a course is not required by the law of the United Kingdom, it has become almost universal practice under the so-called 'Ponsonby rule' to lay the texts of international agreements before both Houses of Parliament before ratification.[7]

Generally, decisions about the state of relations between the United Kingdom and foreign states have been treated as 'political matters' and have been left by the courts entirely in the hands of the government. In such cases a certificate may be sought from the Foreign Office as to whether, for example, a person is the sovereign of an independent state, whether or not a state of war still existed with Germany after her unconditional surrender in 1945 and whether or not a state has been recognized by the Crown as an independent state.[8] It has been the practice of the courts to accept these certificates without demur, even where they appeared to conflict with known facts. In *Mighel* v. *Sultan of Johore* (1894), for example, the plaintiff had agreed upon a marriage with someone she believed to be one 'Albert Baker'. 'Mr Baker' had then defaulted on that promise, revealing that he was, in fact, the Sultan of Johore. In breach of promise proceedings the Colonial Office obligingly certified that he was the sovereign ruler of an independent state, although the claim that Johore was an independent state was 'tenuous in the extreme'. Miss Mighell's case thus foundered at the

144

outset.[9] In more recent cases, the courts have accepted Foreign Office certificates as to the status of foreign states, but have appeared more willing to draw their own conclusion from such status. In *Carl Zeiss Stiftung* v. *Rayner and Keeler Ltd (No. 2)* in 1967[10] the Foreign Secretary issued a certificate that East Germany (GDR) was not recognized either *de facto* or *de jure,* but that the Soviet Union was recognized as having *de jure* authority there, as one of the original Occupying Powers. The House of Lords, none the less, attributed legal effect to a decree of the GDR government as being a subordinate arm of the legal government. It would seem that the court has the power to apply its own interpretation to the consequences of a certificate, even though such consequences might not be those contemplated by the Government. It may well be, in the current post-GCHQ climate, that the courts would be prepared to question a certificate that was inherently self-contradictory, or in conflict with widely accepted facts.

Some of the difficulties concerning the recognition of states, and the status of heads of state and their representatives, have been removed by changes in practice by the Foreign Office and by the intervention of Parliament. Under the State Immunity Act 1978, a head of state, his or her family and personal servants continue to enjoy the immunity conferred upon them by common and international law. State-owned ships no longer enjoy immunity *per se.* If they are engaged in commercial activity, they no longer do so. Diplomats, members of visiting forces and members of international organizations enjoy various immunities, including varying degrees of immunity in the courts, according to status, and immunity from immigration control under the Visiting Forces Act 1952, the International Headquarters and Defence Organisations Act 1964, the Immigration Act 1971, s. 8(4) and the Diplomatic and Other Privileges Act 1971. Since 1989, the Foreign Office has abandoned the practice of according recognition to governments, although it continues to do so in relation to new states. Whether, in fact, a government exercises control over a territory will, in some cases, have to be determined by courts on the evidence presented to them.

THE EFFECT OF INTERNATIONAL AGREEMENTS

Although a treaty, agreement, exchange of notes or other international commitment has no automatic direct legal effect in the United Kingdom, and cannot (except in the case of agreements made with the European Union – see below) be relied upon in the courts until it has been incorporated by Act of Parliament or statutory instrument, international agreements may, none the less, have some important indirect effects on the rights of British citizens *outside* the UK. An extradition agreement may be given effect by a foreign state before the necessary legislation has been enacted in the UK. Prisoners may be returned to the jurisdiction and be subject to trial, when hitherto they had been secure in the foreign state. A right to operate an airline route may be blocked by agreement with the state where the aircraft is to land, effectively denying the holder of the right under British law from benefiting from it. Agreements between states as to the type of travel document required may result in British passengers being refused admission in foreign states. The extent to which British legislation may be flouted or common law rights or legitimate expectations may be infringed in this way depends, in part, on the extent to which the government in its foreign relations is prepared to sanction such conduct, and, in part, on the attitude of the courts of this country, and the type and content of the legislation or common law rights in question.

DEPORTATION AND EXTRADITION

Even where a promise has been made by a British minister to return foreign nationals to their state of origin, in the absence of statutory authorization the agreement cannot be put into effect in this country. Seizure will amount to unlawful detention and the individual should be able to obtain his or her release by habeas corpus and obtain damages.[11] Similarly, the return of individuals to the UK, simply by agreement with the foreign state, and in breach of existing extradition arrangements, or in their absence, is likely to be regarded as an abuse of process by the court. The procedures laid down in the Extradition Act 1989 must be followed. Lord Griffiths declared, in *R. v. Horseferry Road Magistrates' Court ex p. Bennett* (1994), that 'If a practice developed in which the police or prosecuting authorities of this country ignored extradition procedures and secured the return of an accused by a mere request to a police colleague in another country they would be flouting extradition procedures and depriving the accused of the safeguards built into the extradition process for his benefit.'[12]

The Extradition Act 1989, like its predecessor of 1870, contains a prohibition against the surrender of individuals alleged to have committed offences of a political or military character, or if it appears that the real reason for the request for their return is to try them, or restrict their liberty, for reasons relating to their race, religion or political opinions. The return of an individual to another state should therefore be preceded by an inquiry about the nature of the crime which the individual is alleged to have committed before he is returned.[13] States often attempt to avoid these restrictive provisions, which are to be found not only in the national legislation but also in the relevant bilateral or multilateral extradition agreements. This is most commonly done through the process of deportation. Deportation is simply intended to secure the departure of a person from the state, whereas extradition follows the request by one state to another for his return, and his transportation to the requesting state if the request is granted. Although there were limited deportation provisions in the Aliens Act 1905, the first general powers conferred on the Home Secretary appeared in the Aliens Restriction Act 1914 and the Aliens Restriction Order 1914. The alien was required to 'forthwith leave and thereafter remain out of the United Kingdom'.[14] The scope of the new power was tested in R. v. *Secretary of State for Home Affairs ex p. Duke of Chateau Thierry* in 1917.[15] The government had made an agreement with the French authorities to return to France all French men of military age who had not submitted themselves to military service. The applicant, a French national, had refused to return. He was ordered to be deported and was placed on a ship sailing non-stop to France. Under the Aliens Order, the Home Secretary was able to order that deportees be placed on board any ship. The choice of the ship and the notification by the British authorities to the French of the deportee's imminent arrival were, strictly speaking, not an 'extradition', but the actions achieved exactly the same effect. At first instance, the King's Bench Division came unanimously to that apparently inevitable conclusion. The Court of Appeal, however, also unanimously, reversed the decision.[16] It ignored the apparent conflict with the Extradition Act 1870, except to the extent that it held that, since the applicant might jump off the ship before his arrival in France, his arrival there was not inevitable. The majority relied on the supposed power of the Crown to expel aliens, a power hitherto held to have derived, ironically, from French law, and applicable only in French territories[17] (see Chapter 4). The decision can only be explained by the excessive tenderness shown by the courts to the executive at a time when the war was going very badly. In effect, it allowed the government to implement the handover agreement through the use of a prerogative power, in clear conflict with the *Parlement Belge* decision and previous authority, even though a one-line Bill put through a compliant British Parliament could have, legally, achieved the required effect.

The danger of giving effect to agreements for the return of fugitives in wartime is amply demonstrated by the case of the Yalta refugees. At the Yalta Conference in 1944, the British delegation gave an undertaking to the Soviet government that all Russian and other Soviet nationals liberated by British forces during the advance in Western Europe would be returned to the Soviet Union. Many Soviet citizens, including men, women and children, had been forcibly conscripted by the German army into the notorious *Tod* battalions to build the Western defences along the Atlantic shoreline. Others, including many Ukrainians, had defected to the Germans. Others again had ended up in Britain through the various accidents of war. All were to be returned. There was no problem for the British authorities in relation to those held on the continent of Europe. They were entrained, often at the point of a gun, and, to the anguish of the British soldiers compelled to carry out the order, forcibly shipped back to Soviet territory. There would have been no fear of a legal challenge. The plea of 'act of state' (see below) would have been sufficient to oust the jurisdiction of any English court if one had been mounted. The difficulty arose in relation to Soviet nationals in the United Kingdom. Few had committed criminal offences and there was, at the time, no extradition treaty with the Soviet Union. Although a case could have been made for the deportation of some of the Soviet nationals on security grounds in specific cases, it could not have been advanced for a deportation *en bloc*. The Home Office and the War Department hit on the ingenious solution of describing all the Soviet citizens as being 'members of the Soviet Armed Forces' and, hence, subject to the control of Soviet officers under the Allied Forces Act 1940. The fact that most of those affected, including women and children, had never been members of those forces, and were, in any event, either too old or too young to function as soldiers, was conveniently ignored. The refugees were confined in camps and prepared for shipment back to the Soviet Union. Instructions were given to keep them under close confinement, but if any escaped, not to seek to recapture them because they might be brought before a court and it might come to light that their detention was illegal. They were all, but for a tiny handful of escapees, returned to Soviet territory. Many, like those returned by the British land forces, were shot on arrival, and others perished in the *gulags*. The whole discreditable episode is described in graphic and well researched detail in Nikolai Tolstoy's *Victims of Yalta*.[18]

Despite its exceptional context, the *Chateau Thierry* decision was followed in rather different circumstances in *R. v. Brixton Prison Governor ex p. Soblen* in 1962. In this case, the applicant, who was charged with espionage in the United States, had jumped bail there and fled to Israel. He was arrested in Israel by a US marshall and taken via the United Kingdom on a plane bound for the United States. While the plane refuelled at Heathrow, Soblen inflicted serious wounds on himself, and was admitted to a London hospital for treatment. After a request by the US government, the Home Secretary ordered the deportation of the applicant on to an aircraft flying direct to the United States. The Home Secretary had a power to deport, *inter alia*, when he deemed that the deportation was 'conducive to the public good'. As in the *Chateau Thierry* case, he had, under the Aliens Order 1953, power to designate the ship or aircraft, but not to specify the destination. On an application for habeas corpus, Soblen claimed political asylum, and argued that espionage was a political offence for which he could not be extradited. The request by the US State Department for his return (reported in *The Times*) indicated that he was being returned to the USA to satisfy that request. In effect, the deportation order was a 'disguised extradition'. The Court of Appeal held otherwise. There was no evidence before the court that the order was made in response to the request (the Crown had claimed privilege for its correspondence with Washington), and the court could not assume that the Order had been made in response to the request. The return of the applicant to Washington could, in any event, be deemed by the Home Secretary to be in the public interest. Czechoslovakia had indicated that it was willing to receive him, but the court appreciated that his arrival there might not be in the public interest either. The court held that, in the absence of bad faith (which is, in almost every case, impossible to prove, even when present), the deportation order was valid. Both Donovan and Pearson LJJ were agreed that in the unlikely situation of the Home Secretary being shown to have ordered the deportation solely to comply with the request from the US State Department, and not because he thought it was in the public good to accede to the request, the deportation order would have been invalid. Soblen, however, never reached the United States. He committed suicide on the morning he was due to be escorted to the airport for the return journey.

A consequence of this decision is to be seen in the Immigration Act 1971, which now authorizes the Home Secretary to specify the country of destination when the deportation order is made. To prevent serious abuse, the current Immigration Rules now also provide that 'a deportation order will not be made against any person if his removal would be contrary to the United Kingdom's obligations under the Convention and Protocol relating to the Status of Refugees'. This rule and the Asylum and Immigration Appeals Act 1993 are effective to prevent the return of an individual to a country of persecution but they are much less so to prevent the expulsion of an individual to a country where he is wanted for a non-extraditable offence in circumstances where trial for the offence falls short of actual persecution under the Convention.[19] In that situation, deportation can, if abused, operate as a disguised form of extradition, although the availability of an appeal against the deportation destination means that the possibility of abuse can be canvassed before the Immigration Appeal Tribunal.

ASYLUM APPLICATIONS AND FOREIGN POLICY ISSUES

All decisions on the grant or refusal of refugee status involve important, and sometimes delicate, foreign policy decisions. The grant of refugee status implicitly criticises the standards of the departed country and advertises the comparative values of the host society. The desire to maintain friendly relations with another state for commercial or political reasons may outweigh concerns for individual welfare. In 1972, in *Amekrane*, for example, a Moroccan air force officer involved in a plot to overthrow King Hassan's government fled to Gibraltar and requested political asylum. The request was immediately refused, and, although no extradition treaty existed with Morocco, Amekrane was immediately handed back to the Moroccan government for execution. An application by his widow to the European Human Rights Commission that he had been subjected to inhuman treatment by the United Kingdom government in returning him to certain death for a political offence was declared admissible. The government avoided a hearing before the Court by making a 'friendly' settlement of £37,000, paid, *ex gratia*, to the widow.[20]

A decision on the grant or refusal of an asylum application will usually involve an assessment of the political circumstances in the state of origin by the Home Office Refugee Unit and the Foreign Office, and a decision whether or not it would be safe for the applicant to be returned there. Where the applicant has lived in or passed through another 'third' state, an assessment will also have to be made as to whether the third state will abide by its Convention obligations, and not return the applicant to the country of persecution.

Such decisions were originally thought to be entirely political and non-justiciable. Although courts might feel able to decide whether or not a decision on the likelihood of an applicant having suffered torture or discrimination was within the bounds of *Wednesbury* reasonableness, they did not believe themselves to be competent to make a judgment as to the political situation in a state, nor did they feel that it was their business to do so. After the *GCHQ* decision, a slight shift in that position can be detected. In *Bugdaycay* v. *Secretary of State for the Home Department* (1987), the issue was whether or not Kenya was a 'safe' country to which the applicant, who claimed that he had suffered political persecution in Uganda, could be returned. In judicial review proceedings, in which it was argued that the Foreign Secretary's conclusion that Kenya was indeed 'safe', with no appreciable risk that the applicants might be returned to Uganda, affidavits from the Foreign Office were relied upon. On the basis of these affidavits, which were variously described by Lord Bridge and other Lords of Appeal as 'strange' and 'even stranger', 'doing little to inspire confidence in its procedure', the decision of the Secretary of State was quashed and was referred back to him for reconsideration. One commentator has said of the case that 'it is impossible to read the facts, as set out in the speech of Lord Bridge, without despairing at the Home Office's consistent failure to inform itself of the political realities in East Africa'.[21] This important decision indicated that the House of Lords was prepared to apply *Wednesbury* criteria of reasonableness even to foreign policy decisions, where those decisions impacted directly on the lives and liberties of individuals in the United Kingdom.

In the subsequent case of *Sivukumaran*, however, the House made clear that whether or not there existed a 'real and substantial danger of persecution' in a state was a matter to be determined, objectively, by the Home Secretary. The court, in an application for judicial review, could only intervene if the process by which the decision had been arrived at, or the facts disclosed to the court, were wholly at variance with the decision to such a degree as to constitute *Wednesbury* unreasonableness.

In another case, not involving asylum issues, *R.* v. *Secretary of State for the Home Department ex p. Samuel* (1990), concerning steps taken by the Foreign Office to protect an unoccupied foreign embassy, the Court of Appeal refused to intervene to consider whether or not the actions of the Foreign Office were in accordance with international law. It observed that foreign affairs were a matter for the executive, and that it would not be desirable to create a situation which might lead to differences of opinion between the Secretary of State and the United Kingdom courts.[22]

FOREIGN POLICY AND FOREIGN TRADE

Foreign policy decisions are often intimately connected to their effect on trade, and the potential commercial gain or loss to the UK. For the Crown, until the royal revenues became part of a larger national budget, there was also, frequently, the additional question of how the growth or diminution of trade, especially that relating to the excise duties on wines and spirits, might affect tax receipts. For that reason, the Crown, before the establishment of the constitutional monarchy, frequently attempted to regulate trade, to sell trading monopolies to foreign merchants and to prevent the entry of ships or goods which threatened domestic or foreign monopolists. The creation of monopolies by the Crown was declared unlawful by statute in 1624, except in the case of grants to cities and trading companies, but the Crown continued to use powers of arrest and detention of foreign traders competing against the holders of such monopolies in the United Kingdom, and of English traders abroad, at least until the Revolution of 1688. After that date, restrictions on trade without statutory authority in peacetime were, almost universally, regarded as unlawful without statutory authority. Writing in 1820, Chitty observed that, 'The freedom of trade and the general inability of the King to restrain it, or to exercise any discretionary power on the liberty of the subject in this respect, by virtue of his common law prerogatives, and independently of any legislative authority, appears to be clear both on sound constitutional principles and from authorities of first weight and character.'[23]

In wartime the regulation of trade became a matter of national defence and survival, both to secure essential supplies for the UK and to deny them to the enemy. As a consequence, the Crown enjoyed, and continues to enjoy, the widest power at common law for controlling trade with both belligerents and neutrals. That power consists, in the first place, of the laying of a general embargo on goods where required by necessity, and in the second place, in the taking of action against offenders for 'trading with the enemy', a form of common law treason. These powers have been explored more fully in Chapter 5 on the prerogative of defence.[24] In peacetime, controls on both the import and export of goods in modern times have always had to be by statute.

THE EFFECT OF STATUTORY PROVISIONS ON FOREIGN POLICY DECISION-MAKING

Although statutes directly regulating the conduct of foreign policy are rare, it is quite common for Parliament to enact provisions which indirectly fetter the scope of foreign policy making by ministers. For a great many years the Navigation Acts restricted colonial trade to ships owned in England, Ireland or the colonies and manned by crews three-quarters of whom had to be British subjects. These Acts bound the Crown, and effectively prevented it from granting trading concessions to foreign traders in British colonies.[25] More recently, in *Laker Airways* v. *Department of Trade* (1977), for example, Laker Airways had been granted a licence under the Civil Aviation Act 1971 to operate a service to the United States. There was a change of government. The incoming Labour government did not want the service to operate. It could not cancel the licence but it agreed with the United States administration, through the machinery established under the Bermuda Agreement, that landing rights in the United States would not be granted to Laker. Laker successfully challenged the action of the British government in the courts. The issue for the majority in the Court of Appeal (Roskill and Lawton JJ) was 'whether the relevant prerogative power has been fettered so as to prevent the Crown seeking by the use of the Prerogative to withdraw the plaintiff's designation under the Bermuda Agreement and thus in effect achieve what it is unable lawfully to achieve by securing the revocation by the Authority of the plaintiff's air transport licence'.[26] The Court decided that the minister could not use the foreign policy prerogative in this way, and his action in doing so in conflict with the legislation was unlawful.

Legislation may be more explicit in the regulation of foreign affairs. For example, the Overseas Development and Co-operation Act 1980 provided that the Foreign Secretary 'shall have power for the purpose of promoting the development or maintaining the economy of a country or territory outside the United Kingdom, or the welfare of its people, to furnish any person or body with assistance, whether financial, technical or of any other nature'. Authorization for a programme of assistance was given by the Foreign Secretary to the government of Malaysia to build a dam at Pergau, even though he had been advised that the project was uneconomic and did not meet the criteria for aid funds. The decision was challenged by the World Development Movement. The Foreign Secretary argued that there were other, political, considerations, involved in the decision, of which he was the sole judge, and that he could provide aid even for projects which did not meet ordinary economic criteria. In an observation that echoed that of the House of Lords in the famous 'fares fair' decision of 1983 (*Bromley LBC* v. *Greater London Council*), Rose LJ remarked that 'if Parliament had intended to give the Secretary of State power to use funds for unsound projects, it could have said so expressly'.[27]

Although the sale of arms and other goods useful to an enemy in wartime may be prohibited by either proclamation or declaration in a general embargo, such sales in peacetime were, after 1879, regulated by proclamation or Order in Council. During the First World War, the scope of the legislation was widened, but those powers were limited to the period in which there was a state of war. During wartime, the Crown, despite the legislation, granted licences to export or import otherwise prohibited goods. The same practice applied in the Second World War. As the Vice-Chancellor, Sir Richard Scott, observed in his Report on the export of arms to Iraq 'Since the conduct of war was, historically, one of the prerogatives of the Crown, the grant of permission to export where export would otherwise have been illegal may, in wartime, have been regarded as justified under the same prerogative'. The sale of arms and arms-related goods has for many years been a substantial source of revenue for the UK, and successive governments have negotiated major sales with the governments of foreign states. Such negotiations have, not infrequently, been in secret, not least because the purchasers have not always been too scrupulous about how the arms were employed, sometimes using them for purposes prohibited by international law. Sales have also caused concern to the British armed services, because, both in the Falklands and in Iraq, they have found themselves confronted by opponents equipped with the most modern British technology. Sales of such weapons were prohibited by Orders in Council made under the Import, Export and Customs Powers (Defence) Act 1939, but licensed, in specific cases, by the Department of Trade.

The 1939 Act was passed to remain in effect for the duration of 'the emergency that was the occasion of the passing of this Act'. There was no power in the Act for the Crown to licence exports, but it did so during the Second World War on the basis of the war prerogative. After the war was over, the basis of the licensing system became more tenuous. The war prerogative no longer provided a basis for licensing, and clearly, after 1961, when the war with Germany officially came to an end, the 'emergency' which formed the basis for the Act no longer existed. Successive governments failed to approve an Order in Council recognizing the fact, which would have terminated the act. The failure to do so was, said Sir Richard Scott, 'a reprehensible abuse of executive power by successive administrations'.[28] The 1939 Act was, finally, put on a permanent, peacetime, footing by the Import and Export Control Act 1990. It still, however, failed to confer a licensing power on the government. The power to license purported to derive from the implicit power to do so contained in individual Orders in Council which in each case provided, as a defence to anyone charged with a breach of the Order, the possession of a licence issued by the Board of Trade. It is, however, very doubtful if the donee of a power can enlarge that power, and surprising that the licensing of arms exports, which comprise a large part of Britain's foreign trade, rests upon a foundation which, Sir Richard said, has 'at most ... by implication, authorised the Secretary of State to grant licences'.[29]

In the field of immigration and asylum law some essentially foreign policy decisions are now subject to appeal. Under the Asylum and Immigration Appeals Act 1993 some asylum applications are dealt with in a 'fast-track' appeal process if an applicant has passed through a 'safe' third country to which he or she may be returned without the asylum application being fully considered in the UK on its merits. Special adjudicators have had to consider whether or not those destinations, certified by the Home Secretary as 'safe', were indeed safe for the applicant in terms of the Convention on Refugees. During the first two years of the operation of the Act a surprisingly high percentage, including destinations in the European Union, were found not to be safe. This was not because the applicants were liable to suffer persecution in those states, but because there was a real possibility that, because of the inadequate or unsatisfactory nature of their procedures, the applicant was at risk of being sent back to the country of persecution. In these cases, evidence is examined of asylum practices in the relevant states, and the number of successful appeals must give rise to real concern that, as suggested in the *Bugdaycay* case, statements by the Home Office and Foreign Office on the situation in other states cannot, and should not, simply be taken at their face value by the courts. Regrettably, the Asylum and Immigration Act 1996 removed the right of in-state appeal against certificates issued by the Home Secretary that a third state is safe where that state is a Member State of the European Union. Applicants will be left, once again, to the unsatisfactory process of a challenge by judicial review.

The short history of this appeal process, as well as the much longer history of substantive appeals on the merits of asylum applications, clearly demonstrates that the hitherto 'unjusticiable political questions' about the situation in another state are well within the competence of a court or tribunal. Whether or not a court should make such an appraisal, and whether or not it should draw political conclusions from an appraisal, is a different matter, and raises difficult questions about the proper relationship between judicial and executive functions. The argument of Lord Bridge in the *Bugdaycay* case, discussed above, that where 'an administrative decision under challenge is said to be one which may put the applicant's life at risk, the basis of the decision must call for the most anxious scrutiny', seems unanswerable. The short history of appeals against return to supposedly 'safe' countries provides strong support for the review of such decisions by a tribunal in possession of all the relevant facts and able to make a legally binding decision.

THE EUROPEAN UNION: LIMITS ON FOREIGN POLICY DECISION-MAKING

It would be difficult to overstate the importance, in relation to foreign policy-making, of the decision to join the European Economic Community in 1972. Membership has meant, first, that the UK's relations with other states of what is now the European Union are subsumed within the decision-making structure of the Union; second, that, within the competence of the Union, its relations with states outside the Union are now determined by Union rather than national policy priorities; and, third, that, to a more limited extent, UK foreign and economic policy towards states outside the Union is constrained by Community law.

Internal Relationships of Member States within the EU

The Treaty of Rome of 1957, although mainly directed at the achievement of a common market in goods, services, labour and capital, had a longer-term goal, expressed in the preamble to the Treaty, of laying 'the foundation of an ever closer union among the peoples of Europe'. The Treaty, which contains no mechanism for withdrawal or denunciation, created institutions whose decisions were binding on Member States, and a court empowered to enforce those decisions against them. Although the original Treaty was not intended to be the constitution for a new European federal state, the way it has developed through amendments to the original Treaty and through the decisions of the European Court of Justice has moved it, inexorably, in that direction. This is not the place to examine the internal institutional structure of what is now the European Union, but some points need briefly to be made to illustrate the extent of constraints on national decision-making *vis-à-vis* other Member States.

The competence of the Community under the original Treaty was confined to the economic sphere. The consequences of that alone were considerable. Member States were effectively prevented from restricting the import of any goods or services originating in the Community except where they could demonstrate a clear threat to public health, security or other very narrowly defined criteria. Their control over immigration at the point of entry over Community citizens became minimal. Restrictions on the export of capital were abolished. Breaches by Member States of any of these rules resulted in action against them in the European Court, fines and even claims for compensation against them in their own courts. Decisions about their economic relations with each other became matters for policy

156

initiatives by the European Commission, on which the United Kingdom could be out-voted in the final decision-making forum, the Council of Ministers. Effectively, United Kingdom 'foreign' economic policy within Western Europe had became a matter for collective decision-making which had legal force and over which the United Kingdom had lost control.

Successive British governments attempted to reassure their more sceptical citizens, anxious about loss of national sovereignty, that Britain could protect its vital national interests where the Treaty called for qualified majority voting in the Council of Ministers by reliance on the Luxembourg Accords. The Accords, which have been described by a former judge of the Court of Justice as 'a mere press release', without any legal effect, were a declaration that Member States would attempt to reach a politically acceptable compromise where, in a majority-voting situation, a Member State claimed that vital national interests were at stake. The Accords do not make it clear what is to happen if a compromise is not reached. It is, at best, a political agreement not to press matters to a majority vote in certain circumstances, but it is absolutely without legal effect. On several occasions claims to protection by the Accords by a Member State have been ignored, and the Council has taken a majority vote. It is significant that no Member State has ever attempted to enforce the Accords in the Court of Justice. The Single European Act, an amendment to the Treaty in 1986, significantly increased the competence of the Community into the areas of environmental policy, economic and social cohesion, health and safety, academic and professional standards, excise duties, frontier controls and taxation. The inclusion of these areas effectively limits the ability of Member States to make bilateral or multilateral arrangements where these would conflict with legally binding Community measures. The Single European Act also recognized, for the first time, the European Council, a six-monthly meeting of European heads of government which, although lacking the power to make legally binding decisions, effectively sets the general direction of Community policy and the parameters in which the Commission operates.

Political cooperation among the Member States in relation to foreign policy has been developing for more than twenty-five years, and this political cooperation is now a requirement of the Treaty. Article 224, for example, provides that 'Member States shall consult each other with a view to taking steps needed to prevent the functioning of the common market being affected by measures which a Member State may be called upon to take in the event of serious internal disturbances ... or in order to carry out obligations it has accepted for the purpose of maintaining peace and international security.' Article 113 authorized the Community to take measures to implement a common commercial policy in relation to the world market. The Single European Act also committed the Member States 'to formulate and implement a European foreign policy' (Article 30). Neither of these measures was legally binding, but they could result in proposals by the Commission having, as their outcome, a binding Regulation, such as that prohibiting the sale of dual-use (military and non-military) goods within or beyond the territory of the Community.[30] The Treaty on European Union significantly extended the foreign policy dimension of European decision-making. It must, however, be emphasized that the foreign policy, justice and home affairs dimensions that were added by the Treaty on European Union are outside the structure of legally binding Community decision-making. The Treaty changed (and complicated) the whole structure of the European enterprise. The term 'European Union' is now used to indicate the whole structure, including what used to be the European Economic Community, the Coal and Steel Community and Euratom, and 'European Community' now normally means that area of Community policy (within the European Union) which is subject to a legally binding decision-making process, justiciable in the European Court of Justice.

These institutional changes were negotiated by the Foreign Secretary with other Foreign Ministers, and, in accordance with British constitutional convention, were laid before Parliament for approval. There are limits to the extent to which ministers can take steps to implement Community obligations under the European Communities Act 1972. The Schedule to the Act prohibits the use of Orders in Council for the purposes of the imposition of taxation, the conferment of new subordinate legislative powers or the creation of new criminal offences carrying a penalty of more than two years' imprisonment. Any changes of this kind would require, under United Kingdom law, parliamentary legislation. The safeguards are considerably weakened by the fact that Community regulations which conflict with the 1972 Act may be approved by the Council of Ministers. Since these are directly applicable under Article 189 of the EC Treaty, they do not need Orders in Council to give them effect. Directives do require implementation, but the developing doctrine of direct effect of directives may also mean that provisions in UK law may have to be interpreted in such a way as, for example, to increase the burden of taxation. The Court of Justice has, however, itself rejected the possibility that national courts should be obliged to interpret national law in a way which creates or increases criminal liability.[31]

Although, as will be discussed below, Community treaties have immediate effect under Community law after ratification, it has been the practice of the United Kingdom government to seek parliamentary approval of major institutional changes. The European Communities (Amendment) Act 1986 and the European Communities (Amendment) Act 1993 gave effect, in UK law, to the Single European Act 1986 and the Treaty on European Union 1992 respectively. The practice of obtaining legislative approval is, in fact, required under the European Parliamentary Elections Act 1978, which provides that 'No treaty which provides for any increase in the powers of the [European] Parliament shall be ratified by the United Kingdom unless it has been approved by an Act of Parliament.' This provision is effective, as Lloyd LJ noted in *R*. v. *Foreign Secretary ex parte Rees-Mogg* in 1994, 'to fetter the Crown's treaty-making power in relation to Community law'.[32] In the *Rees-Mogg* case the applicant argued that by participating in the establishment of a European Union common foreign and security policy the Crown attempted to transfer to the Council of Ministers its ancient prerogative powers in relation to foreign policy, security and defence, without statutory authority. The court quite summarily rejected this argument, on the basis that the provisions of Title V of the Treaty on European Union did not restrict, but merely provided the means by which foreign policy decisions could be exercised. Lloyd LJ commented that Part V no more divested the Crown of its prerogative powers than did British membership of the United Nations or of NATO. He was, perhaps, a little too dismissive. Although Title V does not, in general, bind Member States to act in a specific way in relations with states outside the Union, and its provisions are excluded from the jurisdiction of the Court of Justice, there are the means, in clause K.1 in Title VI, for immigration and asylum policy in relation to third states to be decided collectively. Under Article 110c of the Treaty, the Council of Ministers can, by a qualified majority vote (after 1 January 1996), give effect to that policy by determining which nationals of which foreign states should hold a visa. A third state national holding such a visa issued by another Member State would, undoubtedly, enjoy certain rights under Community law in the United Kingdom.

External Relations of the European Union

In relation to matters within the competence of the Community, it has long been the case that it can negotiate commercial, trade and aid agreements under Article 113, and association agreements under Article 238. Article 238 also covers the negotiation of agreements with international organizations. Article 228(7) provides that international agreements concluded by the Community bind the Community and are part of Community law. In the most recent GATT negotiations, terms were negotiated by the Commission and subsequently approved by the Council of Ministers. In this situation, at least, the British government will participate to approve the text of the negotiated agreement. However, agreements negotiated before British entry, such as the Lomé Agreement or the Association Agreement with Turkey, also bind the United Kingdom. The terms are directly effective, and can be enforced against the government in the courts of the United Kingdom.[33] Even the last GATT Agreement negotiated before entry was held enforceable in national courts, and was to be interpreted uniformly in the way laid down by the Court of Justice.

Membership of the Community has thus meant that the United Kingdom is bound by agreements which it has not negotiated, and which are directly effective in this country without incorporation by the British Parliament. Besides the consequences of agreements formally negotiated by the Community/Union with external or third states, the operation of the internal rules of the Community frequently affect the UK's external relations. Most obviously this is evident on the level of the common external tariff and the way in which it affects British trading policy outside the Community. Other Community rules may have a more indirect impact. For example, although state aids to industry are generally regarded as anti-competitive, state aid could be regarded as compatible with the common market if it complied with the terms of a Directive on development assistance to a developing country. In one case, the Commission told the German government that it would have to recover aid that had been given because the beneficiary was not a genuine developing country.

The Council of Ministers has adopted a great many common positions on foreign policy issues. None of these is legally binding, but they do, on occasion, have the effect of leading to decisions, like that on the sale of dual military/non-military equipment, which are ultimately translated into binding Community and/or binding national law. The largest number of decisions affecting foreign policy taken at Community level directly affecting the law of the UK are in relation to asylum and immigration policy. The Council has adopted common positions on, for example, what constitutes a 'manifestly unfounded application for asylum' under the Geneva Convention what is a 'safe' country of origin, what constitutes 'persecution' for the purposes of the Convention and how applicants are to be dealt with. Some of these 'common positions' have been translated into British law in the Asylum and Immigration Appeals Act 1993 and the Asylum and Immigration Act 1996. In addition, the Member States have signed the Dublin Convention, which determines which states will have the primary obligation to deal with asylum-seekers. The Convention effectively abrogates the obligation which the Convention was thought to impose on each state to consider each application made to it by each asylum-seeker.[34]

ACTS OF STATE

An 'act of state' means an act of the executive as a matter of policy performed in the course of its relations with another state, including its relations with the subjects of that state, unless they are temporarily within the allegiance of the Crown. It was suggested by Warrington LJ in re Ferdinand, ex-Tsar of Bulgaria (1921) that 'prerogative properly describes the power and authority of the King in relation to his own subjects, and not rights vested in him in relation to persons owing no allegiance to him'. This distinction is misconceived. Although it is true that decisions affecting foreign states do not usually directly affect British subjects (except, perhaps, those resident in them or having dealings with them), they are undoubtedly made as part of the traditional executive functions of the Crown and there are many references to such decisions as being made under the prerogative in the cases, including the making of peace and war, and the granting or withholding of recognition of a foreign state or government.[35] Indeed, in Rustomjee v. The Queen, Blackburn J remarked that the making of treaty was done by the Queen 'in the exercise of one of the highest branches of her prerogative'.[36]

The Ferdinand decision seems to have given rise to the view that all executive acts of the Crown abroad must be acts of state, since they could not be prerogative acts. But the two concepts are not mutually exclusive. Some actions in foreign countries based on the prerogative may be acts of state, some may not. Clearly, all executive actions, in terms of the allocation of the armed forces, the making and carrying out of agreements and the necessary actions by the armed forces and administration by foreign office staff, are carried out as prerogative acts. They may, if carried out negligently, or by means of unauthorized methods, such as detentions of individuals or invasions of property, give rise to actions in tort. In such circumstances, the defence of act of state may or may not be raised. Whether or not the facts justify the plea, once raised, is a matter for the court. Neither the fact that the action was abroad nor the raising of the plea by the Crown means that, without more, there must be acceptance by the court that the action in question was an act of state. Each plea must be assessed on its own facts. Although the courts have, for example, held that the requirement that foreign nationals obtain an entry certificate issued by the embassy or High Commission in the state of origin, before coming to the United Kingdom, is imposed and administered under the prerogative, it has never been suggested that the issue of such a certificate is an act of state.[37] In the case of *Nissan* v. *Attorney-General*, although Winn LJ, in the Court of Appeal, was quite clear that the making of an agreement between the governments of the United Kingdom, Cyprus, Greece and Turkey for the location of a United Nations truce force in Cyprus was an act of state, 'an infinite multiplicity and variety of acts done after the making of that agreement, and in order to carry it into effect, were in their nature quite incapable of constituting acts of state'.[38]

The claim may be made in relation to acts approved either before or after ratification by the Crown. In *Madrazo* v. *Willes* (1820), a British warship, carrying out the government's policy of suppressing the slave trade, seized a Spanish slave ship off the coast of West Africa. The legislation only prohibited the trade by British subjects. The plaintiff, a Spanish ship-owner, obtained damages for trespass in the Court of the King's Bench against the captain of the warship. No plea of act of state was raised; nor was the action of the warship considered in such terms. It was simply a question of whether or not the seizure was authorized by the statute. The court held that it was not. In *Buron* v. *Denman* (1848) the facts were almost identical, but the outcome of the case was very different. On this occasion, the action of the warship captain was subsequently ratified by the Crown. When the claim for damages came before the court, the plea of act of state was raised. Little was said as to what characterized an act of state, but the court decided that subsequent ratification could give it that character. Once the act was recognized by the court as an act of State, the claim for damages could not be maintained.[39] A successful plea, therefore, has the effect of ousting the jurisdiction of the court.

Acts of state are acts relating to the conduct of foreign and defence policy conducted *abroad*. With the single exception of the imprisonment and deportation of enemy aliens, the plea cannot be raised in relation to any action by officers of the Crown in the United Kingdom against either a British subject or a friendly alien. Friendly aliens enjoy, with a few limited exceptions, all the civil and legal rights of a British subject. While within the country they are, in the words of Coke LCJ, 'local subjects' owing local allegiance, and reciprocally entitled to the protection of the common law.[40] Since they are entitled to protection, they are entitled to a remedy against those officers of the Crown who commit torts against them. No wrong can be sanctioned within the country by an officer of the

Crown, because, since the King can do no wrong, he cannot authorize one against a subject. Nor can state or political necessity constitute a defence.[41]

This doctrine, which is based upon the rule of law and the related concepts of allegiance and protection, extends to acts committed against British subjects abroad. It does not, however, protect British subjects living abroad who suffer indirectly as a result of an act of state committed against the government of the country in which they are resident, because the wrong done is not done to them, but to the government under whose laws they currently enjoy protection.[42] It was held in *Walker* v. *Baird* that act of state could not be pleaded against British subjects on British Dominium territory, and, in *Nissan* v. *Attorney-General*, where the majority in the House of Lords seem implicitly to have supported the view that immunity from a plea of act of state depended on the allegiance owed by British subjects abroad, and their consequent entitlement to protection.[43]

An interesting dimension to this rule is raised by the emergence of European Union citizenship, created by the Treaty on European Union and incorporated (from an English constitutional perspective: see *Rees-Mogg*, above) into English law by the European Communities (Amendment) Act 1993. Article 8c confers a right to diplomatic or consular protection on European Union citizens from other Member States, including the United Kingdom, in territories outside the European Union where the citizen's own state is not represented. It might well be that this obligation of protection, although not giving rise to a reciprocal duty of allegiance to the British Crown, would be taken by an English court as barring a plea of act of state by the Crown from being raised against a citizen of the European Union.

CONCLUSION

The conduct of foreign policy remains a major function of the royal prerogative. The limited degree of control and supervision to which it is subject comes, as we shall see, largely from the House of Commons. To an increasing, but still limited, extent, relations between the United Kingdom and foreign states have become the subject of legislation and consequently of judicial review. The scope for judicial review has, in any event, been extended by the decision of the House of Lords in the *GCHQ* case. By far the greatest impact on the use of prerogative powers in the foreign sphere has, however, been made by British membership of the European Union, the development of a common foreign and security policy and the cooperation in justice and home affairs, especially in the field of asylum and immigration. So far, these areas are largely outside the realm of law, but the Court of Justice has shown a remarkable capacity for using non-legally binding decisions of the Council of Ministers to inform its decisions in those areas which are within its competence. In the long term the scope for national foreign policy-making is likely to become increasingly constrained by common policies adopted by the European Union.

NOTES AND REFERENCES

1. Chitty J., *The Law of the Prerogatives of the Crown and the Relative Duties and Rights of the Subject* (1820) pp. 39, 40 (1968 edn).
2. *Commentaries I*, C. 7, para. 11.
3. Maitland, *op. cit.*, p. 424.
4. 12 Co Rep 74. Maitland F.W., *Constitutional History* (1909) p. 424; *Walker* v. *Baird* [1892] AC 491.
5. Keir and Lawson in *Cases in Constitutional Law* (1954) p. 107 make the point that, although the Crown may, in law, make an agreement with a foreign state that will involve a change in the law, such an agreement will, in fact, be of no value in the United Kingdom, because it will, in the absence of legislation, be unenforceable. Whether or not an act by a sovereign state is of a private kind, not protected by state immunity, is a matter for the court, determined under established principles of international law: *I Congreso del Partido* [1981] 2 All ER 1064 HL. See now the State Immunity Act 1978.
6. In 1850 Queen Victoria informed her Foreign Secretary that he had to inform her of any action which he proposed to take, and must not depart from what she had agreed to: Keir, *op. cit.*, p. 408. On King George VI's view on Indian independence, see Kingsley Martin, *The Crown and the Establishment* (1963) p. 117.
7. Hall W.E., *International Law* (1924) p. 380; Brierley *The Law of Nations* (1963) p. 320; De Smith, *op. cit.*, p. 152.
8. *Mighell* v. *Sultan of Johore* [1894] 1 QB 149; *R.* v *Bottrill ex p. Kuchenmeister* [1947] KB 41; *Duff Development Co. Ltd.* v. *Kelantan* [1924] AC 797; *Carl Zeiss Stiftung* v. *Rayner and Keeler Ltd (No. 2)* [1967] 1 AC 853.
9. De Smith, *op. cit.*, p. 154.
10. [1967] 1 AC 853.
11. *The Case of the Russian Sailors*, related in Dicey A.V., *The Law of the Constitution* (9th edn) p. 224; Forsyth, *Cases and Opinions in Constitutional Law* (1869) p. 468; *Diamond* v. *Minter* [1941] 1 All ER 391.
12. *R.* v. *Horseferry Road Magistrates' Court ex p. Bennett* [1994] 1 AC 42 at p.62.
13. S. 6(1) Extradition Act 1989.
14. Art. 6 SR & O 1914 No. 1374.
15. [1917] 1 KB 552.
16. [1917] 1 KB 922.
17. *In re Adam* (1837) Moore 470 (Mauritius); *A-G for Canada* v. *Cain* [1906] AC 542 (Lower Canada). See Chapter 3.

18. Tolstoy N., *Victims of Yalta* (1977) especially Chapter 5, 'The Allied Forces Act: the Foreign Office versus the law'.

19. Immigration Act 1971, Schedule 3, para. 1(1); Asylum and Immigration Appeals Act 1993 s.2; Statement of Changes in Immigration Rules, HC 395 (23 May 1994) para. 380.

20. *Amekrane Case*, 16 Yearbook ECHR 356 (1973); Robertson G., *Freedom, the Individual and the Law* (1989) p. 329; Bailey S.H., Harris D.J. and Jones B.L., *Civil Liberties: Cases and Materials* (1980) p. 31.

21. In the GCHQ case (*Council of Civil Service Unions* v. *Minister for the Civil Service* [1985] AC 374), foreign policy was described as 'unsuitable for discussion and review in the law courts' (Lord Fraser). However, foreign policy matters affecting individual immigration rights were held reviewable in *R.* v. *Secretary of State for Foreign and Commonwealth Affairs ex parte Everett* [1989] 2 WLR 224 (passports). The comment on *Bugdaycay* (*R.* v. *Secretary of State for the Home Department ex p. Bugdaycay* [1987] AC 514 at 533) is by Robertson G., *Freedom, the Individual and the Law* (1989) p. 330.

22. *R.* v. *Secretary of State for the Home Department ex p. Sivakumaran* [1988] 1 AC 958, 996 (Lord Templeman). *R.* v. *Secretary of State for Foreign and Commonwealth Affairs ex p. Samuel, The Times*, 17 August 1989 [1990] C.O.D. 17.

23. Chitty J., *Prerogatives of the Crown* (1820) p. 163. Impeachment was used by Parliament to deal with abuses of monopolies granted to Michell and Mompesson: Keir D.L., *Constitutional History of England*, p. 192; and see *East India Company* v. *Sandys* (1686) 10 St. Tr. 461, 530 (Jefferies CJ); *Otto* (1674) Lord Nottingham's Chancery Cases, Selden Society (1957) Vol. I, p. 121.

24. *The Hoop* (1799) 1 C.Rob. 196, 198; Chitty, *op. cit.*, pp. 164, 165; McNair and Watts, *The Legal Effects of War* (1966) p. 344; *The Scott Report* (1996) HC 115, Vol. I, para. C1.3.

25. Chitty, *op. cit.*, pp. 162, 163; Keir D.L., *op. cit.*, p. 348; Hertz G.B., *The Old Colonial System*, p. 37.

26. [1977] QB 643, CA; [1977] 2 All ER 182, 266 (Roskill LJ).

27. S. 1(1); *R.* v. *Secretary of State for Foreign Affairs ex parte the World Development Movement, The Independent*, 11 January 1995; Grosz S., 'Pergau be dammed', *New Law Journal*, 9 December 1994, p. 1708. On the successful challenge to the GLC's attempt to provide cheap, subsidized public transport for London, *Bromley LBC* v: *Greater London Council* [1983] 1 AC 768.

28. *Scott Report*, Vol. I, para. C1.64.

29. *Ibid.*, para. C1.129; for the limited powers of the donee of a power, see *Customs and Excise Commissioners* v. *Cure and Deeley Ltd* [1962] 1 QB 340.

30. Council Regulation 3381/94; See *Scott Report*, paras K2.8, K2.9.

31. The Court of Justice held, in Case 41/74, *Van Duyn* v. *Home Office* [1974] ECR 1337, that even directives which had not been implemented in a state could be enforced against the state and against state agencies, and in Case C-106/89, *Marleasing* [1990] ECR I-4135, it decided that national laws had to be interpreted in accordance with directives, even those directives which had not yet been transposed into national law. In Case 80/86, *Kolpinghuis Nijmegen* [1987] ECR 3969, however, the court held that this interpretative principle did not extend to the creation or extension of criminal liability.

32. S. 6 European Parliamentary Elections Act 1978. *R. v. Secretary of State for Foreign and Commonwealth Affairs ex p. Rees-Mogg* [1994] 2 WLR 115, 124.

33. Case 12/86, *Demirel* [1987] ECR 3719; Cases 267-269/81, *SPI* [1983] ECR 801; Hartley T.C., *The Foundations of the European Community* (1994) pp. 165–76, 228–30, 272–3.

34. D'Oliveira H.U.J., 'Expanding external and shrinking internal borders: Europe's defence mechanisms in the area of free movement, immigration and asylum' in O'Keeffe D. and Twomey P. (eds) *Legal Issues of the Maastricht Treaty* (1994) pp. 261, 273.

35. *In re Ferdinand* [1921] 1 Ch 139. For cases taking a broader view of the prerogative: *Duff Development Co. v. Kelantan Government* [1924] AC 824; *Blackburn v. Attorney-General* [1971] 1 WLR 1037; compare Wade H.W.R., *Constitutional Fundamentals (1980)* pp. 46, 47, who disputes that the conclusion of a foreign agreement is the exercise of a prerogative power.

36. (1876) LR 1 QBD 487, 493.

37. *Amin v. Entry Clearance Officer, Bombay* [1983] AC 818; *R. v. Secretary of State for the Home Department ex p. Ounejma* [1988] Imm AR 75.

38. [1967] 3 WLR 1009, 1063.

39. *Madrazo v. Willes* (1820) 3 Bar. & Ald. 353; *Buron v. Denman* (1848) 2 Ex. 167, 12 Jur. 82.

40. Enemy aliens are not beyond the protection of the law, but their detention or deportation are acts of state: *R. v. Vine Street Police Station Superintendent ex p. Liebmann* [1916] 1 KB 268; *Netz v. Chuter Ede* [1946] Chj. 224. Friendly aliens are local subjects (*Calvin's Case*, 7 Co. Rep. 1, 20a) and entitled to full access to the courts: British Nationality and Status of Aliens Act 1914.

41. *Johnstone v. Pedlar* [1921] 2 AC 262; *Walker v. Baird* [1892] AC 491; *Nissan v. Attorney-General* [1970] AC 179; see Holdsworth W. 'The growth of the English constitution', in *Essays in Law and History* (1946) pp. 92, 93.

42. *West Rand Gold Mining Company v. The King* [1905] 2 KB 391.

43. [1892] AC 491; *Nissan v. Attorney-General* [1970] AC 179. Only Lord Reid actually based his decision on the status of Nissan as a British subject, however. See Hartley T.C. and Griffith J.A.G., *Government and Law* (1981) p. 315; Collier J.G. [1969] CLJ 166.

7

The Civil Service

All the ordinary administrative functions of government are carried out by civil servants. In addition, senior civil servants provide expert advisory support to ministers. A civil servant has been defined as 'a Crown servant (other than the holder of a political or judicial office or a member of the Armed Forces) appointed directly or indirectly by the Crown, and paid wholly out of funds provided by Parliament and employed in a Department of Government'.[1] The service consists of three services, the Home Civil Service, the Diplomatic Service and the Northern Ireland Civil Service. The Diplomatic Service comprises those officials working at home and abroad for the Foreign and Commonwealth Office. A small number of Home civil servants, in the Home Office Immigration and Nationality Service, also work abroad, on secondment to British missions.

Although the relationship between Crown and civil servant is contractual, the power of the Crown to enter into the contract is derived from the royal prerogative, and subject to the limits placed by Parliament on the power of dismissal, the terms of the engagement of civil servants can by changed at will by the Crown. The basis for this wide discretion enjoyed by the Crown probably derives both from the traditional immunity which the monarch personally had (and still enjoys) from actions in contract and the more modern concept that it would be contrary to the public interest for the Crown to be fettered in its administrative and other decisions by contractual obligations, especially where national security is involved. The latter consideration appears to have been uppermost when the House of Lords, by a majority, declined to intervene in the removal of trade union rights from the conditions of service of civil servants employed at GCHQ, Cheltenham, although they made it clear that in the absence of the security element that was present in this case, decisions altering the terms of service of civil servants should comply with rules of fair procedure.[2]

A recognition of the existence of a contractual or semi-contractual relationship between the Crown (personified, in this case, by ministers exercising the prerogative power of civil service regulation) and civil servants is only the first step in defining the scope of executive authority. In legal terms, what are the limits of what civil servants can be told to do? Are there instructions from ministers which they should disobey? Civil servants, with ministers, comprise the executive power under our constitution. Much of what they do is required or authorized by statute, but much more is not defined at all. 'The principle motive force of the executive power in the British constitution has always been the royal prerogative', declares Holdsworth.[3] That statement, although undeniably true, does not take one very far. As we have seen, Dicey refers to the prerogative as the 'residue of discretionary or arbitrary authority which at any given time is legally left in the hands of the Crown'.[4] The definition begs many questions, some of which have been discussed in Chapter 2. In the context of the general powers within which civil servants operate, it is possible to say that, adopting a narrow approach, 'legally left' means (a) that a traditional power (the 'residue') has not been removed, reformulated or rendered unexercisable by statute and therefore remains exercisable in its original form and (b) that that power, and the manner of its exercise, has been recognized by the courts.

The need for judicial recognition derives from the clear words of *Entick* v. *Carrington*.[5] It is, of course, possible to confine the rationale of that case to the exercise of prerogative powers which interfere with personal or property rights. On this basis, the executive can only exercise recognized prerogative powers interfering with personal and property rights which have received judicial recognition. Taken literally, this approach would only enable ministers and civil servants to do those things recognized by the courts as within the prerogative, or which have been authorized by statute. A broader view, taken by Harris and other recent writers, is that the executive can do (a) anything falling within the traditional, recognized prerogative powers that have not been statutorily curtailed and, in addition, (b) anything else which an ordinary individual can do with full legal capacity. Some of these latter activities, like the power to make contracts, have received judicial recognition; others have not. It does not matter, under the broader view, that an executive function is without specific judicial approval.[6] The narrow view has the advantage that executive power is limited to that which is expressly authorized by common law or by statute and is reasonably certain in its scope. It has the disadvantage that public administration may be confined by a restrictive legalism, with little room for creative discretion by civil servants. The broader view is open to the criticism that there is no analogy between the executive and the ordinary citizen. The executive is not spending its 'own' money. It is an artificial construct, unrestrained by the moral principles which bind ordinary people, and it needs to be made to operate within clear legal parameters.

Neither broad nor narrow view could yet be said to be dominant, although the executive tends to be given the benefit of the doubt by the courts where the legal basis of a power is uncertain, but its exercise is perceived to be in the public interest, and it does not interfere with the enjoyment of rights by citizens. In practice, the Civil Service operates within a wide range of statutes which regulate its external relations with citizens and others. Internally, with regard to recruitment, training, promotion and relations between different departments of the service, Parliament has, until recently, intervened very little, and the Civil Service has largely regulated itself by custom and convention and the strong collegiate ethos it has developed over more than a century. In this respect, the British Civil Service has a remarkable degree of autonomy when compared to the executives of other comparable West European states.[7]

The professional Civil Service is a Victorian invention. Civil servants were originally no more than the handful of employees of the royal household. For that reason, important governmental tasks were put out to commission. The commissioners of tax, for example, would be entitled to a percentage of what they collected. Opportunities for corruption, partiality and extortion abounded.[8] In the seventeenth and eighteenth centuries there was a gradual increase in the number of Crown servants, but the quality of service provided varied greatly. Nepotism was rife, posts were bought and sold, and those appointed frequently engaged others to undertake the work they were supposed to do. The modern civil service still owes much to the spirit of the Northcote-Trevelyan Report of 1854. The Report, whose recommendations were implemented by Gladstone in 1870, called for the creation of a civil service to which recruitment was to be by competitive examination. Recruits were to be 'men who have been engaged ... in studies which have no immediate connection with the business of any profession ... [and whose studies have] the effect merely to open, to invigorate and to enrich the mind'.[9]

The effect of the Northcote-Trevelyan reforms was to create a highly dedicated, committed and competent Civil Service. Drawing on the brightest Oxbridge, largely arts and humanities, graduates, it became a first-class meritocracy, without specialist skills except in administration, but with a strong collegiate sense.

Individual civil servants in the Administrative Grade, the elite of the service, would spend a life-time in a Department. Departments developed their own culture and loyalty. Governments might come and go. There remained a distinctive departmental approach, an identifiable Home Office, Foreign Office or Treasury policy, which incoming politicians found extremely difficult to change. Ironically, although the contracts of senior civil servants were like those of all civil servants, theoretically terminable at will, both convention and their obvious commitment to political impartiality and public service made their removal by an incoming administration, in practice, almost impossible.

Many civil servants would still argue that the stability of their appointments, and the enduring nature of their approach to what are the inevitably recurring problems of government, gives the process itself both continuity and consistency. They are 'the permanent ballast of the constitution.'[10]

Although governments became increasingly involved, from the First World War onwards, in the planning of the economy, the running of the railways, the coal, steel industries, the management of education and housing, the service eschewed, except in wartime, the recruitment of experts. In 1945 the Attlee government, surprisingly in view of its major programme of public ownership, dropped the specialists recruited to the service in wartime, and the service reverted to its pre-war recruitment practices. Until the implementation of the Fulton Report in 1968, leading to the establishment of the Civil Service College in 1970, there was no proper system of training for civil servants. The members of the Administrative Grade were, as Anthony Sampson described them in 1965, 'highly-educated amateurs'. Even after Fulton, the Civil Service remained largely detached from business and the professions. Politicians arriving to take charge of departments were often impressed by the quality of the advice which they received, but were frustrated by the detachment of the service from what they saw as the 'real world'. R.A. Butler, a former Home Secretary who lived most of his life in politics and university administration, remarked that 'the civil service is a bit like a Rolls Royce – you know it's the best machine in the world, but you're not quite sure what to do with it. I think it's a bit too smooth; it needs *rubbing up* a bit.'[11]

CIVIL SERVICE REORGANIZATION

The service had to wait more than twenty years after the Fulton Report before it received the rubbing up that Lord Butler thought it needed. The process was gradual at first. A whole range of measures to increase efficiency, to improve responsiveness to the public and to monitor performance were tried with varying degrees of success: organization and methods, programme analysis and review, the Finance Management Initiative, Citizens' Charters and market testing.[12] The great change came in 1990. Within a few months of Margaret Thatcher leaving office, the 'Next Steps' programme for transferring large chunks of Civil Service work to semi-autonomous agencies was initiated. By April 1996, there were 125 agencies established, with more than 70 per cent of the Civil Service working in them. In 1993, the minister responsible for the Civil Service described the changes as 'a genuine revolution in Whitehall' and the most radical changes in our public services since the Northcote-Trevelyan reforms of 1870.[13]

The 'Next Steps' reforms were widely regarded as essentially managerial in nature, designed to secure the more efficient delivery of services by the contracting-out of public services, market testing, privatization and a more decentralized system of Civil Service pay. They had, as Vernon Bogdanor has observed, very important constitutional consequences, which seem not to have been fully grasped when they were initiated. The rationale behind the reforms in the public services was that they would be delivered more effectively if the government operated along business lines. The delivery of good government is not, however, a business. Lord Rayner, a former director of Marks & Spencer, once remarked that 'Government has to provide services which no sane business would undertake.' A casualty in the process may be the ethos of public service, which is much harder to retain in a business climate and among far-flung agencies. One aspect of the self-regulation of the Civil Service comes from that ethos 'whereby people ... want to do their best; they are aware colleagues are watching and that there are disciplinary procedures'. Nor is there any counterpart in the business world to the constitutional principles designed to ensure the accountability of ministers and the integrity and impartiality of civil servants.[14] The new arrangements have not been in place for very long, but it is already clear that the setting up of the 'Next Steps' agencies has had a significant effect upon the role of the senior civil servants and their relationship with ministers, Parliament and the public.

MINISTERIAL ACCOUNTABILITY AND THE NEW CIVIL SERVICE STRUCTURE

A great many decisions which by statute or under the prerogative are supposed to be taken by ministers are, in fact, taken by civil servants. It would be impossible to run a large department if every minor matter had to be referred up to the minister. Many of these decisions, although within the competence of the department, will be quite outside the knowledge of the minister. The courts have long recognized that, in the absence of specific legislative provisions to the contrary, delegations of decision-making of this kind are perfectly lawful, and, although not actually taken by the minister, may properly be attributed to him or her.[15] Before the Crown Proceedings Act 1947, a minister could be held personally liable for any wrong committed by his department. Since the Act came into force, the practice is now to sue the department itself. Ministers are both legally and politically responsible for their own personal conduct. Much the commonest reason for a ministerial resignation in recent years has been some failure in the area of sexual conduct (associated, in some cases, with an alleged security risk). Resignations for personal misjudgments and for departmental errors have, on the other hand, become a rarity. Whether or not a minister should be held politically to account for the wrongdoing of civil servants in his or her department is much less certain than it used to be. In principle, since all civil servants act in the name of the responsible minister, he or she should take responsibility for them when mistakes are made. As Professor de Smith has observed, 'The political answerability of Ministers has helped to preserve the impartiality and anonymity of civil servants; they have been reasonably secure from public censure and, therefore, find it easier to give unstinted loyalty to a succession of political masters.'

It seems clear that there is a duty placed on the responsible minister to account to Parliament; that is, to explain the circumstances in which a mistake has been made in his or her Department. In that sense, the responsible minister is always accountable to Parliament for the acts of his or her civil servants. More than that, as Hugh Gaitskell, the Leader of the Opposition, said in the debate on the Commander Crabbe affair in 1956, he or she should take at least formal responsibility for it.

> When a Minister comes to the House and says, 'One of my officials made a mistake', thereby implying that he, the Minister was not directly responsible for that mistake, nevertheless it is a sound and vital constitutional principle that the minister takes responsibility for what has happened. [It] is fundamental to our democracy, because if we were to depart from it, it would imply that the Civil Service is in some way independent and not answerable to this House.[16]

Although a minister should always accept formal responsibility for what has happened in his department, that is not to say that he should

172

always accept *blame* for it. Sir David Maxwell Fyfe, the Attorney-General, said in the debate on the *Crichel Down* affair in 1954: 'Where action has been taken by a civil servant of which the Minister disapproves and has no prior knowledge, and the conduct of the official is reprehensible, then there is no obligation on the part of the Minister to endorse what he knows to be wrong, or to defend what are clearly shown to be errors of his officers.'[17]

While a minister may not be expected to take the blame for every wrongful action by a civil servant in his department, he will, in relation to his obligation to *account* to the House, have to explain what has been done to avoid, as far as possible, a repetition of the wrongdoing. This may, of course, involve the disciplining or removal of the offender. In recent years senior civil servants have been increasingly identified with specific policies, creating, at least, what one observer has described as 'a dent rather than a gaping hole in official anonymity'.[18] They give evidence about those policies to Select Committees and, if the policy results in maladministration, they may be named in a report by the Parliamentary Commissioner for Administration. They may also be singled out, as a number were in the *Scott Report on the Sale of Arms to Iraq*, for criticism in relation to the way in which they either assisted in the formulation of a policy or put it into effect.[19] As witnesses before Select Committees, civil servants are expected to explain what the relevant policies are and why they have been adopted. The Osmotherly Rules, which govern the conduct of civil servants on these occasions, do, however, require civil servants to be careful to 'avoid ... comments which ... are politically contentious'. The Rules have, perhaps uncharitably, been described as 'twenty-five pages of how to say, "I'm sorry, Chairman, I can't answer that question. May I refer you to my Minister?"'. Nominally, the Rules are intended to protect the independence and impartiality of the civil service, but, in fact, governments are the chief beneficiary, because they have the effect of ensuring that as little information as possible about government policy is released, and only as and when the government requires it. In this they are also assisted by the instincts of the senior civil service. As Lord St John of Fawsley (who, as an MP, was largely responsible for the current select committee system) put it: 'The whole instinct of the Civil Service, admirable beings though they are, is to conceal information, not to impart information, and to slow things down rather than quicken things up.'[20]

Under the new 'Next Steps' agency structure, each new agency created by statute, such as the Benefits Agency, the Child Support Agency and the Prison Service, is headed by a person not appointed from within the Civil Service, but recruited by advertisement from the world of business or elsewhere. Each chief executive leads a group of civil servants who operate within the new statutory framework. They are still civil servants whose relationship with the Crown is governed partly by the prerogative, partly by their contractual conditions of service and partly, in relation to the work they do, by the statute setting up their agency. The appointment of chief executives from outside the Civil Service has the advantage of bringing new expertise into the operation of public services, and was quite widely welcomed. It has, however, a downside, in that it removes civil servants from the daily control of ministers who are, nominally, at least, responsible for them. How this affects the doctrine of ministerial responsibility to Parliament will be discussed in Chapter 10.

The removal of civil servants to agencies and the reorganization of the service has had a significant effect on the ethos of the service and on the way civil servants work. Since 1979, the number of civil servants has fallen from 735,400 to 499,000. Two-thirds of those who are left have been moved into Next Steps agencies. A report by the *Observer* in April 1996 on research carried out by two civil service unions, the IPMS and the PTC, representing the middle and lower ranks of the service, indicated serious concern about the future of the service. Personal contracts and performance-related pay were said to 'have shattered the jobs-for-life culture that persuaded generations of middle-class families to enter public service'. A trade union official is reported to have said, 'At the top levels, you have permanent secretaries and chief executives of Next Steps agencies with performance-related pay, and often on short-term contracts, which produce enormous personal pressure to give their political masters what they want. At the lower end of the service, you have total disenchantment. Every time voluntary severance schemes come up, they are massively oversubscribed'.[21] Another writer, a former senior civil servant in the Home Office, while welcoming a new emphasis on achieving results rather than administering a process, condemns the way the changes have been carried out, threatening the ostensible objectives of reorganization, 'The result has often been a culture of anxiety, blame and risk avoidance. Politically convenient but intellectually obscure distinctions between policy and operations – and between accountability and responsibility – have added to the decline in confidence.'[22]

Some writers take a more sanguine view of the recent changes. Peter Hennessy, an acute observer of the Civil Service for many years, believes that the essential features of the Civil Service, as envisaged by the Northcote-Trevelyan reforms, 'recruitment and promotion on merit inside a permanent, politically neutral, career public service ... still mercifully fashion the service today'. Simon Jenkins claims that there was little resistance to the reforms from within the civil service, and that able officials wanted to take advantage of the new opportunities to exercise their skills. The reforms promised more responsibility, more career flexibility and more money.[23] The perception may have differed according to the seniority of the official and the extent to which the new structure offered him or her real opportunities for advancement. It may be some years before it will be possible to come to any firm conclusions as to how far the changes have affected the fundamental culture of the service.

POLITICAL NEUTRALITY

The Civil Service, it was declared by a Select Committee in 1985, 'as such has no constitutional personality or responsibility separate from the duly-elected Government of the day'.[24] The convention is that civil servants advise ministers on policy matters and are then involved in the necessary administration to put those ideas into effect, but that they do not themselves hold any preferred view as to what policy ought to be adopted. As we have seen, this is altogether too simplistic a view. Departments develop their own views on what should be departmental priorities, or how policies should be conducted, which ministers find very difficult to overturn. Furthermore, senior civil servants may well present a range of options to ministers, but make it clear which course should be adopted.[25] The point is not that civil servants should not have opinions, but that they should, as far as possible, keep them to themselves. Most importantly, they should ensure that any difference which they may have with a minister about a policy adopted should not become public. It is the appearance of neutrality that is important. The convention is a two-sided one. Civil servants should ensure that the minister is not embarrassed by the expression of open dissent and the minister is required to protect the civil servant from being required to compromise his or her constitutional position of neutrality in public. The consequence of this convention is the almost obsessive secrecy that has characterized British public life for more than a century. It was a characteristic known to Walter Bagehot and was well formulated by Kellner and Crowther-Hunt:

> The unspoken heart of the argument for closed government is
> that private debate amongst civil servants and ministers
> produces more rational policies, freed from public pressure,
> which is assumed to be irrational. Wise men, cogitating quietly

on the nations problems, will produce 'right' answers, if they are shielded from the political hubbub of the marketplace. But once exposed to pressure-groups and vested interests and newspapers that will get it all wrong, who knows what absurdities will result.[26]

Such a view certainly exaggerates the ability of ministers and civil servants to reach sensible and appropriate decisions if left to themselves, and probably underestimates the value of pressure groups in ensuring that better decisions are reached. The reality, in any event, is not that pressure groups are uninvolved in decision-making, but that their involvement is often secret and the participants are not representative of a broad sweep of opinion. The Ministry of Agriculture and Food, for example, is assisted by advisory committees dominated by the food and agricultural businesses. Consumer groups have lobbied for many years for a separate government department to represent consumer interests, but were long unsuccessful. The new Government has acknowledged that there is a problem and has committed itself to the establishment of an independent Food Safety Agency. There is a widely held belief that the pressure for deregulation and lower costs to business have been at the expense of safety. Rightly or wrongly, the lowering of safety levels in relation to the treatment of cattlefeed is seen by the public to have contributed to the spread of BSE. The food industry successfully resisted the licensing of food processing premises. Following a score or more deaths from food-poisoning in Scotland it now seems likely that provisions in the Food Safety Act 1990 will need to be implemented to set up a licensing system.[27]

The pressure by select committees for more open decision-making has produced, in a few instances, some striking revelations about departmental decision-making, and provided opportunities for pressure groups to make a real impact. The decision to provide assistance to the Malaysian government to build the Pergau Dam is a case in point. The evidence given to two select committees showed that Sir Tim Lancaster had gone to considerable lengths to advise the then Foreign Secretary, Douglas Hurd, not to support the Pergau Dam project. When reconsidering his original advice, Sir Tim had written, '[He] had looked again at the papers to see whether there was any material counter argument to be set against the clear economic case against the project, such that reasonable individuals could agree to disagree about the balance of arguments with regard to the intrinsic worth of the project ... he saw no serious counter to the arguments.' Despite this advice, the Foreign Secretary decided to support the project on political grounds. Aid was only permissible under the Overseas Co-operation and Development Act 1980 if it was granted 'to promote the development ... of a country or territory outside the United Kingdom.' It was Sir Tim's view that the aid would not do this, and that on no reasonable view could it achieve the required aim. In the proceedings brought by the World Development Movement which are discussed in Chapter 6, the Foreign Secretary gave evidence that 'no suggestion was made by officials that any illegality would arise were ministers to approve the project'. Rose LJ charitably described this evidence as 'manifestly incomplete'.[28]

The Next Steps reforms are likely to have a significant effect on the public profile of civil servants. Many of those appointed to head the new agencies have acquired their management skills outside the Civil Service. They are used to accepting responsibility for their decisions and to defending them in public. Recognition is given to their new status in the reforms. For the first time in the history of Parliament, letters addressed by MPs to ministers about the operation of an agency and written parliamentary questions were answered not by the responsible minister, but by the chief executive of the agency. The division between 'policy', for which ministers remain responsible, and 'operational decisions', for which responsibility lies with the chief executive, is often not an easy one to draw. There have been allegations that, despite the nominal independence of the agencies, ministers are sometimes incapable of resisting the temptation to get involved in their day-to-day running, especially where the work is politically sensitive. The dismissal of the head of the Prison Services Agency in October 1995 over escapes of prisoners and other alleged failures of the service resulted in demands by the dismissed Chief Executive, Derek Lewes, to be allowed to explain his conduct to Parliament, and also to active consideration by the First Division Association as to whether all senior officials should be allowed to be accountable for their actions, and not just give evidence to select committees on behalf of their ministers.[29]

The traditional neutrality of senior civil servants requires that they should not themselves become actively involved in public politics or take up public political positions. Since civil servants are citizens as well as servants of the Crown and the public, the rules prohibiting their active involvement have been drawn as loosely as possible to reflect both their seniority and the sort of work which they do. There are three categories, which were originally devised following an official inquiry in 1949.[30] The most politically restricted are senior members of the service, who are debarred from national political activities, but are entitled to take part, with the permission of their department, in local political activities, provided that they act 'with moderation and discretion, particularly in matters affecting their own Department'. Officers in the executive grade, mainly falling in the clerical and technical category, are much less restricted, and can normally take part in both national and local politics, unless their work takes them into direct contact with the public. Other civil servants are not restricted at all.

The most direct threat to the neutrality of the Civil Service is the use of civil servants in publicity and in the presentation and development of party policy by the party in power. Politicians are increasingly obsessed about the control and manipulation of information. The lower they stand in public esteem, the more the 'presentation' of policy takes over from the substance. Policies do not, as such, fail. It is the public perception of the policy that fails. There is always a temptation for governments to co-opt the civil service, with all the resources at the disposal of the state, to enhance the standing of the government and to present its policies in the most favourable light. At the highest level in the executive, in the Prime Minister's private staff, there has, since the days of Ramsay Macdonald, been a press officer at Number 10 Downing Street. Harold Macmillan had one. Harold Wilson had two: Trevor Lloyd-Hughes, an ex-newspaper man whose press statements were so bland that he was described as 'more of a civil servant than the civil servants'; and Joe Haines, the Prime Minister's press secretary, who never pretended to be neutral and was always a Labour partisan. By the mid-eighties, relations with the media assumed a central role. At the heart of that process was a civil servant, the Prime Minister's press secretary Bernard Ingham. Like Haines, Ingham never pretended to be neutral. Sir Frank Cooper, the Permanent Under Secretary at the Ministry of Defence, who had tangled with Ingham over the reporting of the Falklands War, said in 1986,

> The aim now is the management of the media with a much higher degree of central control from Number 10 Downing Street and with the connivance of a part of the media. There is now public relations – which I would define as biased information. I suggest that the post of Chief Information Officer at Number 10 Downing Street is in fact a political job in a party sense and is not a job which it is proper for a civil servant to fill unless he or she resigns from the Civil Service on appointment.[31]

Other civil servants have also worked with similar dedication for the Prime Minister. Charles Powell, a career diplomat and Margaret Thatcher's Principal Private Secretary, is even rumoured to have dined with Conrad Black, the owner of the *Daily Telegraph*, to discuss the political reliability of the paper's then editor, Max Hastings.[32] David Faulkner, a former senior Home Office official, recently observed that 'the pressures on civil servants to contribute to political initiatives are greater than ever before', but that opinion is not universal. Peter Hennessy does not believe that Mrs Thatcher politicized the senior ranks of the Civil Service, despite one or two well publicized cases and a widespread impression that she had, and it is likely that the politicization, if it existed, extended only to her press secretaries and her personal advisors. The latter would, in any event, leave government service on a change of government. The politicization has been, in the case of the Home Civil Service at least, not of a party-political kind, but has involved a fundamental change in the philosophy of the service towards a more market-led, cost-conscious approach. The evidence of politicization is much stronger in the case of quangos (quasi-autonomous non-governmental organizations, funded by the taxpayer), for which the 'one of us' test did apply.[33] *Questions of Procedure for Ministers*, which the Cabinet Office has issued for a number of years to newly appointed ministers, but which was first published in 1992, contains a clear prohibition against ministers asking 'civil servants ... to engage in activities likely to call in question their political impartiality, or to give rise to the criticism that people paid from public funds are being used for political purposes'. Whether or not there are adequate means to enforce such a prohibition, should it be breached, remains a matter of dispute.[34]

THE CONTROL OF INFORMATION

As we have seen, the dissemination of information is one of the most politically sensitive aspects of the work of senior civil servants. Until the Central Office of Information received statutory recognition as an agency, information was issued by the Crown under the prerogative. As long ago as the *Case of Proclamations*[35] in 1611, Coke LCJ held that the King might by proclamation 'admonish his subjects to keep the law'. It is, presumably, on this basis that advertisements are published giving details of new legislation and specifying how those affected by it – motorists, employers, farmers and so forth – must act in order to comply with it. In *Jenkins* v. *Attorney-General*, Clive Jenkins, a trade union leader, sued the government in an attempt to stop it distributing a free pamphlet on the Common Market at a cost to the taxpayer of £20,000. The judge is reported to have rejected the action on the basis that the distribution was a prerogative power of the Crown which the court could not question.[36] There would appear to be no legal constraints on the distribution of information by departments, except that the distribution is authorized by the responsible minister and that the cost is met out of funds allocated in the annual expenditure round and approved by Parliament.

The release by civil servants of individual pieces of information without the necessary authorization could, under the Official Secrets Act 1989, lead to their prosecution. In the case of people who are, or who ever have been, members of the security or intelligence services, or who have worked as defence contractors, or who have been notified that the work that they do is connected with the intelligence services, any disclosure, of whatever kind, relating to those services will be an offence. In the case of other civil servants, the disclosure will be a breach if the material released is 'damaging' and relates in some way to defence, international relations, crime and special investigatory powers. The 1989 Act modifies the effect of section 2 of the Official Secrets Act 1911, under which the unauthorized release of *any* information by a civil servant constituted an offence, however trivial the information. The concept of 'damaging' information is very wide. In relation to international relations, for example, it means any 'disclosure is "damaging" if it damages the interests of the United Kingdom abroad'. 'International relations' includes a disclosure affecting the relations of the United Kingdom with an international organization. This would, it would seem, involve disclosure by a civil servant of discussions between Member States about proposed legislation in the Council of Ministers. Much criticism has been directed at this secretive body for its unaccountable processes, not least by the European Court of Justice. A leak of its proceedings might well be embarrassing to a British government, but disclosure could, in some circumstances, be in the public interest even though relations with another state might well be 'damaged'. Despite attempts during the Committee Stage of the 1989 Bill, the government resisted the inclusion of a 'public interest' defence. The courts have, regrettably, refused to recognize any interest requiring protection in cases where national security was claimed except the interests of the state as defined by the government of the day.

The rules on secrecy have sometimes placed conscientious civil servants in an invidious position. The civil servant owes a duty of allegiance to his or her employer, the Crown. Although often called a 'public servant', he or she, under the law at least, owes no duty to the public which pays his or her salary. The senior Civil Service does, however, have a strong corporate sense of commitment to preserve what has been called 'an idea of Britain', which may transcend its immediate loyalty to the government of the day. Lord Sherfield, who served as deputy head of the Foreign Office and joint head of the Treasury, said, after his retirement, 'we attempted to moderate the more extravagant demands of Ministers'. When asked on whose authority, he replied, 'In the interests of what one saw as sound policy.'[37] Although that might sound presumptuous, such an ethos may, on occasion, provide civil servants with the confidence to resist improper instructions from ministers, or from their seniors. As we have noted, what civil servants can and cannot do within the confines of the service is largely regulated only by precedent and convention and, in recent years, by their new Code of Practice and by their Conditions of Service. The creation of the Next Steps agencies has had the effect of fragmenting the service, and raises difficult questions about how essential standards of propriety can be maintained in the new environment. In the past, if a civil servant was directed to do something which breached the law, an established convention or his or her conditions of service, the proper course was to make a formal complaint to the person in the hierarchy immediately above the official who had given the improper instruction. Civil servants were naturally reluctant to do this because, whether or not the complaint was successful, they might be labelled as 'difficult' and 'obstructive' and refused further promotion.

Evidence given to the House of Commons Select Committee on Defence, investigating the Westland Affair, suggests that Collette Bowe, Chief Information Officer at the Department of Trade and Industry, was instructed by the then Secretary of State at the Department, Leon Brittan, to leak a letter containing legal advice about the conduct of Michael Heseltine, then Secretary of State for Defence, provided, however, that the release of the letter was agreed by Downing Street. She was unhappy about doing so, because it was a clear rule of Civil Service practice that legal advice of this kind was to be kept secret. The letter from the Attorney-General was, in any event, marked 'confidential – unauthorized disclosure'. It so happened that her Principal Personnel Officer, her Permanent Secretary, was not available, so she sought the advice of Bernard Ingham, the Senior Information Officer and the Prime Minister's Press Secretary at Downing Street. What transpired in the conversation she had with him is disputed. Contemporary press reports indicated that she was told to 'do what she had ******* well been told'. Whether or not these reports are true, it is accepted that, following the conversation with Ingham, Bowe released a paraphrased version of the Attorney-General's letter to the Press Agency room at the House of Commons.[38]

Authenticated reports concerning the involvement of civil servants in the Foreign and Home Offices in the detention and expulsion of Russian refugees as 'prisoners of war' and 'members of the Soviet forces' in 1945/6, when they were clearly neither, and where the officers involved knew that they were acting illegally, indicate that the problem is not a new one.[39] The Scott Report makes clear that some civil servants have, for many years, been involved, in relation to the sale of arms and arms-related equipment to Iraq, in the provision of information to Parliament that was seriously misleading, in conniving in activities which they knew were illegal and in attempts to obstruct witnesses and interfere with the course of justice. It is generally agreed that such incidents are rare, and that the ethical standards of the British Civil Service are second to none.

It is also, however, acknowledged that where ministers or senior civil servants are involved in some kind of wrongdoing, junior officials who do not wish to be a party to such action have been in a dilemma. They cannot complain to the senior officers who are involved in the impropriety, because to do so would not only be useless but would be very damaging to the prospects of the civil servant concerned. If they draw the matter to the attention of the press, they are liable to prosecution under the Official Secrets Act, or, at the very least, dismissal from the service for breach of confidence. Even if they did so anonymously, the newspaper concerned would not be protected, and could, despite section 10 of the Contempt of Court Act 1981, be compelled to disclose its source of information. As we have seen, there is no protection against disclosure on the grounds of public interest, and a breach of the Official Secrets Act 1989 might, as in the Sarah Tisdall case in 1984, be committed where a document belongs to a certain category of documents, even though the content of the document in issue is, in itself, in no way 'damaging', as otherwise required under the Act.[40] In the *Tisdall* case the defendant, an official in the Ministry of Defence, had leaked a memorandum to the *Guardian* newspaper about how the public relations aspects of the arrival of cruise missiles in the United Kingdom would be handled by the government. The House of Lords supported the order against the *Guardian*, requiring it to identify its source. While the document itself constituted no threat to security, the fact that the defendant had released a document from the Ministry of Defence of a non-risk type did not mean that one could safely assume that other more risky documents of the same type might not be released by her. The use of this 'class of document' approach in the Act very much weakens the 'non-damaging' defence that the Act provides.

Nor is it any defence, as the jury was directed in the *Ponting* case, also in 1984, for the defence to argue that the information was given to an MP, despite the principle of accountability. It is, of course, a fundamental principle of our constitution that ministers should keep Parliament informed about the matters for which they are responsible. But it is the *minister*, as we have seen, who is accountable to Parliament, and not individual civil servants. Following the Ponting case, Sir Robert Armstrong, the then Head of the Civil Service and Cabinet Secretary, drew up a memorandum, entitled *Note of Guidance on the Duties and Responsibilities of Civil Servants in Relation to Ministers*. It states that 'Civil servants are servants of the Crown. For all practical purposes the Crown in this context means and is represented by the Government of the day ... The Civil Service serves the Government of the day as a whole, that is to say Her Majesty's Ministers collectively ... the duty of the individual civil servant is first and foremost to the Minister of the Crown who is in charge of the Department in which he or she is serving.'[41]

Effective parliamentary accountability depends, as Sir Richard Scott acknowledged in his Report, upon ministers giving a full and frank account of the work of their departments to Parliament. If they fail to do so, should there be an obligation on civil servants to ensure that Parliament is not misled? It is one thing to ensure that civil servants are not compelled to compromise their integrity, or the political neutrality of their position, but it would be going much further to cast on them the obligation to ensure that their own department or agency acted properly by reporting any impropriety to Parliament. Professor Carol Harlow has observed that 'the idea of the faceless civil servant has broken down, and there is increasing concern for personal accountability, with public servants being accountable to select committees and to the courts'. The need for such identifiability has arisen at least in part because of the devolved budgets of agencies, and because of the responsibility of individual civil servants for them and for the 'operations' which they fund.[42] There is clearly a danger that full accountability of civil servants to Parliament may raise the possibility of a conflict between minister and civil servant in a select committee, and draw him or her directly into the party political fray. It is likely that the development of individual Civil Service accountability will continue to be resisted, and will be limited to contact between select committees and the most senior departmental civil servants and the chief executives of Next Steps agencies.

There has been widespread political pressure in recent years for more openness in government decision-making. 'Ironically, the power of Parliament to extract information from the executive declined as the volume of official information has expanded.'[43] Although it was common in the nineteenth century for the House of

Commons to pass motions that papers be laid before the House concerning certain topics or that select committees be set up to investigate alleged abuses, the growth of party discipline has gradually ensured that such committees are either not set up, or, even following the St John Stevas reforms of the select committee system in the early 1980s, not very effective. Some acknowledgement of the lack of information underlying government policy decisions has been made by successive governments. Starting with the Croham Directive issued in 1977 and the White Paper on Open Government in 1993, there have been attempts at ensuring that there is more information about the making of public policy and its implementation. The Directive and the White Paper resulted in the release of a great deal of information, but there remain many exceptions to what is available. Most importantly, even in the areas where information is not restricted, there is no legal obligation to disclose it. This is not the place for a full discussion of the progress made towards open government, and the continuing need for full release of official information in a participatory democracy, enforceable through a Freedom of Information Act. The extent to which official information is available does, however, have an important bearing on the position of civil servants and their relationship to the community at large, as well as to ministers and to Parliament. The position of ministers in this process is discussed in Chapter 10.

THE CIVIL SERVICE AND DEMOCRATIC ACCOUNTABILITY

Where a civil servant works for a department or an agency in which the service provided is being operated inadequately, dishonestly or even dangerously, and where public money or the lives of users are being put at risk, does the civil servant owe a duty to the public at large? In most cases these problems can be dealt with by taking the matter to the line manager. There are, however, two cases where this course of action may be inadequate. The first is where the line manager is directly involved in the wrongdoing, or where he or she does not wish to come into conflict with the wrongdoer. The second case is where the risk to the public is so great and immediate that internal procedures are too slow to provide an effective remedy or protection for the public.

The inadequacy in the first case may be cured by having an alternative line of complaint that has the means to provide a quick and effective solution if one is possible and appropriate. That procedure may not provide a solution where the situation is urgent. As we have seen, the First Division Association has been unhappy about the internal procedure in the civil service because it exposes the complainant to dismissal or loss of career prospects, even if the complaint is well founded. Following evidence of these misgivings, the Nolan Report on Standards in Public Life addressed the issue of complainants, or 'whistleblowers' in public life, and recommended that a complaint system independent of the line of management be set up. The government accepted the recommendation in July 1995, and such complaints are now referred to the Civil Service Commission. How effective this will be, especially if the complaint is about the conduct of a minister, is yet to be seen. There seems to be a great reluctance to enact any of these processes, or to make them legally binding. To do so is seen to be contrary to the culture of Bagehot's constitution. As Grey declared in 1864, 'Law would be too clumsy an instrument for regulating the conduct of Ministers of the Crown and the permanent Civil Servants of the State in their relations with one another.'[44]

Where the matter is urgent, or where an internal complaint has been made and nothing has been done, the employee is in a dilemma. If the act is clearly criminal, then the police can be informed. If the issue involves health and safety at work, civil servants, like other employees, can raise the matter internally. If no action is taken, they are empowered by European Community law to report the matter to the appropriate authority.[45] If the matter raises no obvious breach of criminal law, and he or she goes to the press, the consequence of publication is almost certainly going to be dismissal. Newspapers who publish the information, even if supplied in breach of the employee's duty of confidence, will be protected against an action in tort if publication is genuinely in the public interest, but they may still, as in the *Guardian* case, have to disclose their source.[46] The employee, in practice, will be severely exposed, and may, in practice, have no protection. Civil servants, although employed on the basis of contracts made under the royal prerogative, have the benefit of protection against unfair dismissal provided by the Employment Protection Consolidation Act 1978 (s. 138). Although it will not be a proper ground for dismissal where an employee has disclosed information in the public interest, it may well be open to an employer to argue, and for an industrial tribunal to accept, that the trust which forms the basis of the relationship between employer and employee has been breached, and the relationship can no longer be sustained.[47]

A number of ways of protecting public service informants have been attempted. The then Secretary of State for Health announced in August 1995 that a duty to report on wrongdoing and malpractice at work will be imposed in doctors' contracts, although such contracts will also contain a prohibition about talking to the press about such matters! The European Community, concerned about dealings in drug-related money by the banks, has imposed a duty on banks and their employees, in the so-called Money Laundering Directive (91/308/EC), to breach the normal duty of confidentiality and report any suspicion of unlawful dealings to the authorities. The Community could attach a similar duty on public servants and other employees where they suspect that Community-derived funds were being misapplied. More recently, two private member's bills, with all-party support, have attempted to protect the security of employment of employees who report illegal or improper behaviour at their place of work. The Whistleblower Protection Bills failed to find sufficient time, and were lost in both the 1984/5 and 1985/6 parliamentary sessions.[48]

None of these approaches addresses the central question, which is to whom the civil servant owes his or her primary loyalty. Is it to the Crown (that is, the minister and the department) as the employer? Or Parliament, to which the Civil Service, through its ministers, is responsible? Or the public, to whom ministers and Parliament, are all ultimately accountable? Our pragmatic, unwritten constitution tends to dodge such questions of principle. As we have seen, there is now an attempt to create a greater degree of autonomy for the Civil Service, with a code of behaviour for both civil servants and ministers. The elevation of *Questions of Procedure for Ministers* into what Peter Hennessy has described as 'the crucial and acknowledged instrument of decency and proper procedure at the apex of the political and governmental system' has not altered the fact that the only parts of the existing system that have much substance in either legal or political terms are the controls which ministers exercise over civil servants. As the Scott Report made clear, without the information which is routinely denied it, and without the independence from the executive to give it the will to demand information, Parliament is not in a position to make civil servants account directly to it, except to the extent allowed by the executive, as in the case of the new Next Steps agencies. And, as Professor John Stewart said to the Scott Inquiry, 'public accountability ... depends on the adequacy of the "account" which should be tested by open government and access to information'.[49]

CONCLUSIONS

The scope of the prerogative under which the process of government is carried on is wide and largely undefined. Provided that a civil servant does not exceed the bounds of a statute, or use the powers of the prerogative to invade the rights of citizens recognised by statute or common law, he or she has a more or less unfettered discretion in the way in which government policy is implemented. Only the need to obtain approval for the necessary funds will make specific parliamentary approval necessary. In other respects, the only restraining influence on a civil servant, either on ministerial instructions, or on his or her own initiative, will be the civil servant's own conscience, and the ethics of his or her profession.

Other civil services in Western Europe, such as those in Italy and Sweden, have created an elaborate body of legal rules, which tend to discourage initiative and foster a contempt for the law. For its own internal regulation of the Civil Service, the United Kingdom has relied on a series of ill-defined constitutional conventions, and what Peter Riddell has called the 'good chaps know how to behave' principle. It is now widely recognized that the prerogative is no longer a sufficient legal basis for executive action, and that a broad structure of legally enforceable rules binding on both ministers and civil servants, is necessary. The purpose of the new legislation should be, as a Danish commentator has said of reforms to his own civil service, 'To underline the limits of the subordination of civil servants to the politically nominated minister ... [and to emphasize] the legal right and ethical duty of civil servants to set aside normal loyalty and secrecy concerning the affairs of the service. Such ethical and quasi-legal considerations emphasise that the civil service is in service to society at large rather than just to the politically appointed minister.'[50]

NOTES AND REFERENCES

1. De Smith *op. cit.*, p. 204.
2. *Council of Civil Service Unions* v. *Minister for the Civil Service* [1985] AC 374. The Order in Council, made under Art. 4a of the Civil Service Order in Council 1982, refers to 'conditions of service', which clearly implies a contract of employment. The Civil Service Pay and Conditions Code states that 'It should be understood ... that in consequence of the constitutional position of the Crown, the Crown has the right to change its employees' conditions of service at any time, and that they hold their appointment at the pleasure of the Crown' (quoted by Lord Roskill).
3. Holdsworth W., *A History of English Law*, Vol. X, p. 339.
4. Dicey A.V., *The Law of the Constitution* (10th edn, 1959) p. 424.
5. (1765) 19 St. Tr. 1030; Lord Camden, having described the breadth of the power claimed by the Crown, continued, 'Such is the power, and therefore one should naturally expect that the law to warrant it should be clear in proportion as the power is exorbitant. If it is law, it will be found in our books. If it is not to be

found there, it is not law.' Later he observed, 'It is then said that it is necessary for the ends of government to lodge such a power with a state officer ... With respect to the argument of State necessity, or a distinction that has been aimed at between State offences and others, the common law does not understand that kind of reasoning, nor do our books take notice of any such distinction.'

6. Nourse L.J., in R. v. *Secretary of State for the Home Department ex p. Northumbria Police Authority* [1988] 2 WLR 590 referred to the 'scarcity of references in the books to the prerogative' [of keeping the peace] and said that it 'does not disprove that it exists. Rather it may point to an unspoken assumption that it does.' That observation seems completely at odds with the dictum of Lord Camden in *Entick* v. *Carrington*. See also Harris B.V., 'The third source of authority for government action' (1992) 109 *Law Quarterly Review* 626; Page A., 'Executive self-regulation in the United Kingdom', in Daintith T. (ed.), *Constitutional Implications of Executive Self-regulation: Comparative Experience* (1996).

7. Page, *op. cit.*, pp. 60, 61.

8. Ogg, D., *England in the Reign of James II and William III* (1955) pp. 400–7.

9. Sampson A., *Anatomy of Britain Today* (1965) p. 257.

10. Lord Bancroft, quoted by Hennessy P., *Muddling Through: Power, Politics and the Quality of Government in Postwar Britain* (1996) p. 57. Richard Crossman recounts numerous battles with his Permanent Secretary, Dame Evelyn Sharpe, at the Ministry of Housing and Local Government, in *Diaries of a Cabinet Minister*, Vols 1–3 (1975–7).

11. Sampson, *op. cit.*, p. 263.

12. Hennessy, *op. cit.*, p. 57.

13. Bogdanor V., 'Ministers, civil servants and the constitution: a revolution in Whitehall?', *Institute of Advanced Legal Studies Bulletin*, 15 October 1993, p. 10.

14. *Ibid.*, p. 11. Nursaw J., in Daintith, *op. cit.*, p. 80.

15. *Carltona* v. *Commissioners of Works* [1943] 2 All ER 560. Ss 13(5), 14(3) and 15(4) Immigration Act 1971 specify that certain immigration decisions have to be taken personally by the Home Secretary; *R.* v. *Secretary of State for the Home Department ex p. Oladahinde* [1991] 1 AC 254.

16. Extracted in Wilson G., *Cases and Materials on Constitutional and Administrative Law* (1976) p. 153.

17. HC Debates (5th series) Vol. 530, col. 1285 (20 July 1954).

18. Drewry G., 'Select committees and back-bench power' in Jowell J. and Oliver, D., *The Changing Constitution* (1989) p. 161.

19. See, for example, *The Third Report of the Parliamentary Commissioner for the Session 1968–69* HC 316. Sir Richard Scott describes, for example, the attempt by two named officials of the Foreign and Commonwealth Office to persuade Iraqi diplomats not to waive their diplomatic immunity in order to give evidence for the defence as 'interference in the course of a criminal trial ... [and] thoroughly reprehensible'. *Report of the Inquiry into the Export of Defence Equipment and Dual-Use Goods to Iraq, and Related Prosecutions* (1996), Vol. IV, para. J5.20.

20. Hennessy, *op. cit.*, p. 77. The Osmotherly Rules were updated in 1994 to reflect the more liberal information climate created by the Open Government White Paper of 1993. See Hennessy P., *The Hidden Wiring: Unearthing the British Constitution* (1995) pp. 158–9.

21. Ghazi P. and Bevins A., 'Now only "Yes Minister" will do', *The Observer* 14 April 1996. See also Faulkner D., 'Self-serving system leaves out the citizen', in the same issue.
22. Faulkner D., *The Observer*, 14 April 1996.
23. Hennessy, *op. cit.*, p. 58. Jenkins S., *Accountable to None* (1996) p. 236.
24. *Seventh Report from the Treasury and Civil Service Committee, Vol. II* (1985–86) HC 92-II, Note by Head of the Home Civil Service (p. 7), para. 2; and see Turpin C., 'Ministerial responsibility', in Jowell J. and Oliver D., *The Changing Constitution* (1989) p. 64.
25. Crossman, *op. cit.*, Vol. 1, pp. 79, 90; Meacher M., 'Whitehall's short way with democracy' in Coates K. (ed.), *What Went Wrong: Explaining the Fall of the Labour Government* (1979) pp. 170–86.
26. Kellner P. and Lord Crowther-Hunt, *The Civil Servants* (1980) pp. 275, 276.
27. Burrows N., and Hiram H., 'The official control of foodstuffs', in Daintith T. (ed.), *Implementing EC Law in the United Kingdom: Structures for Indirect Rule* (1995) pp. 150, 163.
28. Grosz S., 'Pergau be damned', *New Law Journal*, 9 December 1994. *R. v. Secretary of State for Foreign Affairs ex p. World Development Movement Ltd.*
29. Bogdanor, *op. cit.*, p. 13 describes the new responsibility of chief executives in relation to written parliamentary questions as 'a striking constitutional innovation'. Peter Riddell, in 'Cabinets, codes and the courts', *The Times*, 13 May 1996, refers to the 'policy/operational' distinction as sounding 'neat ... but it can be distorted into a doctrine of ministerial irresponsibility ... While it is obviously daft to blame Mr Howard every time a prisoner escapes, there is no clear-cut distinction between policy and operations.' The new Home Secretary announced on 15th May 1997 that, in future, questions on the prisons would be answered by a minister and not an official: HC Deb. vol. 294 col. 1.
30. De Smith, *op. cit.*, pp. 205–6; Masterman J.C., *Report of the Committee on the Political Activities of Civil Servants* (Cmd 7718, 1949); and the Armitage Committee (Cmnd 7057, 1978).
31. Harris R., *Good and Faithful Servant: the Unauthorized Biography of Bernard Ingham* (1990) p. 99.
32. *Ibid.*, p. 181.
33. Hennessy, *op. cit.*, p. 296. *Top Jobs in Whitehall: Appointments and Promotions in the Senior Civil Service*, Royal Institute of Public Administration (1987). Compare Young H., *One of Us* (1989) pp. 336–8.
34. Questions of Procedure for Ministers, Cabinet Office (1992) para. 55. After 1986, a limited internal appeals procedure was introduced where civil servants were being asked to do something unethical or improper, or where their conscience prevented them from doing something which they had been asked to do. The appeal procedure was used only once in eight years. The First Division Association explains the paucity of appeals by the overwhelming reluctance of civil servants to use the procedures for fear of adverse effects and because the procedures are entirely internal and require civil servants to use the same chain of command from whence the initial instruction came. Tomkins A., 'A right to mislead parliament?' (1996) 16 *Legal Studies* 63, 72, 73.

35. (1611) 12 Co. Rep. 74.
36. (1971) 115 SJ 674 [1971] *Current Law* 1628. Wade H.W.R., *Constitutional Fundamentals* (1980) p. 49 offers the case as 'a choice example of a non-prerogative ... since all the Crown's subjects are at liberty to issue as much free information as they like'. So they might, but not at the taxpayer's expense!
37. Paxman J., *Friends in High Places: Who Runs Britain* (1990) p. 132.
38. Harris, *op. cit.*, pp. 130–3; *Fourth Report of the House of Commons Defence Committee, Session 1985–86*, paras 174, 1289.
39. Tolstoy N, *Victims of Yalta* (1977) Chapters 5 and 6.
40. S. 1(4). The section seems to be based on the view of the majority of the House of Lords about the threat posed by the release of a document of a particular type: *Secretary of State for Defence* v. *Guardian Newspapers* [1985] AC 339. Stone R., *Textbook on Civil Liberties* (1994) p. 144.
41. HC Deb, Vol. 74, cols 128–130 (WA) (26 February 1985); revised HC Deb, Vol. 123, Cols 572–575 (WA) (2 December 1987). See Brazier R., *Constitutional Texts* (1990) pp. 488–92; Tomkins, *op. cit.*, pp. 63, 70.
42. Daintith *op. cit.*, p. 55.
43. Austin R., 'Freedom of information: the constitutional impact', in Jowell J. and Oliver D., *The Changing Constitution* (2nd edn, 1989).
44. Grey, *Parliamentary Government* (1864) p. 327, quoted by Page, *op. cit.*, p. 68; Riddell, P., 'Cabinets, codes and the courts', *The Times*, 13 May 1996.
45. The Health and Safety Directive (89/391/EC); See *Whistleblowing, Fraud and the European Union*, Public Concern at Work (1996) para. 5.0.
46. *Secretary of State for Defence* v. *Guardian Newspapers* [1985] AC 339. Another threat to the anonymity of public servant informants by para. 3(5) of Schedule 7 Prevention of Terrorism Act 1987 was demonstrated in *Director of Public Prosecutions* v. *Channel Four Television, The Times*, 14 September 1992, where the defendant was ordered to disclose the identity of an informant following the showing of a programme about collusion between the security services and paramilitary death squads. Channel Four refused on the grounds that to do so would put the informant's life at risk, and was fined. The quite inadequate protection given to journalistic sources by s. 10 Contempt of Court Act 1981 was severely criticized by the European Court of Human Rights in the *Goodwin* case, and may result in the amendment of the section; see Stephens M., 'Snowing in Strasbourg', *New Law Journal*, 5 April 1996, p. 472. On public interest and breach of confidence, see *Lion Laboratories* v. *Evans* [1984] 2 All ER 41.
47. Vickers L., 'Whistleblowing and freedom of speech in the NHS', *New Law Journal*, 18 August 1995, p. 1257.
48. See 'Safeguards for whistleblowers sought in bill', *The Independent*, 28 June 1995; *Four Windows on Whistleblowing*, Public Concern at Work (1995); Vickers L., *Protecting Whistleblowers at Work* (1995). The second Bill, published in February 1996, was the Public Interest Disclosure Bill.
49. Riddell, *op. cit.*; Scott Report, paras K8.2, K8.3.
50. Jarvad I.M., 'Executive self-regulation in Denmark', in Daintith, *op. cit.*, p. 32.

8

The Crown and the Courts

THE COURTS

The Judiciary

The national courts in England and Wales have always been the Queen's (or the King's) courts, administering royal justice. The judges were appointed by the Crown. In the early days, the appointment would have been made by the monarch personally, and, subsequently, after the rise of Conciliar and Cabinet government, by the Lord Chancellor. The medieval enforcement of the criminal law became not, as in Saxon times, a process of ensuring that the victim or his family was adequately compensated, but a matter of upholding the King's peace. Cases were initiated and judgment was executed in his name. Civil cases were, of course, instituted by the injured party, but the royal judges adjudicated in civil suits, and their judgments were backed by the warrants executed by the officers of the courts. The monarch was the fount of justice. It was only in the seventeenth century that kings abandoned their claim to preside in their own courts, but they still persisted with their right, under the prerogative, to appoint judges favourably disposed to a wide interpretation of monarchical power, and to dismiss at will judges who delivered politically unacceptable judgments. They only held office *durante bene placito*, during the King's good pleasure. After the Revolution of 1688, and the rise of Cabinet government, the monarch lost the right, in the Act of Settlement of 1700, to remove judges. Their appointment remained, nominally at least, with the monarch, but, in fact, came to be exercised in practice by the Lord Chancellor. Judges acquired a new status and a new independence. Thereafter, they could not be removed except for conviction of an offence or the passage of an address by both houses of Parliament calling for their dismissal.[1]

Judges are, today, still appointed on the recommendation of the Lord Chancellor, on whom Parliament has conferred the title 'President of the Supreme Court'.[2] Unlike the other judges, although head of the judiciary, his position is like that of other political members of the Cabinet and he holds office 'during Her Majesty's pleasure'. Chancellors can, therefore, be dismissed as summarily as other Cabinet ministers.[3] The functions of judges and their jurisdiction now owe little to the prerogative under which they were originally appointed. At common law, they are protected from liability in damages for any act which is, or which the judge believes to be, within his or her jurisdiction. The principle probably derives, originally, from their position as the king's judges, but the link with the Crown, at least as far as actual or potential liability for their actions is concerned, is severed by section 2(5) of the Crown Proceedings Act, which excludes the liability of the Crown in relation 'to anything done or omitted to be done by any person … discharging or purporting to discharge responsibilities of a judicial nature … or … in connection with the … judicial process'. Although Her Majesty's judges continue, in theory, to dispense royal justice, they have not, since the constitutional settlement of 1688 and the separation of executive and judicial functions, been comprehended in the term 'the Crown'. They are, however, paid out of public funds, swear an oath of allegiance to the Queen and can properly still be said to be in the service of the Crown.

The jurisdiction of the courts was originally derived from the most general obligation owed by the judges to the Crown through the judicial oath to do justice according to law and equity. It has now become almost completely statutory in origin. Little is left of its original jurisdiction. What remains, although in part derived from the time when the courts were no more than an arm of monarchical government, could no longer be called prerogative power. Although the Supreme Court Act 1981 specifically preserved the non-statutory jurisdiction of the Supreme Court, which the constituent courts of the Court of Appeal, the High Court and the Crown Courts exercised before the Act came into force, the scope for its exercise is limited to making the operation of the court effective. It is largely limited to procedural matters. It has, however, been described by Jacob as 'a virile and viable doctrine of English procedural law'.[4] Some evidence of the court's original jurisdiction can be seen in the inherent power of the High Court to appoint new trustees of a trust where none are capable or willing to act, and to create new types of remedy where the circumstances require it. The old prerogative remedies of *mandamus*, prohibition and *certiorari* have now been incorporated subjected to limitation by statute in the Supreme Court Act 1981.[5]

The one specific prerogative power which the courts continued to exercise, either on application or on their own motion, was that of the Crown as *parens patriae* in relation to wards of court. The prerogative in this context originally related to the property of 'infants', 'idiots' and 'lunatics', and the benefit which successive monarchs were able to derive from managing the estates of those incapable of doing so. Chitty describes the King's role rather as 'the guardian of his people and, in that amiable capacity [he] is entitled, or rather it is his Majesty's duty, in return for the allegiance paid him, to take care of such of his subjects as are legally unable'. The function of the Crown in relation to those affected by mental disability was removed by the Lunacy Acts and is currently dealt with under the Mental Health Act.[6] The power in relation to the wardship of children was specifically preserved by the Supreme Court Act 1981, but it has been largely supplanted by the Children Act 1989. The Act makes wardship and local authority care incompatible. If a ward of court is committed to care, the wardship ceases, and while a child is in care he or she cannot be made a ward of court. Of course, unless and until such a care order is made, the possibility of a wardship order remains, and the court continues to enjoy an inherent jurisdiction to do whatever is necessary to protect a child, which it will exercise where there is no conflict with the use of statutory powers conferred on another agency.[7]

Judiciary and Executive

Although judges are now distanced from the executive, and exercise judicial rather than prerogative power, their backgrounds, their manner of appointment, their previous links with the government as legal advisors and Treasury Counsel and a natural preference in Lord Chancellors for judges who could be regarded as 'a safe pair of hands' have all tended to result in a certain homogeneity of outlook with the executive when judges determine what is, and what is not, in the public interest. Indeed, it has been said that until the expansion in the number of judges in the 1960s the High Court was staffed, to a significant extent, with judges with executive or political experience. Many had also served regularly as Crown advocates.[8]

Some of the important judgments in cases in the latter part of the nineteenth and the early years of the twentieth centuries relating to the scope and reviewability of Crown powers and Crown immunity were delivered by judges such as Lords Halsbury, Atkinson, Hewart,

Dunedin and Simon, who were either Lord Chancellors and closely identified with the government of the day, or former law officers in previous administrations. In addition, by 1914, following the implementation of the Northcote-Trevelyan reforms, 'all the upper echelons of the civil service were populated by men, a remarkable proportion of them with firsts and double firsts, who had shared their schools, universities and clubs with the barristers who became the judiciary of the inter-war years'.[9] That is not to say that the judiciary showed conscious bias, but their personal proximity to the decision-takers gave them an excellent insight into the political significance of what had been decided and its impact on the process of government, and they were, perhaps, less attuned to the expectations of individuals and to the need for open government in a modern democracy. They continued, also, to have faith, or at least to express faith, in the process of ministerial accountability to Parliament. In addition, as we have seen in Chapter 3, the late nineteenth century had seen a conscious attempt to build up the monarchy around a relaunched 'Queen-Empress'. The consequence, as J.D.B. Mitchell observed in 1965, was that a certain deference was shown to the administration by the courts because that adminstration was conducted by the Crown, 'with its overtones of feudalism, a mystic air of being related to monarchy (an air perhaps all the more dangerous when monarchy had become innocuous but the rules are in truth applicable to a government with much greater power than a monarch ever had)'.[10]

Political experience is now, except in the case of the Lord Chancellor, regarded as a disqualification for judicial office. Former Treasury Counsel are still prominent on the bench and deliver important judgments on constitutional and administrative issues, but they no longer have the dominance of former times. Decisions limiting the exercise of prerogative and statutory powers are more frequent and there has been a flowering of the judicial review of executive action. The new vigour of the courts was noted in a *Times* editorial in 1995. 'Judicial review of administrative decisions has been a welcome evolutionary development in the unwritten constitution, a necessary check upon the centralisation of power and the growth of the royal prerogative.'[11] Gone, at least, is the automatic sympathy, even deference, which many judges once felt towards those engaged in public administration. The relic of such deference is still to be found in a large body of case law which is only gradually being whittled away by a less executive-minded modern judiciary. Although it would perhaps be going too far to say that the judiciary has been 'transformed' – its almost instinctive genuflection when the words 'national security' are uttered belies such a comforting conclusion – it is true to say that judges now owe nothing to executive experience and generally adopt a much more robust and practical approach to rules about Crown privileges and immunities.[12] The distance between judiciary and executive could not have been made more plain by judicial reaction to attempts by the government to limit the discretion of judges in the sentencing process by increasing the number of mandatory sentences.

The tension created by these measures has been such as to put the Lord Chancellor, who is both head of the judiciary and a member of the Cabinet, in a very difficult position. He is bound, like his colleagues, by the doctrine of collective Cabinet responsibility but at the same time must be conscious of the need to maintain the independence of the judiciary from executive control. His office is a paradox. In a country which, it is said, gave rise to Montesquieu's theory of the separation of powers, the Lord Chancellor is the living embodiment of the fusion of all three. He presides over the House of Lords as a debating chamber, sits on the judicial committee of the House as a Lord of Appeal and acts, in effect, as a minister of justice in the Cabinet. Lord Steyn, a Law Lord himself, has recently observed that 'the proposition that a Cabinet minister must be head of our judiciary in England is no longer sustainable on either constitutional or pragmatic grounds'. He said that the Lord Chancellor gave an appearance of speaking neutrally and impartially as head of the judiciary but 'the truth is different. Under governments of all complexions, the Lord Chancellor is always a spokesman for the government in the furtherance of its political agenda.' Much of the recent tension has been caused by the financial limitations placed on the working of the courts by the Treasury and what is seen by all levels of the judiciary as a complete failure by the Lord Chancellor to stand up for it in Cabinet. Lord Steyn suggested that the Lord Chief Justice would be better able to lead the judiciary from a position of total political impartiality.[13] A further distancing of the judiciary from the executive could be achieved by removing the appointment of judges from the Lord Chancellor and transferring it to an independent body, such as the Judicial Services Committee, a proposal of Sir William Goodhart reflected in the 1991 IPPR constitution and now, apparently, supported by the new Government.[14]

The Law Officers of the Crown

The law officers were originally appointed under the prerogative but now hold office under statute.[15] None the less, they still continue to exercise a number of important prerogative powers in relation to the civil and criminal process. The Attorney-General's chief function is to act as the principal legal advisor to government departments. His or her advice is not published unless, as in the case on the debates on the ratification of the Maastricht Treaty, the advice is given to the House of Commons, of which he or she is a member. Only as a result of an improper disclosure, as happened in the Westland Affair, or in the course of an inquiry, as was the case in the Scott inquiry into the export of arms to Iraq, do details of such advice become public. The advice given may have a crucial effect on important policy decisions.

However, during the debates on the Maastricht Treaty, in which the legal status of the protocol to the Treaty on social policy was a central issue, the Attorney-General consistently refused to disclose his advice to the government. He acknowledged that 'the Law Officers advise the Government on a variety of issues every week – the variety is fascinating and remarkable ... [but] I cannot recall any occasion when [that] advice has been disclosed'.[16] The Westland Affair was probably one of the few occasions when this occurred (see Chapter 7). Ministers are not obliged to follow such advice, although, as the Scott Report made clear, they appear generally to do so. He also scrutinizes parliamentary bills in draft, and may be appointed to sit on standing committees, especially when bills with a high level of legal technicality are under consideration. Much of this aspect of his work will be undertaken by the junior Law Officer, the Solicitor-General.[17]

Although the Attorney-General is a member of the government, he has a number of non-political functions. He may, either on his own initiative or at the prompting of a private individual, and as the guardian of the public interest, initiate civil proceedings in the High Court to assert or vindicate some public right. He may also defend as the nominated officer of the Crown in proceedings, where there is no appropriate government department, although it would seem that this function does not apply where the disputed act takes place abroad, outside the Commonwealth, although undertaken by British armed forces.[18] In doing this he is exercising a prerogative power which, it would seem, despite the more liberal approach of the courts since the GCHQ case, is still not subject to control or review.

In *Gouriet* v. *Union of Post Office Workers* in 1977 the applicant, a member of an organization called the National Association for Freedom, attempted to obtain an injunction to prevent a trade union from blocking, as a protest against its policy of *apartheid,* the delivery of mail to South Africa. An obstruction of the delivery of mail in this way would have amounted to a breach of the criminal law. Since Gouriet had no personal or financial interest in South Africa, he had to persuade the Attorney-General in the then Labour government to take up the case in the public interest. In this he was unsuccessful. In the course of the proceedings which he attempted none the less to pursue, he sought to impugn the refusal of the Attorney General to lend him support. The House of Lords unanimously and unequivocally rejected the idea that such decisions were, or should be, subject to control or review by the courts. A former Conservative Lord Chancellor, Lord Dilhorne, declared:

> The Attorney-General has many powers and duties. He may stop any prosecution on indictment by entering a *nolle prosequi*. He merely has to sign a piece of paper saying he does not wish the prosecution to continue. He need not give any reasons. He can direct the institution of a prosecution and direct the Director of Public Prosecutions to take over the conduct of any criminal proceedings and he may tell him to offer no evidence. In the exercise of these powers, he is not subject to direction by his ministerial colleagues or to control and supervision by the courts.[19]

In cases with political implications, the Attorney-General may consult his government colleagues but, at the end of the day, his decision to continue with or to withdraw from a prosecution should be a non-political one. It is a difficult exercise. A government has fallen because of a decision to withdraw a prosecution for, it was alleged, political reasons. And more recently, the decision of the Attorney-General not to draw matters to the attention of prosecuting counsel in one of the arms to Iraq trials, allegedly to spare the government political embarrassment, has also attracted critical comment.[20] Recent events would suggest that the observation of J.H. Morgan, Professor of Constitutional Law at the University of London, in a letter to *The Times* in 1927 is still relevant: 'There has been during the last twenty years a most unhappy tendency on the part of successive Law Officers of the Crown to regard themselves, not *parens patriae* and guardian of the rights of the subject, but as the docile instruments of Government Departments going into Court to strain every prerogative in practice and pleading.'[21] Lord Steyn, whose views on the role of the Chancellor are quoted above, would not dissent today. He has said that the Attorney-General is 'a political figure responsive to public pressure'. Although there are safeguards against any abuse of his office, these depend on weak conventions, such as that he does not take orders from government but can seek ministers' views, and that, although he is not influenced by party political considerations, he can take account of public policy.[22]

There is an important public and citizenship dimension to the decision of the Attorney-General to support, or to decline to support, actions brought in relator proceedings on behalf of certain individuals or groups. As we have seen in *Gouriet*, civil proceedings, either by ordinary action or by an application for judicial review, cannot be brought unless the plaintiff or applicant has a direct personal or proprietorial interest – a 'sufficient interest' – to protect. The common law has, traditionally, taken a very narrow view of what constitutes such an interest. In some cases, where there is a public right, such as a right of way, proceedings may be brought to vindicate that right by a local authority under the Local Government Act 1974. Local authorities have, however, a limited competence, and their resources are scarce. The relevant authority may not be able, or willing, to act. The Attorney-General has, on the other hand, a wide discretion. In addition, private individuals may be deterred from taking action by the amount of costs they may have to pay if they lose. The Attorney-General may meet that burden out of public funds and may even, when an injunction is sought before the proceedings to stop an alleged wrongdoing from continuing before the hearing takes place, be compelled to give an undertaking to compensate the other party for any consequential losses caused by such an order if, in the substantive hearing, the claim of wrongdoing is eventually held to be unfounded.[23]

The failure of the Attorney-General to authorize relator proceedings used to be fatal where there was no person with an interest able or willing to bring proceedings. In certain areas of public law, there may be no one who has been specifically affected in such a way as to give them a sufficient interest to apply for judicial review. Legislation that is intended to benefit the community at large, or to protect the environment, is by definition unlikely to affect any specific individual or body in such a way as to confer an interest on them which the court will recognize. To some extent this problem, and the difficulty of engaging the support of the Attorney-General, has been mitigated by the willingness of the courts to adopt an increasingly liberal approach. They have recognized such bodies as the Child Poverty Action Group, Greenpeace and the World Development Movement as having an interest in matters within their area of concern, although their interest is not personal, proprietorial or financial. Being a taxpayer used not to be sufficient, although it now might be. Even 'a sincere concern for constitutional issues' has, in one case, been held to suffice.[24]

LIABILITY OF THE CROWN IN CONTRACT AND TORT

The Crown and Statute

One of the privileges of the Crown unaffected by the Crown Proceedings Act 1947 is the general immunity which it enjoys from statutory provisions, unless the statute expressly refers to the Crown or applies by necessary implication. There is a converse principle expressed in the rule that the Crown may take the benefit of a statute even if the statute does not expressly (or by necessary implication) mention the Crown as a beneficiary. The basis of both rules has been simply stated. 'Since an Act is made by the Queen in Parliament for the regulation of subjects, it follows that, unless the contrary intention appears, the Act does not bind the Crown itself.' Lord Diplock expressed the principle as 'laws are made by rulers for subjects'.[25] Both statements bear little relation to the modern world. Although the direct control which governments have exercised over such diverse fields as postal services, transport, health and the more traditional functions of defence and foreign policy has been reduced considerably in the past decade, the ambit of legislation, especially that originating in the European Union, is frequently wide enough to cover activities of both civil servants and those who, although not involved in the new Next Steps agencies, are actively employed in doing government work. The distinction, therefore, between legislation aimed at 'subjects' and that aimed expressly at the Crown itself becomes increasingly difficult to draw. Nor is the principle capable of justification in a constitution publicly committed to the rule of law, especially the option which the Crown has of 'having its cake and eating it'; that is, enjoying a principle of exclusion from onerous statutes, while at the same time enjoying an implication of their application where the consequences are beneficial to the Crown. A proposal to extend penalties for the late payment of bills by instructing clients to building and other contractors and to subcontractors to government agencies, such as the Highways Agency, was vigorously resisted by the Treasury, on the ground that it would increase public expenditure. Without such a provision, government agencies will continue to be immune from penalties for late payment.[26] There seems to be no reason, in principle, why such a rule of good business practice should not apply to the Crown unless there are good grounds, argued before Parliament, for Crown immunity. In other words, the presumption should, arguably, always be that statutes *do* bind the Crown, except where the Crown is expressly excluded.

The main difficulty in the application of the rule of exclusion of the Crown from the effect of statutes is the uncertainty which surrounds the identity of 'the Crown'. Clearly, the term covers the Sovereign personally, the 'Crown as monarch'. She assented to the legislation and could, under the old common law rule, do no wrong by breaching the terms of a statute unless she had expressly agreed to be bound by it. But where she had not agreed to be bound by it (by, for example, the inclusion of such words as 'This Act shall bind the Crown'), how far could the immunity derived from that lack of assent be held to extend? In other words, what is meant by 'the Crown as executive' (see Chapter 1)? In *Town Investments Ltd* v. *Department of the Environment* in 1978 Lord Diplock declared that the expression 'the Crown' covered 'ministers of the Crown and members of the Civil Service acting under the direction of ministers'. Public corporations which are essentially autonomous in the way in which they carry out their functions are not part of the Crown. Lord Denning drew the distinction when he considered the application of the Rent Restriction Acts to the British Transport Commission in *Tamlin* v. *Hannaford* in 1950. The minister had power, in certain circumstances, to direct the Commission in the national interest, and the Commission was a corporate body. Despite the 'great powers' possessed by the minister over the Corporation,

> still we cannot regard the corporation as ... his agent ... In the eye of the law, the corporation is its own master and is answerable as fully as any other person or corporation. It is not the Crown and has none of the immunities and privileges of the Crown. Its servants are not civil servants and its property is not Crown property. It is as much bound by Acts of Parliament as any other subject of the King ... [It] is not a government department nor do its powers fall within the province of government.[27]

The decision in *Tamlin* v. *Hannaford* contains two tests, both used in subsequent cases to determine whether or not a public person or body was within the expression 'the Crown' and was, consequently, protected by Crown immunity. Was the individual or body acting as a servant or agent of the Crown? And did the person or body purported to be affected carry out a function 'within the province of government'? The first question is essentially a matter of fact and would seem easier to answer than the second, although the courts have not always come to consistent decisions on apparently similar facts. In *Pfizer Corporation* v. *Ministry of Health* in 1965 the court held that the supply of drugs to the National Health Service was 'for the services of the Crown', yet, in *British Medical Association* v. *Greater Glasgow Health Board* in 1988, the Inner House of the Court of

Session held that although the Greater Glasgow Health Board, acted as agent of the Crown and, as a health board, 'exercised functions delegated only through servants or agents [of the Crown]', there was 'no justification for holding that every agent or servant of the Crown was to be equiperated with the Crown'.[28] Fortunately, the position of health authorities has been clarified by Parliament since these two cases. They have been largely stripped of any actual or presumed Crown immunity and will, in most circumstances, be criminally and civilly liable in the same way as a private individual.[29] However, the difficulty of trying to use an agency, direction or service test to ascertain whether or not any other body has Crown status remains. The new Next Steps agencies clearly act as agents of the Crown, but they do not act under the day-to-day direction of the Crown, any more than the old nationalized industries of the kind described by Lord Denning in *Tamlin* v. *Hannaford* used to do. They act, as we have seen in Chapter 7, in *operational* matters, independently of the minister who is responsible for them, although he or she remains ultimately responsible for the *policy* within which the agency operates.

The second test suggested by Lord Denning in *Tamlin* v. *Hannaford* is not of very much assistance. What is, or is not, properly within the province of government is a question that would probably be answered differently today, compared to fifty years ago. During the debates on the Crown Proceedings Act in 1947, the Attorney-General explained the purpose of the legislation as assimilating, as far as possible, the position of the Crown and the private citizen. He warned, however, that the analogy cannot be carried too far. 'The private citizen does not have the same kind of responsibility for protecting the public, such as the Crown possesses; he does not have the defence of the realm to consider; he is not responsible for the organization of such services as the Post Office.'[30] Even after more than fifteen years of privatization of public utilities, it would probably still be possible for most people to agree that defence is an essential function within the province of government. The provision of a mail collection and delivery service, although traditionally run by the state, could not, however, now be classified as a necessary function of government.

Decisions of the European Court of Justice on the scope of Article 48(4) EC Treaty, under which member states are entitled to exclude European Union citizens from employment in 'the public service', make an interesting comparison. The Court has consistently held that payment from the public purse does not automatically result in the categorization of an appointment as within the public service exception, and that the Post Office (*in casu*, the Deutsche Bundespost) fell outside the 'public service' exception. Nor does the designation of the individual as a 'civil servant' bring him or her within the exception.[31] As with Article 48(4) EC Treaty, until Parliament has tackled the problem, and enacted that there is to be a *presumption* that all persons and bodies, including the Crown, are bound by legislation, every claim to Crown immunity will have to be examined by the courts on a case-by-case basis. It will continue to be a difficult task, since, as one writer noted after the Glasgow Health Board case, 'the concept of the Crown, so central in Scottish and English constitutional law, is not merely vague but elastic'.[32] The binding of the Crown by the 'necessary implication' of legislation has also proved difficult to establish. The fact that there are specific sections of an Act from which the Crown is excluded in their application has not resulted in the courts inferring that the Crown is bound by the remaining sections. Nor will the fact that the legislation will not work effectively if the Crown is not bound result in the Court drawing an inference that the Crown must necessarily be bound.[33]

Finally, in this context, the impact of European Community law must be taken into account. A large number of statutes now give effect to Community directives. Some of those directives are clearly intended to bind the state, such as those relating to the award of public works contracts. It seems clear that, whether or not the Crown is referred to in the implementing legislation, it will be bound if it is the purpose of the directive to bind it. Directive 71/305, for example, which deals with the advertising of public works contracts, defines contracting authorities as 'the State, regional or local authorities, bodies governed by public law'.[34] Even where the state is not referred to by the directive, its scope may be such as to cover it. The Sex Discrimination Act 1975, for example, was intended to implement Directive 76/207. The Directive has the purpose of ensuring the equal treatment of male and female employees. Although they are not excluded by the Directive, section 85(4) of the Act purported to exclude from its ambit 'the naval, military and air forces of the Crown'. Despite this exclusion of the Crown, Morison J sitting in the Employment Appeal Tribunal in *Ministry of Defence* v. *Cannock*[35] in 1995, and applying Community law, held that 'where the State is the employer, the employee may rely directly on the principle of equal treatment contained in the Directive, even though such a right was not conferred by, or was excluded by the domestic legislation'. Can one detect a note of regret in the judge's further observation that 'It is not our function to comment on the fact that the incoming tide of European law has swept away the provisions of our domestic law; but for the Directive the applicants would have had no claim'? That tide, before very long, is likely to sweep away much more of the immunity which the Crown currently enjoys in relation to statutory provisions.

Liability of the Crown in Tort

Until the enactment of the Crown Proceedings Act 1947, no action could be brought against the Crown. The only practical remedy was a Petition of Right, an ancient process later regulated by the Petition of Rights Act 1860. To bring a claim, the consent of the Home Secretary had to be obtained. In practice, it was never refused if the applicant had the shadow of a claim. The Petition procedure was, however, only available in relation to contract claims. It did not lie in tort. If the Crown had committed a wrong it was, in theory at least, under ancient rules, totally immune from action. From a simple procedural rule in the medieval courts, that a feudal lord cannot be sued in his own court, came the rule that the King, the supreme feudal lord could not be sued in the royal courts. In the language of sixteenth- and seventeenth-century monarchical supremacists, the feudal rule of procedural incapacity became elevated to the maxim 'The King can do no wrong', meaning that the King could not be guilty of crimes or torts. In addition, under the same principle, the King could not be sued for breach of contract.

Such a doctrine did not sit well with the triumph of the common law and the fall of the Stuart monarchy. During the period following the Revolution of 1688 the problem of Crown immunity was overcome by confining that immunity to the *person* of the monarch. Officials who acted unlawfully and caused loss or damage were held personally liable. They could not plead authorization by the King, because the King could no more authorize wrong than he could commit it himself. The early reports abound with cases brought by individuals against officers of the Crown. All were liable to civil actions where they exceeded their powers and invaded the rights of others. 'The law', Lord Wilmot CJ memorably remarked in 1769 in the last of the actions arising from the attempts of the government to suppress the newspaper *The North Briton*, 'makes no difference between great and petty officers. Thank God, they are all amenable to justice'.[36]

It was not, however, always possible to identify the Crown servant who had committed or authorized the wrongdoing. In such cases the Crown would nominate the servant who was to be deemed responsible. In some cases, where, for example, the Crown was responsible simply as occupier, the connection with the nominated civil servant was extremely tenuous. He or she may have had nothing to do with the premises which the Crown occupied. The practice was described by the Attorney-General in the debates on the Crown Proceedings Bill in 1947: 'Although the Crown could not be sued for civil wrongs or torts it would normally – not, I think, invariably but normally – stand behind its servant, who could always be sued personally for any wrong he had committed in the course of his duties, since the fact that what he had done might have been done on the orders of his superior, afforded him no defence. The Crown would in such cases stand behind its servant, and if damages were awarded against the servant, the Crown would see that they were paid.'[37] The courts refused to go along with what, in some cases, was clearly a fiction. In *Adams* v. *Naylor* in 1946, the House of Lords expressed strong disapproval of an obvious fiction in that case, and in *Royster* v. *Cavey* in 1947 they actually rejected a claim on the ground that the nominated defendant could not possibly have been in occupation of the premises the condition of which, it was alleged, made him liable. Both cases were influential in persuading the government to bring forward the Crown Proceedings Bill which had been under contemplation for at least twenty years.[38]

The Act preserved the personal immunity of the sovereign.[39] It did not establish a general principle of Crown liability in tort, but the object of the Bill, as the Attorney-General declared, was to assimilate the position of the Crown to that of the subject. The Act made the Crown liable in the same way as a private person of full age and capacity. The Crown has, since the Act came into force, been liable for torts committed by its servants or agents acting in the ordinary course of their functions, and for breach of the common law duties owed by employers.[40] Which persons or bodies are its servants or agents is not exhaustively defined by the Act, but 'agents' includes, under section 38(2), independent contractors but not, it would seem, bodies which are autonomous statutory corporations and which do not act under the instructions of officers of the Crown on a daily basis. The applicable law as to who, or what, is 'the Crown', and what are acts of the Crown for these purposes has been discussed above, in relation to *Tamlin* v. *Hannaford*. The Crown is also liable in the same way as any other owner or occupier of property and, subject to some limited exceptions in relation to the armed forces, as employer. It is not intended here to attempt a full analysis of the Act, some provisions of which are so obscure and contradictory that in one instance Lloyd LJ was moved to remark, in relation to section 31: 'the court must do its best to make sense of what is, in truth, nonsense'.[41] We will only attempt to evaluate the extent to which it has been successful in its aim of bringing the Crown within the bounds of ordinary tortious liability.

Although the Act purported to create a regime under which the Crown was liable for any wrong committed in the same way as a private individual, the self-evident difference between a government body carrying out prerogative and statutory functions and a private person going about his or her daily business was reflected in a number of provisions which distinguished and limited the liability of the Crown. Subsequent case law has had the effect of extending, rather than diminishing, these distinctions. Section 2(2) of the Act provides, for example, that the Crown will only be liable for the tort of breach of statutory duty if the statute in question binds not only the Crown and its servants but others too, and is capable of creating tortious liability. Potential liability of the Crown is already limited by the fact that statutes do not, as we have seen, bind the Crown unless they state as much expressly, or it can be inferred from the statute by necessary implication. This subsection, confining the tortious liability of the Crown in relation to statutes to those also binding on third parties, seems to have no purpose other than to limit Crown liability. There seems to be no reason in principle why the Crown should be any less bound to avoid the tort of breach of statutory duty in relation to a statute aimed exclusively at the Crown, than any other person or body on whom a statutory duty is imposed is obliged to avoid it. This rule does not apply to local authorities or other statutory bodies operating in the public interest. In each case, the courts will also have to determine if the statute is intended to create a tort of breach of statutory duty.

Where Parliament has considered the issue it may well have made a specific provision either creating civil liability for breach, as, for example, in the Nuclear Installations Act 1965, or expressly excluding it, as in the Guard Dogs Act 1975. Very often no consideration will have been given to this aspect of the legislation in the House, and the courts will simply have to attempt to discern Parliament's 'intention', even though it may not have had one.

Where the Crown is specifically bound, the court will be reluctant to infer tortious liability, except where no other, or no satisfactory, remedy is provided in the Act and the plaintiff is one of a class of intended beneficiaries under the Act. The cases are not easy to reconcile. Indeed, one writer has observed that 'there are no standards, no principles and no pattern'.[42] In *R. v. H.M. Treasury ex p. Petch*[43] in 1989, for example, the plaintiff was a civil servant who had suffered physically as a result of delays in dealing with his claim to a pension arising from an illness contracted at his work. Popplewell J accepted that a failure to deal promptly with his application for a pension under the Superannuation Act 1972 could give rise to a claim for breach of statutory duty. The Act provided no sanction for breach, there was no express statutory remedy and it was designed to deal with a specific class of which the plaintiff was a member. The respondent in the proceedings was the Prime Minister, as minister for the Civil Service. The court held that she was bound as 'an officer of the Crown', that therefore the Act bound 'a person other than the Crown', as required by section 2(2), and there was, therefore, no Crown immunity on that account. In relation to the nature of the statutory duty giving rise to potential liability, the decision is, in some ways, surprising because, in *Yuen Kun Yeu* v. *Attorney-General of Hong Kong* in 1988 the Privy Council had held that an omission by the Commissioner of Deposit-taking Companies to monitor the solvency of the companies for which he was responsible gave rise to no liability.[44] Although the case turned on the construction of the relevant legislation, the Privy Council decision indicates a more general unwillingness to hold a public body liable for non-performance of a duty, especially when it appears to have a discretion as to how, and when, to perform that duty. In *R.* v. *Deputy Governor of Parkhurst Prison ex p. Hague*[45] in 1992, the House of Lords concluded that the Prison Act 1952 and the Prison Rules did not create a statutory duty giving rise to an action for breach of that duty. Although there were some provisions dealing with the protection of prisoners in the Act and the Rules, they were primarily about the administration of prisons, were not, unlike the Health and Safety at Work Act or the Factories Act, directed at the protection of prisoners and could not, therefore, confer on prisoners an action for their breach. The decision is not altogether surprising. But in *Olutu* v. *Home Office and Another*[46] in 1996, the Court of Appeal held that a provision under the Prosecution of Offences Act 1985, under which regulations were made defining the maximum period of detention for those awaiting trial, did not create a right to sue for breach of statutory duty, even where, as it was accepted in this case, the plaintiff had been unlawfully detained. In this case the relevant section of the Act and the regulations were clearly intended to protect detainees who had not yet been convicted of an offence. There was no remedy, except to apply for bail. Bail may be useful in securing the release of a person who is in custody, but it does not provide a means of securing redress once a person has been released. The decision could hardly be said to be in the best judicial tradition of concern for the liberty of the subject.

Where the Crown is exercising either a prerogative or statutory power it may be liable for such torts as nuisance, negligence or misfeasance in office. There is, in principle, no reason why an act based on the prerogative might not give rise to such liability. In practice, actions relating to prerogative acts abroad may be blocked by a claim that they are acts of state. Such a plea effectively ousts the jurisdiction of the court, if the court accepts that the circumstances justify such a plea.[47] If, on the other hand, the plea is not made, or it is not accepted by the court, then ordinary liability may arise.

The main exception to this general principle is where the claim is made by a member of the armed forces. Section 10 of the Crown Proceedings Act 1947 provided that neither the Crown nor a member of the armed forces would be liable for death or personal injury caused by acts or omissions of a member of the armed forces while on duty, if the deceased or injured person was also a member of the armed forces on duty, or was on land, premises, ships, aircraft or in vehicles used for the purposes of the armed forces and the injury was certified by the Secretary of State as attributable to service for entitlement to a pension. After a number of training accidents in which soldiers were precluded from making claims, the blanket protection of section 10 was removed in 1987, but it could be revived by order of the Secretary of State 'for the purpose of any warlike operations in any part of the world outside the United Kingdom'.[48] The effect of the provision seemed to be that, where no order had been made to revive section 10, the Crown could be liable, for example, for negligence or for failure to provide a safe system of work. No order was made to revive section 10 during the Gulf War in 1991. Gunner Mulcahy suffered serious damage to his hearing during the Gulf War as a result, he alleged, of the careless firing of a howitzer at the Iraqis by his battery sergeant. The Court of Appeal agreed that two of the elements for a successful negligence claim, proximity and foreseeability of damage, were present in this situation, but it refused to accept that either a duty of care or a duty to provide a safe system of work was owed in battle conditions. It would not be fair, just and reasonable to impose one. The decision was, the Court admitted, based exclusively on policy considerations.[49] However, since the Crown had not chosen to clothe itself with the revived immunity of section 10, the decision seems to be a striking example of the court proving itself *plus royaliste que le roi*. In earlier times, successful actions have been brought against senior military and naval officers by junior soldiers when they had acted unlawfully or maliciously, or by foreign nationals when assault or trespass had been committed against them by members of the armed forces.[50]

The *Mulcahy* decision is characteristic of a recent tendency of the courts not to impose liability in negligence on public bodies discharging statutory or other functions. In the case of statutory functions, a distinction is drawn between policy decisions made under the statute, which are generally immune from liability if made within the discretion given to the decision-maker, and operational decisions, carried out in execution of the policy, which are, in theory at least, capable of giving rise to a claim in negligence.

The distinction is not easy to draw and the decisions are not wholly consistent. Some recent decisions seem to have abandoned any attempt at detailed analysis, and move straight to a general consideration, as in *Mulcahy*, of whether or not a duty of care should be imposed. As Peter Cain has observed, the current criteria for liability in relation to the careless exercise of statutory powers is open to criticism on the ground that 'there is no non-circular way of classifying a decision as policy or operational: a policy decision is simply one which can lead to liability in negligence only if it is *ultra vires*, whereas an operational decision is one to which the ordinary law of tort applies, and it was ultimately up to the court, according to its own willingness to award a tort remedy, to decide into which category to place any particular decision'.[51]

Attempting to define the circumstances in which a duty of care would be imposed by the courts, Lord Browne-Wilkinson in *X (minors)* v. *Bedfordshire CC* said that 'a common law duty of care cannot be imposed on a statutory duty if the observance of such a common law duty of care would be inconsistent with, or have a tendency to discourage, the due performance by the local authority of a statutory duty'. On this basis, the courts have refused to impose a duty of care on local authorities in relation to children with special educational needs, the police in relation to the prevention and investigation of crime, the fire brigade and shipping classification societies.[52] In the last case, the majority in the House decided that it would not be right to impose a duty of care on classification societies because they are charitable non-profit making organizations, promoting the collective welfare and fulfilling a public role. The arbitrary nature of such exclusion from liability was forcefully pointed out by Lord Lloyd in a strong dissenting speech. Referring to the public role of the societies on which the majority relied, he said 'Why should this make any difference? Remedies in the law of tort are not discretionary. Hospitals also are charitable non-profit making organisations. But they are subject to the same common law duty of care under the Occupiers Liability Acts 1957 and 1984 as betting shops and brothels.'[53]

It has become almost as difficult to predict the circumstances in which an officer of the Crown, or some other person or body exercising statutory or prerogative powers, will have a duty of care imposed upon them by the courts in relation to the exercise of those powers, as it is to predict when the courts will infer a parliamentary intention to give a remedy in tort for the breach of a statutory obligation by a government minister or other public officer. If the law continues to develop in this way, some at least of the immunity from liability in tort which was removed by the Crown Proceedings Act 1947 may be reimposed, in relation to negligence, on grounds of public policy by the courts.

Another basis for the liability of public officials that has been considered by the courts relates to the ancient, but until recently wholly neglected, tort of misfeasance in public office. This tort, which was described by a leading authority in administrative law as recently as 1980 as 'not firmly rooted in the case law', has been urged by counsel on several occasions in the past few years as a possible basis for the liability of a public official, including a government minister, for the wrongful use of powers conferred on him, but it has only very rarely resulted in an actual finding of liability. The reason for this is that a plaintiff must show that the act of the defendant involved 'failure to exercise, or the exercise of, statutory powers either with the intention to injure the plaintiff or in the knowledge that the conduct is unlawful'.[54] Intent to do wrong and knowledge of wrongdoing are as notoriously difficult to prove as the lack of good faith which is closely linked to misfeasance and which, for the many years of judicial deference, was the only limitation placed by the courts on decision-makers exercising a wide discretion given to them by common law or statute. Misfeasance has, consequently, been described as a tort of 'quite limited value'.[55]

In *Bourgoin SA* v. *Ministry of Agriculture, Fisheries and Food* in 1986, a poultry importer claimed damages from the ministry for a ban imposed on the import of poultry into the UK in the period before Christmas 1981. The ban purported to be on health grounds but the European Court of Justice decided that it was essentially a protectionist measure designed to protect the domestic poultry market, and that the ban therefore breached Article 30 of the EC Treaty as a restriction on the free movement of goods. Community law did not, at the time, specify the type of remedy which national courts should provide for breach of a Community obligation, and the Court of Appeal considered the claim as an alleged misfeasance in office by the minister. It refused to accept that there could be a tort in this case of breach of statutory duty in relation to the European Communities Act 1972. But it also held that there was no misfeasance by the minister, because it could not be shown that the minister knew that he was acting contrary to his Treaty obligations and that his action could affect the plaintiffs. It was not, however, necessary to prove malice. The plaintiff had failed to establish a knowledge of wrongdoing by the minister and, accordingly, his claim failed.

The *Bourgoin* case arose out of the making by the minister of a statutory instrument prohibiting the import of turkeys. The courts of the United Kingdom have consistently shown extreme reluctance to impose legal liability for the exercise of legislative powers. Parliament is immune from action, even if it has clearly acted in breach of the law. Provided that its actions are 'proceedings' in Parliament they are immune. Ministers are protected by absolute privilege.[56] The exercise of delegated legislative powers, has, however been held to be subject to judicial review where they conflicted with a statutory requirement that they had to be approved by Parliament before they were exercised. In *R. v. HM Treasury, ex p. Smedley* in 1985, the Court of Appeal expressed its willingness to intervene if the Chancellor of the Exchequer approved an Order without first obtaining parliamentary approval. *Bourgoin* made it clear, however, that even an unlawful exercise of legislative powers would only result in tortious liability if the decision resulting in legislation was one which met the extremely stringent requirements for a finding of misfeasance in office.

The Effect of European Community Law: State Liability

European Community law is likely to have a major impact on the whole field of Crown and ministerial liability in tort in the United Kingdom. The decision of the European Court of Justice in *Francovich* v. *Italy*[57] in 1991 is only beginning to be felt, but it carries forward a concept which can be traced back to *Van Gend en Loos* in 1962. Community law confers rights on individuals which they can enforce not only against other individuals but against their own states. As the court said in *Van Gend*:

> Independently of the legislation of Member States, Community law ... not only imposes obligations on individuals but is also intended to confer upon them rights which become part of their legal heritage. These rights arise not only where they are expressly granted by the Treaty, but also by reason of obligations which the Treaty imposes in a clearly defined way upon individuals as well as upon Member States ... The vigilance of individuals concerned to protect their rights amounts to an effective supervision in addition to the supervision entrusted by Articles 169 and 170 to the diligence of the Commission and of the Member States.[58]

The court's decision in *Francovich* enabled individuals to obtain compensation from the Italian government after they had suffered from its failure to implement a Community directive which required the government to set up a fund to protect employees in the event of the insolvency of their employers. Although the case concerned the implementation of a directive, the court made it clear that the principles on which the decision was based went much wider than Member States' obligations in relation to directives.

In *Brasserie du Pecheur SA* v. *Federal Republic of Germany* and *R.* v. *Secretary of State for Transport ex p. Factortame (3)*[59] in 1996, the court set out the principles under which Member States could be liable for any breach of Community law. The Treaty does not lay down any express provisions for the consequences of the breach of Community law by Member States, but the court decided that, to make Community law effective, it would have to provide them. It held that, for there to be liability imposed on the state, three conditions must be satisfied. The rule of Community law must be intended to confer rights on individuals, the breach must be sufficiently serious and the breach must have been shown to have caused damage to the individual. From an English point of view, the most important aspect of the *Brasserie/Factortame (3)* decision is that it will be unlawful to make the right to recover damages dependent on establishing a duty of care.

The consequences of the lack of a need to establish a duty of care can be seen most clearly in the recent *Traders Ferry Case.*[60] The case was an application for judicial review of the degree of police protection against demonstrations by animal rights protesters provided to haulage companies involved in the export of livestock. The case was not a private law claim in negligence, but, as an application for the review of the legality of the Chief Constable's decisions, it involved an assessment of the way in which police personnel were deployed by the Chief Constable to protect the hauliers in Shoreham Harbour. The Divisional Court would not interfere with the discretion of the Chief Constable and emphasized the breadth of the powers within which local police forces operate.

It was on this basis, it will be recalled, that the court also held. in *Hill* v. *Chief Constable of West Yorkshire*, that no duty of care was owed by the police to members of the public in relation to the way in which they carried out their duties.[61] In European Community law, however, the court was satisfied that the policy matters which informed the Chief Constable's decision, such as shortage of resources and a desire not to exacerbate the confrontation with the protesters, did not constitute a defence to a breach of Article 34 of the EC Treaty, which conferred a directly enforceable right to export goods. The Divisional Court did not deal with the issue of damages, but it seems clear from this case, and the more recent decision of the Court of Justice in relation to the unlawful restriction by a Member

State on the export of goods in *R.* v. *Ministry of Agriculture, Fisheries and Food, ex p. Hedley Lomas (Ireland) Ltd* in 1996, that damages would now almost certainly be payable in these circumstances by the Chief Constable, and perhaps also by the Home Office for having failed to provide the level of financial support to make local policing effective.[62]

The crucial issue in the new criteria laid down by the European Court of Justice is the *seriousness* of the breach by the state. A breach by the state is 'serious' if there is a judgment of the European Court of Justice defining an infringement which is matched by the act forming the basis of the claim, there has been a preliminary ruling to that effect or there is settled case law of the court. Put simply, the state (or the Crown/government in the UK) will be liable if its action or inaction infringed a clearly established rule of European law. Liability does not, therefore, depend on any consciousness of fault, as the Court of Appeal had held in *Bourgoin*, or any lack of care. The standard is both strict and objective.

In *Dillenkofer and Others* v. *Federal Republic of Germany*, the Court of Justice recently spelled it out. It said the right to reparation where a Member State had failed to implement a directive cannot depend 'on the existence of intentional fault or negligence on the part of the organ of the state to which the infringement is attributable'.[63] This ruling is clearly incompatible with the *Bourgoin* decision. The House of Lords had, in any event, in *Kirklees MBC* v. *Wickes Building Supplies*, doubted, after *Francovich*, whether *Bourgoin* had been correctly decided. It is now clear that it was not. Secondly, the cases have opened up the possibility of a wide range of claims against the United Kingdom government for failure to implement Community law, or for failing to implement it properly. This has very considerable ramifications, because a large percentage of UK legislation, both primary and secondary, has its origin in Community law. Any failure to legislate, or to legislate effectively, can give rise to a *Brasserie du Pecheur* type claim.

Some cases which have previously given rise simply to a declaration that a UK statute is in conflict with EC law should now, in appropriate cases, result in an award of damages against the Government for failure to implement a directive. In *R.* v. *Secretary of State for Employment ex p. Equal Opportunities Commission*[64] in 1994, the House of Lords held that the Employment Protection (Consolidation) Act 1978, which protected full-time workers against unfair dismissal, was sexually discriminatory and contrary to Directive 76/207, since it did not apply to part-time workers, the overwhelming majority of whom were women. The court refused, however, to entertain a claim in damages in the proceedings for judicial review by a woman who claimed to have suffered from the government's failure to legislate, and directed her to bring her claim against her employer in an industrial tribunal.

Following the *Brasserie du Pecheur* and the *Factortame (3)* decision, it would seem that British courts will have to deal with such claims for damages, even in applications for judicial review. Normally, such actions will be against the responsible minister or government department, but there is no reason why, in the absence of specific ministerial responsibility, there should not be a private action against the Attorney-General as representative of the Crown. None of the restrictions in the Crown Proceedings Act 1947, or the common law rule that any statutory or other provisions should only bind the Crown where it is clearly intended to do so, should, under European Community law, preclude such an action. It is now well established that national law must provide 'effective' remedies and, as the European Court of Justice held in the *Factortame* case, any national rules, such as that which apparently precluded interim injunctive relief from being granted against the Crown, should be set aside.[65]

Although the Court of Justice has spoken of reliance on individuals as a means of ensuring that Community obligations are observed by Member States, there are limits to the extent to which the English law of tort can be used to ensure compliance by the state/Crown in this country at the suit of individuals. Where, for example, a Community directive has been inadequately implemented by statute or statutory instrument, the courts will, as we have seen, be reluctant to recognize that a duty has been imposed by statute which gives rise to tortious liability if breached. Individuals may have trouble in showing that they were intended to be the beneficiary in the case of some statutes, such as public health or food safety legislation, even if they have suffered as a result of the breach.[66] If it is possible to show that the directive on which the statute was based was intended to benefit individuals, the failure of the courts to recognize that interest may, of course, give rise to a claim against the state on that account. Although the doctrine of the separation of the powers creates difficulties for dealing effectively with what one writer has called 'deviant judicial decisions', the European Court of Justice in *Factortame (3)* made it clear that a Member State may be liable irrespective of which organ of the state is responsible for the breach of Community law.[67]

Where there are no obvious and identifiable human beneficiaries, such as Community legislation affecting the environment, a claim in damages against the state or an agency of the state is not a viable option. Although environmental groups, such as Greenpeace, may be recognized as having sufficient *locus standi* to apply for judicial review, they will not be entitled to a private law remedy in tort, or to claim damages in judicial review proceedings, because they will not be able to show that they themselves have suffered actual damage or loss. The European Court of Justice has itself refused to recognize that a general environmental framework directive is capable of creating direct effect,[68] which is an essential precondition for a claim in damages. As Jane Holder has noted, this is primarily because the doctrine has been judicially developed in the entirely different context of cases in which individuals assert financial and employment rights or 'individual interests'. In contrast, environmental law deals with problems of general interest: the quality of air, conservation of flora and fauna and the effects of development on the environment.[69]

The development of the doctrine of direct effect, the recognition by the Court of Justice of the importance of the citizen in the enforcement of Community law, the related acknowledgement of the value to citizens of Community rights transcending the limits of national law and the liability of the state in damages are all likely to be profoundly important in the development of English law. The decision of the House of Lords in the first *Factortame* case on the immunity of the Crown to coercive action in judicial review proceedings, except in the case of the enforcement of Community law rights, has been reversed by in the highly significant decision of the House in *M.* v. *Home Office* in 1993, so that ministers of the Crown are now subject to the same injunctive orders in matters relating to national law as they are in relation to Community law.[70] The House has taken a similar approach in the law of restitution, where Lord Goff commented, in *Woolwich Equitable Building Society* v. *IRC* in 1992, 'at a time when Community law is becoming increasingly important, it would be strange if the right of the citizen to recover overpaid charges were to be more restricted under domestic law than it is under Community law.'[71]

Liability of the Crown in Contract

The Crown Proceedings Act 1947 abolished the immunity which the Crown had hitherto enjoyed in contract. Thereafter, government departments could be sued for breach of contract in the same way as ordinary citizens. The Act provided that proceedings could be instituted against the appropriate authorized government department, or, if there is none applicable, against the Attorney-General.[72] Contracts with the government are often made by an officer or agent acting on behalf of the relevant department. The Crown, can of course, only contract through some natural or legal person acting on its behalf. Such contracts are enforced 'against the Crown as executive'.[73]

Government contracts can be conveniently grouped into three kinds: construction contracts, supply contracts and conditions of service for civil servants. The last type of contract has been discussed in Chapter 7. The first covers the whole range of defence and building contracts, and the second an array of contracts for the supply of both goods and services. These latter have come to assume a growing significance in the past few years, in which many government functions have been privatized or put out to contract. Functions which were previously regulated by statute, and subject to direct control through the management of the Civil Service, are now the subject of contractual terms. Some prisons, for example, are no longer subject to the direct control of the Prisons Agency, which, although now a semi-autonomous Crown agency, is still staffed by civil servants. They are run by private security companies according to the terms of contracts negotiated by the Home Office but supervised by the Prisons Agency.

This relationship raises a number of important issues about control and accountability to Parliament, but, more immediately, it brings into focus the extent to which the contractual relationship between Crown and service-provider offers a satisfactory means by which the relevant service is delivered. The starting point must be an examination of the extent to which the Crown and government departments are free to enter into contracts and to enforce them, and be subject to enforcement, in the same way as ordinary individuals. Patently, the Crown as the executive is not in the same position as an ordinary individual, but the common law has always proceeded on the basis that the Crown is entitled to benefit from the general philosophy of freedom of contract and to enter into whatever contracts it pleases and for whatever purpose. Its ability to do this has been assisted by the judicial view that the power of the Crown to contract is either a prerogative power or, at the very least, one of the common law powers enjoyed by the Crown in its capacity as a corporation sole; that is, a natural consequence flowing from its identity as a corporate body under the common law. Unless the corporate body is limited by charter or by the statute by which it is established, it is able to contract in much the same way as a private individual.

Statutory bodies, such as local authorities, are almost invariably restricted to the making of contracts for the purpose for which they are established. A local authority was, on this account held incapable of entering into contracts connected with speculative interest-swap transactions since such transactions went far beyond the investment powers permitted to local authorities by the Local Government Act 1972.[74] Nor can an authority make a contract which prevents it from exercising or 'fetters' the discretion conferred on it by statute. A local planning authority could not, for example, agree to give sympathetic consideration to planning applications by a supermarket which agrees to build a school or a road for the local community, because the effect of the contract would be to bind the authority not to give proper consideration of each such future planning application on its merits.

The Crown's contracting powers are much greater, although not unlimited. Contracts which a government department has made for which Parliament has not voted the necessary funds were originally thought to be void. The better view now seems to be that they are not void but unenforceable.[75] At common law, contracts with civil servants were terminable by the Crown at will, but they are now protected from dismissal by the Employment Protection (Consolidation) Act 1978. The general rule, however, is that the effect of a Crown contract can be avoided at will in the public interest.

The scope of this rule is uncertain. It originates in a decision made in the aftermath of the First World War, *Rederiaktiebolaget 'Amphitrite'* v. *The King*. In March 1918 the Swedish owners of the ship *Amphitrite* approached the British government for an assurance that, if the vessel entered a British port, its cargo would not be seized and the vessel would not be detained. The British legation in Sweden gave such an assurance. The vessel arrived in the UK and it was seized, in breach of the undertaking. The owners sued for breach of contract. Rowlatt J doubted if the exchanges between the parties actually gave rise to a contract. Even if they did, he said, it was 'not a contract for the breach of which damages can be sued for in a Court of Law ... it is not competent for the Government to fetter its future executive action, which must necessarily be determined by the needs of the community when the question arises. It cannot by contract hamper its freedom of action in matters which concern the welfare of the State.'[76] The decision did not, the Court emphasized, apply to commercial contracts, but it was severely criticized at the time. The legal historian Sir William Holdsworth called Rowlatt J's dictum 'sweeping ... without any cases to support it'.

It is far from clear what is, and what is not, 'a commercial contract'. As Holdsworth says, 'The ambit of the rule is, too the last degree, vague.' It has, however, been followed and still appears to be good law. A much more appropriate response in such cases would be for the contract to be treated as valid, but, in the event of circumstances arising which would make the performance of the contract contrary to the public interest, to treat it as frustrated. The court would have to ensure that the frustration was not self-induced by the Crown. In that event, damages would be payable by the Crown.[77]

It should, however, be emphasized that government departments and the new agencies will all contract on standard-form contracts which, since the Crown is the dominant party, enable it to determine the circumstances under which it will be released from the terms of the contract. That power itself is not unlimited, because governments are bound by the Unfair Contract Terms Act 1977 and the more recent EC Directive 93/13 on Unfair Terms in Consumer Contracts, which may invalidate any such terms which are unfair.

The immense economic power which governments have, and the almost complete immunity which the Crown's contractual transactions enjoy from judicial review and investigation by the Parliamentary Ombudsman, has meant that Crown contracts provide governments with a very effective tool for carrying out policy with a minimum of external interference or supervision. In the past, standard terms which were offered in government procurement contracts might go far beyond the matters which were the immediate subject of the agreement, and cover such matters as the working practices of subcontractors, the prohibition of racial and sexual discrimination and the recognition of trade unions.

The Crown's economic power, or *dominium*, as Terence Daintith has called it, may be a more effective way of achieving policy goals than the enactment of primary or secondary legislation.[78] This power has assumed even greater significance in an era in which governments have eschewed social goals, but have sought to place vast tracts of what had hitherto been regarded as governmental functions into a commercial context, by a process of contractualization and privatization. This is not the place to examine the range of means selected to achieve the desired ends, but the means adopted raise profound questions about the continuing accountability of the Civil Service, and the extent to which the use of this contracting prerogative is subject to effective legal and political control. Some of the issues involved are touched on in Chapter 7.

There is a real danger, as Mark Freedland has argued, that the private law notion of privity of contract will invade the arena of public law and be used to exclude legal challenges by individuals adversely affected by government contracts in circumstances in which, had statutory powers been used, judicial review would have been available to them. The fact that one of the parties is a public body does not mean that the courts will accept that the way in which the contract has been entered into, its content or the way in which it is executed are suitable matters for review. The courts will, it seems, look for some other 'public' element. As Susan Arrowsmith has argued, such distinctions seem to have no clear underlying principle. On the contrary, the fact that one party is a public body should raise a

217

presumption of the availability of judicial review. 'A public authority surely has no prima facie claim to the freedom of action enjoyed by private individuals in the exercise of contractual rights: it is the public nature of the body which should give rise to an obligation to treat citizens fairly and reasonably.'[79] Recent legislation which places local authorities under an obligation to contract out services, and to offer work, hitherto carried on 'in-house', to public tender, is subject to residual powers of direction by the Secretary of State. The use of such powers, the Divisional Court has recently held, are subject to judicial review, as are the processes by which local authorities offer work for tender.[80]

It has been said that the new systems of public service delivery, including the Next Steps agencies, and the wider contracted out privatized functions have 'by the test of the efficient delivery of services ... begun to show signs of yielding some significant dividends'.[81] The great growth in the use of contractual and quasi-contractual powers in the delivery of public services hitherto provided by civil servants is, however, of interest not only to those in the Treasury whose primary concern must be to reduce public expenditure, nor to those who have contracted with the Crown to deliver them, or who failed to obtain the contract to do so, but also to those for whose benefit the services are supposed to be delivered. It is much easier to specify in quantitative terms, for example, how long a patient should wait before receiving medical attention, or how many prisoners should be confined in a cell and for how long, than to assess the value of patient care delivered by a nurse employed by a commercial agency who may never be in the same ward more than once, or prison reform by a security firm more concerned with containment and profit margins than with rehabilitation. The still largely unanswered question is how far the delivery of a high quality of public service can be secured by contract.

Public Interest Immunity

As part of the process of ensuring that a fair trial takes place, whether the proceedings be civil or criminal, plaintiff and defendant, prosecutor and accused are all required to disclose or, in the old terminology, 'to discover' to one another all relevant material. Section 28(1) of the Crown Proceedings Act 1947 provides that, in any proceedings to which the Crown is a party, it may be 'required by the court to make discovery of documents and produce documents for inspection'. The Act, however, preserved the power of ministers of the Crown to secure non-disclosure where it is 'injurious to the public interest'. Non-disclosure was achieved by the issue of a certificate, now called a 'Public Interest Immunity Certificate', by the relevant minister. The great expanse of this power had been established not long before the Crown Proceedings Act was passed in *Duncan* v. *Cammel Laird* in 1942.[82] It was open to the appropriate minister to claim what was described as a 'prerogative power' and then called 'Crown privilege' in any proceedings, whether or not the Crown was a party to them.

The danger of allowing confidential material to be considered in open court was made clear in *Duncan* v. *Cammel Laird* itself. The case was brought by family members of the crew of the naval submarine *Thetis*, which had been lost with all hands during its trials off Birkenhead in 1939. The plaintiffs believed that the loss of the vessel was caused by structural defects, and sought disclosure of the submarine's plans from the defendant shipbuilders. The Crown had intervened, claiming that disclosure would be damaging to the UK's defences at a crucial time in the war at sea.

The House of Lords unanimously upheld the Crown's claim, but its decision went far beyond the requirements of national defence. Claims by ministers should, Lord Simon the Lord Chancellor said, be accepted either where the documents were of a *class* which, by their very nature, it would be damaging to the public interest to allow disclosure of them, or where, because of their *content*, it would be damaging to do so. Documents or information in the first category would include those concerned with national defence, the security services, foreign policy and Cabinet papers; those in the second, where disclosure of the content would inhibit 'candour' between civil servants and prevent 'the proper functioning of the public service'. The 'class claim' became very popular with ministers. The practice arose of issuing certificates claiming class immunity 'on a regular basis, as if pronouncing a spell ... In this way immunity from production could be secured for ever-widening classes of material, even if the subject matter had nothing to do with security, the prevention of crime or sensitive economic matters. It could be claimed for matters such as correspondence regarding the lease of a hotel, or documents concerned with reorganisation of local authorities.'[83]

A new low point in the claim to immunity was reached in the case of *Ellis* v. *Home Office*[84] in 1953. Here, a prisoner was attacked by a fellow inmate with a long history of dangerous and unpredictable behaviour. The two had been placed in the same cell, and the plaintiff believed, and the court seems to have accepted, that a medical report on the assailant would have indicated that there was an obvious risk of such an assault on the plaintiff. The plaintiff's claim failed, however, because the Home Office claimed immunity for the

219

report. The court was left with a strong suspicion that immunity was claimed not to protect the public interest, but to defeat the plaintiff's action. The practice continued to cause widespread dissatisfaction. Joseph Jacob quotes the concern of the Inns of Court Conservative and Unionist Society that ' "public interest" determined by the Executive itself is too easily equated with "administrative convenience" '.[85]

An opportunity for the House of Lords to review the whole law of disclosure came in the case of *Conway* v. *Rimmer*[86] in 1968. In its new, more interventionist mode, already demonstrated in its wide-ranging decision in *Ridge* v. *Baldwin*[87] in 1963, opening the opportunity for judicial review into new fields of natural justice, the House was ready to respond to current concerns about the widespread, and apparently indiscriminate, claims to public interest immunity. The case concerned a former trainee police constable, who claimed that he had been maliciously prosecuted. He wished to have disclosed for the proceedings reports made about him while in the police service. Crown privilege was claimed for the reports. The House of Lords refused to accept that a mere ministerial certificate would suffice to deny the reports to the plaintiff. It held that the responsibility of deciding whether or not evidence should be withheld from a court of law rested with the courts and not with ministers. The court had to examine the documents or other evidence for which immunity was claimed. Having examined the documents, the court had to conduct a 'balancing exercise', weighing up, on the one hand, the public interest in non-disclosure against, on the other, the public interest in the proper administration of justice. Although claims to immunity, henceforth to be called 'public interest immunity', could still be made on either a contents or a class base, they should both be examined.

The way seemed to be set for a more careful consideration of the public interest issues involved in disclosure in particular cases. Very soon, however, the process seems to have gone into reverse: as the availability of the new public interest immunity extended way beyond the bounds of the Civil Service, so too did the grounds for non-disclosure proliferate. Instead of making decisions on a case-by-case basis, the courts came to lay down general rules as to when documents and other evidence could be withheld, without the need even to weigh up the effects of such a denial to individual litigants. From denying discovery of any information supplied by private informants to the Gaming Board, a blanket was thrown over information supplied to the social services, to voluntary agencies and by and to the police in the course of investigating a complaint against the police. The latter rule, established in *Neilson* v. *Laugharne* in 1983, effectively prevented complainants against the police using information obtained in the course of the investigation of their complaint in any subsequent proceedings against the police. The House of Lords, in *R. v. Chief Constable of West Midlands Police, ex parte Wiley* in 1996, held that a blanket exclusion of evidence in police complaints cases was never justified and that such evidence should be examined, evaluated and weighed to decide if it should be disclosed.

Many other categories of information continued to be immune from disclosure, and the weighing of conflicting public interest claims seems to have become a fiction. Immunity was routinely claimed by civil servants on behalf of ministers for broad categories of information and, it would seem, routinely accepted as such by the courts. Rupert Allason, the Conservative MP and spy-story writer, describes how, in a civil case in which he was defendant, he was in receipt of a PII certificate signed by a minister. When urged to examine the documents in contention, he reports that the judge replied 'Who am I to gainsay the Secretary of State?'.[88]

It was not only the courts that, during the years following *Conway v. Rimmer*, seem to have abdicated their obligation to make a proper evaluation, in individual cases, of the public interest in withholding and in securing a fair trial. The old practice of wide class claims re-emerged. Ministers, it appeared from the Scott Inquiry, were told that, if documents fell into a certain class disclosure of which was, in a general sense, harmful, they were obliged to claim immunity for them, whether or not they believed the disclosure in the specific instance was in fact harmful. Although the placing of documents in a certain category produced what Sir Richard Scott called in his Report 'a knee-jerk reaction for a PII class claim to be made', ministers should not have been compelled to act in that way, as is clear from the circumstances of the *Ponting* trial, where edited versions of highly sensitive documents were produced in the trial, after careful consideration by the then Secretary of State for Defence, Michael Heseltine. Sir Richard Scott makes the position plain enough:

> The proposition that a Minister who did not think that the public interest required the documents to be withheld from the defendant, let alone a Minster who thought that the public interest required the disclosure of the documents, was nonetheless, obliged to make a claim for PII in respect of the documents has no place in the principles of PII/Crown privilege enunciated by Lord Simon [in *Duncan v. Cammel Laird*].[89]

The position on disclosure in criminal cases ought to be more clear, because the outcome affects, in many cases, not merely any right to compensation but the liberty of the defendant. There has, however, been some confusion between the criteria applicable in civil and criminal cases. The starting point is clear enough. As the Master of the Rolls, Lord Esher said in *Marks* v. *Beyfus* in 1890, 'if upon the trial of a prisoner the judge should be of the opinion that the disclosure of the name of the informant is necessary or right in order to show the prisoner's innocence, then one public policy is in conflict with another public policy, and that which says that an innocent man is not to be condemned when his innocence can be proved is the policy that must prevail.'[90] There is, in this situation, no balancing exercise, although, unfortunately, the then Lord Chief Justice, Lord Taylor, in *R. v. Keane*[91] in 1994 said the decision in that case 'resulted from performing the balancing exercise, not from dispensing with it'. As Sir Richard Scott says, 'The firm conclusion is, in my opinion, justified that in criminal cases the only question should be whether the documents might be of assistance to the defendant. This is not a "balancing exercise". The issue does not depend on the weight of the PII factors that are being invoked.'[92]

The Government sought to argue in the MATRIX Churchill and the related arms export cases that it was obliged to claim public interest immunity. It was then a matter for the trial judge to determine if the claim was justified. It is now clear that this was wrong. Besides the danger of important evidence in favour of the defendant being missed by the trial judge if, as in *Keane*, the prosecution was, as Lord Taylor LCJ said, 'simply to dump all its unused material into the court's lap and leave the trial judge to sort through it, regardless of its materiality', it also removed the double filter established by *Conway* v. *Rimmer*. The issue of damage to the public interest and importance of the material to a fair trial should be considered in relation to each piece of material by *both* the minister and the trial judge.

There is some hope of more openness and a greater concern for justice in the aftermath of the Scott Inquiry. As a result of the debate which followed criticisms in the Report of the blanket claims to immunity made by ministers, the Attorney-General announced in the House of Commons on 18 December 1996 that the government would no longer claim immunity for documents on a class basis, but Public Immunity Certificates would only be signed by ministers when disclosure would cause 'real damage or harm'.[93]

It should, however, be emphasized that disclosure is for the purpose of court proceedings. In some cases it may be so limited by order of the court that it will be contempt for a newspaper to publish the information. It is not part of any general duty for ministers or government to provide information which those in authority may wish to conceal, either for perfectly laudable or for less creditable reasons. The courts have certainly not placed themselves at the head of the movement for freedom of information. Lord Reid, in *Conway v. Rimmer* in 1968, thought Cabinet minutes ought to be protected from disclosure until such time as they were of mere historical interest: otherwise disclosure would 'create or fan ill-informed or captious public or political criticism. The business of government is difficult enough as it is, and no government could contemplate with equanimity the inner workings of the government machine being exposed to the gaze of those ready to criticise without adequate knowledge of the background and perhaps with some axe to grind.' Lord Wilberforce was more specific in *Burmah Oil* v. *Bank of England* in 1980: 'I do not believe that ... it is for the courts to assume the role of advocates for open government.'[94] Lord Reid's view of the process of government seems inherently inconsistent. Public opinion is likely to be more, rather than less, ill-informed about why decisions have been made if it is totally excluded from the debates which preceded decisions. The position is changing, however.

This is not the place to discuss freedom of information, but attitudes towards it do have an important bearing on the readiness of ministers and senior civil servants to make documents available, so that they may be read or discussed in open court. The last government published a White Paper favouring more openness. The new Government has promised a Freedom of Information Act. There is no doubt that such legislation would be welcomed by some judges. In *R.* v. *Secretary of State for Defence ex p. Sancto*, Rose J, while refusing judicial review of a decision by the Defence Secretary to deny to the parents of a soldier the report of the board of inquiry investigating his death because they (the parents) were not parties to any proceedings and had no right to such information, he said, 'In the absence of a Freedom of Information Act there is no public right to know. There is no litigation between the parties which would allow an order for discovery, and although the category of bodies susceptible to judicial review has expanded, it is still a remedy operating only either to protect legal rights or enforce legal duties.[95]

Coercive Orders against the Crown

Some consideration was given in Chapter 2 to the extent to which decisions made under the prerogative are subject to judicial review. Where ministers of the Crown are found to have acted unlawfully, usually where they have defied the terms of a statute, they may, occasionally, be directed under an order of *mandamus* to act according to law.[96] Public duties have, since the eighteenth century at least, been the subject of control by the courts by orders, formerly called the Prerogative Writs. Individuals wrongly detained could achieve their liberty by application for the ancient writ of habeas corpus. The old writs were issued in the name of the Crown, but they very early on ceased to have any direct connection with the Crown, despite the 'prerogative' tag, and were, after the constitutional struggles of the seventeenth century, entirely in the hands of the courts.

Today, those writs have been replaced by the forms of relief referred to in the Supreme Court Act 1981, section 31, namely *mandamus*, prohibition, *certiorari*, declaration and injunction, which can issue following a successful application for judicial review. Defiance of such orders can result in contempt proceedings against defaulters. This is not the place to discuss the scope of the relief available, which is considered at length in books on judicial review. Some aspects of the law are, however, relevant to consideration of the extent to which the Crown is subject to the same degree of control as other administrative bodies and individuals. Decisions of ministers may, for example, be quashed by *certiorari*, but the relevant minister will have, then, to consider the matter again and/or to apply the appropriate rule of law or to follow the appropriate procedure. Coercive orders have not been made against the Crown itself, because it has always been thought inappropriate that the Crown should be subjected to such orders in its own courts. The remedy normally sought against the Crown will be a declaration. Applications for judicial review may also be coupled, under Order 53 of the Rules of the Supreme Court, with a claim to damages, where these would have been available in an ordinary action. A failure by a minister of the Crown to observe the terms of a statute rarely gives rise to a claim for damages. Simply acting *ultra vires* is not, as we have seen, *per se* sufficient to entitle the person adversely affected to claim damages unless the conduct of the minister is malicious and constitutes misfeasance in office, or the statute, specifically or by implication, creates a new tort which binds the Crown, or the *ultra vires* action results in, say, an unlawful invasion of land constituting a trespass, or an act of negligence causing loss or harm where the court recognizes that a duty of care is owed to the plaintiff.

The extent to which the Crown can be ordered to desist from acting unlawfully against a plaintiff remains unclear. It was established, for example, in the nineteenth century that *mandamus* could not be used by a subject against the Crown or to compel a servant of the Crown to perform a duty which he owes the Crown under the prerogative, but it is clear that a minister may be compelled to perform a *statutory* duty.

Duties which the Crown is said to owe subjects, such as the duty of protection while they are abroad, will not be enforced by the court. They are said to be duties of imperfect obligation.[97] It is hard to see how this principle can be reconciled with the duty of protection imposed by Article 8 of the EC Treaty in relation to other EC citizens. It would be anomalous if EC citizens, other than, UK citizens, had a right of protection under the Treaty which was denied to UK citizens under the common law. In *M.* v. *Home Office* in 1993 the position of the Crown was broadly stated by Lord Templeman:

> The judges cannot enforce the law against the Crown as monarch because the Crown as monarch can do no wrong but judges enforce the law against the Crown as executive and against the individuals who from time to time represent the Crown. A litigant complaining of a breach of the law by the executive can sue the Crown as executive, bringing his action against the minister who is responsible for the department of state involved. To enforce the law the courts have power to grant remedies including injunctions against a minister in his official capacity.[98]

This statement of the law has been criticized as going rather further than the majority of the House of Lords actually went in *M.* v. *The Home Office*. The case does not appear actually to enlarge the scope of coercive action against the Crown as executive, as Lord Templeman describes it. Rather, the intention of the decision appears to be to separate remedies available against *officers* of the Crown, which could include injunctions, from those available against the Crown itself, which are very limited and do not include any coercive relief.[99]

A great many powers which ministers exercise are conferred on them specifically by statute, like the power of the Home Secretary or officers of his department to deport, which gave rise to the proceedings in *M.* v. *Home Office*. In such cases an order will be made against the minister as an officer of the Crown, charged by Parliament with the duty in question. The problem is that statutes may not be specific and may simply confer a duty or power on 'the Crown' in general, or the power concerned may derive from the prerogative. Since the prerogative is now, since the GCHQ case in 1985, in many respects reviewable in the same way as statutory powers, why should its exercise not attract the same remedies? Why should a minister, for example, not be ordered to reconsider an application by a British Citizen for a passport? As we have seen, under Community law, a British citizen who wishes to exercise his right to free movement may be entitled to be issued with one. Or why should not an order require the Foreign Secretary to provide the protection to other European citizens as required the EC Treaty?

Professor H.W.R. Wade puts the question in a broader constitutional context. Can there be some hidden cause which makes judges prefer to wander in a maze of restrictive technicalities rather than grant the full range of remedies against the Crown and its officers in accordance with, respectively, the reforming purpose of the Crown Proceedings Act and the constitutional principles which impose liability on Crown officers?[100] The answer, at the moment at least, is that it would not be acceptable to the current House of Lords. Lord Woolf emphasized, in *M.* v. *Home Office*, that 'The Crown's relationship with the courts does not depend on coercion, and in the exceptional situation when a government department's conduct justifies this, a finding of contempt should suffice ... It will be for Parliament to determine what should be the consequence of that finding.'[101]

As we shall see in Chapter 10, it would be a mistake to pitch expectations of an effective parliamentary response very high. In the meantime, lack of coercive powers, or the will to operate existing powers, will, as in *Factortame* in 1991, continue to create difficulties for individuals seeking to enforce rights derived from Community law. The European Court of Justice held in 1978 in *Amministrazione delle Finanze* v. *Simmenthal* that conflicting provisions of national law should be 'automatically inapplicable'. This meant that not only provisions of substantive national law should be disregarded when they conflicted with Community law, but also, as demonstrated in *Factortame*, procedural rules which inhibit the enforcement of Community rights. In *Factortame*, the Court of Justice held that the common law rule that interim injunctions would not lie against the Crown must be set aside to provide the relief required by Community law. The case law of the Court of Justice has incorporated Articles 6 and 13 of the European Convention on Human Rights, which requires both effective judicial control of executive action and an effective remedy.[102] The Court of Justice has shown itself increasingly ready to pass judgment on the effectiveness of national remedies, and it is unlikely that the immunity of the Crown from coercive action (as opposed to the individual liability of ministers as Crown servants) will survive for very much longer in its present state.

CONCLUSIONS

The reform of proceedings against the Crown in 1947 was intended, as far as possible, to bring the Crown in litigation into line with the subject. This has not been fully achieved, in part because the Crown as executive is in an intrinsically different position and must, to operate effectively, enjoy a much wider discretion than individuals, and in part because the courts have shown what can only be called deference to certain areas of executive action. This has been reflected in the way in which courts have allowed the Crown as executive to avoid the effect of statutes, to limit, on public policy grounds, the extent to which it could be the subject of claims for breach of statutory duty and negligence, and claims for breach of contract.

Such judicial policies are likely to be modified by the growing impact of European Community law. The English courts have, traditionally, respected the separation of powers and have been especially careful not to appear to challenge the supremacy of Parliament. Community law is increasingly casting the courts, and particularly the House of Lords, in the role of constitutional court. This will, as national law continues to follow Community law, mean that English courts will extend their role into the review of executive actions under the prerogative and ministers' and Parliament's legislative functions. Claims for damages will follow, opening up the possibility of litigation in areas which have hitherto enjoyed complete immunity, to ensure that rights which Community law confers on individuals will be given proper effect.

Whether the increased use of litigation by individuals against public officials will result in better administration is open to doubt. The American experience would seem to indicate that public decision-makers become more defensive, showing more concern to protect their backs than to engage in innovation. Litigation of this kind is, however, often a symptom of the failure of the political system to provide an effective means of redress. In the European Community, the court of Justice has frankly acknowledged that the creation by the Court of what one writer has called 'the judicial liability system' is a consequence of the failure of the European Commission, with its limited resources, to ensure by both political and legal methods that the governments of the Member States met their obligations under the Treaty. In the United Kingdom, it is still only incompletely recognized by courts that Parliament no longer provides an effective means of control and review of ministerial action.

NOTES AND REFERENCES

1. Maitland, F.W., *Constitutional History* (1909) pp. 107-14, 312, 313. Kenyon J.P., *The Stuart Constitution* (1969) pp. 421, 422. The security of tenure of judges is now provided for by s. 11(3) Supreme Court Act 1981.

2. Supreme Court Act 1981 s. 1.

3. For example, Viscount Kilmuir was dismissed by Harold Macmillan in his major 'purge' of the Cabinet in July 1962.

4. Ss 15(2)(b), 19(2)(b), 29(1), 45(2)(b). On the inherent jurisdiction of the court see Jacob J., *op. cit.*, p. 60, and Jacob J., *The Inherent Jurisdiction of the Court* (1970) 23 CLP p. 23.

5. The inherent power of the court to remove and appoint trustees is discussed in *Letterstedt* v. *Broers* (1884) 9 App. Cas. 371 at 386, PC. More recently the High Court has used its inherent jurisdiction, in the absence of statutory authority to do so, to prevent the defendant's assets from being removed from the country, to secure relevant documents and other evidence and to make a party submit to a medical examination: *Mareva Compania Naviera SA* v. *International Bulk Carriers* [1980] 1 All ER 213, CA; *Anton Piller KG* v. *Manufacturing Processes Ltd* [1976] Ch. CA; *Edmeades* v. *Thames Board Mills Ltd* [1967] 2 QB 67. The power of the court to make *Mareva* injunctions has been specifically recognized by Parliament in s. 37(3) Supreme Court Act 1981; Jacob J., *The Fabric of English Civil Justice* (1987) pp. 136–47. Jurisdiction to make the old prerogative orders of *mandamus*, prohibition and *certiorari* is now contained in s. 29 Supreme Court Act 1981.

6. Chitty J., *A Treatise on the Law of the Prerogatives of the Crown and the Relative Duties and Rights of the Subject* (1820) p. 155. The position on protection and guardianship is now governed by s. 8 Mental Health Act 1983.

7. Children Act 1989 s. 91(4); Bainham, 'The Children Act 1989: the future of wardship' [1990] Fam Law 270. Under the old law, the Court of Appeal held that the prerogative power was not ousted by the taking of a child into care under the Children Act 1948: *Re M. (An Infant)* [1961] 1 All ER 788; Bromley P.M., and Lowe N.V., *Bromley's Family Law* (1992) p. 478. Despite the restrictive provisions of the 1989 Act, where the statutory powers are inappropriate even a local authority may still invoke the court's wardship powers: *Devon CC* v. *S.* [1995] 1 All ER 243, 247 Fam D (Thorpe J).

8. See the figures quoted by Jacob J.M., 'From privileged Crown to interested public' [1993] *Public Law*, 123, 125.

9. Sedley, S., 'The sound of silence: constitutional law without a constitution' (1994) 110 LQR 270, 280.

10. Mitchell, J.D.B., 'Causes and effects of the absence of a system of public law' [1965] PL 95, 114.

11. *The Times*, 3 November 1995.

12. Jacob, 'From privileged Crown to interested public', pp. 146–8.

13. Lord Steyn, in an address to the Administrative Law Bar Association, *The Times*, 28 November 1996: see also Lord Ackner, 'The erosion of judicial independence', *New Law Journal*, 6 December 1996.

14. Goodhart, W., 'Lions under Downing Street: the judiciary in a written constitution', *IALS Bulletin*, 9 October 1991; Institute for Public Policy Research, A Written Constitution for the United Kingdom, Arts 103 and 104; 'Public to help in choosing judges', *The Times*, 27th May, 1997.

15. Law Officers Act 1944.

16. Sir Nicholas Lyell, HC Debates, Vol. 219, No. 128, Col. 735 (23 February 1993).

17. Edwards, J.L.J., *The Law Officers of the Crown* (1964).
18. *Burmah Oil Co. Ltd* v. *Lord Advocate* [1965] AC 75; *A-G* v. *Nissan* [1970] AC 179 at 210; *Trawnik and Another* v. *Lennox and Another, Times* Law Report, 14 December 1984.
19. *Gouriet* v. *Union of Post Office Workers* [1978] AC 435, 487, HL.
20. Norton-Taylor R., *Truth Is a Difficult Concept: Inside the Scott Inquiry*, pp. 172–3; Edwards, *op. cit.*, Chapters 10 and 11. See De Smith, *op. cit.*, pp. 392–3.
21. Morgan J.H., 30 April 1927, quoted by Jacob, *op. cit.*, n.27, p. 128.
22. *The Times*, 28 November 1996.
23. *Hoffman-La Roche & Co. Ltd* v. *Secretary of State for Trade and Industry* [1975] AC 295; *Barratt (Manchester) Ltd* v. *Bolton Metropolitan Borough Council*, 18 September 1991, Court of Appeal; Crawford C., 'Undertakings in damages by the Attorney-General', *New Law Journal*, 15 May 1992, p. 687.
24. *R.* v. *Secretary of State ex p. World Development Movement* [1995] 1 All ER 611, 620 QBD DC (Rose LJ); *R.* v. *Secretary of State for Social Services ex p. Child Poverty Action Group* [1990] 2 QB 540; *R.* v. *Inspectorate of Pollution ex p. Greenpeace Ltd (No. 2)* [1994] 4 All ER 329. For recognition of the interest of one taxpayer: *R.* v. *HM Treasury ex p. Smedley* [1985] 1 All ER 589 [1985] QB 657, 670. For a 'constitutional concern', see *R.* v. *Secretary of State for Foreign and Commonwealth Affairs ex p. Rees-Mogg* [1994] 1 All ER 457; [1994] QB 552.
25. Bennion, F.A.R., *Statutory Interpretation* (1984) p. 100; *British Broadcasting Corporation* v. *Johns (Inspector of Taxes)* [1965] Ch 32 at p. 78.
26. McSmith, A., 'Treasury ducks new bill rules', *The Observer*, 7 January 1996.
27. [1950] 1 KB 18, CA.
28. [1965] AC 512; 1988 SLT 538.
29. National Health Service (Amendment) Act 1986, ss 1 and 2; National Health Service and Community Care Act 1990, s. 60.
30. HC Debates, Vol. 349, Col. 1679 (Sir Hartley Shawcross).
31. *Sotgiu* v. *Deutsche Bundespost* (Case 152/73) [1974] ECR 153; *Lawrie-Blum* v. *Land Baden-Württemberg* (Case 66/85) [1987] 3 CMLR 389.
32. Wolffe J., 'Crown immunity from regulatory statutes' [1988] *Public Law* 339, 340.
33. *Bombay Province* v. *Bombay Municipal Corporation* [1947] AC 58, 61–62; Bennion, *op. cit.*, p. 103.
34. Article 1(b); implemented by the Public Works Contracts Regulations, SI 1991/2680.
35. *Ministry of Defence* v. *Cannock* [1995] 2 All ER 449, 453, 457, EAT.
36. *Wilkes* v. *Lord Halifax* (1769) 19 St. Tr. 1406; *Entick* v. *Carrington* (1765) 19 St. Tr. 1030.
37. HC Debates, Vol. 439, Col. 1677.
38. *Adams* v. *Naylor* [1946] AC 543, HL; *Royster* v. *Cavey* [1947] 1 KB 204, CA; Jacob, J., 'The debates behind an Act: Crown proceedings reform 1920–1947', [1992] PL 452.
39. S. 40.
40. S. 2.
41. *R.* v. *Dairy Produce Quota Tribunal, ex p. Caswell* [1989] 1 WLR 1098 at p. 1095, affirmed [1990] 2 WLR 1320.

42. Harlow, C., *Compensation and Government Torts* (1982) p. 69.

43. [1990] COD 19, 20.

44. [1988] AC 175.

45. [1992] 1 AC 58, 171 (Lord Jauncey of Tullichettle).

46. *Independent* Law Report, 5 December 1996 (Lord Bingham CJ).

47. *Madrazo* v. *Willes* (1820) 3 Bar. & Ald. 353; *Buron* v. *Denman* (1848) 2 Ex. 167; 12 Jur. 82. Such claims had, of course, to be brought against the officer personally, rather than the Crown itself: *Tobin* v. *R.* (1864) 16 CB (N.S.) 310; 33 LJCP 199.

48. S. 2(2)(b) Crown Proceedings (Armed Forces) Act 1987.

49. *Mulcahy* v. *Ministry of Defence*, CA, *The Times*, 27 February 1996.

50. *Benson* v. *Frederick* (1766) 3 Burr. 1845; *Madrazo* v. *Willes* (1820) 3 Barn. & Ald. 353.

51. Cane P., *An Introduction to Administrative Law* (1992) p. 254.

52. *Rich (Marc) & Co. AG* v. *Bishop Rock Marine Co. Ltd* [1995] 3 All ER 307, HL; *X and others* v. *Bedford CC* [1995] 3 All ER 353; *Hill* v. *Chief Constable of West Yorkshire* [1989] AC 53; but see also *Swinney and Another* v. *Chief Constable of Northumbria Police*, CA, *The Times*, 28 March 1996, where the Court held that there could be liability where the police had undertaken a specific duty in relation to the safe-keeping of confidential information.

53. *Rich (Marc) & Co. AG* v. *Bishop Rock Marine* [1995] 3 All ER 307, 320, HL; *X and Others* v. *Bedfordshire CC* [1995] 3 All ER 353, HL. *Hill* v. *Chief Constable of West Yorkshire* [1989] AC 53, HL.

54. The quotation on misfeasance is from De Smith's *Judicial Review of Administrative Action* (4th edn, 1980) p. 339. Harlow C., *Compensation and Government Torts* (1982) p. 68 adds: 'It is not likely to become so. It is not that the common law *cannot* generate such an action, it is that the judges *do not wish* to develop it.' The definition of misfeasance is by Lord Browne-Wilkinson in *X (minors)* v. *Bedfordshire CC* [1995] 3 All ER 353 at 364a. *Racz* v. *Home Office* [1994] 1 All ER 97,101 HL (Lord Jauncey).

55. Cane, *op. cit.*, p. 254. In *Jones* v. *Swansea City Council* (1989) NLJL Rep 503; [1990] 1 WLR 54 it was alleged that a licence to use council premises leased to the plaintiff as a club had been refused out of political malice. The Court of Appeal accepted that, if such a motive could be proved, it constituted the necessary wrongful intention to give rise to a successful claim for misfeasance in office.

56. *R.* v. *HM Treasury ex p. Smedley* [1985] QB 657; *Bradlaugh* v. *Gossett* (1884) 12 QBD 271; *Pickin* v. *British Railways Board* [1974] AC 765. *Church of Scientology* v. *Johnson Smith* [1972] 1 QB 522.

57. Cases C-6, 9/90 [1991] ECR-5357, [1993] 2 CMLR 66.

58. Case 26/62 *Van Gend en Loos* v. *Nederlandse Administratie der Belastingen* [1963] ECR 1.

59. [1996] 2 WLR 506.

60. *R.* v. *Chief Constable of Sussex, ex p. International Trader's Ferry Ltd* [1995] 4 All ER 364.

61. [1989] AC 53, [1988] 2 WLR 1049, HL.

62. *R.* v. *Chief Constable of Sussex ex p. International Trader's Ferry Ltd* [1995] 4 All

ER 364, 372, 377, 378 (Balcombe LJ); *R.* v. *Coventry CC ex p. Phoenix Aviation* [1995] 3 All ER 37, DC; *R.* v. *Ministry of Agriculture, Fisheries and Food, ex p. Hedley Lomas (Ireland) Ltd, Financial Times,* 4 June 1996; Gordon R., and Miskin C., 'European damages', *New Law Journal,* 19 July 1996.

63. Joined cases C–178 and 179/94, *Dillenkofer and Others* v. *Federal Republic of Germany, The Times,* 14 October 1996. A mistake made in good faith in the transposition of a directive which was 'imprecisely worded' did not, on the other hand, constitute a sufficiently serious breach giving rise to liability: case C–392/93, *R.* v. *HM Treasury, ex p. British Telecommunications plc, The Times,* 16 April 1996.

64. [1995] 1 AC 1.

65. Case C–213/89, *R.* v. *Secretary of State for Transport ex p. Factortame* [1991] 1 All ER 70; case C–87/94 R, *Commission* v. *Belgium* [1994] ECR I-1395; Vincenzi, C., 'Private initiative and public control in the regulatory process', in Daintith T. (ed.), *Implementing EC Law in the United Kingdom: Structures for Indirect Rule* (1995).

66. *Square* v. *Model Dairy Co.* [1939] 2 KB 365.

67. Joined cases C–46/93, *Brasserie du Pecheur* v. *Germany,* and C–48/93, *Factortame (3)* [1996] 1 CMLR 889; Szyszczak, E., 'Making Europe more relevant to its citizens' (1996) 21 *European Law Review* 351, 360.

68. Case C–236/92, *Comitato di Coordinamento per la Difesa dell Cava and Others* v. *Regione Lombardia and Others* [1994] ECR I-483; Holder J., 'A dead end for direct effect? Prospects for enforcement of European Community law by individuals' (1996) 8 *Journal of Environmental Law,* 313.

69. See n. 64. In case C–72/95, *Aanemersbedrijf PK Kraaijeveld BV and Others* v. *Gedeputeerde Staten van Zuid-Holland,* unreported, 24 October 1996, the Court of Justice indicated that the national court should, where it was under national law able to do so, raise relevant provisions of Community environmental law on its own motion where these were not raised by the parties. This may enable environmental issues to be dealt with by national courts, where relevant, where no one who has an interest, wishes to raise them.

70. *R.* v. *Secretary of State for Transport ex p. Factortame* [1990] 2 AC 85; *In re M.* [1993] 3 WLR 433.

71. [1992] 3 WLR 366, HL; case 199/82, *Amministrazione delle Finanze dello Stato* v. *San Giorgio SpA* [1985] 2 CMLR 647; D'Sa, R., *European Community Law and Civil Remedies in England and Wales* (1994) p. 248; Lord Goff and Jones G., *The Law of Restitution* (1993) pp. 549–53.

72. Ss 1 and 17.

73. *Town Investments Ltd* v. *Department of the Environment* [1978] AC 359; *M.* v. *Home Office* [1993] 3 All ER 537, 540 (Lord Templeman).

74. *Hazell* v. *Hammersmith and Fulham LBC* [1991] 2 WLR 372.

75. *Churchward* v. *R.* (1865) LR 1 QB 173 at 209; *New South Wales* v. *Bardolph* (1933–4) 52 CLR 455; De Smith, *op. cit.,* p. 627.

76. [1921] 3 KB 500.

77. (1929) 35 LQR 162, 166; *Commissioners of Crown Lands* v. *Page* [1960] 2 QB 274. Cane P., *Introduction to Administrative Law,* pp. 264-6 believes that the principle may still apply in exceptional cases involving national defence, but

that now recognized but separate principles that the Crown can be bound by an undertaking, and that the Crown may be prevented from going back on conduct which has raised a legitimate expectation, will make the courts reluctant to apply it. *R. v. Commissioners of Inland Revenue, ex p. Unilever plc* [1996] STC 681; *M. v. Home Office* [1993] 3 All ER 537; Gordon R. and Ward T., 'The billowing fog', *New Law Journal*, 15 November 1996; *Barratt (Manchester) Ltd* v. *Bolton Metropolitan Borough Council* (1991) *New Law Journal*, 15 May 1992.

78. Daintith T., 'Regulation by contract: the new prerogative'[1979] CLP 41; Daintith T., 'The techniques of government', in Jowell J. and Oliver D., *The Changing Constitution* (3rd edn, 1994).

79. Freedland M., 'Government by contract and public law' [1994] *Public Law* 86, 99; see generally Harden I., *The Contracting State* (1992). Cane P., *An Introduction to Administrative Law* (2nd edn, 1992) pp. 41–3. Arrowsmith, S., 'Judicial review and the contractual powers of public authorities' (1990) 106 LQR 277, 288.

80. *R. v. Secretary of State for the Environment ex p. Oldham Metropolitan Borough Council, The Times*, 16 December 1996.

81. Drury G., 'Revolution in Whitehall: the Next Steps and beyond', in Jowell and Oliver, *op. cit.*, p. 173.

82. [1942] AC 624.

83. Zuckermann, A.A.S., 'Public interest immunity and judicial responsibility' (1994) 57 MLR 703, 706; *Merricks* v. *Nott-Bower* [1964] 1 All ER 717, 722; *Re Grosvenor Hotel, London (No. 2)* [1964] 3 All ER 354; *Wednesbury Corporation* v. *Ministry of Housing and Local Government* [1965] 1 All ER 186.

84. [1953] 2 QB 135, [1953] 2 All ER 149.

85. Jacob J.M., 'From privileged Crown to interested public' (1993) *Public Law*, 123, 141; *Ellis* v. *Home Office* [1953] 2 QB 135; De Smith, *op. cit.*, p. 637.

86. [1968] AC 910, [1968] 1 All ER 874.

87. [1964] AC 40.

88. *Neilson* v. *Laugharne* [1981] QB 736; *R. v. Chief Constable of West Midlands Police ex p. Wiley* [1994] 3 All ER 420, HL, *The Times*, 15 July 1994. Letter by Allason R., *The Observer*, 20 November 1995.

89. Scott Report, Vol. III, paras G18.58, 62.

90. (1890) 25 QBD 494, 498; Pavlou P., 'Public interest and Scott', *New Law Journal*, 8 March 1996, p. 345.

91. *The Times*, 19th March 1994.

92. Scott Report, Vol. III, para. G18.79.

93. Norton-Taylor R., 'New rules put paid to easy recourse to gagging orders', *The Guardian*, 19 December 1996.

94. *Conway* v. *Rimmer* [1968] AC 910, 952 (Lord Reid); *Burmah Oil Co* v. *Bank of England* [1980] AC 1090, 1112 (Lord Wilberforce).

95. *R. v. Secretary of State for Defence ex p. Sancto, The Times*, 9 September 1992; *White Paper on Open Government*, 1993, Cmnd 2290, HMSO.

96. See, for example, *Padfield* v. *Minister of Agriculture, Fisheries and Food* [1968] AC 997.

97. *China Navigation Co.* v. *Attorney-General* [1932] 2 KB 197; *Mutasa* v. *Attorney-General* [1980] QB 144.

98. [1993] 3 All ER 537, 540 HL.
99. Wade H.W.R., 'Injunctive relief against the Crown and ministers', 107 LQR 4 (1991); Gould M., '*M. v. Home Office*: government and the judges' [1993] *Public Law*, 568.
100. Wade, *op. cit.*, p. 10.
101. [1993] 3 WLR 433, 466, HL.
102. Case 106/77, *Amministrazione delle Finanze dello Stato* v. *Simmenthal SpA* [1978] ECR 629; case C-213/89 R, R. v. *Secretary of State for Transport ex. p. Factortame and Others (No. 2)* [1991] 1 All ER 70, [1990] ECR I-2433. On procedural rights and effectiveness of national remedies, see case 222/86 *UNECTEF* v. *Heylens* [1987] ECR 4097, [1989] 1 CMLR 901.

9

Miscellaneous Prerogative Powers

One of the distinguishing features of prerogative powers, rights and immunities is their residual nature. They have survived the attention of Parliament, either because they were thought to be too insignificant to be worthy of attention or to merit the expenditure of Parliamentary time, or, alternatively, because they were deemed to be too useful to the executive to be curtailed or abolished. Chitty's *Prerogatives of the Crown* of 1820, probably the only attempt at a comprehensive account ever published, runs to no fewer than seventeen chapters, and describes a large number of prerogative rights and powers, many of which have been overtaken by statute or have fallen into disuse, and were probably long disused even at the time he was writing. As Maitland observed in 1909:

> Since the settlement of 1688 very little has been done towards depriving the king by any direct words of any of his legal powers. Those powers were great and they were somewhat indefinite ... [But] the old prerogative powers have become clumsy and antiquated, and have fallen into disuse: the very uncertainty as to their limits has made them impracticable ... Remember this, that we have no such doctrine as that a prerogative may cease to exist because it is not used ... Thus our course is set about with difficulties, with prerogatives disused, with prerogatives of doubtful existence, with pre-rogatives which exist by sufferance, merely because no one has thought it worthwhile to abolish them.[1]

Some of these ancient powers have been abolished, others have fallen into disuse, others remain but in a new, statutory form, yet others survive in their original state because there remains a clear need for them in that way. It is to these extant powers that we now turn.

THE POWER TO PARDON

The power to pardon offenders after the commission of an offence, and even before trial and conviction, has belonged to the Crown since medieval times. It was originally a personal function of the monarch, as the fount of justice. Even after it was clearly established in the case of *Prohibitions del Roy* in 1607 that the king could not adjudicate personally at trials, he still retained what was seen essentially as an *executive* rather than a judicial function, the power to *dispense* with effect of a criminal conviction. Pardon before trial is possible, but unusual. Since the Crown, through the Attorney-General and the Director of Public Prosecutions, has a discretion in deciding whether or not to prosecute, or to issue a *nolle prosequi* to halt a prosecution brought by a private individual, a pre-emptive pardon will not, generally, be necessary.

The pardon, granted under the prerogative of mercy, was the only kind of *individual* dispensation to survive the Revolution of 1688 and the Bill of Rights of 1689. In 1948, after a vote by the Commons to abolish the death penalty for murder, but before the House of Lords had passed the Bill, the Home Secretary declared that he would, in all cases of murder, advise the Crown to exercise the prerogative of mercy. Such a declaration, although justified in the political circumstances of the time, was probably rightly criticized by the then Lord Chief Justice Goddard, on the grounds that it amounted to both a suspension and a *general* dispensation, both of which were prohibited by the Bill of Rights.[2]

Crimes may be pardoned absolutely or conditionally. A free pardon wipes out not only the sentence, but the conviction and all its consequences. From the time it is granted, it leaves the person pardoned in exactly the same position as if he or she had never been convicted. Sentences may also be commuted. Commutation is the substitution of a punishment of a different character from that which has been awarded by the court. Remission, on the other hand, is the reduction in the *amount* of a sentence or penalty without changing its character. These powers have long been exercised on behalf of the monarch by the Home Secretary. Pardons may only be granted in respect of criminal proceedings, and are not available for civil wrongs.

Since commutation is the substitution of a lesser penalty for a greater one, it can only take place where the defendant consents, because only a court, and not the Home Secretary, can impose a sentence. Indeed, in the case of *William Smith O'Brien* in 1848, the defendant was convicted of treason, and sentenced to being hanged, drawn and quartered. He was offered a commuted sentence of transportation instead, but refused.[3] Special legislation had to be enacted to enable the transportation to be effected. The creation of the Court of Criminal Appeal in 1907 and the abolition of the death penalty in 1965 (except for certain offences against military discipline, piracy and treason) together reduced the use of the pardon and the commutation of sentence, but executive release under the prerogative is still not infrequently used in the case of prisoners sentenced to mandatory life imprisonment or for those to be released on parole.

The power of the Home Secretary in relation to prisoners serving mandatory life sentences for murder has attracted the attention of both the courts of the UK and the European Court of Human Rights. When a judge passes a sentence for murder, life imprisonment is mandatory. The judge may add a recommendation that the offender serve a particular minimum term, but this is done in fewer than 10 per cent of the cases. In the majority of cases the judge notes down the term of detention 'necessary to meet the requirements of retribution and deterrence'. The papers then go to the Lord Chief Justice, who adds his own opinion, and passes the case to the Home Secretary. The views of the judges do not bind him and, in fact, evidence given to a House of Lords Select Committee indicated that the Home Office frequently sets a higher tariff than that suggested by the judges. In addition, the Parole Board, set up under the Criminal Justice Act 1967, can review these cases and make recommendations which are not, however, binding on the Home Secretary, who makes the ultimate decision himself. The process has been the subject of severe criticism.

> Decisions on the effective tariff for different kinds of murder are made largely by the executive behind closed doors, without giving reasons and without representations from or on behalf of the prisoner ... This is not so much an argument about judicial independence, or even about constitutional responsibilities – the prerogative may be thought to establish the Home Secretary's right, as a Minister of the Crown, to release lifers sooner or later. It is more an argument about the judicial function and the rights of individuals.[4]

After considering this system, the European Court of Human Rights in *Gunnell, Thynne and Wilson* in 1990 decided that once the tariff period of the sentence had expired, any subsequent detention on the grounds of public protection should be capable of being challenged through proceedings in a court or tribunal which is independent of the executive.[5] The 1991 Criminal Justice Act went some way to meet these criticisms, and section 34 now provides that the Home Secretary has a duty to release a life sentence prisoner after the expiry of the initial period set up by the trial judge, as long as the Parole Board is satisfied that the protection of the public does not require the prisoner's further confinement. In the case of prisoners not serving a life sentence, there are also powers under the 1967 Act for early release to be ordered by the Home Secretary. Although the power of release in this case is statutory, the decision-making process is executive, secretive and again, for that reason, unsatisfactory.

These decisions on the commutation or remission of sentence, whether made under the prerogative or on the basis of statutory provisions, are heavily underscored by their prerogative origins. Although the courts have, on occasion, criticized the procedures adopted, they have displayed reluctance to look at the merits of the decision made by the Home Secretary and the procedures adopted by him are given considerable latitude.[6] Technically, in judicial review proceedings, the merits of cases cannot be considered, but it is open to the court to reach a conclusion that a decision is irrational, on the basis of a complete lack of facts on which a rational decision-maker could come to the decision reached. Home Secretaries have, it is true, taken public opinion into account when exercising the prerogative power of mercy, but there has been some suspicion in recent years that the executive decision of the Home Secretary to release or refuse to release a prisoner has been based almost wholly on the need to appease public opinion rather than with regard to objective grounds, such as the continuing dangerousness of the prisoner.[7]

However, although the House of Lords indicated in the *GCHQ* cases that certain matters, including the exercise of the prerogative of mercy, would remain non-justiciable, the Divisional Court has quite recently shown a surprising flexibility in allowing judicial review of the decision of the Home Secretary to refuse a posthumous pardon to Derek Bentley. Following an application by the defendant's sister, the Divisional Court concluded that 'although the court had no power to direct the way in which the prerogative of mercy should be exercised', it did have a role to recommend that the Home Secretary 'look at the matter again and ... examine whether it would be just to exercise the prerogative of mercy in such a way as to give full recognition to the now generally accepted view that this young man should have been reprieved'. Following the decision, the Home Secretary announced that he was recommending the grant of a pardon, limited to sentence.[8]

PREROGATIVE REVENUE RIGHTS[9]

It will be recalled from Chapter 3 that the monarch traditionally derived income from Crown lands, such as those in Cornwall, the Duchy of Lancaster and the Palatinate of Durham. The income from these lands, and the royal forests, together with excise duties on wine and spirits, which also used to form part of the royal revenue, were all surrendered to the nation in exchange for the regular income supplied by the Civil List. The first surrender was made on the accession of George III in 1760 and a formal surrender of these revenues is made on the occasion of the accession to the throne of each monarch. In addition, there is a category of revenue rights called, collectively, *bona vacantia*; that is, unclaimed goods. The term is applied to things in which no one can claim ownership, and includes the residuary estate of people who die intestate and without husband or wife or near relatives, wreck, treasure trove, waifs and estrays, and all property and rights of a dissolved corporation, but not goods lost or abandoned on purpose.

TREASURE TROVE

Treasure trove is where any money, coin, gold, silver, plate, or bullion, is found hidden in the earth, or other private place, the owner thereof being unknown. And in such case, the treasure found belongs to the Crown; but if he that hid it be known, or afterwards found out, the owner, and not the sovereign, is entitled to it. It is the hiding, we may observe, and not the abandonment that gives the king a property.[10]

The Treasure Act 1996, when it is brought into effect by statutory instrument by the Secretary of State, will replace the old law of treasure trove with new rules on the ownership of lost valuables. Although the old law was intended to swell the royal treasury, it came to be a useful weapon in the protection of antiquities. The invention of the metal detector led to an enormous growth in the number and diversity of antiquities found and led to a realization of the inadequacy of the old law. The requirement that the object was composed of a substantial amount of gold or a substantial amount of silver greatly limited the category of protected antiquities. No matter what the historical, cultural or artistic value of objects made of other metals or non-metals, they were not treasure trove and not protected.

The second requirement depended upon the intention of an unknown and long-dead person. It had to be shown that the person who had left the object intended to return and retrieve it. This second requirement had the effect of excluding from the definition such objects as burial offerings, such as the treasure at Sutton Hoo and single items which appeared to have simply been lost by their owners.[11]

Under the old system, the coroner usually held an inquest, with a jury, to determine if the object was treasure trove. If the requisite requirements were met, the coroner declared the object as treasure trove and it then became the property of the Crown. The British Museum or another museum were enabled to retain the object upon paying the finder a reward. The reward was usually the full market value, as assessed by the Treasure Trove Reviewing Committee.

The Treasure Act 1996 was passed with the object of correcting the inadequacies of the old treasure trove law, namely a change in the definition of treasure, a simplification in the process of determining whether or not an object is treasure and the creation of a new offence of failing to declare the finding of treasure. There is also an entitlement to a reward for either the finder or the owner or occupier of the land, or both. Under the Act, treasure is any object which is at least three hundred years old when found and, if not a coin, has a metallic content of silver or gold of at least 10 per cent of its weight. Insofar as it is not included in the new definition, anything that would have been treasure trove under the old definition is also included.

'Treasure' will include objects associated with the find, such as the pot in which coins are found. Other objects may also become treasure within the terms of the Act. The Secretary of State has the power by statutory instrument to designate other types of object as treasure, provided that they are at least two hundred years old. Ownership of treasure vests in the Crown, but subject to the rights of the original owner. There is now no need to prove that the goods were hidden, or the owner's intention to return. The coroner's inquest may now be held without a jury. If the coroner decides that the treasure falls within the terms of the Act, and the treasure is to be transferred to a museum, the Secretary of State must decide the market value of the treasure, the amount of the reward, which is not to exceed the market value, to whom the reward is to be paid and how it is to be divided if there is more than one person with a claim to the reward. It has been said that the Act buries the medieval law of treasure trove, together with the difficulties of its application. It is yet to be seen whether or not those difficulties might be resuscitated by the new definition.[12]

MISCELLANEOUS SOURCES OF REVENUE FOR THE CROWN

Royal Fish

Royal fish are whales and sturgeons which were either thrown ashore or are caught near the shore. These are the property of the sovereign, on account of their 'superior excellence'. It is one of the prerogatives set out in the incomplete list in the statute *De Praerogativa Regis*, attributed, probably incorrectly, to the Parliament of Edward II. A distinction appears to have been made between the sturgeon, the whole of which belonged to the monarch, and the whale, of which he was only entitled to the head.

Shipwrecks

Wrecks were also declared to be the king's property by *Praerogativa Regis*. Under the early law, the Crown was entitled to all unclaimed wrecks, including flotsam, jetsam, ligan and derelict, which came to the shore or were in any tidal water adjoining the sea. This is now the case under both common law and the Merchant Shipping Act 1995. 'Flotsam' is where a ship is wrecked and the goods float on the sea, 'jetsam' where they are thrown into the sea in order to lighten a ship and then sink, and 'ligan' where they are cast into the sea to mark the spot of a wreck. Wreckage which does not come ashore is the property of the finder where the true owner cannot be discovered.[13] It was held in the case of *The Lusitania* in 1986 that the right of the Crown to wrecks does not apply to wrecks found outside territorial waters.[14]

Waifs

Waifs are things stolen and thrown away by the thief in his flight. They belong to the Crown by prerogative right, it is said, as a punishment to the owner for not having pursued the thief and retaken the goods. The goods do not belong to the Crown until they have been seized on its behalf. Until this time, the owner can retake them. Even when they are in the hands of the Crown, they still belong to the true owner if he pursues the thief with due diligence, or if he afterwards brings him to justice and secures a conviction.[15]

Estrays

Estrays are valuable animals of a tame or reclaimable nature which are found wandering within the bounds of any manor or lordship. They belong to the Sovereign as the residual owner in her capacity of tenant in chief, or lord paramount, under the old system of feudal tenure. Normally they are kept in the village pound, and will pass if not claimed within a year and a day, either to the lord of the manor or to the Crown if they are not claimed by him.[16]

Swans

Provided that they are wild and unmarked, the ownership of all white swans swimming on open rivers belongs to the Crown under the prerogative. Tame swans, or swans which have been marked with an owner's mark, belong to that owner. Swans were thought, at one time, to be a delicacy for the table. The Crown used formerly to make an annual claim to the swans on the River Thames. This is a practice that endures in a now largely formal ritual carried out annually by the Dyers and Vintners Association, called 'swan upping'.

Gold and Silver Mines

By prerogative right the Crown is entitled to all mines of gold and silver within the realm, whether the mines are located in Crown lands or land belonging to a subject. This prerogative right does not, however, extend to mines containing base metals, such as copper, tin, lead and iron. British subjects, and towns or boroughs in which the ore of these metals is discovered, may own and mine them as the wish. Any mine, however, which primarily produces gold, along with some base metal, belongs to the Crown.[17]

GRAND SERGEANTY

All the above rights are part of the revenue of the Crown, but they belong to the nation under the settlement of 1763. A few feudal rights, of a largely symbolic kind, survived the Abolition of Feudal Tenures Act 1660. There are a dozen or more, but grand sergeanty is typical. Under the feudal system, freehold land was held in return for services, very much in the same way as leasehold land is now. Sometimes payment was in the form of a money rent, or the performance of agricultural services, such as helping at hay-making or getting in the harvest.

Sergeanty simply means service. The most exalted form of sergeanty, grand sergeanty, was rendered by the richest and most powerful feudal tenants. Many of these services were symbolic, such as supporting the king's head when he crossed the sea to Normandy or performing some service, such as carrying the royal gloves, at the Coronation. Whether or not one can perform such a service is at the discretion of the Sovereign, to whom the service is personally due. It can, however, only be performed by the owner of the manor land to which the obligation of grand sergeanty is attached. A number of ritual services were performed for the Queen by large landowners at the Coronation of 1953.[18]

ROYAL CHARTERS

Before the creation of the limited company in the nineteenth century, towns, cities and groups of traders would acquire corporate status – that is the right to be treated in law as a legal person – by incorporation by royal charter. Two of the most celebrated companies in Britain's trading history, the East India Company, which operated in India and the Far East, and the Hudson's Bay Company, trading largely in northern Canada for hides and furs, were established in this way. Not only were cities and towns established to carry on and regulate trade within their areas, but they were authorized to operate often lucrative markets. The City of London itself was incorporated in this way, and it received charters from the Crown which conferred on it the right to hold markets in Smithfield in 1444. The grant of such a charter effectively gave the holder a monopoly of trade in the market area, and of the right to hold a market in the area of the borough. Such charters may still give rise to disputes as to the extent of the land over which they are exercisable.[19]

The rights they confer may be in perpetuity, or for a fixed period of time. Besides local boroughs, and trading companies, the bodies which have most frequently been granted corporate status by royal charter are non-profit making organisations, such as the Royal Institute of Chartered Surveyors, the British Broadcasting Corporation and the older universities. The Crown formerly enjoyed a power to grant sole entitlement to an inventor to exploit an invention by letters patent, but the grant of patents is now subject to statute. The power to grant a monopoly for the sale of a product was much used by Queen Elizabeth I and James I to increase royal revenues. These monopolies were often called 'patents', but comprised such unlikely 'discoveries' as 'the patents for currants, iron, powder, cards, horns, ox-shin bones, train-oil ... ashes, bottles, glasses, bags, aniseed, vinegar', which were the subject of bitter complaint in the Commons in November 1601. The prerogative power to create such monopolies was abolished in 1624.[20] It could, in theory, revive if the current statute, the Patents Act 1977, is repealed, but unilateral action by any government in this area is extremely unlikely because it is increasingly governed by European Community intellectual property law.

THE BRITISH BROADCASTING CORPORATION

The BBC was originally established by royal charter in 1927, and is continued by renewals of the charter, with the main object of providing, as a public service, sound and television broadcasting services. It has nine governors who are appointed by the Crown on the advice of the Prime Minster. It was given special authority by the Broadcasting Act 1996 to broadcast television through the new digital broadcasting medium. Under the terms of the charter, the BBC is a body corporate with perpetual succession, but the charter is renewable. The last charter was granted on 23 July 1981 and continued in force until 31 December 1996. The current charter was granted on 1 May 1996 and runs until 31 December 2006. Like the commercial broadcasting companies which were authorized for the first time to operate in 1954, the BBC is licensed for operation as a broadcasting station. There are conditions attached to the licences to both the BBC and the commercial companies.

Although there were no other broadcasting companies before 1954, the BBC did not, in law, have a monopoly. The government simply chose not to license any other broadcaster. Although corporations granted royal charters have been held to have exclusive rights in their area, the Crown was held in 1965 by the House of Lords not to have conferred a monopoly on the BBC in relation to broadcasting and, indeed, to have been prohibited by the Statute of Monopolies of 1624 from doing so. In *BBC* v. *Johns* in 1965, it was argued that, because the BBC was set up by a royal charter, it was an agent of the Crown, and hence tax legislation did not apply to it. The House of Lords rejected this argument, and any suggestion that the Crown held a natural monopoly of broadcasting which it could delegate by conferment by a royal charter to a body created for the purpose. A charter can only enable the body incorporated by it to operate within the law, and cannot confer on it any power to curtail the rights or liberties of others. 'The limits within which the executive government may impose obligations or restraints upon citizens of the United Kingdom without any statutory authority are now well settled and incapable of extension.'[21]

The restraints which are imposed on broadcasters in the charter and in the Licence Agreement are, however, very wide. By section 13(4) of the Licence Agreement the Home Secretary has the right to prohibit the BBC from transmitting any item or programme at any time. The charter is not subject to full scrutiny, although there is always a debate on the new charter. When the last Licence Agreement was made in 1981, which remained in force until 1996, it was unanimously approved by Parliament. The commercial television and radio stations operate as ordinary public limited companies under rules contained in the Broadcasting Acts. These Acts are subject to full parliamentary debate and scrutiny.

The BBC is one of the largest broadcasting companies in the world, widely respected for its independence. That independence is, however, not formally protected, except by a fairly weak constitutional convention. The 1978 White Paper on Broadcasting stated that 'the provision and content of programmes are the responsibility of the broadcasting authorities, and their independence in matters of programme content is central to the constitutional arrangements for broadcasting in the United Kingdom'.[22] The ineffectiveness of those arrangements was demonstrated in 1990, when the Home Secretary issued a directive under Article 31(4) of the Licence Agreement proscribing the broadcasting of statements made by certain organizations, including the IRA. Although no threat was posed by the statements, the intention behind the directive, the Prime Minster said, was to deny them the 'oxygen of publicity'. Little was achieved by the ban, because the statements were still read, but by an actor with a Northern Irish accent! The ban was lifted during the 1995–6 ceasefire.

The weakness of the European Convention on Human Rights in the UK was also demonstrated when the House of Lords heard a challenge to the directive by two journalists. Although Article 10 of the Convention is intended to protect freedom of expression, the House decided that it was not a relevant matter to be taken into account by the Home Secretary when making the directive, because the Convention has not been incorporated into United Kingdom law. Only when UK law was ambiguous was there any need for reference to be made to it, and in this case the power to make the directive was in the widest terms and was clear enough.[23] The incorporation of the Convention will undoubtedly strengthen the independence of the BBC.

The lack of legal safeguards for the independence of the BBC partly derives from the extent to which its whole structure and organization is so directly in the hands of the government in its power to shape the royal charter without any direct involvement of Parliament. The Corporation is, of course, forced to rely upon the government to fix and collect the licence fee. The commercial companies are also open to direction by the Home Secretary under the Broadcasting Acts, and are subject, like the BBC, to the Broadcasting Standards Council, but their management is not appointed by the government, and they stand more at arm's length from it.

THE UNIVERSITIES

The so-called 'new universities', the former polytechnics, are the creatures of a statute, the 1988 Education Act. As such, they are subject to control and review by the courts in the same way as any other statutory body. The 'old' universities, on the other hand, were incorporated by royal charter. It is not intended to examine the structure or organization of these universities, which varies considerably. The dominant feature which they have in common, however, is their legal autonomy.

Each university charter empowers the governing council, or other governing body, to approve statutes for the university's internal regulation. University decisions under the internal statutes may usually be appealed to a representative of the Crown called 'the Visitor', who has an exclusive power of adjudication. In an important decision, the House of Lords has recently decided that decisions made by the Visitor, although clearly of the public law type now generally regarded as attracting judicial review, are an exception to this general rule. It was argued in *R. v. Hull University Visitor, ex p. Page* in 1992, that, in view of the important public role occupied by universities, they should not be immune from the general law of the land. Lord Browne-Wilkinson accepted that the position of the Visitor was anomalous, but he was not prepared to go as far as to say that the circumstances justified 'sweeping away the law which for so long has regulated the conduct of charitable corporations ... It is not only modern universities which have Visitors: there are a substantial number of other long-established educational, ecclesiastical and eleemosynary bodies which have visitors.' The university Visitor system provided a speedy, cheap and final answer to internal disputes. The effect of this decision is to protect charitable bodies set up in this way by royal charter from effective control and review by the courts.

COLONIAL GOVERNMENT

One prerogative power which has diminished rapidly in application and significance with the decline of Britain's empire has been the prerogative power of colonial government. In conquered or ceded territories – that is, in relation to the United Kingdom's remaining colonial territories – the Crown, under the royal prerogative, has full power to establish executive, legislative and judicial institutions, and to act executively and legislatively in whatever way it thinks proper until those institutions are established, provided that its actions do not conflict with those statutes of the United Kingdom Parliament which are applicable to colonial territories or, once it is established, with acts of the colonial legislature.[24] Once a legislature has been established in a colony, the Crown's legislative function is in abeyance, but it may revive if either there is a power of revocation in the grant establishing the legislature, and the power of revocation is exercised, or, even when there is no power of revocation, when the legislature has ceased to function.[25]

In settled colonies, the prerogatives of the Crown and the rights and immunities of British subjects were similar to those enjoyed in the United Kingdom. Settlers from the United Kingdom were said to have carried the common law and statute with them, as far as they were applicable to the new situation. That position was modified when the colony had been settled by another European nation and had been conquered or ceded to the Crown. Colonial territories seized from another colonial power have frequently been formally ceded to the UK by the treaty which concluded hostilities: for example, Gibraltar under the Treaty of Utrecht, and the former French colonies of Canada and Mauritius. Such treaties usually contained a formal recognition by the Crown of the existing system of law, and a pledge to maintain it.

It has been held that, even before the establishment of the legislature, the Crown had no general power of legislating, since it lacked this power in the United Kingdom unless specifically given it by statute. It may be doubted, however, whether these limited legislative, or indeed, executive and judicial powers of the Crown prevailed in all colonies, especially those in which the new British government promised to respect the existing laws of the settlers. In these colonies, the powers of the governor, as the Queen's representative, might be greater, even to the point of absolutism. In *Re Adam* in 1837, for example, the Governor of Mauritius was held by the Judicial Committee of the Privy Council, under the 'peculiar provisions of the French law', to be able to deport a local settler under *le droit d'aubaine*, an old code of pre-revolutionary French law which put the persons of foreigners completely at the disposal of the King. A similar power, under the same French law, was available to the executive in Canada and enabled it to deport two aliens in circumstances which, at that time, would have been impossible under the prerogative in the United Kingdom.[26] In these cases, the content of the local law, and the extent to which it has been curtailed by any established local legislature, will need to be proved as a matter of fact. On this basis the court, in *Mostyn* v. *Fabrigas* in 1774, accepted evidence that the Crown had no power, under the local Spanish law, to expel the plaintiff from the Island of Minorca; nor was the Court persuaded, in the trial of the Governor of Trinidad, *R. v. Picton*, in 1806, that the local Spanish imperial law enabled the Governor to extract a confession from a ten year old child by means of torture.[27]

In colonies where there was no recognized antecedent law, the common law operated from the beginning, modified either by the local legislature or, where none was established, by statutes of the United Kingdom Parliament, if these were applicable, or the decrees or ordinances of the colonial Governor. Hong Kong, for example, until it reverted to China in 1997, was governed under a constitution based upon Letters Patent of 19 January 1955 and Royal Instructions of 14 February 1917. The legislation comprised ordinances made under the prerogative. Until 1992 both the Executive and the Legislative Councils were comprised of nominated officials. This position, it seems, has been re-established by the new administration of mainland China.

Only a handful of colonies remain, most of which are sparsely inhabited islands such as Tristan da Cunha, St Helena, the Pitcairn Islands, Ascension, the Falklands and the Turks and Caicos Islands. Bermuda is now probably the largest. They continue to be administered under prerogative powers. There is an expectation that the colonies will, at some stage, achieve a form of representative government. Some, like Bermuda, St Helena and the Turks and Caicos, have this, while Pitcairn, for example, does not. Although those born in the colonies, or whose parents were born there, are British Citizens of Dependent Territories, they have no citizenship rights in relation to the United Kingdom. Except for a small group of Hong Kong citizens and Falkland Islanders (who only acquired the right after the Falklands War), they have no right to enter the United Kingdom. In the case of St Helena, the 1981 Act ended a guarantee of 'perpetual' citizenship contained in a royal charter of 1673.[28] Those who have no legislature or representative council could be said to be without the basic political rights in Marshall's categories of citizenship (see Chapter 11).

CONCLUSIONS

The miscellaneous powers, rights and privileges described in this chapter have no unifying characteristic except, perhaps, that they could all be properly described as prerogatives in the sense described by Blackstone. They are all incidents of government which are not shared with the governed. The powers to override the law by granting a pardon, to confer legal status on a group of persons, for the purpose of business or learning, to govern colonies or to receive payments or property in kind when no one else has title to it could all be said to be functions of the head of state. Like all the prerogative powers, their scope is uncertain. It is even not clear whether some still exist. While it may be desirable that the executive should enjoy some, at least, of these powers, the way in which they survive is hardly compatible with the rule of law, the central proposition of which is that both governors and governed should be subject to the same law, and that the law to which both are subject should be clear and certain.

NOTES AND REFERENCES

1. Maitland F.W., *Constitutional History* (1909) pp. 418–21.
2. *Prohibitions del Roy* (1607) 12 Co. Rep. 63; Arts 2 and 12 Bill of Rights 1689; *R*. v. *LCC* [1931] 2 KB 215, 228 (Scrutton LJ); Heuston, R.V.F., *Essays in Constitutional Law* (1964) pp. 67, 68.
3. 12 & 13 Vict., c. 27; Heuston, *op. cit.*, p. 70; Brett P., 'Conditional pardons and the commutation of the death penalty' (1957) 20 MLR 131.
4. Ashworth A., *Sentencing and Criminal Justice* (1992) p. 47.
5. 5 October 1990.
6. *R*. v. *Secretary of State for the Home Department ex p. Findlay and Others*, *The Times*, 16 November 1984.
7. Troup E., *The Home Office* (1925) p. 25, observed that the 'Home Secretary may even properly take into account popular feeling in the matter and intervene in a case in which the execution of the death sentence would do more harm than good by the shock it would give to the great mass of the public.'
8. *Council of Civil Service Unions* v. *Minister for the Civil Service* [1985] AC 374 per Lord Roskill; *R*. v. *Secretary of State for the Home Department ex p. Bentley* [1994] 2 WLR 114.
9. See Halsbury's *Laws of England*, Vol. 8, paras 1503–20.
10. Coke's *Institutes*, Part III (1817 rd) c.58 p. 32, cited with approval in *Attorney-General of the Duchy* v. *GE Overton Farms Ltd* [1982] 1 Ch 277 at 288 per Lord Denning MR. The last part of the quotation is by Serjeant S., *New Commentaries on the Laws of England* (13th edn, 1899) Vol. II, pp. 476–7.
11. *Waverly BC* v. *Fletcher* (unreported, High Court of Justice, Queen's Bench Division, 17 February 1994) reversed on appeal [1995] 4 All ER 756, [1995] 3 WLR 772; see MacMillan C., 'Burying treasure trove', *New Law Journal*, 20 September 1996, p. 1346.
12. MacMillan, *op. cit.*
13. *Eyston* v. *Studd* (1574) 2 Plowd 463; *Hamilton* v. *Davis* (1771) 5 Burr 2732.
14. *Pierce* v. *Bemis, The Lusitania* [1986] QB 384.
15. 1 *Blackstone's Commentaries* (14th edn) p. 297.

16. *Nicholson* v. *Chapman* (1793) 2 Hy Bl 254.
17. *Case of Mines* (1567) 1 Plowd 310, 315; Royal Mines Act 1688 s. 3.
18. Jessel C.R., 'Grand Sergeanty', *New Law Journal*, 10 January 1997.
19. *Crown Estate Commissioners* v. *City of London, The Times*, 11 May 1992.
20. Prothero G.W., *Select Statutes and Other Constitutional Documents* (1913) p. 113; Maitland F.W., *Constitutional History* (1908) p. 261; Monopolies Act 1624.
21. *British Broadcasting Corporation* v. *Johns* [1965] 1 Ch. 32, 79, CA.
22. Para. 100, *White Paper on Broadcasting*, Cmnd 7294, 1978.
23. *R.* v. *Secretary of State for the Home Department ex p. Brind* [1991] 1 All ER 70.
24. *Campbell* v. *Hall* (1774) 20 St. Tr. 239 at 323; *Phillips v. Eyre* (1870) LR 6 QB 1; Colonial Laws Validity Act 1865 s. 2; *Sammut* v. *Strickland* [1938] AC 678, PC; *Halsbury's Laws of England* (4th edn, 1974) Vol. 6, para. 1029.
25. *Sabally and N'Jie* v. *Attorney-General* [1965] 1 QB 273 at 293, per Lord Denning MR.
26. *In re Adam* (1837) 1 Moo. PC 460; the quotation is from the opinion of Lord Brougham, the Lord Chancellor; see also *Donegani* v. *Donegani* 3 Knapp 85 (1834), in which the Privy Council accepted that the *droit d'aubaine* became the law of Lower Canada, with regard to aliens, on the ancient French law being established there by the statute 14 Geo. III, Ch. 83; and *Attorney-General for Canada* v. *Cain* [1906] AC 542.
27. (1774) 1 Cowp. 1020; 'The trial of Thomas Picton', in Thomas D. (ed.) *The Public Conscience: State Trials* (1972) Vol. 2, pp. 158, 170.
28. Black I., and Wigglesworth A., 'St Helena longs for home', *The Guardian*, 11 February 1997.

10

The Myth of Parliamentary Accountability and Control

In a famous motion proposed by John Dunning, the House of Commons declared on 3 April 1780 that 'the power of the Crown has increased, is increasing and ought to be diminished'. Dunning's motion did not refer to the monarch whose inept intervention had contributed so significantly to the recent loss of the American colonies, but to the growing powers which ministers exercised in his name. The effectiveness of the eighteenth-century constitution owed much to the dominance of the House of Commons, which was controlled for most of the century by the Whigs through a mixture of bribery, blackmail and patronage. The Crown, which during the reign of Queen Anne still counted for something in political terms, was reduced, until the advent of George III, to a cypher. Sir Robert Walpole engineered control of the court. His methods were 'crude but immediately effective ... quite simply he bought it – hard cash for the King and titles for his mistresses.' Although Walpole's ministry went the way of all ministries, the system he established was strong enough to survive him. His efforts, and the revolutionary settlement of 1688, enabled an aristocratic oligarchy to use Parliament to govern in the name of the Crown.

The eighteenth century established patronage as one of the essential features of the British structure of power.[1] The name of the Crown enabled that process to be carried off with at least the appearance of grace. Executive power still derived largely from the prerogative, but a recognition by the Commons of the need for the extensive use of prerogative war powers during the American War of Independence and the Napoleonic Wars, supplemented by additional

250

statutory authority, placed a growing administration in an increasingly powerful position.

The government machine remained small. In 1861 the whole Civil Service still numbered no more than 39,000. However, by 1929, it had increased tenfold.[2] In that year Lord Salisbury noted the shift of power away from Parliament. Nothing, he said, was more clear than that, whatever party was concerned, 'the Government is absorbing more and more of the power which used to belong to Parliament. Those who are familiar with public affairs have seen the difficulty under which Parliament itself was conducted, and how the power of the State was concentrated in the Government. In regard to the House of Commons matters had undoubtedly been carried to such a point that complete freedom of speech did not seem to be any longer possible, and a good deal of details as to important measures could never be discussed there.'[3]

To an extent, the weakening role of Parliament was an inevitable consequence of the growing interventionism of the state. From the late nineteenth century, the state became involved in education, transport, pensions, housing and planning. The change that this effected to the constitution was, at first, hardly noticed by constitutional lawyers. Atiyah has observed that England stumbled into the modern administrative state without design and even contrary to the inclinations of most Englishmen.[4] The truth is that most Englishmen probably neither knew nor cared what was happening to the constitution. They would only have been aware of the growing involvement of the state in a whole range of matters which had previously been thought to have been the province of private business or private charity. After the First World War, emergency powers over the availability of food, power and other essential supplies were modified or withdrawn but the experience of state involvement left an indelible impression on the participants. During the post Second World War period, the state moved from being a facilitator in the provision of services by private industry to being the owner and controller of major industries such as coal, steel, railways, gas, electricity and water. The Civil Service increased proportionately to serve in the new ministries which Parliament had created to supervise the new public utilities. By 1979, the number of civil servants stood at 732,000.

Another feature of the growth of state power and the diminution of the power of Parliament was the immense increase in the use of legislation by ministers and by other bodies to whom the power to legislate had been given by Parliament. It was these powers, largely generated in the first instance by the exigencies of wartime, and almost always immune from proper parliamentary scrutiny, which so concerned Lord Hewart, the Lord Chief Justice, in his book *The New Despotism*, published in 1929. The volume of such legislation has continued undiminished in the intervening years. In 1979, there were 543 statutory instruments laid before Parliament. By the early 1980s, the number of statutory instruments had risen to an average of 1,900, and in 1994 it had risen again to 3,334.

Under the classic concept of the British constitution as described by Bagehot and Dicey, and taught to generations of students, the Crown as executive operates within a system of checks and balances maintained by the legislature and the judiciary. The system, as misdescribed by Montesquieu, was perceived to work to protect individual property and liberty, because the legislature called the executive to account, the legislature in turn depended on the executive to execute the laws which it had made, and individuals looked to an 'indifferent judiciary' to enforce the law against both executive and individual. Although Locke recognized the danger of a situation where everyone is 'Judge, Interpreter and Executioner ... in his own case', he did not, paradoxically, in the case of the state, regard it as any more than coincidental that the 'Legislative and Executive Power come often to be separated'.[5]

In fact, there has never been a complete separation of executive and legislature in the United Kingdom. In the early days of conciliar government, the Royal Council issued decrees and ordinances. Later, after parliamentary government was established in 1688 and developed by Walpole, the dominant party in the Commons, which governed through the Cabinet in the monarch's name, had an almost complete control of the legislative process. The judiciary became, as we have seen, genuinely independent or 'indifferent', as Locke described it, under the Act of Settlement 1700, but the Commons remained largely the instrument of the party in power. Some element of independence remained to backbench MPs as long as they were recognized by their constituents as separate from the party which they represented, and had the means to finance their own re-election. The rise of mass parties put an end to that, but the convention of ministerial responsibility, which was intended as the means by which ordinary MPs were able to check individual and collective abuses of power by ministers and government, had by then become well entrenched, and it remains, at least as a nominal check on the executive government.

Ministerial responsibility, which is closely associated with ministerial accountability, means, in the words of G. Marshall and G.C. Moody, 'that Ministers are responsible for the general conduct of the government, including the exercise of many powers legally vested in the Monarch, and ultimately, through Parliament and parties, to the electorate'. One part of the doctrine is the individual responsibility of ministers, which makes them politically answerable in Parliament in respect of matters lying within their field of responsibility. They are responsible not only for their personal acts but for the conduct of officials in their department, and the principle is said to be that a minister takes the praise for the success of the department and the blame for its failures. The sanction for misconduct of government is that a minister is exposed to criticism or censure in the House, and, if the misconduct is serious, may be expected to resign.[6] In relation to accountability, Marshall has said that it is 'about requiring a person to explain and justify – against criteria of some kind – their decisions or acts, and then to make amends for any fault or error, whether by reversing the decision, or paying compensation or in some other way – even resigning from office'.[7] That is the theory. The practice is, however, far removed from principle. This is caused, in part, by the dominance of party in the process of government and, in part, by the immense complexity of a modern central government administration, operating at European Community, national and local levels, which makes attribution of blame so difficult.

The close association between the success of the party in control of Parliament and the ambitions of members, so that the careers of 'disloyal' members are inevitably short when the whip is removed, has guaranteed that the 'check' which Parliament is supposed to impose upon the executive is almost always a weak one. The party in control has no interest in holding its own ministers to account and the opposition has not the means to do so. The government in power is further reenforced by a 'payroll vote' of senior and junior ministers. It is certainly arguable that there are too many junior ministers for the work to be done. At the present time, there are 86 ministers and whips in the Commons, nearly three times as many as a century ago. As we have seen, the size and scope of government has increased enormously during that time, but decision-making is still actually concentrated in about three dozen members of the Cabinet and senior ministers, who have a very heavy workload. The government chief whip, however, likes to have as many posts as possible as patronage.[8] Albert Dicey, with whom the concepts of both parliamentary supremacy and the rule of law are most closely associated, had already recognized the total inadequacy of parliamentary control over ministers before he died. Commenting on the hollow reassurance offered by Lord Haldane in the House of Lords, in refusing to intervene in *Local Government Board* v. *Arlidge* in 1915, that 'the Minister at the head of the Board is directly responsible to Parliament like other Ministers', he wrote:

This reference to so-called ministerial responsibility is some-what unfortunate. It is calculated to promote the belief that such ministerial responsibility is a real check upon the action of a Minister or a Cabinet when tempted to evade or override the law of the land. But any man who will look plain facts in the face will see in a moment that ministerial liability to the censure not in fact of Parliament, nor even by the House of Commons, but by the party majority which keeps the Government in office, is a very feeble guarantee indeed against action which evades the authority of the law courts.[9]

Dicey's comment loses some of its force by virtue of the fact that, in the *Arlidge* case, the House had decided that the Board was acting in an administrative way that was *within its legal powers*. If that exercise of discretion, though legal, was in fact in some way inappropriate, the remedy was *political*, the House said, and not legal. The court was the forum for controlling excesses of power which went so far as to be illegal, while Parliament was the place to challenge decisions which, although wrong on their merits, were within the law. Dicey was, however, more perceptive than other constitutional lawyers of the early years of the twentieth century in recognizing the inadequacy of parliament as a means of political control, and his words have as much resonance today as when they were delivered eighty years ago. Few judges acknowledged the inadequacy of parliamentary scrutiny. The outburst of Farwell LJ in *Dyson* v. *Attorney-General* in 1911 is a solitary voice: 'If ministerial responsibility were more than the mere shadow of a name the matter would be less important, but as it is, the courts are the only defence of the liberty of the subject against departmental aggression.'[10]

The extraordinary thing is that, time and again, most judges would, like Lord Haldane, attempt to justify a refusal to intervene in a matter concerning the exercise of powers which were essentially legal, on the grounds that a minister's or civil servant's decision was, in fact, based on 'political' considerations and was, therefore, non-justiciable. The applicant's appropriate remedy, it was said, was to raise the matter in Parliament with the minister, or for Parliament to legislate. The fact that a minister has resisted taking what the applicant regards as appropriate action right up to the doors of the court is, however, likely to be a strong indication of the ministerial response in the House to the applicant's Member of Parliament. And, as Dicey and, indeed, the reception in the House of Commons to the Scott Report made plain, the fall of ministers or governments as a result of injustice done to litigants is as rare as ice in mid-summer. Ministers resign when they have lost the confidence not of the House, but of the Prime Minister, or when the Prime Minister believes that a minister's personal behaviour is likely to damage the government.

Lord Hailsham, in his now celebrated Dimbleby broadcast in 1976 entitled 'Elective dictatorship', declared that

> in present conditions, the whole absolute powers of Parliament, except in a few matters like divorce or abortion, are wielded by the Cabinet alone and sometimes by a relatively small group within the Cabinet ... The decreasing leisure and increasing economic pressures upon Private Members, few of whom live upon their Parliamentary salaries, make it more and more difficult to bring a Minister to book. Even when he is wrong, he can usually make it look sufficiently as if he were right to get his own supporters into the lobby when the division bell rings.'[11]

Lord Hailsham, like Margaret Thatcher, shared, as Simon Jenkins has observed, 'a familiar syndrome among British politicians: an aversion to "elective dictatorship" when out of office and a sudden conversion to its glorious subtleties when in power'.[12]

To share a concern with Dicey, Hewart and Hailsham that Parliament, as it is currently operated, is an inadequate forum for the maintenance of political control and accountability is not necessarily to share their suspicion of the involvement of government in what, in the mid-nineteenth century, was exclusively the private sphere. Tony Prosser has described three broad approaches to the application of public law. They are not mutually exclusive, and range across what is essentially a political spectrum. At one extreme stand Dicey, Hewart and Hayek, for whom the crucial aspect of the exercise of public law is 'control'. State intervention is a necessary evil, probably best confined to law and order and the defence of the realm. Public law should primarily be concerned with creating techniques, largely legal, for the control of the exercise of public power. These are often called the 'red light' theorists. At the other end of the spectrum stand those who accept, or even welcome, state involvement, and who argue that the exercise of power by the state over a wide range of social and economic policies is quite proper, and is, indeed, inevitable, given the inadequacies or failures of alternative mechanisms, especially the market. These theorists, usually called 'green light theorists', prefer to see accountability of government achieved primarily through the political process, rather than through the law. The third school of thought, containing the so-called 'amber theorists', concedes the desirability and need for the exercise of public power, and rejects the view that public law should be seen exclusively in terms of the control of such power, but would argue that reliance on traditional political techniques for promoting accountability, such as parliamentary questions, political debates, ministerial responsibility, select committees and the like, is, as a matter of practical reality, inadequate, and that forms of political control need to be buttressed by forms of legal control[13]

Few today would embrace the minimalist state of the red light theorists, or accept, as green light theorists appear to do, that after the experience of the past thirty years Parliament still provides an effective means by which to scrutinize the process of government. There are a number of reasons for this which require consideration, especially in relation to the use of prerogative powers. These still provide an important underpinning of much governmental activity, as we have seen. As Holdsworth observed in 1938, 'The principal motive force of the executive power in the British constitution has always been the prerogative.' It is rarely formally acknowledged, although section 5(5) of the Ministers of the Crown Act 1975 provides that the powers conferred by the Act are without prejudice to 'any power exercisable by virtue of the prerogative power of the Crown in relation to the functions of Ministers of the Crown.' Legal remedies may provide a solution where individual interests or European Community rights are affected, or where statute has provided a tribunal or other appeal system, or recourse to an Ombudsman, but broader issues affecting the use of defence powers by ministers, or involving national security, foreign policy and the regulation of the Civil Service and the Next Steps agencies, for example, will still in many cases be regarded by the courts as raising non-justiciable issues, and will have to be dealt with by the political process or not at all. Legal and political solutions are not, of course, mutually exclusive, and one may be pursued where the other has failed, or they may even be sought concurrently. Political and legal accountability are, therefore, intimately connected.

POLITICAL ACCOUNTABILITY IN THE 1990s

The political events of the years of the Thatcher administrations had an enormous impact on the distribution of power within the British constitution. Paradoxically, the government that was elected to 'roll back the frontiers of the state' saw an increase of state power to an extent which the post-war planners of the Morrison era would have envied. State industries were turned into private monopolies, but under a very tight system of statutory regulation. Education, which had been in the hands of locally elected education committees, was effectively removed from their control. Schools achieved a nominal autonomy, but within a new national curriculum devised in and monitored from Whitehall. Local authorities lost their autonomy in relation to housing policy and their budgets became, effectively, subject to Treasury diktat. The localized health service became market-orientated, but again, under overall direction from London. In many areas of government, locally elected representatives were removed and replaced by people from the business world who shared the government's philosophy. The arts, sport, housing, social services and many other local provisions became the concern of government-appointed quangos. *The Times* journalist Simon Jenkins described the acceleration of a process that had started at the beginning of the century but now seemed to have destroyed any balance between central and local power:

> Mr Major already runs every prison in the land, every hospital, every motorway, every railway, every job-centre, every training council. He is set on running every police force, every university, every county, every town ... The strain is beginning to show – not least on hapless ministers who must answer for everything remiss in their master's burgeoning empire ...
>
> We have witnessed not a rational argument over the best distribution of constitutional power in a modern state. We have witnessed a turf war. The debate over centralization is not about efficiency, democracy or uniformity, but about power. As long as Britain has no written constitution and concentrates all government power in the hands of the leadership of a Commons majority, that leadership will always seek more. In this matter the only law it need recognize is that of the jungle.[14]

According to the traditional view of the constitution, all these new functions of central government or quasi-governmental action could be kept under review through the processes of parliamentary scrutiny, the doctrine of ministerial accountability, the processes of parliamentary questions and investigation by select committees. We have already considered some of the problems of accountability in relation to the civil servants who now find themselves in the Next Steps agencies. These problems are compounded in the case of the privatized utilities because the minister who is nominally responsible for the industry has very little control over it. The real power lies with the regulator. In 1995, Clare Spottiswood, the director of Ofgas, the gas industry regulator, delivered a candid speech in which she admitted that she felt wholly unaccountable. Regulators do not hold public hearings and they reach decisions in private. Neither the public nor Parliament could take her to the Monopolies Commission if she was felt to be in the pocket of the industry. She admitted that her reports to Parliament were 'not worth the paper they are printed on'. She was scrutinized by the National Audit Office and was subject to judicial review, but as for accountability, it is, she said, 'in truth very little'.[15]

The difficulty of accountability where those exercising power are at more than one remove from the House of Commons can be contrasted with the situation where there is a responsible minister in the House, who has the necessary information with which to render an account of the work of his or her department to individual MPs, the whole House or a select committee, but who, for a number of reasons, both good and bad, refuses to do so. There are established conventions that ministers do not answer parliamentary questions on a whole range of issues. These are listed in seven pages of Erskine May, and, besides such obvious areas falling within the prerogative as defence, the secret services and sensitive information about the economy and the national currency, they include such unexpected items as information about agricultural workers' wages, curricular matters and trade statistics for Scotland.[16]

Even when questions are answered, the information supplied may be of minimal utility. Anyone who has examined old ministerial files in the Public Records Office will have been struck by the ingenuity shown by civil servants in providing draft, alternative answers, denying any information, supplying some or, if the minister so desires, supplying the fullest reply. Under paragraph 27 of Questions of Procedure for Ministers, it is stated that ministers have a duty 'to give Parliament, including its Select Committees, and the public as full information as possible about the policies, decisions and actions of the Government, and not to deceive or mislead Parliament and the public'. Sir Richard Scott identified at least eight serious breaches of that duty in his Report on the arms to Iraq affair, and he observed that 'the obligation of Ministers to give information about the activities of their departments and to give information and explanations for the actions and omissions of their civil servants lies at the heart of Ministerial accountability'.

The problem is that it is ministers who determine what information they will give and to whom. Self-evidently, if a minister decides to conceal information, neither Parliament nor the public will be aware of the fact. Only if a civil servant leaks the information to Parliament or the press will the information come into the public domain. The consequences of such a disclosure will be serious for the informant, including at worst a criminal prosecution, and at best dismissal and even loss of pension rights. Nor will the press be protected from attempts by the Crown to obtain details about the identity of the informant.

In its 1994 Report, the Treasury and Civil Service Select Committee emphasized that the system of ministerial accountability 'depends upon two vital elements: clarity about who can be held to account and held responsible when things go wrong; confidence that Parliament is able to gain the accurate information required to hold the Executive to account and to ascertain where responsibility lies'.[17] Neither of these conditions is currently being fulfilled. As we have seen, recent government reforms have resulted in ministers having a greatly increased load of responsibility, without the same degree of connection with those who actually make and execute decisions as existed under the old departmental system. Simon Jenkins describes the consequences of such recent reforms:

> In May 1995 the Prime Minister found himself explaining at the dispatch box why an emergency patient had been moved from London to Leeds, and his health secretary why part of an Edgware hospital accident department should close. A sports minister negotiated a special payment for teachers for one games period a week. Alternative conduits of accountability had either been stripped out of government or rendered impotent. The 'minister' stood alone, exhausted, battered, usually confused, defending decisions of which he had little knowledge and over which he had little direct control.

This disconnection between ministerial responsibility and actual control has led to a demand that accountability and responsibility should be separated. The chief proponent of this view is Sir Robin Butler, the former Head of the Civil Service and Secretary to the Cabinet. According to Sir Robin, ministerial accountability is a constitutional burden that rests on the shoulders of ministers and cannot be set aside. It does not necessarily, however, require *blame* to be accepted by a minister in whose department some blameworthy error or failure has occurred. A minister should not be held to blame or be required to accept personal criticism unless he or she has some personal responsibility for or some personal involvement in what has occurred. Sir Richard Scott has accepted this new concept of ministerial responsibility, because, he says, 'government has become so complex and the need for the delegation of responsibilities to and reliance on the advice of officials has become so inevitable as to render unreal the attaching of blame to a Minister simply because something has gone wrong in the department of which he is in charge'.[18]

The difference between personal and non-personal decisions has been developed into the policy/operational distinction which ministers have attempted to argue in relation to the functions of agencies. The distinction was most forcefully argued by Michael Howard, the then Home Secretary, in relation to various prison escapes and matters relating to prison administration discussed in the House of Commons in October 1995. Prison policy was what the Home Secretary was responsible for, while Derek Lewis, head of the Prison Services Agency, was responsible for the operation of the prisons. The distinction, as Peter Riddell of *The Times* has said, 'sounds neat and is, in part, intended to counter knee-jerk demands for resignations whenever something goes wrong. But it can be distorted into a doctrine of ministerial irresponsibility. While it is obviously daft to blame Mr Howard every time a prisoner escapes, there is no clear-cut distinction between policy and operations.'[19] The new doctrine is concerned with apportioning blame according to what a minister knew or ought to have known. But it is based on a false premise. The traditional doctrine may or may not involve fault by the minister concerned but it cannot, and should not, only apply when the Minister is morally at fault. The Minister is 'where the buck stops'. As Vernon Bogdanor has said:

> Ministerial responsibility is a widely misunderstood concept. It ought not to mean, and indeed it has hardly ever been interpreted to mean, that a minister is to *blame* for any mistake in his or her department, only that he *takes* the blame for such mistakes. The principle means, not that the minister is necessarily at fault, but that it is he or she who is responsible for taking corrective action, for putting things right, and for ensuring that the department is run effectively. (Emphasis added.)

Bogdanor acknowledges that the creation of the Next Steps agencies makes the operation of ministerial responsibility much more difficult. There is no constitutional doctrine of Civil Service responsibility, yet agencies are headed by civil servants who under the last Government even answered parliamentary questions. Ministers remain responsible to Parliament, as Mrs Thatcher accepted when she introduced the reforms. Since they remain responsible, ministers are tempted to interfere, as, Derek Lewis alleges, did Michael Howard on a daily basis. Bogdanor argues that the new relationship between ministers and agencies needs to be put on a proper legal basis, defining the roles of chief executive and minister quite specifically. The Framework Agreement, which is presently an informal arrangement governing the relationship between minister and agency, would be converted into a legal document that could be subject to judicial interpretation, and would put the chief executive in a stronger position to resist ministerial interference. It would also clearly delimit the matters for which a minister would be responsible, in the sense that it would be known for which matters a minister might, as a final sanction, be called upon to resign and avoid the endless opportunities for buck-passing offered by the current system.[20]

What might be called the Butler doctrine of political irresponsibility does not sit well with the *Carltona* principle under which ministers are said, in law at least, to be the authors of decisions which (unless Parliament has specifically required that they be made by ministers) are, in fact, the decisions of civil servants. Legally too, the ministry may be vicariously liable for acts of Crown servants carried out in the course of their work, of which members of the ministry concerned may have had no actual knowledge, provided that the act in question was performed as part of the duties of the Crown employee, albeit carried out in an unauthorized way.[21] It is true that the courts have attempted, in the law of negligence, to draw a distinction between policy decisions, for which the policy-maker will not be liable, and operational decisions, which may, in appropriate cases, attract liability.

It would seem appropriate that action which does not attract legal liability should at least carry some potential political liability for the decision-maker, and conversely, operational decisions which may not attract the political censure of the policy-maker should give rise to a duty of care. But the distinction is as hard to draw in law as in politics. The problematic nature of the policy/operational distinction is illustrated by *Rigby* v. *Chief Constable of Northamptonshire* in 1985.[22] In this case, a decision not to acquire a particular type of CS gas canister (the use of which did not create a fire risk) was held to be a policy decision, whereas a decision on a particular occasion to use a canister of a type which did create a fire risk was an operational decision. In practice, it is very difficult to determine where a policy decision ends and an operational decision begins. The difficulty of the distinction in a complex chain of responsibility undoubtedly puts traditional ideas of ministerial responsibility in question. 'Political authority does not in and of itself enable ministers to exercise the degree of control over the processes of government implied by exclusive reliance on the notion of ministerial responsibility as the mechanism of accountability. In other words, the role of the cabinet, and of ministers in relation to their departments, is partly a matter of constitutional myth.'[23]

SELECT COMMITTEES

Select committees were originally set up by the House of Commons to address a specific issue, such as reform of the rules of procedure, MPs' salaries and other matters of immediate concern.

It was usual in the nineteenth century for the House of Commons to pass motions that papers be laid before the House concerning specific topics or that select committees be set up to investigate and extract information about a particular issue. As party discipline ensured executive control of the House of Commons, such motions were successfully resisted by governments, so that the regular flow of information to the House of Commons had become much diminished by the early years of the twentieth century, at the very time when the role of government was expanding.[24] Except for the Committee of Privileges, now called the Standards and Privileges Committee, such committees were disbanded when their final report was delivered.

The growth in the size and power of the executive, the greatly expanded use of delegated legislation which was not subject to proper supervision and the increasing dominance of Parliament by the executive led, in 1918, to recommendations by the Haldane Committee for the establishment of a new form of select committee to monitor the performance of each government department. Nothing was done, but renewed demands were made for reform by Ivor Jennings and the Fabian Society in the 1930s, and these continued until the Haldane recommendations were finally adopted by the House of Commons, under the leadership of Norman St John Stevas, in 1979.[25] Fourteen departmental committees were established that year. By the end of the 1994–5 session, the number had grown to sixteen.

The Procedure Committee reviewed the working of the new select committees ten years after they were set up and gave them a clean bill of health. The Committee's judgment was that they were effective, 'ministers considered they were effective and they had now become an integral part of the working of Parliament'. This sanguine view was not universally shared. Lord St John of Fawsley, who had, in his earlier persona, set up the committees, thought that it 'was an extraordinarily complacent report. It could have been written by Candide. All was for the best in the best of all possible worlds.'[26]

The committees are effective at monitoring the more routine work of departments, but serious difficulties arise in relation to politically sensitive issues. An important obstacle to the work of the committees in relation to such issues is often the acquisition of information. Hearings before the committees can become an elaborate pantomime in which the committee tries hard, but not too hard, to get the relevant information, and the civil servant or minister tries to disclose as little as possible. Robert Hazell, Director of the Nuffield Foundation and a former senior civil servant, has described the process of giving evidence to a select committee: 'I've seen senior officials from my old department, the Home Office, putting up very effective and stone-walling performances in front of the Home Affairs Select Committee. If it is courteously done I think the select committee genuinely accepts that the officials are playing within the rules and it doesn't press them too hard for information.'[27]

David Judge, Reader in Government at the University of Strathclyde, has noted that the main, recurring, problem, in relation to information which the committees do obtain, is that politically sensitive issues are evaded, or the relevant committee splits along party political lines when it considers them. Select committees, although often chaired by opposition members, always have a government majority when, which is the usual situation, the government has a majority in the House. For that reason, select committees rarely press government ministers to the point of political embarrassment.

Some Conservative select committee chairs have, on occasion, shown a remarkable independence of mind. A persistent stand of this kind is, however, likely in the end to result in the loss of the chairmanship of the select committee and in terminal damage to the parliamentary career of the member. The dangers of excessive independence were made clear in 1992. In July of that year, Nicholas Winterton, the Conservative member for Macclesfield and chair of the health select committee, and another Conservative MP, Sir John Wheeler, were both removed from their posts by the committee of selection. Winterton, described by Patricia Wynn Davies, the *Independent's* political correspondent, as 'one of the government's most outspoken critics', accused the committee of selection of succumbing to pressure from government whips. In a subsequent vote on the recommendations of the committee of selection an attempt was made to reinstate both Winterton and Wheeler. Although it is customary to allow members a free vote on such occasions, the attempt was defeated by a determined mobilization of the government's 'payroll vote' of senior and junior ministers. Winterton complained that the select committees, 'the last bastions of defence' against excess of government, had been severely compromised.[28]

The event is not reassuring, if one looks to the select committee system as an effective check on the governmental process. Professor John Griffith may be right when he accepts government dominance of all parliamentary processes as inevitable under the system as it is currently constituted.

> The whole structure of the Constitution, the way in which Parliament works, is that it is a party machine, and that means that the majority party and the government have a common interest and they are interdependent. The government majority backbenchers have an interest in making sure the government does its job, but also that it manages to put into effect the policies of a government. So there's a relationship and it's very close. Now, unless you can crack that detailed connection between the two, then you 're not going to get anywhere in the end.[29]

He is probably going too far in suggesting that, in order to have select committees which are as powerful and as effective as the committees of the United States Congress, you must necessarily have a complete separation of powers, and expel members of the executive from Parliament. Congressional committees are extremely well resourced. They also have extensive powers to obtain material and to compel individuals to give evidence under oath. As Peter Hennessy has written, 'even allowing for the separation of powers and the institutionalised importance of the Congress which flows from that, and even acknowledging, too, America's relative wealth, the support system of Westminster's 650 MPs, compared to those of Washington's 100 senators and 435 Representatives, are extraordinarily meagre – all the more so considering how centralized a nation we are compared to the United States, and how few our checks and balances compared to theirs.'[30]

Strengthening our select committee system would involve giving such committees greater resources, and would also involve 'constitutionalizing' them. This would involve giving select committee chairs a legally protected status with power to compel the taking of evidence under oath, the power to direct the production of evidence and to treat as the criminal offence of contempt a refusal to do so. Ironically, the Parliamentary Ombudsman has power to order the production of evidence by government departments in relation to which complaints are permissible under the Parliamentary Commission Act 1967, but the parliamentary committee to which he reports has no such power.

Select committee chairs could, perhaps, have security until such time as they should retire voluntarily, until they are removed by a two-thirds majority of the committee which they chair or until Parliament is dissolved. There are signs that Parliament, following the Willetts affair in November 1996, is making a hesitant move in this direction. Recognizing, perhaps, that its procedures stand very low in the public esteem, the report of the Standards and Privileges Committee on the affair has stated that, in future, evidence to the committee should be given on oath. Although the committee will not be able to deal itself with the giving of perjured evidence, it would be a criminal offence which, in theory, could be dealt with by the ordinary criminal courts. For this to happen, it would seem that the Bill of Rights would have to be amended so that such perjured evidence would not be protected as a 'proceeding' of the House under Article 9. Allegations of impropriety are currently subject to investigation by the new Parliamentary Commissioner for Standards, who reports to the Standards and Privileges Committee.

This committee, which is the oldest and most 'judicial' of Parliament's select committees, seems to have been the subject of an attempt, in the Willetts case, to pervert its processes by 'exploiting the good Tory majority' on the committee. As the Winterton case made clear in 1992, ordinary departmental select committee chairs are even more vulnerable to pressure from government whips. Much needs to be done if the departmental select committees, which were launched with such high expectations in 1979, are to have their credibility and effectiveness restored and enhanced. Perhaps what is most needed is a change of attitude by select committee members. Lord St John of Fawsley has noted that 'deference has grown within the political system and deference in the House of Commons is now at a historic high; despite all the noise, despite all the appearance of rebellion, the deference to those holding office, the deference to civil servants, has grown, is growing and I think could profitably be diminished'.[31]

THE SELECT COMMITTEE ON EUROPEAN LEGISLATION

Of the non-departmental select committees, the Select Committee on European Legislation is probably the most constitutionally important. As we have noted in relation to the making of foreign policy decisions, membership of the European Union has, in effect, given ministers the power to legislate through their use of the foreign policy prerogative. Since the Council of Ministers has the final word on most legislative decisions, it is, in practice, the legislature of the Union, although legislative proposals are actually drafted by the Commission. Draft Community regulations and directives are sent for scrutiny by national parliaments at the same time as they are sent to the European Parliament. The European Parliament has only limited powers of amendment under the so-called 'cooperation procedure'; no powers of amendment at all under decisions made under the 'consultation procedure'; and only power to block legislation under the 'condition procedure'.

It might be thought, therefore, that some cooperation between the European and United Kingdom Parliaments was desirable, and that some attempt would be made to ensure that legislation is effectively examined and important measures are discussed before they reach the Council of Ministers. A report by the Department of Trade and Industry in 1993, *Review of the Implementation and Enforcement of EC Law in the UK*, estimated that almost 70 per cent of UK law affecting business would soon derive from Community law.[32] Other areas of law will also be significantly, though less substantially, affected. Given the volume of legislation, and its importance, the extent of scrutiny is highly unsatisfactory. There are two main reasons for this. The first can only be called philosophical, while the second is, in essence, practical.

The greatest difficulty is that the Westminster Parliament is not used to operating at different levels with another legislature. Not being part of a federal structure, like, for example, the *Bundesparliament* in Germany, it is not accustomed to a division of legislative functions. The European Parliament is simply seen as a competing parliament, and one to which successive British governments have been most reluctant to allocate greater powers. Legislation is considered by the European Parliament by standing committees, which not only examine it in draft, but may call expert witnesses and examine Commission officials in a way which is unknown at Westminster in relation to the examination of draft legislation by standing committees at Committee Stage. Westminster politicians are used to examining draft legislation that may have been redrawn many times and is regarded, in Whitehall at least, as the 'final' draft. The whole approach of the European Parliament is so different that communication between it and Westminster is a serious problem. It is not just a matter of language. As Vernon Bogdanor has said, 'It is not surprising that the two Parliaments find it difficult to communicate with and understand each other. Their attempt to do so resembles a dialogue between two incompatible computers.'[33]

In theory, since the Council of Ministers has the last word on most Community legislation, national parliaments can exercise some control over the Council's legislative process through the accountability of ministers to those parliaments. In the case of the Westminster Parliament, the effectiveness of that accountability is much diminished, as we have seen, by the grip of the government party machine. In addition, the growth of qualified majority voting under the Single European Act 1986 and the Treaty on European

Union in 1992 has resulted in a growing inability of ministers to block legislation which is opposed by a majority in the House of Commons.

The Westminster Parliament is intended to be protected by the so-called scrutiny reserve. This is a government undertaking not to agree in the Council of Ministers to any proposal for European legislation which has been recommended by the select committee for debate, unless there are special reasons for not doing so. These reasons are, broadly, that measures are confidential, routine, trivial or substantially the same as an item which has already been scrutinized. By a Declaration annexed to the Treaty of European Union, Member States committed themselves to ensuring that 'national parliaments receive Commission proposals for legislation in good time for information or possible examination' (Declaration 13). According to a recent report of the select committee, this is not happening. Decisions are often made by the Council of Ministers on the basis of a French text for which no English translation is available, and the select committee frequently only sees the English translation *after* the measure has been approved by the Council of Ministers.

Members of the select committee have expressed concern that the Brussels legislative process was being operated beyond the scrutiny of national parliaments.[34] Given that discussions in the Council of Ministers are held in secret, and that the European Parliament can, at best, only amend or block legislation, but cannot initiate it, and can neither question nor hold the Council to account (unlike its powers in relation to the Commission), there can be no doubt that there is a serious democratic deficit in relation to the accountability of the Council of Ministers at both Community and national level.

Although a Protocol to the 1997 Amsterdam Treaty provides for a six-week period for national parliaments to dicuss proposed legislation before it is approved by the Council, there has been no attempt in the Treaty to integrate the process of approving and amending legislation between the European and national parliaments, or to make the Council of Ministers more open and accountable. Any such attempt would, in any event, almost certainly be resisted at Westminster as the first stage in the creation of a federal structure. It is ironic that resistance to the imposition of a more effective system of control and accountability over the growing use of the foreign policy prerogative, which, in effect, enables Ministers of the Crown to legislate in the Council of Ministers without effective prior scrutiny by the United Kingdom Parliament, is raised in the name of maintaining the sovereignty of that same Parliament! The irony is increased by the fact that the 'sovereignty of Parliament' for which such a brave defence is made in Brussels by successive governments was long ago ceded in practice, if not in law, to the executive.

HOLDING THE EXECUTIVE TO ACCOUNT: THE ROLE OF MEMBERS OF PARLIAMENT

Ministerial accountability can only work if individual Members of Parliament are both able and willing to make it work. According to traditional constitutional theory, the individual member has a duty to listen to his or her constituents and then to make a judgment, whether it be of proposed legislation or the conduct of government. In 1774, Edmund Burke made his celebrated declaration to the electors of Bristol:

> It ought to be the happiness and glory of a representative to live in the strictest union, the closest correspondence, and the most unreserved communication with his constituents. Their wishes ought to have great weight with him; their opinions high respect; their business unremitted attention. It is his duty to sacrifice his repose, his pleasures, his satisfactions, to theirs; and above all, ever, and in all cases, to prefer their interest to his own. But, his unbiased opinion, his mature judgment, his enlightened conscience, he ought not to sacrifice to you, to any man, or to any set of men living. These he does not derive from your pleasure; no, not from the law and the constitution. They are a trust from Providence, for the abuse of which he is deeply answerable. Your representative owes you, not his industry only, but his judgment; and he betrays, instead of serving you, if he sacrifices it to your opinions.[35]

Burke's declaration of an MP's duties is a counsel of perfection but, even after more than two centuries, it is still one to which most modern MPs would, in principle, aspire. MPs receive a mass of correspondence each week from their constituents, and attend 'surgeries' with their constituents at weekends. They tender advice, pass on cases to other bodies to deal with and seek the help of individual ministers where the constituent's grievance concerns their department. Any MP who is concerned to retain his or her seat will, as Burke advocates, attend industriously to the constituents' business and attempt to hold ministers to account where the minister's department has failed them. The MP will also make it his or her business to keep in touch with local opinion.

If there is no satisfactory outcome to representations by the member to a minister, he or she may put down a question or even open a debate on the adjournment of the House. But if the minister produces an anodyne and uninformative reply and brushes aside any further challenge on the floor of the House, then most MPs will pursue the matter no further. A few may, if appropriate, refer the case to the Ombudsman, the Parliamentary Commissioner for Administration, for further investigation. Only the most committed and persistent member can use Parliamentary Questions to secure answers when the minister does not want to give them. MPs of the calibre and determination of Tam Dalyell in pursuit of information about the sinking of the battleship *Belgrano* in the Falklands War are rare indeed, and are as rarely rewarded with the information they desire.[36] As we have noted in relation to the work of select committees, there are some matters, especially those involving the use of prerogative powers of defence, foreign policy, the security services and the organization of the Civil Service, where no answers will be forthcoming, as sanctioned by parliamentary custom and detailed in Erskine May.

When it comes, however, to exercising independent judgment on the performance of government, or acting solely in the public interest on a matter of general policy, the position of MPs is very different from that in which they are pursuing a concern on behalf of an individual constituent. 'Each individual is interested not only in his own affairs but in the affairs of the state as well.'[37] The interest to which Thucydides refers is not only the citizen's own property and material well being (which was the original basis of the franchise), but the interest which all citizens have in securing honest and effective government. The closest most individuals come to affairs of 'the state' will probably be to a government department or to a Member of Parliament. The state of general knowledge about our political institutions is such that many members of the public will think that all MPs are part of the state or, regardless of party, are 'the government'. For whatever reason, they will look to their Member of Parliament to redress individual grievances or to correct what they may see as abuses of power or misguided policies. Few will regard the expression of such concerns as 'participation in the process of government', but the combined effect of numerous representations should at least inform the judgment of the member, in the sense recognized by Burke, although it should not, on the same premises, dictate the way in which the member votes.

Participation in this modest way by citizens in the formation of policy and in the scrutiny of government is an essential, though neglected function of citizenship in liberal democracies. It has been forcefully argued that lack of participation by citizens in the political process has resulted in the poor quality of representation, which has, in turn, further discouraged public participation in the process of government. David Selbourne, in his *Principle of Duty*, has observed that

> the inadequacy and even entire unfitness for office, of many who hold such office in the corrupted liberal orders is the outcome itself of the failure to uphold the principle of duty, as it applies both to the civic order's duty of self-protection and protection of citizens, and the citizen's co-responsibility for the condition of the civic order; expressed here, in the particular duty of regular and vigorous scrutiny of the merits of those who hold and seek office in such civic order.[38]

While the overwhelming majority of MPs are honest and conscientious, all of them are subject to pressures which prevent them from responding effectively to constituents' general concerns about the performance of the executive. The main form of pressure is from the party whips, and from their own political aspirations. They are also hampered by lack of resources. If they are lucky, they will have a research assistant, or the share of one. Most will not have the time to carry out their own research, or be able to pay for someone else to do it. As a consequence, there is a growing tendency to rely upon pressure groups and public relations consultants to brief them on current issues, and even, in some cases, to use questions which have been drafted for them by someone with an axe to grind. Worse still, some MPs will use their opportunity to put an oral question to a minister in order to make some sycophantic statement in the hope of preferment, or to ask some 'planted' question so that the minister can disclose information as part of a 'spontaneous' response. Other questions, as the Nolan Committee has heard, have been put simply in exchange for the payment of money. The question may be one with which they, in principle, may agree but it is not *their* question and it may have little to do with the interests of their constituents or the public at large. Party conferences and other political events are dominated by lobbyists of all kinds. MPs, by West European standards, are poorly paid, and many have neither the time nor the opportunity to undertake paid work outside the House. It is probably undesirable that they should have such work, which may well create a conflict of interest, but they do need some form of additional resources.

The consequences of the lack of support, and the vulnerability of MPs to inducements offered by lobby organizations, have become plain, and have done little to encourage electors to see their members as a political conduit through whom they can express their opinions and on whose independent judgment or action they can rely. This may be unfair, but recent surveys have shown that MPs stand little higher than estate agents and journalists in the public estimation. Parliament's attempts to prevent abuses by its own members have not been notably successful. Rules and conventions which worked well when members, ministers and civil servants had all reached their positions through 'the velvet drainpipe' of the great public schools and Oxbridge, Parliament was the best club in town and 'understandings' between politicians of all parties carried the whole process of legislation and scrutiny forward, no longer carry much conviction or work very well in a very different and much more complex world.

What Martin Loughlin has called 'conservative normatism', symbolized by the concept of 'the Crown in Parliament' and supported by a belief that society constitutes an immutable order in which each is assigned its place, is fast disappearing.[39] The institutional structure and most of the conventions remain intact, but they have become increasingly empty. The convention that ministers do not lie to Parliament has, for example, become that 'they must not lie, but that they can be 'economical with the truth'. It is but one aspect of the loss of legitimacy of Parliament and of the political process. It would seem that national confidence that Parliament has either the will or the means to make political accountability work effectively, or to regulate itself when its processes are abused, is at a low ebb.

THE RELEVANCE OF POLITICAL ACCOUNTABILITY

Anyone writing about constitutional reform should be uncomfortably aware how little the constitution and the political process seem to matter to most people. Many live their lives with no contact with their local MP, except, perhaps, when he or she appears every four or five years on their doorstep to solicit their vote. Probably a majority have no idea which functions are provided by central government, and which by local or by private utilities. Between general elections some electors, usually no more than 30 or 40 per cent of the registered electorate, may turn out for a local election. Furious media activity, poster campaigns, extravagant promises and mutual recrimination by politicians usually generate sufficient interest to persuade a larger percentage of the registered electorate to vote at general elections, but a popular television programme on election night might be sufficient to keep them at home. Harold Wilson is reputed to have persuaded the BBC not to show an episode of *Steptoe and Son* for fear that potential voters might be tempted not to fulfil their electoral duty. Some people eligible to vote never even make it on to the electoral register. One of the most serious consequences of

271

the Community Charge was to discourage young people from completing the annual return to enable them to be entered on the register. Some have remained off it even after the abolition of the tax. Non-registration seems to be highest among young people from black minority groups, who feel most alienated from the political system. A survey published by the *Guardian* on 9 January 1997 indicated that up to 90 per cent of young black people were not intending to vote at the forthcoming general election.

Quite why there is this widespread lack of enthusiasm for the political process is clearly a matter for political scientists and sociologists rather than constitutional lawyers. It may be, however, that the failure of our constitutional system to do what it claims to do has played some part in the growth of disillusionment. As we have seen, recent political developments have resulted in an immense increase in the centralization of power, and in a corresponding diminution in centres of local power, especially within the education, health, fire and police services. Devolution of some powers to a parliament in Scotland and an assembly in Wales will, undoubtedly, go some way to reverse the trend, but much still needs to be done. Over the last twenty years central government has been strengthened, but through a whole range of agencies in which actual control is at least one remove from a nominally responsible minister. The problem is much deeper than a failure of institutions to deliver an effective system of government, which is, at the same time, politically accountable, and in which citizens participate more than once every four or five years. 'Elective dictatorship' is probably only an attractive system of government for the politicians who pull the levers of power, but its growth has tended to mask the diminishing power of the nation state in Western Europe and elsewhere. In the United Kingdom over the past twenty years power has tended to gravitate more to the centre and has generated expectations about what governments can do which cannot be fulfilled. A general disillusionment with governments of nation states is partly a consequence of the fact that they tend to promise to their electorates much more than they can deliver.

As Jonathan Eyal, Director of Studies at the Royal United Services, has written:

> The problem is that all Western leaders continue to derive their legitimacy from national elections but, in practice, they have little control over an economy that is truly global. Although not familiar with the intricacies of financial transactions, people everywhere are only too painfully aware of realities: those who do affect their lives are usually unknown and unelected; those

who ostensibly hold political power prove unable to exercise it ... The real rulers of the world today are the chairmen of multi-media companies and multi-national institutions.[40]

It is clear that problems of a globalized economy cannot be addressed at a national level, and the current obsession in the United Kingdom with the maintenance of national autonomy either within or without the European Union has an air of complete unreality. Large business conglomerates, some with turnovers which exceed the gross domestic product of the smaller European Union states, make decisions about transfers of capital, the opening and closing of plants and inward and outward investment according to criteria which have little to do with the welfare of their employees, the inhabitants of the states in which they are located or the global environment. Their primary obligation is to their shareholders. It is a situation to which we have not yet adjusted in either our political or legal thinking. 'We have been used, for too long, to think of the world as being constituted by nation states ... But it will be more useful ... to think of the world as constituted by the 200 or so global corporations. Their internal trade, their treasurer's decisions to shift the petty cash – an odd billion dollars or so – can cause an exchange rate crisis. Their production decisions bind countries together in an international division of labour.'[41] The obligation of nation states, on the other hand, is to their citizens. Corporations are not citizens, although there have been claims to 'corporate citizenship' and even to the protection of corporations' 'human' rights. These claims are considered in the next chapter.

The new world order poses a serious challenge to the old nation state. States have the choice of engaging in a Dutch auction, in which security of employment and welfare provision are driven down to their lowest levels, in the hope of providing a low-cost environment for inward investment, or of combining with each other to provide a trading regime in which minimum employment and social welfare standards are protected. The history of Western Europe between the wars taught the nation states that national protectionism was ultimately self-destructive. Post-war experience has taught them that cooperation in attaining high standards of welfare provision in the European Community is not necessarily incompatible with the attainment of high levels of productivity. Citizenship, as we shall see, is not only about the exercise of legal and political rights, but also about creating the sort of economic environment in which those rights can flourish.

If these issues are to be tackled in the interest of the majority of the citizens of this country, it will, in the first instance, have to be at a

European Union level. Writing in 1985, Harry Shutt, in a prescient book, *The Myth of Free Trade*, criticizes 'the tendency of much of the international establishment to insist upon the essential primacy of market forces, in the teeth of all the evidence of their own policies and behaviour', and advocates international collaboration in the structuring of world trade, starting with a nucleus of developed and less developed states. 'Given the traditions of its member states, it would seem that the EEC might well be an appropriate vehicle for such an experiment, although it would have to seek partnership with a far weightier group of LDCs than the weak and fragmented collection of states associated with the Lomé Convention.'[42]

The future of the European Union is, in any event, inextricably bound up with its relations with its penumbra of associated states and other states with which it has close trading relations. The Union's developing immigration policy, its common visa and its common asylum policy are all closely related to its trading policies with the states from whence come the majority of the third state nationals who comprise most of the Community's long-term foreign residents. A policy of fair trade with those states would remove the current incentive to illegal immigration, increase their political stability, reduce the political repression caused by instability and the asylum-seeking which such repression causes, and diminish the danger of racist violence on the mainland of Europe. The current approach to asylum-seekers is not promising. Member States, through their agreement, in the Dublin Convention, not to give substantive consideration to any asylum application made by an applicant who has passed through the territory of another Member State, seem to be attempting to avoid the international obligation of all the Member States under the Geneva Convention to give substantive consideration to *all* asylum applications made to them. Member States are right to look to the European Union for a supranational solution to its external trade and asylum policy, but they are going to have to take a much longer, harder look at their longer-term goals and to move beyond their current negative and reactive mode. The Union already has its own citizenship, which is still too closely tied to its original economic nexus. European citizenship confers rights of free movement on its holders, but only upon those who are economically active, or who are self-supporting. Citizenship of the Union is, in effect, a means-tested benefit.

If, as is probably inevitable, the European Union plays an increasing role in the development of a common economic policy (irrespective of whether or not the United Kingdom joins the single currency), and the European Court of Justice becomes progressively more important in shaping our law, the United Kingdom will be involved in attempts to make the decision-making processes of the Union more open and accountable to both the European and the Westminster Parliaments. The major task for both Union and national politicians is going to be to make the people of the United Kingdom, along with the people of all the Member States, feel more involved in the whole European Union enterprise. Most people feel remote from it, even hostile. Jonathan Eyall comments that 'the Union remains a bureaucratic construction, founded on the premise that regulating the size of eggs (usually without bothering to tell the hen) would gradually draw Europeans closer together'. Unless we progress beyond this kind of stereotype of the European Union, we remain in the blind alley of nationalism.

LEGAL ACCOUNTABILITY

Until a more effective system of political accountability is devised to meet the complexities of modern government, providing more appropriate means of scrutiny at the supranational, national and local levels at which political and administrative decision-making takes place, much reliance will have to be placed on legal accountability, at both a national and a European level. Although litigants are still not infrequently referred by the courts to Parliament for a political or legislative solution to their problem, some members of the judiciary now seem prepared to recognize that all is not well with the old constitutional structures. Sedley J has recently observed that

> The British paradigm of a parliament elected on a universal
> adult franchise making laws which the courts enforce and
> calling to account ministers whose executive departments carry
> out prescribed duties according to publicly announced policies
> is recognized as unreal. In particular, the fact that the
> government of the day now controls both Parliament and the
> executive has profound implications both for the constitutional
> separation of powers and, less often recognized, for the political
> distinction between party and state.[43]

Few would now quarrel with the observation of Sedley J. Not so many would follow his prescription. He observes that the royal prerogative has grown as the power of the state has grown. He goes much further than most members of the judiciary, denies 'the constitutional immunity of the Crown in all its incarnations from legal process' and holds that 'once the prerogative is grasped in its modern form as being not a historic residue of extra-legal power held by executive government, but the power, within the law, to fill constitutional spaces and exercise governmental choice, it takes its place within and not beyond the rule of law'. In some ways it is reassuring that a High Court judge should be prepared to look at any prerogative decision in the same way as any other decision made under common law and statutory powers. We have seen many executive decisions which are, for a variety of reasons, beyond the reach of effective parliamentary scrutiny, because they are made by some agency of whose activities the responsible minister is unaware, or about which no information can be obtained. Many of these are made in the exercise of prerogative powers.

The disturbing aspect of the approach of Sedley J is the great power which it places in the hands of the judiciary. As we have seen in Chapter 2, we lack any clear, fundamental principles of law by which such constitutional spaces can be filled. Sedley J is not worried by such a lack of principle. 'The great thing about the organic development of law as against the ad hoc enactment of statutes and making of regulations is that, if it is informed by what Montesquieu called *l'esprit des lois*, it furnishes at each stage some of the materials for the next stage of growth.' That sounds suspiciously like substituting for the 'ad hoccery' of Parliament the 'ad hoccery' of the judiciary.

Incorporation of the European Convention on Human Rights will provide a clearer set of principles by which the substantive exercise of prerogative powers could be judged. Hitherto we have had nothing, except the vaguest observations about public morality and reasonableness enunciated by Lord Diplock in the *GCHQ* case.[44] Those who oppose incorporation of the Convention or of a Charter of Rights, because to do so would place too much power in the hands of the judges, often fail to acknowledge that the present system already gives judges very great power to develop constitutional law, but without the guidance of any clear principles approved through the democratic process. Although incorporation, as envisaged by the Human Rights Bill, will not provide a comprehensive statement of fundamental overriding rights, it will give a framework within which constitutional decision-making can develop. It may, ultimately, lead to a general recognition that a more comprehensive rewriting of our constitution is necessary.

Both the *Smith* case, concerning gay men and women in the services, and the *Sancto* case, which involved an attempt by the parents of a dead soldier to obtain a report about the circumstances of his death, cried out for a clear statement of principle about privacy in the first case, and freedom of information in the second.[45] No accumulation of *dicta* by the judiciary is ever likely to take us to that point. Only Parliament can do it. In the meantime, ministers reach into the historic recesses of the prerogative, from time to time, like old retainers ransacking the attic for some forgotten relic, whenever they are confronted with a situation in which they feel they need to act and for which they have no statutory authority. No one can predict with any certainty whether the courts will approve their action. That is not, surely, the way to run a country.

Stephen Sedley has criticized the incorporation of the European Convention or the enactment of a Charter of Rights on the ground that it may 'ensure that ... those with the sharpest elbows and loudest voices ... are continually at the head of the queue for the enforcement of *their* entrenched rights'. That may be so, and it will be necessary to create some agency along the lines of the Equal Opportunities Commission, or the Human Rights Commission envisaged in the IPPR constitution. An option to create such a Commission was considered in the White Paper *Rights Brought Home: The Human Rights Bill* (October 1997), but was, unhappily, rejected. There is, undoubtedly a need that others, besides victims, should be able to bring proceedings, particularly in a period of reduced legal aid funding. Without a Commission, there is a risk that only the most powerful victims of breaches of the Convention will be able to sue.[46] Such a risk does not detract from the value of establishing a set of principles by which executive decisions may be judged, and for breach of which ministers and administrators may be held to account in the courts.

NOTES AND REFERENCES

1. Plumb J.H., *The Growth of Political Stability in England 1675–1725* (1967) pp. 178, 188.
2. Drewry G., 'Revolution in Whitehall: the Next Steps and beyond' in Jowell J. and Oliver D., *The Changing Constitution* (1994) pp. 156–9.
3. *The Times*, 16 May 1929, quoted by Lord Hewart in *The New Despotism* (1929), p. 159.
4. Atiyah, P.S., *The Rise and Fall of Freedom of Contract* (1979) p. 13, quoted by Harden I. and Lewis N., *The Noble Lie: the British Constitution and the Rule of Law* (1986) p. 31.
5. *De l'Esprit des Lois*, Livre 2, C. 4; Locke J., *Second Treatise on Government* (Laslett P., ed., 1960) p. 365; Vile, M.J.C., *Constitutionalism and the Separation of Powers* (1967).
6. Marshall G. and Moodie G.C., *Some Problems of the Constitution* (5th edn, 1971) p. 37, quoted by Munro C.R., *Studies in Constitutional Law* (1987) pp. 36–7.
7. Marshall G., *Constitutional Conventions* (1994), quoted by Oliver D., 'Law, politics and public accountability' [1995] *Public Law*, 238, 246.
8. Riddell P., 'Too many junior ministers chasing too little work', *The Times*, 14 February 1995.
9. *Local Government Board* v. *Arlidge* [1915] AC 120; Dicey, A.V., 'The

development of administrative law in England' (1915) 31 LQR 148, 152. Sir Frederick Pollock added the following somewhat over-sanguine comment to Dicey's article: 'As to the Cabinet being secured by the support of a party majority, it has to be remembered that all party majorities become minorities sooner or later, and that one of the surest ways in which any Government can hasten that process is to acquire a reputation for arbitrary interference with ordinary rights' (*ibid.*, p. 153).

10. [1911] KB 410.

11. Lord Hailsham, reproduced in Lively J. and Lively A. (eds) *Democracy in Britain: a Reader* (1994) p. 58.

12. Jenkins S., *Accountable to None: the Tory Nationalization of Britain* (1995) p. 267.

13. Prosser T., 'Democratisation, accountability and institutional design: reflections on public law', in McAuslan P. and McEldowney J.F. (eds), *Law, Legitimacy and the Constitution* (1985) pp. 192, 193.

14. Jenkins, *op. cit.*, p. 258; Jenkins S., 'School for control freaks', *The Times*, 25 October 1995.

15. Speech to Charter 88, reported in *The Times*, 15 March 1995; Jenkins *op. cit.*, n. 12, p. 34.

16. Erskine May, *Parliamentary Practice* (21st edn) pp. 287–94.

17. *Report of the Inquiry into the Export of Defence Equipment etc.*, Sir Richard Scott (1996) Cmnd 115, Vol. IV, para. K8.2; HC 27 (1993–1994) Vol. 1, para. 132.

18. Sir Robin Butler in evidence to the Scott Inquiry, Transcript, Day 62, 9 February 1994, pp. 22–6, Scott Report Vol. IV, para. K8.15. The 1994 Treasury and Civil Service Select Committee expressed its disagreement with the distinction: Report (1993–1994) Vol. 1, paras 132, 133.

19. *The Times*, 13 May 1996.

20. Bogdanor V., 'Ministers, civil servants and the constitution: a revolution in Whitehall', *IALS Bulletin*, 15 October 1993.

21. *Carltona Ltd* v. *Commissioner of Works* [1943] 2 All ER 560; *Racz* v. *Home Office* [1994] 1 All ER 97.

22. [1985] 1 WLR 1242.

23. Harden I. and Lewis N. *The Noble Lie: the British Constitution and the Rule of Law* (1986) p. 119.

24. Mackintosh J.P., *The Government and Politics of Britain* (5th edn, 1982) p. 138; Austin R., 'Freedom of information: the constitutional impact', in Jowell J. and Oliver D. (eds), *The Changing Constitution* (3rd edn, 1994) p. 395.

25. See Ministry of Reconstruction, *Report of the Machinery of Government Committee*, Cd 9230 (HMSO, 1918), p. 15; Jennings I.W., *Parliamentary Reform*, New Fabian Research Bureau (1934) pp. 140–60. As adopted by the Procedure Committee, see Select Committee on Procedure (Session 1977–8), First Report, Vol. 1, *Reports and Minutes of Proceedings*, HC 588-I (HMSO, 1978); Hennessy P., *Muddling Through* (1996) pp. 63, 64.

26. Hennessy, *op. cit.*, pp. 64, 68.

27. *Ibid.*, p. 65.

28. Wynn Davies P., 'Deposed health chairman condemns "dictatorship"', 'Payroll vote stifles rebellion', *The Independent*, 14 July 1992.

29. Hennessy P., *op. cit.*, p. 67.

30. *Ibid.*, p. 70.
31. *Ibid.*, p. 78.
32. An Efficiency Scrutiny Report Commissioned by the President of the Board of Trade, July 1993, para. 4.14.
33. Bogdanor V., 'Britain and the European Community', in Jowell and Oliver, *op. cit.*, p. 9.
34. *The Intergovernmental Conference 1996: the Agenda. Democracy and Efficiency: the Role of National Parliaments*, 24th report, Vol. 1, Select Committee on European Legislation, Session 1994–1995, HMSO.
35. Burke E., 'The MP as Representative: speech to the electors of Bristol', in Lively and Lively *op. cit.*, p. 62.
36. Jennings I., *Parliament* (2nd edn, 1970) p. 27; Ponting C., *The Right to Know: the Inside Story of the Belgrano Affair* (1985) pp. 136, 137.
37. Thucydides, *The Peleponnesian War* (trans. Warner R., 1954) pp. 118–19.
38. Selbourne D., *The Principle of Duty: an Essay on the Foundations of the Civic Order* (1994) p. 211.
39. Loughlin M., 'Courts and governance', Paper delivered to SPTL seminar, 'Frontiers of Liability III; the Limits of Judicial Review', 23 January 1993.
40. Eyal J., 'Conspiracy of silence', *The Guardian*, 28 November 1996.
41. Desai M., Professor of Economics, LSE, in a letter to *The Independent*, 24 October 1995.
42. Shutt H., *The Myth of Free Trade: Patterns of Protectionism since 1945* (1985) pp. 184–5.
43. Sedley S., 'The sound of silence' (1994) 110 LQR 270, 282.
44. *Council of Civil Service Unions* v. *Minister for the Civil Service* [1985] AC 374.
45. *R.* v. *Ministry of Defence ex p. Smith* [1995] 4 All ER 427, QBD; *R.* v. *Secretary of State for Defence ex p. Sancto, The Times*, 9 September 1992, QBD.
46. Article 26. *A Written Constitution for the United Kingdom*, Institute for Public Policy Research (1991); *Rights Brought Home: The Human Rights Bill. CM 3782* para. 3.10. Sir Robert Fellowes, the Queen's Press Secretary, has indicated that he will seek to use the Convention to obtain injunctions to prevent the press from inquiring into the private lives of the royal family; Norton Taylor R., 'Gagging Orders abuse of power', *Guardian*, 3rd November 1997.

11

From Subjecthood to Citizenship

In its most neutral sense 'citizen' means no more than 'an inhabitant of a city', but from the time of the old Greek city-states it came to refer to a status which carried with it a bundle of rights and duties. Aristotle saw it in essentially political terms. For him, a citizen was simply one who had a share in 'both ruling and being ruled'.[1] Whatever attributes are given to citizenship, they are, broadly, either active or passive in character. In other words, they either require or enable a citizen to participate in the life of the state in a number of different ways, or they entitle him or her to be treated according to certain principles which might, for example, include equality before the law and an entitlement to certain welfare benefits. The content of citizenship is essentially open-ended. It probably has a core of rights and entitlements on which most would agree, but thereafter, its definition becomes a matter of political choice. 'The particular interpretation of citizenship taken by each person will reflect his or her ideology in general about the proper relationship between the individual and society.'[2]

Citizenship, in its modern sense, is a republican concept and derives from the Enlightenment, the French Revolution and the republican constitutions which followed in the path of armies of the First Republic. In its later manifestations in the constitutional monarchies of Europe, it was grafted on to the much older feudal notions of mutual duties of allegiance and protection which subsisted between monarch and subject. It is this last process which has formed the basis of its development in the UK. It has continued to evolve and has recently become very much part of the currency of the political debate about the relationship between state and individual, and in connection with proposals for constitutional reform. In the context of the European Union, a new dimension has been added in the shape of European Union citizenship, which, although at present lacking in much content, is likely to have a growing impact on the national citizenship debate.

Citizenship has been classically defined by T.H. Marshall as comprising three main components: civil, political and social.

> The civil element is composed of the rights necessary for individual freedom – liberty of the person, freedom of speech, thought and faith, the right to own property and to conclude valid contracts, and the right to justice. The last is of a different order from the others because it is the right to defend and assert all one's rights on terms of equality with others and by due process of law. This shows us that the institutions most directly associated with civil rights are the courts of justice.
>
> By the political element I mean the right to participate in the exercise of political power, as a member of a body invested with political authority or as an elector of the members of such a body. The corresponding institutions are Parliament and councils of local government.
>
> By the social element I mean the whole range from the right to a modicum of economic welfare and security to the right to share to the full in the social heritage and to live the life of a civilised being according to the standards prevailing in the society. The institutions most closely connected with it are the education system and the social services.[3]

These three categories require some modification but they are broad enough to include most concepts of citizenship and they still represent the best analysis so far made. They have, however, been criticized as deficient in three aspects, namely that they fail to address the need for individual and collective identity, a common culture and obligations and responsibilities. Whether these are, or ought to be, essential elements of citizenship in either the United Kingdom or the European Union will be dealt with in the context of the relevant elements of citizenship identified by Marshall.

The debate on citizenship has generated a growing body of literature, and has ranged widely over economic, political and legal issues affecting the position of individuals in the modern state, the nature of community, interdependence and autonomy.[4] This chapter will, however, concentrate on the way in which national views on citizenship in the United Kingdom have been moulded by our constitutional, political, economic and social development, and, in particular, by the relationship between individuals and the Crown in its many manifestations.

CIVIL CITIZENSHIP

One of the consequences of Britain's very gradual evolution from absolute to constitutional monarchy has been that until as recently as 1983, British people were defined in terms of their nationality as 'subjects' rather than 'citizens'. Although the British Nationality Act 1981 abolished subject status for all but a handful of individuals, the ideology of subject status permeates the common law, and the whole relationship of state and citizen in this country. It appears, most obviously, in the Oath of Allegiance which those who become British Citizens, British Dependent Territories Citizens, British Overseas Citizens and British subjects have to swear, 'I, A.B., swear by Almighty God that, on becoming [a British citizen, etc.] I will be faithful and bear true allegiance to Her Majesty Queen Elizabeth the Second Her Heirs and Successors according to law.' Judges, magistrates, bishops, Privy Councillors and Members of Parliament all also take an oath of allegiance to the Queen and her successors.

Although 'the Crown' has come to be the term which is used to represent the executive and even, in some circumstances, the state in the United Kingdom, the oath involves neither. Nor does it involve, as it does in so many countries, a promise to defend and support the laws and the constitution. The Privy Councillors, who hold the greatest range of political and legal powers in the land, promise 'to keep secret all matters revealed unto' them and to 'assist and defend all Jurisdictions, Pre-eminences, and Authorities granted to [Her Majesty] and annexed to the Crown by Acts of Parliament or otherwise, And Generally in all things ... [that they] will do as a faithful and true Servant ought to [Her Majesty].' It is a promise of faith and allegiance to the present monarch and her successors, and is delivered kneeling, holding the Bible, kissing the hand of the Queen and retiring from the room by moving backwards in a bowing position. These oaths are much more than mere symbolism. 'Underpinning the constitutional arrangements of the Crown is a hidden written constitution – the network of ancient oaths of allegiance to the Crown.'[5]

Allegiance does not entail very much, except in wartime, when even the wrongful possession of a passport by someone who was not a British subject was held to impose a duty of loyalty, breach of which amounted to capital treason. In *Calvin's* case in 1608,[6] the court defined the relationship by the Latin maxim *protectio trahit subjectionem et subjectio protectionem*: protection draws the subject and the subject protection. This meant, at common law, that those who were subjects were entitled to protection from (and to a limited extent, by) the Crown and in return subjects were obliged to abide by the laws of the UK, particularly those relating to treason and sedition. The maxim is an old one, and appears to derive from a passage in Glanville as to the relationship between the landlord and his tenant by homage. 'The result was to make subjecthood a passive or negative status ... No rights of a permanent or fundamental or contractual kind arose from the subject's status, yet it carried permanent obligations which could not be shaken off.'[7] 'Allegiance implied a duty of unquestioning obedience and loyalty and the lack of any right to question one's ruler. The individual was subject to arbitrary power, in the sense that the King could make many laws by proclamation without obtaining the consent of Parliament, and he could suspend or dispense with the law to favour certain classes or individuals.'

The power to make law by proclamation is gone, and there have been changes in the way in which prerogative and statutory powers are used, but the dispensation from the effect of statutes in relation to certain favoured groups of taxpayers and immigrants is still with us. The pattern of thinking that *Calvin* set is still far from dead and was reflected in a section of the Green Paper on British Nationality Law published in 1977:

(f) Civic privileges

66. An important aspect of citizenship is the privileges associated with it. In this country the common status of British subject, held in our law not only by citizens of the United Kingdom and Colonies but by all other Commonwealth citizens, carries with it voting and other privileges.[8]

Note that citizenship was not distinguished from subjecthood and was perceived as having *privileges*, not rights, attached to it. Nowhere in the statute book are there enumerated even the *privileges* to which those who have either British citizenship or subjecthood are entitled. The negative aspect of subjecthood is best illustrated by the fact that its benefits are almost entirely definable in the way in which subjects do not suffer the disabilities of aliens. Unlike aliens, they can vote in parliamentary and local elections, they can stand for Parliament, they can take up an appointment in the Civil Service and they may be the owners of a British ship. The only positive right specifically attaching to British citizens is the right of entry to and abode in the United Kingdom conferred by the Immigration Act 1971. This right is not, however, possessed by British Overseas Citizens, who have no right of entry to or residence in the United Kingdom, or anywhere else for that matter, or British Dependent Territory Citizens, who have a right of entry and residence in the colony through which they acquired their citizenship, but no rights in relation to the United Kingdom.

British Overseas Citizenship is not, in fact, citizenship at all, but a national label for the purposes of immigration law and Britain's obligations under international law in relation to statelessness.[9] Nationality is the external face of citizenship in most West European states, but in the United Kingdom there is no internal aspect. It will also be recalled from Chapter 4 that those who have British citizenship have, under United Kingdom law, no right to a passport, which is issued at the discretion of the executive under the royal prerogative. The White Paper on British nationality published in 1980 made the position clear: 'people holding the new citizenship would be *eligible* to have passports describing them accordingly', while the British government 'would be entitled to afford consular protection'.[10] There is no right to protection. It is entirely in the discretion of the government whether or not to provide it.

All the apparently fundamental *rights* which Marshall describes in his first category – liberty of the person, property ownership, freedom of speech, thought and faith, the right to contract and the right to justice – are, in one sense at least, no more than privileges. The effect of the Revolutionary Settlement of 1688 was to transfer the remains of the absolute power of the monarchy to Parliament. Parliament had in the course of the sixteenth and seventeenth centuries acquired most of those powers, but under the 1688 Settlement, those powers became absolute. The Crown-in-Parliament became more powerful than the Crown had ever been in its own right. The consequence is, of course, that all the rights described can at any time be taken away by the narrowest of parliamentary votes. Some of them have been removed in time of war. Removal in peacetime would put this country in breach of its obligations under the European Convention on Human Rights, but there would be nothing to stop Parliament, under the present constitution, from negating the effects of the Convention by Act of Parliament, in exactly the same way as its provisions are now being incorporated. In this sense, at least, all the civil rights and liberties we possess are at the whim of what a Parliament may, at any one time, choose to do. This is an inevitable consequence of parliamentary sovereignty. Parliamentary sovereignty must, however, give way to political reality. As long as British membership of the European Union continues (and there is no viable alternative on offer at present), rights derived from Community law, such as freedom from discrimination on grounds of nationality, the right of men and women to be paid equal wages for work of equal value and the right to go to another member state to look for work under Articles 6, 119 and 48 of the EC Treaty, are rights to which the courts of the United Kingdom must give effect and which the United Kingdom Parliament cannot repeal. The loss of sovereignty of Parliament in these spheres has resulted in the protection or entrenchment of those rights. The obvious implication which a number of advocates of major constitutional reform have drawn is that loss of parliamentary sovereignty is a price that we shall have to pay if our other nationally based 'rights' are to be protected.

In a legal sense, many of the civil 'rights' we enjoy are no more than liberties. Even the *right* to personal liberty which British subjects are supposed to share with 'local subjects' – that is, aliens resident in the country – is not unqualified. Besides the obvious and necessary qualifications which are recognized by the European Convention, such as the detention of criminals and those suspected of committing criminal offences, illegal immigrants and those suffering mental illness, we have seen that the prerogative may allow the Crown to detain subjects in order to prevent them from leaving the country for some reason of public policy, to use force to conscript seamen into the royal navy and to arrest and expel friendly aliens who have committed no crime and are regarded at common law as 'local subjects', but whose presence is thought by a minister of the Crown not to be 'conducive to the public good'. These powers of the Crown may or may not be upheld by the courts, depending on the circumstances in which the Crown may claim to use them.

Property rights are probably more secure in the UK than any other, but the courts have shown an indulgence to trespasses committed by the police in pursuit of evidence which runs wholly contrary to the rule of law, and successive Home Secretaries have 'sanctioned' the placing of bugging devices on private premises when neither statute nor common law enabled them to do so.[11] The Police Act is said to put the placing of such devices on 'a statutory basis', as though it *had* some other legal basis before! It also appears from reports that emerged from the security services in the *Spycatcher* cases, summarized in Chapter 5, that some senior members of the services were engaged in extensive bugging and burglary operations that were wholly illegal, although Lord Donaldson, Master of the Rolls, came to the extraordinary conclusion that it was 'absurd' to claim that every breach of the law by the security services amounted to a 'wrongdoing'.[12] It would seem that, in some circumstances, at least, the security services and the police are seen by the courts to be above the law, although comments by members of the senior judiciary on the Police Bill seem to indicate that this is a far from universal view. Property rights are narrowly construed by the common law, and privacy, particularly in relation to family life, has no protection under the common law, although that position will change once the Convention is incorporated.

Freedom of speech, thought and faith are no more than freedoms. They are never absolutes in any constitution, but under the common law, the restrictions which are accepted as necessary in any liberal democracy are unclear and unpredictable. They are not, in any sense, *rights*. There is some protection of religious beliefs, but only those of the established church. We live in a society with a great diversity of faiths, but only one, the Church of England, of which the Queen is the Head, is protected by the law of blasphemy.[13] This is not the place to explore the scope of freedom of expression, but censorship has been associated with the Crown for centuries. Originally a function of the church courts, it was taken over by the Council of State in the sixteenth century. The courts have inherited from the Star Chamber a residual, and wholly anomalous, role of creating common law offences to effect a form of censorship where none exists under statute.[14] Even after the abolition of the Star Chamber, which operated an extensive system of censorship of books and pamphlets, censorship of plays by the Royal Chamberlain, a Palace official, continued, at first under the royal prerogative, and later under the Theatres Act 1843 until it was abolished by Parliament by the Theatres Act 1968.[15] Censorship was not confined to matters which were deemed to be obscene. No representations of reigning monarchs were permitted on stage and irreverent references to fascist dictators were suppressed throughout the 1930s. Even in 1939 a revue song was banned by the Lord Chamberlain on account of its opening line: 'Even Hitler had a mother'.

There is a kind of bossy paternalism about English censorship. It has the two principal aims of suppressing criticism or mockery of those in authority, on the one hand, and protecting the lower classes against exposure to reading and other material which their weak and untutored minds would be unable to resist, on the other. In the early days of printing, the royal prerogative was used to license printers and to destroy heretical tracts. After the abolition of licensing at the end of the seventeenth century, the task was taken up by the common law courts. It was not until 1857 that the country acquired its first Obscene Publications Act. Printing and almost universal literacy had, by the beginning of the twentieth century, opened the possibility of contagion to a great number. In the first twentieth century obscenity case, the Common Sergeant of the Old Bailey was confidently able to assert that a book which sold at 1s 11d. would 'clearly tend to corrupt the morals ... In the Middle Ages things were discussed which if put forward now for the reading of the general public would never be tolerated.'[16]

Parliament has laid down restrictions on the disclosure of official information under the Official Secrets Acts, some of which have been considered in Chapter 7 in relation to the Civil Service. The previously blank prohibition on disclosure has been replaced by a less all-embracing regime under the Official Secrets Act 1989. A considerable relaxation has also occurred in the use of Public Interest Immunity certificates and some effort has been made to enable citizens to be better informed through a greater emphasis on openness in the White Paper on Open Government. All these steps fall a long way short of a Freedom of Information Act. There is still a culture of secrecy in Whitehall and a reluctance to include the public in debates which precede the making of policy decisions. 'The root of the problem in Britain is that we have a deeply secretive society in which access to official information is very tightly controlled and parcelled out in small bits to the favoured few that suits the person giving it. There is a presupposition in favour of secrecy where, in a fully democratic system, there should be a presupposition in favour of openness.'[17] As we have seen in relation to ministerial responsibility and the work of select committees in Parliament, there is still much information that will not be disclosed. Freedom of information is an integral part of freedom of expression and, as Geoffrey Robertson has observed, 'is becoming almost a defining characteristic of accountable democratic government elsewhere in the world, at a time when it is implacably opposed by the British Government and its senior bureaucrats'.[18]

Marshall emphasized the role of the courts in the protection of civil rights. Dicey laid great stress on the efficacy of legal remedies as against the high-minded declarations of foreign constitutions. 'The Habeas Corpus Acts have ... done for the liberty of Englishmen more than could have been achieved by any declaration of rights.'[19] But the argument can be overstated. While effective legal remedies are crucial in upholding the maintenance of civil rights, they are not, in themselves, a sufficient guarantee. As we have seen in our discussion of the use of the prerogative in time of war, and in the very wide powers given to ministers under the Defence of the Realm Act in 1914–18 and under the War Powers (Defence) Act 1939, the prerogative is wide enough and Parliament is quite capable of framing statutory discretions which are as wide, and which put them beyond effective control and review by the courts. Dicey tended to ignore the prerogative in his discussion of the subjection of officials to the rule of law, to minimize the significance of statutory discretion and to reject the need for the development of administrative or public law principles.

As we have seen, the twentieth century has seen an immense increase in the development of state power. That has been accompanied by the creation of a wide variety of legal powers and an even greater variety of agencies which have been granted jurisdiction to exercise public law powers. The new agencies include central government and the Next Steps agencies, local authorities, nationalized industries, quangos of various kinds and a number of private bodies, such as the former utilities, which exercise some public powers and are subject to varying degrees of regulatory control. This diversity has created problems of political account-ability which have been discussed in Chapter 10, but it also raises issues about the enforcement of civil rights.

The diversity of agencies exists in a context of a whole mass of legal and quasi-legal rules, and contractual and semi-contractual relationships, all of which may affect the exercise of civil rights. Traditional legal theory works on the assumption that substantive rules of public law must be found exclusively in formal rules of law statutes, statutory instruments, cases and European law. Many legal writers now recognize the inadequacy of such a view.[20] In recent years there has been a rapid increase in the range of non-statutory rules, codes of guidance, discretionary codes, ministerial circulars and directives, agency rules and European Union programmes which are treated as 'rules' even though they do not directly have the force of law. If we take the position of people suffering disabilities, for example, they may experience difficulties exercising rights across the whole range of Marshall's paradigm. Liberty of the person will mean little to someone who is trapped in his or her home because buildings or public transport facilities make access impossible. Contractual rights will have little content if people with disabilities are denied the possibility of contracting for employment or services.[21]

The Disability Discrimination Act 1996 was intended to give a right of action to anyone suffering discrimination on the grounds of disability in relation to the provision of goods and services. The Act makes it unlawful to discriminate against disabled people in employment or the provision of goods, facilities and services. It creates important new rights for the disabled, and imposes corresponding duties on employers and others. The rights are enjoyed only by those who are disabled within the meaning of the Act. To be disabled, the individual must have a physical or mental impairment which has a 'substantial and long-term adverse effect on his ability to carry out normal day-to-day activities'. The courts and industrial tribunals have to decide whether claimants satisfy this substantial adverse effect test when they sue for unlawful disability discrimination. They will also have to decide whether the action of an employer, or other person or body against whom a claim is made, have caused the claimant a substantial disadvantage.

In deciding both whether a person is in fact disabled and whether he or she has been discriminated against, courts and tribunals will have to apply a complex web of regulations, two codes of practice and a guidance issued by the Department of Education and Employment. Unlike government circulars, the guidance is not simply administrative. Where it operates, it will determine whether individuals have legally enforceable rights or duties, and whether particular conduct is or is not contrary to the law of the land. The guidance does not, unlike the regulations, have to be laid before Parliament. The only safeguards are that the minister must consult 'such persons as he considers appropriate' before issuing the guidance. There is no legal aid to assist claimants in industrial tribunals. The new National Disability Council (NDC) set up by the Act has a role which is advisory only. Unlike its counterparts under the race and sex discrimination law, the NDC cannot enforce the law. The effect of the legislation is to create 'rights' which have a variable content and which are not subject to a system of effective control and scrutiny, which are not clearly defined and which cannot, in practice, be enforced in tribunals except by claimants who can pay for their own legal representation.[22]

Problems arise in Marshall's first category of civil rights not only because they are not clearly defined, or because the agencies which affect their exercise are numerous and their legal status complex, but because of the uncertain relationship between citizenship rights and nationality. We have already noted that, in law, citizenship in the United Kingdom is little more than nationality with rights of entry and residence. Other rights which only attach to British citizens can be identified from legislation which excludes specific rights from aliens, such as the right to vote or to be considered for employment in the Civil Service, or the duty to serve on a jury. Most minimum civil rights in this category overlap with the minimum rights contained in the European Convention on Human Rights. It is widely assumed that, in most cases, as far as both civil and human rights are concerned, citizenship/nationality is not relevant. All that is required for a person to enjoy the protection of such basic rights is to be within the country. This is broadly true, but the provisions of the Asylum and Immigration Act 1996 deny people who are lawfully in the United Kingdom, and who have made an application for asylum after they have entered it, any right to welfare benefits. As far as the state is concerned, there is no obligation to provide even the most minimal subsistence. The English courts have described the removal of subsistence rights as 'not the action of a civilised country', and have refused to accept that asylum claimants should be left destitute.[23] Economic rights are not, of course, part of the catalogue of basic civil rights, but without them the exercise of civil rights becomes impossible. Denial of subsistence to those who are pursuing rights of appeal against refusal of asylum has been justly criticized as an attempt to deny the individuals concerned their right of access to the courts. Although ministers have insisted that this is a matter of ordinary domestic policy with regard to entitlement to benefits, denial of subsistence could be regarded as 'degrading treatment' under Article 3 of the European Convention and could even result in denial of the right to life.

Citizenship and nationality are about exclusion as well as inclusion. Citizenship is about identity and belonging. It is 'a status bestowed on all those who are full members of a community. Citizenship requires a direct sense of community membership based on loyalty to a civilisation which is a common possession.' In the British tradition, that loyalty and that belonging were epitomized by a personal loyalty to the monarch.

As the Kingdom grew the personal link between King and subject disappeared and was replaced by a symbolic loyalty to the more symbolic Crown. Subjects owed allegiance and, as we have noted, could expect protection. Aliens owed their allegiance elsewhere, and the protection they received was qualified by their continuing loyalty and presence within the kingdom. Their ambiguous position was reflected in their rights in relation to employment and property and to litigate to protect them. Initially, aliens were not able to own property, and therefore could not bring an action to recover land. Anyone who sold land to an alien effectively forfeited it to the King. Later, aliens were allowed to own moveable property and could bring an action in tort to protect their chattels and their persons. Aliens have only very gradually improved their position as litigants at common law. The courts have acted as gatekeepers on the borders between excluded and resident alien, and between resident alien and subject. The rights of aliens to both liberty and property have been directly affected by the way in which they were seen to have a lesser status than subjects. The effect could be most serious where state security was seen to be involved. As J.M. Evans observed in 1983:

> The reluctance of the courts to challenge the Executive's
> exercise of statutory powers on matters touching national
> security may . . . have been reinforced by the Crown's claim that
> the exclusion and expulsion of aliens was within its prerogative,
> the scope of which was never definitely established in the
> courts, but which still maintains a shadowy existence alongside
> contemporary statutory controls . . . Aliens refused admission
> owed no allegiance and could not expect the protection of the

law; resident aliens, on the other hand, did owe 'local allegiance' and were entitled to the protection of the common law whilst they were on British territory, subject, apparently, to the Crown's prerogative of summary expulsion.[24]

H.W.R. Wade has also noted that 'the courts have shown a marked reluctance to extend to aliens the same principles of procedural protection and fair play that apply to citizens of this country. Public policy requires that the Home Secretary should have drastic powers of deportation, refusal of entry and so forth. But there is no necessary reason why these, like other drastic powers over citizens generally, should not be required to be exercised fairly, particularly since the consequences for the alien are often extremely severe.' More recently the courts have shown some inclination to make decisions involving the liberty of foreign nationals in a way that more closely resembles the approach adopted towards subjects and citizens. In *R. v. Secretary of State for the Home Department ex p. Khawaja* in 1985, Lord Scarman roundly declared that 'every person within the jurisdiction enjoys the equal protection of our laws. There is no distinction between British nationals and others. He who is subject to English law is entitled to its protection'.

In terms of access to civil rights by aliens, a more recent decision of the Court of Appeal is even more significant. The grant of nationality was, originally, a prerogative of the Crown. Aliens were made 'denizens' by letters patent by grant under the royal seal, having taken the oath of allegiance. Such grants were at the complete discretion of the monarch, and usually contained specific benefits, such as 'licence for [the grantee] to dwell within the realm for the term of his life'.

Since 1844, foreign nationals have been able to acquire British nationality by a process created by statute. There is still a wide discretion exercisable by the Home Secretary. Applicants seem to have been refused nationality for any reason and none. In the 1930s a clear policy of anti-semitism prevailed in the Home Office, and Jews were required to complete a much longer period of residence than northern Europeans.[25] Under the British Nationality Act 1981 applicants, who must satisfy certain criteria, including a residence condition and being of good character, may be granted nationality by the Home Secretary 'if he thinks fit', and the Act provides that the Home Secretary 'shall not be required to assign any reason for the grant or refusal ... and the decision ... shall not be subject to appeal to, or review in, any court'.

The brothers Mohammed Al Fayed and Ali Al Fayed, Egyptian nationals, major shareholders in Harrods and long-term UK residents, were denied naturalization by Michael Howard, then Home Secretary, in 1995. No reasons were given, but the brothers suspected, rightly or wrongly, that the refusal was not wholly unrelated to information which they had supplied to the newspapers in connection with the 'cash for questions' investigation in the House of Commons. Surprisingly, despite the clear wording of the Act, the Court of Appeal decided that, although the Home Secretary did not have to give reasons for the decision *after* it was made, he had a discretion whether or not to give reasons *before* the decision was made as to why he was minded to refuse the application, so that the applicants would have an opportunity to rebut any false assumptions on which the final decision might be based. The Master of the Rolls said that the decision was of such importance to the applicants that it displaced the general common law rule that administrators did not have to give reasons for their decisions. The refusal of naturalization 'deprived them of the substantial benefits of citizenship, such as freedom from immigration control, citizenship of the European Union and its accompanying rights, and the right to vote and stand in parliamentary elections'.[26]

The decision is remarkable, not only in the fact that it appears to defeat the clear attempt by Parliament to exclude judicial review, but also because the decision comes to the aid of two aliens who have no right to be granted nationality, even if they meet the criteria laid down in the Act. At best, they only had an expectation that they might be granted it.

Citizenship is, in part, about belonging to a society. It is also about participating in the life of the community and in the political process. The content of the civil rights which are part of that citizenship has largely been defined by the courts and developed through the common law. In a society without a written constitution there are no fundamental rights. There are the liberties we have described, and the rights to personal property and security which are protected by the common law. In the preceding chapters we have considered the scope of those rights where the Crown is involved. We have seen that, although the courts have developed a body of case law which improves on the old common law rules on the legal accountability of officers of the Crown, they are still far from being subject to the same degree of control and review, or liability in tort or contract, as the rest of the community. Further, other aspects of our civil rights depend on presumptions and rules of interpretation by the courts. It has been argued that these reflect some, at least, of the fundamental rights which are enshrined in the constitutions of other West European states.

These include a presumption against retrospective legislation, especially in criminal matters, a requirement of particular precision in defining the scope of criminal liability and tax liability, and a presumption in favour of the protection of private property. The limited number and uncertain scope of these presumptions, which can be brushed aside by clear statutory drafting, illustrate the minimalist extent to which fundamental rights are recognised in our rather unclear constitutional arrangements.[27]

Perhaps the widest assumption made by the courts is that everything is permitted except that which is prohibited, but that goes for the state as well as for the individual.

PARTICIPATION IN THE POLITICAL PROCESS

'We are the freest country in the world. Our constitution is monarchical in form, and full of well-adjusted checks upon popular power, yet in its practical operation it gives more direct and immediate effect to the outspoken will of the people than in any republic.' This bold statement by the then Attorney-General, Sir John Lawson Walton, is contained in a preface to a book by Frederick Peaker entitled *British Citizenship: Its Rights and Duties*, published in 1906, and reflects the comfortable complacency of Edwardian Britain. Peaker's book rejoices in the fact that 'we can now, with truth, say that the people of England govern themselves, and that if they are not at any time well-governed they have nobody but themselves to blame. If citizens take an intelligent interest in citizenship and all that it means, there need be no fear that Britain, "the land of the free", will be the best and most justly governed nation on earth.'

The book is illuminating because it illustrates how closely attached concepts of citizenship are to the values and concerns of the time. It recognizes the civil rights discussed in the first part of this chapter, the political rights in Marshall's second category and even the social right which the citizen has, namely 'the right to live, to be fed, clothed and educated'. However, the fact that at least half the adult population was, at the time, without the franchise is not taken into account in the assertion that 'the people of England govern themselves'. Nor are the separate identities of the Scots, Welsh and Irish acknowledged. The 'British' and the 'English' are casually equated. The absence of the female franchise merits a passing mention. 'Women cannot vote in the election of a Member of Parliament, neither can idiots, persons convicted of crime, aliens or minors.'[28] Such blind spots are easy to recognize with the benefit of hindsight. The really difficult task is coming to grips with the depth and range of the problems presented by political citizenship in our own time.

Marshall identifies as 'political citizenship' the right to participate in the exercise of political power, either as a member of a body invested with political authority or as an elector of the members of such a body. The political process is, of course, much more complex than the deliberations of representative bodies, such as central and local government, and the processes of election to them. This is widely recognized, but lawyers, not unnaturally, tend to be concerned with rules and legal structures created by rules. As Carol Harlow has said, 'lawyers might be described as "flat-earthers" who have created for themselves a narrow, legal universe of "rules" and "rights" which they are reluctant to abandon. They prefer to seal off the world of political scientists, economists and sociologists, drawing arbitrary lines between matters political and matters legal.'[29] This is not a fault peculiar to lawyers, but any examination of political citizenship must take into account the broadest context in which rights of citizenship operate. Some attempt was made to do this in Chapter 10, and there is an obvious overlap between the exercise of political rights as a citizen and the extent of powers and duties of members of the executive. An examination of the legal rights of voters, for example, or the machinery of the electoral system under the Representation of the People Acts will tell you very little about the political process or the practical limits on the exercise of political power.

Marshall epitomized political participation by the work of the parliamentary or local government representative or through the casting of a vote by the elector in central or local government elections. Such a limited involvement seems far removed from effective political participation. The work of six hundred or more Members of Parliament in a chamber, or in committees which have become increasingly dominated by a combination of Cabinet government and the party machine, seems a poor sort of representation. Parliament has become a kind of electoral college, elected every four or five years, whose most important function is to elect the Prime Minister, who in turn appoints the Cabinet. Thereafter, the duty of members of the government party is to support their government and to ensure that it is maintained in power, come what may, until the next election.

In the late twentieth century we have arrived at a form of government which the American, James Madison, described in the eighteenth. Madison's principles of representative government, expressed with those of John Jay and Alexander Hamilton in *The Federalist Papers* (1787–93), were satisfied as soon as the members of government were appointed, either directly or indirectly, by the people. The power of actual decision-taking, the reality of political power, belonged to the government. A modern American political commentator has accurately described the system as a 'satisfying, persuasive and protective ideology for the minorities of wealth, status and power' against the 'popular majority'.[30]

The political oligarchy which our present system creates or renews every five years at Westminster, Lord Hailsham's 'elective dictatorship', is largely sustained by the ambitions of backbench supporters, and the fear of political oblivion that de-selection by the party would involve. Her Majesty's Loyal Opposition is enabled to endure the futility of opposition by the knowledge that it, too, will one day be able to wield as much absolute power as the reduced economic and political circumstances of the British state can deliver. The pleasures of ministerial office, the official car and the deference of Sir Humphrey can all be anticipated with relish.

As we have seen in Chapter 10, local government, which has been stripped of so much of its power over the past twenty years, is viewed with either hostility or indifference by many local electors. This may be a reflection of an appreciation by voters of how little can be accomplished at local level when central government has such an overwhelmingly dominant role, of the generally poor quality of both local representatives and local government officers, and of the entrenched position enjoyed by some parties in the town halls. There is a widespread perception by the people that the system is not working. Any solution will have to embrace what Dawn Oliver has identified as the three central objectives of accountability, effectiveness and citizenship.[31] Our focus is on citizenship and the relationship between the political rights and duties of citizens and the exercise of power by the executive.

This is not the place to make a detailed exploration of solutions, but a number of steps have been suggested which seem to offer a more real political involvement by citizens. At local level, power needs to be returned to local government.

> Courage must be found to return to local democracy much of
> the autonomy taken from it in the past two decades ...
> Functions and powers could revert to elected rather than
> appointed bodies – powers to raise revenue, set services
> standards and monitor them locally. No country in Europe,
> indeed few in the world, have as little autonomy vested in
> subordinate local institutions as has Britain. Even Margaret

Thatcher's favourite philosopher, Hayek, was emphatic on this point: 'Nowhere has democracy worked well without a great measure of local self-government, providing a school of political training for the people at large as much as for their future leaders.'[32]

Citizens could also become more involved in the day-to-day decision-making process. 'Participation' should be in the process of government as much as in the process of selection of governments. Simon Jenkins has put it most trenchantly: 'Citizenship is not a matter of exercising consumer choice of products and services where permitted, and voting once every four or five years. The ceaseless exercise of political freedom is not just a right: it is an obligation.'[33]

One way in which individuals can be involved is through the establishment of local 'citizens' juries'. The use of juries as a method of democratic consultation – instead of commissioning an opinion poll or holding a public meeting – was pioneered in the United States and Germany, and is attracting the attention of the Labour Party. German and American jurors have been involved in such diverse decisions as approaches to the reduction in teenage abortions and the siting of power stations. In Cologne, jurors rejected the city council's entire range of choices for a new civic hall and insisted on a design featuring trees and an open space in front. The juries, which are known in Germany as planning cells, are used by local and national government to test public opinion on construction projects. They have passed judgment on such controversial questions as the routes of motorways and by-passes. American juries have tackled a wider range of subjects than their German counterparts. Nationally they have included President Clinton's health care reforms, and at state level, welfare policy and teenage crime.[34]

The system is open to the criticism that the juries are not selected by the people whose views they purport to represent, may not be a fair representation of public feeling and may be swayed by the way the case is presented to them. These problems can, at least partly, be addressed by ensuring that a genuine cross-section of the public is chosen and by enabling the jury to ask for information from alternative sources. The system does have the merit that, if it is widely used, it will have a considerable educational value in that most of the population will, at some time or other, have participated in a public decision-making process, and will have some idea of how public policy decisions are made and of the sort of factors which influence decision-makers.

Probably the most fundamental criticism that can be made against this type of 'participation' is that it can, of course, be ignored by decision-makers and it can have the appearance of involving citizens when the actual involvement is negligible. This has been the case with participation in planning policy since the days of the Skeffington Report in 1969, which has been described as 'the high-water mark of participatory theory in the English planning system'. Either little weight is attached to submissions to public planning inquiries or when such inquiries are held the crucial policy decisions have already been taken. 'Public participation' in planning was never conceptualized in terms of public law mechanisms for scrutiny and debate of policy, with the result that the instruments used remain discretionary and are ineffective in opening up the policy-making process before significant options have already been closed. The position was most effectively put by a leaflet which was circulated to local householders by protesters against the construction of a motorway in the Aire Valley in West Yorkshire in 1975. It parodied the public inquiry that was about to be held with the question: 'Do you want a motorway to be constructed (a) through your local school (b) through your public library or (c) through your back garden?[35]

The usual response to demands for public participation in policy decisions, either through securing information, so that citizens can make an effective contribution in the ordinary run of political debate, or by a more formal involvement by ordinary individuals in the decision-making process itself, is that politicians and officials are elected and appointed to make decisions and that they should be allowed to get on with it. Hard choices have to be made, and they cannot be made by individuals who may have conflicting financial and other interests. The argument sounds very like the demand made by Madison in the eighteenth century for a government by the elite. It is the same plea that Lord Reid made in 1968 in *Conway* v. *Rimmer* in favour of government secrecy in Whitehall and in support of claims of Crown privilege or public interest immunity. 'The business of government is difficult enough as it is, and no government could contemplate with equanimity the inner workings of the government machine being exposed to the gaze of those ready to criticise without adequate knowledge of the background and perhaps with some axe to grind.' We, as subjects, should be satisfied with the quality of government we get and not make the process of government even more difficult than it is.

David Williams rejected such arguments more than thirty years ago with an eloquence which will still evoke a response from anyone who would like to see a more effective political participation by citizens: 'A steady repetition of arguments about the need for frankness, about the value of a confidential relationship between Minister and civil servant, about the criteria of administrative efficiency, and so forth, has certainly helped the official view ... It has shifted the onus of proof. Those who wish to support publicity wherever possible have been thrown on the defensive. It seems to have been forgotten that in a democratic country the onus should be on those who support secrecy to justify their case.' Getting access to public information is, however, only the first step. Much work still needs to be done in devising ways in which citizens can participate effectively. The idea that ministers and civil servants sit in their ivory towers in Whitehall making decisions without any external intervention is now wholly incredible. They are lobbied in White-hall, Westminster and Brussels by an army of professional lobbyists and special interest groups. There is a clear need for people who have neither the time nor the money to apply that kind of pressure to be brought into the process. Citizens' juries, although obviously imperfect, may provide a useful starting point.

SOCIAL AND ECONOMIC CITIZENSHIP

The social and economic content of citizenship is not new. The belief that everyone in society was entitled to the basic wherewithal for survival, including food, clothing and shelter, was an argument familiar to Liberal collectivists of the turn of the century. The belief was central to Beveridge's welfare state.

It might be said that the new middle class in the seventeenth and eighteenth centuries had concentrated on legal rights, because the protection of their persons, property, right to contract and religious beliefs was their first priority. The Reform Bill and the extension of the franchise were the next step in a process of a broadening emancipation that was only concluded when votes were conferred on women on the same terms as for men in 1929. Neither civil nor legal rights are of much worth if individuals lack the means to live or to make their civil and political rights effective. The welfare state was, therefore, an essential step in the process of giving citizenship a meaning that went beyond the rather empty fusion of patriotism and civic duty. The courts ceased to be, in the famous words of Lord Jowett, 'open to all – like the Ritz hotel'. The Legal Aid Act 1949 enabled anyone who had a legal right to assert to take it to the courts. The great new mass of welfare rights, unemployment, child, sickness and industrial benefits, if denied, could be claimed in the new tribunals, which were open, informal and lawyer-free.

People – and the benefits were not, initially, confined to British subjects – were freed to take a more active part in their local communities. The whole post-1945 generation, taking advantage of the new opportunities offered by the 1944 Education Act, went on to become the new meritocracy in business and the civil service that was to forge the white heat of Harold Wilson's technological revolution of the 1960s. Yet the change was not as deep as it appeared. The Civil Service grew to administer the great new public utilities and the welfare state, but, as we have seen, Attlee shrank from its reform in 1945. The coal mine management that replaced the mine owners became as remote from the miners who now 'owned' their pits as the real owners had been before them. The South Metropolitan Gas Company became the South Eastern Gas Board. The board of directors of the old company became the new board. Little else changed except the name-plates. Morrisonian socialism was at worst distant, bureaucratic and unfeeling, and at best well meaning and paternalistic. The beneficiaries were the passive recipients of welfare. Tawney's idea of equality that inspired the post-war Labour government was preoccupied with a levelling of incomes. Little attempt was made to involve employees in industrial management. 'Sir Stafford Cripps was speaking both as a member of the upper class and of the Labour Government when he stated that workers simply did not have the necessary skills to participate in management.' Real attempts were made to redistribute wealth through the tax and benefit system, and a degree of consensus was achieved when the Conservatives returned to power in 1951. The welfare state became part of the nation's patrimony, but the net effect of all the reforms upon the social and political structure was minimal. It remained dominated by the public schools and Oxbridge. A 'left-wing', public school and Oxford educated jounalist has made the most withering comment. 'Far from introducing "social revolution" the overwhelming Labour victory of 1945 brought about the greatest restoration of social values since 1660. Complacency, parochialism, lack of serious structural change, these are sustainable charges.'[36]

The effect of the welfare reforms was to transform the physical quality of life for the majority of British people in housing, education and the social services. They became contributors to the new welfare system through the national insurance scheme and consumers of the new benefits and of the services provided by the new public utilities. Instead of individual provision, all put resources into the common pool, from which they could draw as and when the need arose. However, the welfare state could only last as long as it was seen to be 'affordable'. By the end of the 1970s, 'middle England', which had benefited so much from the welfare state, was affluent enough not to be so reliant upon it. The decline of the British economy in the 1970s, and the consequent under-investment in and increasing deterioration of the welfare system and the public services, resulted in a dissatisfaction felt by both those who worked in them and those who were supposed to be the beneficiaries, leading to strikes and a general air of crisis, epitomized by the 'winter of discontent' of 1978/9. The neo-liberals who came to power with the Conservative government elected in 1979 were committed to 'rolling back the frontiers of the state'. The epitome of what Mrs Thatcher called 'the nanny state' was the system of health and welfare provision. The welfare state was, however, still popular, although it could not be said to be entrenched. Throughout the 1980s it was therefore subjected not to a frontal assault, but to a gradual process of erosion. Will Hutton has identified the weakness of the welfare state in the face of this attack:

> [The welfare state] satisfies a vague sense of justice, so that the free National Health Service and universal pension, for example, are regarded as inviolable. But this moral sense is not buttressed by any tradition of social citizenship. In Britain we are 'subjects' of the Crown-in-Parliament, and there is therefore no citizenship tradition to draw upon. The welfare state is no more [than] a system of state social assistance, based on collective insurance and enacted by Labour when it had a parliamentary majority.'[37]

Marshall's idea of social citizenship is probably less embedded in our ideas of what is constitutionally 'right' than, say, our belief in the sanctity of personal liberty, property and the franchise, although these are also vulnerable to gradual erosion by parliamentary absolutism. It does, however, have a moral basis, which is an important and often neglected aspect of citizenship. Marshall tended to neglect 'national identity' as an aspect of citizenship, perhaps because he saw a tendency towards equality as being a characteristic of modern citizenship, and citizenship which draws strongly on 'identity' will tend to be exclusive rather than inclusive.

'Equality' is such a diffuse concept that it is not very helpful in the context of citizenship. In terms of civil rights, it means equality before the law. Though this is symbolically important, in practice lack of legal aid for so many, and in so many forums, makes it a right without much content. In relation to political rights, everyone's vote carries the same weight in theory, but in a first-past-the-post system the vast majority of votes have little effect on the final outcome. Only in 'social citizenship', with its assumptions about social obligations and redistributive justice, could it count for much. Citizenship was identified by the Speaker's Commission as the full participation of individuals in the communities to which they belong. For such participation to be effective it must recognize the contribution which each citizen can and ought to make, to the community of which he or she is part. That recognition must, surely, involve acceptance that all participants have all the necessities of life contemplated by 'social citizenship' to make their participation effective. That may involve some transfer of resources from those who have to those who have not, through the agency of the state. It does not, however, necessarily involve an attempt at complete redistribution of wealth. That may be a desirable goal for a socialist party but it is not a necessary condition of citizenship.

Social and political citizenship involves duties as well as rights. Those duties are based on the moral responsibility most people in all societies recognize that we owe to one another if our communities are to function. Social interdependence is crucial to effective participation and, therefore, effective citizenship, although economic equality is not.[38] Selbourne has strongly argued that the principle of duty 'is a positive ethical principle through whose observance the citizen is educated to his true status as a moral being and in turn gains greater moral worth thereby', and contrasts him or her with the lesser citizen 'in the corrupted liberal order' dominated by 'dutiless right and demand-satisfaction'.[39] There may be differences of view as to whether, or when, the moral imperative should drive the citizen to individual or collective action, but the moral view of citizenship tends to emphasize active participation in some form or other. Subjecthood emphasizes obedience. Citizenship, on the other hand, recognizes moral obligations to other members of the community and emphasizes responsiveness and participation.

A recent survey of citizenship in the national curricula of the fifteen states of the European Union is remarkable in that there is so little emphasis in the teaching requirements on the passive elements of loyalty, obedience and tradition, although six of the states are monarchies. The aims of citizenship courses in the Member States give priority to: 'active participation in a democratic society' (Denmark); 'mutual equality ... to function as active critical and responsible members of a society of citizens' (Finland); 'to instil the values of liberty ... democracy, tolerance, support a peaceful attitude internationally ... to awaken the willingness to act in the social interest and to accept political responsibility, to awaken the consciousness of a European identity' (Germany); 'Critical social-political consciousness' (the Netherlands); 'to know, understand and value from a critical perspective ... the human and social community at different levels' (Spain). Only the Austrian curriculum refers to 'loyalty to ... the democratic and Federal Republic of Austria' and the French to 'respect for the law, love of the Republic'. Even the curriculum for England and Wales refers only to 'positive, participative citizenship ... exploring, making informed decisions

... and exercising responsibilities and rights in a democratic society'.[40] The importance of moral and social responsibility to others over loyalty and obedience is well understood in countries which still have a collective memory of totalitarian rule. In extreme circumstances, citizens may have a moral and social responsibility to be disobedient.

Social or welfare citizenship tended towards an inactive citizenship. The neo-liberalism of the 1980s seemed to replace the passive citizenship of the welfare state with the passive citizenship of the consumer and the Citizen's Charter. The new citizen is a 'customer' pursuing 'demand-satisfaction'. At least the citizen of the welfare state was part of a broader system of welfare provision organized on a community basis. However, the new citizen stands alone, with his or her money, buying goods and services from a whole range of public and private service providers. At its extreme, the neo-liberal will declare, like Mrs Thatcher, 'There is no such thing as society, only individuals and families.' There is a strange parallel to be drawn between the new, centralized Britain and post-revolutionary France as described by Tocqueville. The Revolution had supplanted one centralist bureaucracy with another. A monarchical dictatorship was replaced by an elected dictatorship. The new citizenship might have the vote, but it was an 'atomized' vote. Under the Directorate, Frenchmen were privatized.

'I see each citizen standing apart, like a stranger to the destiny of others; his children and personal friends forming for him the entire human race. As for the remainder of his fellow citizens, he is beside them but he does not see them ... Above these people rises an immense and tutelary power.' He did not see the arrival of the newly emerging capitalism as providing an answer to centralized state power. Consumer choice he saw as a necessary, but not sufficient, basis for democracy. Most of all he valued a strong local community, with effective democratic structures in which everyone participated.[41]

There is an awareness of a greater sense of community and community responsibility in the growing recognition of the importance of the environment and the need for its protection. The annual household survey, *Social Trends*, for 1996[42] indicates that, while one person in twenty-five is a member of a political party, one person in ten belongs to an environmental organization. Many people are prepared to sacrifice their time and even their liberty to protect a piece of woodland against a motorway, or animals against cruel methods of factory farming, slaughter, transportation or hunting. Young citizens see these issues as more important than what they see as the Whitehall farce of Westminster politics. Their concerns often bring them into conflict with government agencies, large construction companies and landowners who are engaged in the management of the countryside and in country pursuits. There can be little sense of a community of interest between citizens with such environmental concerns and a royal family which has, traditionally, sought relaxation on its estates in hunting, shooting and fishing. The law has only recently recognized the interest of environmental agencies as meriting recognition for the purposes of standing to initiate application for judicial review. It has not, however, recognised a moral objection to fox-hunting as a relevant consideration to be taken into account when land is managed by a local authority.[43] Citizenship in this context is seen as embracing more than a selfish pursuit of individual economic interests. The UN Conference on the Human Environment in Stockholm in 1972 clearly recognized a link between human rights and the environment. In its first Principle, it declared that 'Man has a fundamental right to freedom, equality and adequate conditions of life, in an environment of quality that permits a life of dignity and well-being, and he bears a solemn responsibility to protect and improve the environment for present and future generations.'[44]

The most difficult question concerning citizenship is that citizenship/nationality has, as we have noted, an external as well as an internal face. It excludes as well as it includes. How far should citizenship rights and duties extend to those who are resident, but are not citizens/nationals, or are not even resident? This is particularly important in relation to free movement and to welfare rights. Piers Gardner has argued that

> if citizenship is to be a dividing criterion between an 'in' and 'out' group, there will be cases of persons who have no right and no claim to enter the United Kingdom and others who may legitimately do so. At least in one respect, however, citizens retain a responsibility even towards non-citizens in this category who cannot participate or even enter the jurisdiction. That responsibility is to ensure that the policies and procedures which are applied in the name of the citizenry reflect the principles and policy which are the embodiment of the values of the state concerned.

For those non-citizens who are physically present in the UK, the issue will be how far citizenship is equated with 'being human'. In other words, how far does our concept of citizenship overlap with the more universal concept of human rights? To put it simply, all citizens are human, but not all humans are citizens. The Draft IPPR constitution significantly confers all Marshall's citizenship rights, including those found in the European Convention on Human Rights, on 'everyone', except the right to vote and participate as a political representative, which is confined to 'adult citizens', whereas, under Tony Benn's Charter of Rights in his Commonwealth of Britain Bill, the same rights are conferred only on 'citizens'.

Much depends on how strictly 'citizen' is interpreted. In the Republic of Ireland, citizenship rights have been extended by decisions of the Supreme Court to resident aliens.[45] Common law and statute law have been less than generous to aliens in the United Kingdom. They entitle the resident alien, who owes allegiance to the Crown, to the protection of the law and welfare benefits, but, for however long he or she remains resident without acquiring British citizenship, there will be no opportunity to stand as a political representative or vote in local or parliamentary elections.

EUROPEAN CITIZENSHIP

We have seen that the Treaty on European Union in 1992 created a new European Union citizenship. The European Court of Justice and the European Commission had been referring to 'European citizens' for more than a decade. The new benefits which the Treaty attached to the new citizenship were modest, and added little, if anything, to the rights which were already conferred by the EC Treaty. The new citizenship did, however, have a considerable symbolic importance. Community law has conferred directly enforceable rights in a whole range of activities which people in Member States can enforce against their own governments. Many of these are economic rights in the fields of employment, health and safety at work and consumer protection, but some extend into the fields of education, science and environmental protection. None, however, specifically attaches to European citizenship. They are, like the social and economic rights in Marshall's third category, available to anyone who lives within the borders of the European Union. Except where European citizens are abroad in another Member State, there are no civil or political rights conferred on them by Community law. Civil and political rights are still very much a matter of national law.

As decisions affecting the lives of all citizens in the member states are increasingly made by the Commission and the Council of Ministers, the same issues troubling constitutional lawyers in the United Kingdom, of openness and accountability, are coming to the fore in the Community and the European Union as a whole. The Treaty on European Union created a new European Parliamentary Ombudsman to protect citizens and those resident in the area of the

European Union against maladministration. In his first report to the Parliament, the first Ombudsman, Jacob Soderman, estimated that lack of transparency by the Community institutions ranks only after failure by Member States to implement Community law in terms of the number of complaints he has received. The most often repeated complaint is that asylum, visa and police cooperation are subject to public scrutiny within each Member State but tend to be debated in almost total secrecy by EU justice and home affairs ministers when they meet in Brussels.[46]

The problem of the 'democratic deficit' in the Community is, in some respects, the same problem that exists in the United Kingdom, but in an even more acute form. The executive, in the shape of the European Commission, is also a party, with the Council of Ministers, to the law-making process. There is thus no separation of powers between legislature and executive. The only elected body, the European Parliament, plays only a peripheral role in the process of law-making. The Commission is accountable to the European Parliament, but the Council of Ministers, as a body, is accountable to no one. Douglas Hogg, the then Minister of Agriculture and a member of the Council, made the point by refusing to appear before the European Parliament's agriculture committee during its 1996/7 inquiry into the Community's role in the BSE outbreak. Individual ministers are accountable only to their national parliaments. We have seen how ineffective this process is in relation to the Westminster Parliament, given the secretive nature of the Council and the inadequate methods of scrutiny of draft Community legislation. The United Kingdom has resisted making the European process more accountable to the European Parliament, but has not come up with anything approaching an adequate national solution.

The lack of power of the European Parliament and the lack of accountability of the European institutions to European citizens has not been the subject of serious debate except among a small group of European politicians, lawyers and political scientists. There is little evidence of public awareness of the issue, although there seems to be an increasing feeling that the institutions are remote and bureaucratic. Elections to the European Parliament in each Member State are conducted almost entirely on the basis of *national* political issues. There can be no proper democratic accountability until European voters see themselves as a group, over and beyond being part of the citizenry of their own states. That will be hard to achieve. Until it is achieved, attempts at greater integration are likely to founder. Monetary union will certainly be imperilled if it is embarked upon without a much greater degree of openness and accountability to the citizens of Europe. The creation of a strong central bank will exacerbate the centralization of the Community. There is, at present, no strong, democratic centre to act as a check on the power of the new bank, nor is there any general recognition of the need for one. 'A strong centre ... needs legitimacy; democracy cannot flourish without a *demos* – a public with a shared loyalty and identity.'[47]

United Kingdom governments have endlessly reiterated their concern about the retention of 'parliamentary sovereignty', but one must doubt the genuineness of their commitment. The foreign policy prerogative power has enabled them to legislate in the Council of Ministers in a way they have never been free to do, even with a large parliamentary majority, at Westminster. It was only with the increase in qualified majority voting following the Single European Act in 1986 and the Treaty on European Union in 1992 that the government started to show any concern about UK parliamentary scrutiny, and only then as the lesser of two evils. It seemed as though the government would do almost anything to prevent the European Parliament gaining a more significant role in legislation, even to the extent of allowing the Westminster Parliament a more formal involvement in the decision-making process. In this context, however, there has been, as David Judge has observed, a complete conflation between 'parliamentary sovereignty' and 'executive sovereignty'. 'National identity' was to be preserved by the involvement of national parliaments. However, 'Governments would still govern, and parliaments would still be expected to authorise and legitimise such actions. Executive sovereignty would still be the operational code of the constitution subsumed under, and obscured by, an overarching theory of "parliamentary sovereignty".'[48]

The significance of European citizenship in the subject/citizenship debate is that it provides an alternative focus for legal rights which are immune from national repeal. Many of the rights which British people enjoy under European Community law are, however, not readily identifiable as European in origin and are not specifically associated with any kind of citizenship. Many of these would, as noted above, fall within the Marshall catalogue of economic and social rights.

It may be, as British citizens continue to work and travel more widely, that there will be growing recognition of the rights which they enjoy as European citizens. In a world where they may work for large corporations operating in a number of Member States and, indeed, in other parts of the world, they may become increasingly dependent on the Community to protect their social and employment rights which their national government may be unable or unwilling to do. It may also become increasingly clear to them that the social and economic rights which they enjoy, and which they are often forced to assert against their own government, like the service-women exercising their equal rights following dismissal on the grounds of pregnancy, are enjoyed under a superior system of law which overrides their own. Such rights are enforced in the courts of the UK. Ultimately, however, they depend on decisions of the European Court of Justice, which, in many respects, has the function of a constitutional court for the Community. The process of giving direct effect to Community law has been described by a judge of the court: 'the unique judicial contribution to the making of Europe ... [taking] Community law out of the hands of politicians and bureaucrats ... to give it to the people'.[49] We have, therefore, two overlapping citizenships, operating at two different levels, the one depending for its protection on the government and the courts of the United Kingdom, and the other, ultimately, on the European Commission and the European Court of Justice. The future development of citizenship in the United Kingdom will clearly take place in what has, increasingly, the appearance of a federal structure.

CORPORATE CITIZENSHIP

The importance of the international company, weighed against the political and economic power of the governments of nation states, was considered in Chapter 10. Such companies play a growing part in the economic and political life of Britain and the European Community. Investment and disinvestment decisions by them have a political as well as an economic dimension. But the company, although it is a legal person, is not driven by the same impulses as human beings. Its only obligation, it would seem, is to earn profits for its shareholders. If opportunities in one country are better than in another, the company should close its plant where costs are higher and move to the more favourable location. Hoover may move from Lyons to Cambuslang, or Ford from Merseyside to Valencia. It has no legal or moral obligation to do anything else but to maximize its return on investment. It does, however, have legal duties in the countries in which it operates. If it breaches a contract it may be sued. If it operates a plant in breach of safety laws it may be prosecuted and fined. But it does not 'regret' its offence.

> The company itself is a legal figment. Its physical embodiment is only a piece of paper – in the case of a registered company, the memorandum of association. It has no feelings. It can hardly be said to be convicted 'justly' or 'unjustly'. Upon being convicted it never becomes neurotic, or spends the rest of its

life writing letters to the Lord Chancellor complaining of having been unjustly dealt with. So any analogy with a human being is inapt. Whether a company should be liable to conviction depends entirely on whether this subserves the general good of society.[50]

Those who manage companies may well view the criminal law in the same utilitarian way, and regard penalties imposed for breach of regulations governing the conduct of the company simply on the basis of risk and cost/benefit. Companies are not human beings, and cannot, it might be thought, be citizens. Such an approach would not, however, accord with the new 'corporate citizenship' embraced by some companies. Sir Allen Shepherd, Chairman of Grand Metropolitan plc, describes corporate citizenship in this way:

Today's good corporate citizen believes that involvement in the community is not something separate from the business of earning profit – but an integral part of it. The motive for it is not altruism, but vision and commonsense ... Modern international businesses affect the lives of millions. Some global corporations generate bigger earnings than the gross national product of small states. Their operations cover most of the world. Inevitably people have started asking some fundamental questions about these multi-national giants: What is their role in society? What is their purpose? ... I believe businesses have a right to certain freedoms – the freedom to operate, to recruit, to manufacture and distribute, and to make a legitimate profit. And the freedom of commercial speech, to sell and advertise their products. They have a right to protection of their property and assets. And a right to expect the community to give them its support in the wealth-creation process. On the other side they have ... a responsibility to be concerned not only for their shareholders but for all those who have a stake in their business. An obligation to respect the environment – local, national and global. An obligation to be open, honest, and fair in all their dealings. And finally, a responsibility to play an active role in the community, to help it prosper and succeed.[51]

The 'vision and commonsense' to which Sir Allen refers are not the sentiments of the company, of course, but of the directors. They are, in any event, as Sir Allen frankly admits, the product of no more than enlightened self-interest. They improve the image of the company. Corporate community involvement has become an increasingly important part of the value of the company in the eyes of the investor.

Citizenship involves obligations as well as rights. Such obligations may be legal, as in the case of contracts, into which companies enter daily. They may also be moral, such as the duty to help fellow citizens when in difficulties, or to assist in the enforcement of the law. No one could say that a company, which is only a person in the strictly legal sense, could be *morally* at fault for failing to do any of those things. The directors may be regarded as morally responsible individuals, but the company has, in law, no *moral* obligation to anyone. Whether we take as our basis of citizenship allegiance and subject status, or a moral obligation to our fellows, the company is not an apt candidate for citizenship. However, despite its wholly artificial character, the limited company, probably the most successful creation of modern capitalism, has started to acquire human characteristics. In certain limited respects, it has been held to benefit from some of the provisions of the European Convention on Human Rights. It is entitled to fair treatment and natural justice in civil proceedings, and its property rights must not be invaded. It is entitled to protection against self-incrimination in criminal proceedings, although it has not yet been accorded protection for its family home.[52] Where is this process to stop? Surprisingly, it has been the European Court of Justice which has tried to set limits to claims by companies to benefit from the Convention, whereas the European Commission on Human Rights and the Court of Human Rights have seemed more willing to extend protection to these wholly artificial entities.

There is a warning here for those who, like the writer, favour the incorporation of a Charter of Rights into a written constitution. Such charters, like the European Convention, can benefit those who, as Sedley J has described them, 'have the sharpest elbows and the loudest voices'.[53] There is no doubt that the new corporations have very sharp elbows, loud voices and a very short attention span for the obligations of the citizenship to which they aspire. It will surely be the case that any attempt to devise some new concept of 'corporate citizenship' will require a careful examination of company credentials in any new European environment. Perhaps the price of access to the new European market of more than four hundred million souls will have to be the inclusion of a code of corporate citizenship into the company's memorandum and articles of association.

CONCLUSIONS

British citizenship means little at present, and is far from attracting the catalogue of the rights and duties which characterize citizenship in many West European states. The subject status that continues to

309

prevail, despite its formal abolition by the British Nationality Act 1981, is a consequence of the individualism and relative 'rightlessness' of the common law. The clearest manifestation of this is the indefinite scope of royal prerogative powers. The state of rightlessness is further exacerbated by the absolute powers possessed by the Crown-in-Parliament to take away any of the rights currently conferred by statute and common law. That power, and the executive powers derived from the prerogative, although nominally constrained by parliamentary accountability and scrutiny, is not, in practice, subject to such controls. Some advance has been made by the courts in the process of judicial review, but the absence hitherto of any fundamental principles which could be supplied by a charter of rights in a written constitution has meant that the process of review, and the protection of the civil and political rights of citizens and others has lacked any clear focus. Much will now depend on how the courts interpret the newly incorporated Convention.

European citizenship and the developing case law of the European Court of Justice have provided a growing corpus of rights, largely in the social and economic field, but the lack of accountability of European institutions and the lack of any sense of European identity have so far failed to give European citizenship much content or sense of direction. Citizenship was barely addressed in the discussions leading to the 1997 Amsterdam Treaty and many related issues associated with the creation of an effective federal structure were postponed until the next Intergovernmental Conference on the consequences of the further enlargement of the Union. Within the United Kingdom, if citizenship is to have any real meaning it will have to be built on a full recognition of the rights conferred by Community law, the incorporation of the European Convention and its development into a full charter of rights in a new constitutional settlement.

NOTES AND REFERENCES

1. Aristotle, *The Politics* (1951 edn) Book III, pp. 167–85.
2. Blackburn R., 'Introduction: citizenship today' in Blackburn R. (ed.), *Rights of Citizenship* (1993) p. 3.
3. Marshall T.H., 'Citizenship and social class', in Marshall T.H., *Class, Citizenship and Social Development* (1977) p. 78.
4. Rosas A. and Esko A. (eds), *A Citizens' Europe* (1995); Heater D., *Citizenship: the Civic Ideal in World History, Politics and Education* (1990); Turner B.S. (ed.), *Citizenship and Social Theory* (1993); Blackburn R. (ed.), *Rights of Citizenship* (1993); Turner B. and Hamilton P., *Citizenship: Critical Concepts*, Vols I–II

(1994); Gardner J.P. (ed.), *Hallmarks of Citizenship: a Green Paper* (1993); Van Steenbergen (ed.), *The Condition of Citizenship* (1994); *European Citizenship 1999*, The Federal Trust (1996).

5. Pimlott B., *The Queen: a Biography of Elizabeth II* (1996) p. 345; Benn T. and Hood A., *Common Sense: a New Constitution for Britain*, p. 42.

6. *Joyce* v. *DPP* [1946] AC 337; *Calvin's Case* (1609) 7 Co. Rep. 1; Statute of Treasons 1351.

7. Dummett A. and Nicol A., *Subjects, Citizens and Aliens: Nationality and Immigration Law* (1990) p. 62.

8. 1977, Cmnd 6795, HMSO.

9. White R.M., 'The relationship of immigration and nationality: how the tail wagged the dog', *Contemporary Issues in Law* (1996) Vol. 1, Issue 4, 25.

10. Cmnd 7987, HMSO.

11. *R.* v. *Khan*, 5 July 1996; Leach P., 'The Police Bill', *New Law Journal*, 29 November 1996; see the comments of Lord Browne-Wilkinson in the debate on the Bill, *The Times*, 21 January 1997.

12. *A-G* v. *Guardian Newspapers Ltd (No. 2)* [1990] 1 AC 109; Ewing K.D. and Gearty C.A., 'Breaches of the rule of law (the "Spycatcher" Case)'. in *Freedom under Thatcher; Civil Liberties in Modern Britain* (1990) p. 163.

13. *R.* v. *Chief Metropolitan Magistrate, ex p. Choudhry* [1991] 1 QB 429. The applicant argued unsuccessfully, in a case concerning Salman Rushdie's book, *The Satanic Verses*, that the protection of the common law given to the Christian religion of the established church should be extended to Islam.

14. *Shaw* v. *DPP* [1962] AC 220; *Knuller* v. *DPP* [1973] AC 435.

15. S. 1 Theatres Act 1968 repealed the Theatres Act 1843 and prohibited the exercise of any 'of the powers which were exercisable thereunder by the Lord Chamberlain of Her Majesty's Household ... by or on behalf of Her Majesty by virtue of Her royal prerogative.'

16. *R.* v. *Thompson* (1900) 64 JP 456, quoted by Robertson G., *Freedom, the Individual and the Law* (1989) p. 181.

17. Trelford D., 'The right to know – a missing link in Britain's democracy', *The Guardian*, 1 October 1984.

18. Robertson, *op. cit.*, p. 145.

19. Dice A.V., *Introduction to the Study of the Law of the Constitution* (9th edn, 1952) p. 221.

20. Partington M., 'The reform of public law in Britain: theoretical problems and practical considerations', in McAuslan P. and McEldowney J.F. (eds), *Law, Legitimacy and the Constitution* (1985) pp. 194–6; Ganz G., *Quasi-legislation: Recent Developments in Secondary Legislation* (1987).

21. Buck T., 'The disabled citizen', in Blackburn, *op. cit.*, p. 179; West J., 'The Americans with Disabilities Act' (1991) *The Millbank Quarterly*, Supplements 1/ 2, Vol. 69.

22. The Disability Discrimination Act 1995; The Disability Discrimination (Meaning of Disability) Regulations 1996, SI 1996 No. 1455; The Disability (Employment) Regulations 1996; the Code of Practice for the elimination of discrimination in the field of employment against disabled persons or persons who have had a disability (Department of Education and Employment); the Code of Practice:

Rights of Access: Goods, Facilities, Services and Premises (Department of Social Security); Guidance on matters to be taken into account in determining questions relating to the definition of disability (DSS and DfEE); Lester A., 'Ministers must be checked', *The Times*, 13 June 1995; Harrison K., 'The Disability Discrimination Act', *New Law Journal*, 6 December 1996, p. 1793.

23. Ss. 9, 10 and 11 Asylum and Immigration Act 1996; on the supposed lack of international implications, see Lord Mackay of Ardbrecknish, Minister of State, Department of Social Security, HL Reports, Col. 605, 24 June 1996; In *R. v. London Borough of Hammersmith and Fulham ex p. XMPA*, *The Times*, 18 February 1997, Lord Woolf, the Master of the Rolls, in the Court of Appeal, said that the plight of the asylum-seekers was 'horrendous' and 'obviously can and should provoke deep sympathy'. The court ruled that, although the 1996 Act had excluded any right to income support, local authorities were bound, under the National Assistance Act 1948, to provide food and shelter.

24. Evans J.M., *Immigration Law* (2nd edn, 1983) pp. 422–33.

25. Aliens Act 1844; Calendar of Patent Rolls, 28 February 1384, p. 413; Dummett and Nicol *op. cit.*, p. 154.

26. *R. v. Secretary of State for the Home Department, ex p. Mohammed El Fayed*, *The Times*, 18 November 1996.

27. Gardner J.P., 'Citizenship, not human rights', in Garner J.P., *Hallmarks of Citizenship* (1993) p. 194.

28. Peaker F. *British Citizenship: Its Rights and Duties* (1906) pp. 31, 32, 148.

29. Harlow C., 'Power from the people? Representation and constitutional theory' in McAuslan and McEldowney, *op. cit.*, p. 62.

30. Harlow, *op. cit.*, p. 66, quoting Dahl R., *A Preface to Democratic Theory* (1956) p. 4.

31. Oliver D., *Government in the United Kingdom: the Search for Accountability, Effectiveness and Citizenship* (1991) pp. 202–3.

32. Jenkins S., *Accountable to None: the Tory Nationalization of Britain* (1995) p. 266.

33. *Ibid.*

34. Elliott V., 'Blair to give public more say with citizens' juries', *The Times*, 28 October 1996; Foster P., 'Notable triumphs for popular will in Germany and US', *The Times*, 11 November 1996.

35. The Skeffington Report, *People and Planning* (1969); Harlow, *op. cit.*, p. 79, note 81; Harden I. and Lewis N. *The Noble Lie: the British Constitution and the Rule of Law* (1986) p. 174; Tyme J., *Motorways versus Democracy* (1978) p. 19.

36. Marwick A., *British Society since 1945* (1996) p. 107.

37. Hutton W., *The State We're In* (1995) p. 196.

38. Report of the Speaker's Commission on Citizenship, *Encouraging Citizenship* (1990); Williams C.J., 'The moral dimension', in Gardner J.P. (ed.), *Hallmarks of Citizenship* (1993) pp. 168–9.

39. Selbourne, *op. cit.*, p. 260.

40. The Federal Trust, *European Citizenship 1999, Report of the Pilot Phase to the European Commission*, (January 1996) pp. 46–8.

41. Siedentop L., *Tocqueville* (1994) p. 64, quoted in Jenkins S., *Accountable to None* (1995) p. 260.

42. *Social Trends 27*, HMSO, 1997; *The Independent*, 30 January 1997.

43. *R. v. Secretary of State for Foreign Affairs, ex p. World Development Movement*

[1995] 1 All ER, QBD; *R.* v. *Somerset CC, ex p. Fewings* [1995] 3 All ER 20, CA.

44. Macrory R., 'Environmental citizenship and the law: repairing the European road' (1996) 8 *Journal of Environmental Law* 219 at 220.

45. Institute for Public Policy Research, *A Written Constitution for the United Kingdom* (1991) pp. 34–48. Benn T. and Hood A., *op. cit.*, Schedule 2, Commonwealth of Britain Bill; *The State (McFadden)* v. *The Governor of Mountjoy Prison (No. 1)* [1981] ILRM 113.

46. *The European*, 30 January 1997.

47. Kellner P., 'Hard facts about Europe's looming currency disaster', *The Observer*, 26 January 1997.

48. Judge D., *The Parliamentary State* (1993) p. 192.

49. Mancini F., 'Democracy and the European Court of Justice' (1994) 57 Mod. L Rev. 175; Lenaerts K., 'Fundamental rights to be included in a Community catalogue', 16 EL Rev. 365.

50. Williams G., *Textbook of Criminal Law* (2nd edn, 1983) p. 975.

51. Sheppard A., 'Corporate citizenship', in Gardner, *op. cit.*, pp. 177–8.

52. In Cases 46/87 and 277/88 *Hoechst* v. *Commission* [1989] ECR 2859 and Case 374/87 *Orkem* v. *Commission* [1989] ECR 3283, the ECJ held that anti-trust proceedings against economic undertakings did not attract the same protection as criminal proceedings against natural – that is, human – persons. In Case A/256 *Funke* v. *France*, the Court of Human Rights, and in *Société Stenuit* v. *France* (1992) Series A, Vol. 232, 14 EHRR 509, the Commission on Human Rights disagreed. The ECJ has shown deference to the inviolability of the home, but not to business premises: Case 85/87 *Dow Benelux* v. *Commission* [1989] ECR 3137. The Convention refers throughout to 'everyone' or 'no one'. The only specific reference to a legal person is in Article 1 of the First Protocol, which provides that 'Every natural *or legal person* is entitled to the peaceful enjoyment of his possessions'(emphasis added).

53. Sedley S., 'The sound of silence: constitutional law without a constitution' (1994) 110 LQR 270, 286.

12

Postscript

The survival of the British constitution for so long has been a triumph of pragmatism over principle. Because it appeared to work, the British people failed to ask uncomfortable questions about it. The genius of those who ruled in the name of successive monarchs has been in using their power to create the myths which sustained it. When the clear line of the hereditary monarchy was broken in 1688 and William and Mary were invited to take the throne, the myth was promulgated that the Stuarts had 'voluntarily' abdicated the throne which had become 'vacant'.

The myth continued to be propagated even after the unsuccessful efforts of the Stuarts to recover it in 1715 and 1745. The throne was open only to the descendants of the Electress of Hannover who were Protestants and communicants of the Church of England. The Glorious Bloodless Revolution of 1688 against the abuse of prerogative powers resulted in a Bill of Rights which sought to address some of the abuses, but like the Petition of Right before it, it was not much more than a request for the restoration of a largely mythical common law constitution. The great powers derived from the royal prerogative continued unabated, but in the hands of the party which dominated the Commons and which had opposed their abuse.

Throughout much of the eighteenth century the fiction was cherished of a patriotic England ruled by an English King. In fact, the royal prerogative was used by an English Cabinet sustained by a corrupted Parliament to govern in the name of an absent German King. Queen Victoria, the future Queen-Empress of India, was, with the handsome, civilized German Prince Albert, the founder of the family of Saxe-Coburg-Gotha, from which so many of Europe's royal families would trace their descent. That family came to represent the best in English family life and the focus of English patriotism. On the continent of Europe wars and revolutions raged. Hereditary kings were replaced by constitutional monarchs, presidents and republics. In Britain there was an industrial revolution, a Reform Bill and an extension of the franchise.

The intervening years have seen many such adjustments: the curtailment of the power of the hereditary peers to block legislation in 1911–49, the final extension of the franchise to all adult men and women in 1929, the abandonment of the selection of the Prime Minister from the Parliamentary Conservative Party when the Conservatives are in office. The monarch has become less directly involved in affairs of state, although still 'consulted and informed' by successive Prime Ministers. It has a diminished role now that the empire has been replaced by a loose association of Commonwealth states. The foreign perspective of Britain has become more focused as its means have diminished with the loss of empire and most of its manufacturing base. The greatest change came with Britain's entry into the European Economic Community in 1973.

British entry was accompanied by a chorus of ministerial assurances that nothing would change and that national and parliamentary sovereignty would be unaffected. In fact, everything had changed. After nearly a quarter of a century of membership the extent of British legal and economic integration is such that it would be very difficult to put in reverse. The Intergovernmental Conference of 1996/7 has moved that integration even further. Greater powers for the European Parliament, more decision-making by qualified majority voting in the Council of Ministers, the creation of a central European bank and a single European currency are pushing the relationship between European and national institutions to the front of political debate. It is no longer possible to isolate discussion about British institutions and British citizenship from the larger European Community, and even global, context.

The centralization of power in Westminster and Brussels has set up a reaction in the form of demands for the greater devolution of power to regional and local level, and for greater participation by citizens in the exercise of political power. The first steps in this process have been taken by the creation of a Scottish parliament and a Welsh assembly. The current institutional structure no longer seems to meet the needs of the people it is intended to serve. It seems an appropriate time to start asking questions about the constitution and about the way we are governed. Much has recently been written about constitutional change. This book has sought to look at the monarchy, at the powers derived from the royal prerogative, and how they have affected the way we are governed and how we see ourselves in the present order as both subjects and citizens.

The monarchy stands at the head and at the heart of the constitution. Its symbolism is ubiquitous. The courts, the military, the civil and diplomatic services and even the Post Office still all function in the name of the Queen. Privy Councillors and Cabinet ministers govern in her name. They swear loyalty to her; so, too, do her subjects. The structure of government is subsumed by a network of oaths of allegiance to the Queen. The Crown-in-Parliament legislates with her assent. The Crown is the fount of honours. Peerages, baronetcies, knighthoods, honours, orders of medieval romance and chivalry cascade forth on royal birthdays and at the New Year. Is this all merely the stuff of tradition that gives colour, weight and dignity to our constitution? Do we not still need to see a family on the throne, representing all our aspirations and the best in family life? Will it still be acceptable in a liberal democracy in the twenty-first century for the Prime Minister to be selected and appointed by a person who holds the post of head of state by inheritance? If that is so, will the argument still hold good when the last hereditary peer has lost his right to vote in the House of Lords?

A monarch lends dignity to the office of head of state. We have a Queen who has earned widespread respect for the way in which she carries out her duties. The great state occasions in which she takes part are grand and uplifting. The doings of the royal family preoccupy the press. A royal divorce rivets the attention of the media only a little less than a royal marriage. The monarchy, it is said, is invaluable to the British tourist industry. But the price for all that may still be too high. It reinforces social divisions and legitimizes privilege. It invests the public offices associated with it with a kind of mystery which excites deference for the office rather than respect for the holder, and discourages openness and accountability. At its worst, traditional pageantry can create a kind of British Ruritania for the tourist industry, a theme park in which people increasingly pursue their daily lives in a historic environment preserved in aspic for the foreign visitor and the media. Although in past centuries rural villages were served by blacksmiths, potters, bakers and shoemakers who had learned their trade in the family workshop, few would now accept inheritance as the mark of qualification for their doctor, dentist, pharmacist or lawyer. Why should inheritance be the qualification for the post of head of state, when all other major offices are derived from election or are appointed by those who have themselves been elected? If the hereditary monarchy is retained, would it not be more appropriate that decisions about the appointment of a Prime Minister or the dissolution of Parliament be taken by the Speaker of the House of Commons, or by a commission established for the purpose?

The royal prerogative remains a crucial, but intrinsically uncertain, power in the hands of government. As we have seen, in the fields of immigration and defence, it is claimed by the executive as enabling it to detain individuals for the purposes of exclusion and expulsion, in peace and in war, in undefined circumstances and where it is not authorized by statute. It is used to override statutory provisions in immigration and tax law when this clearly seems to breach the prohibition in the Bill of Rights against dispensation of statute. In the field of foreign policy, the prerogative enables the executive to deny travel documents to British citizens and the right to travel without any defined cause, and to legislate in the Council of Ministers without effective scrutiny or control. The high degree of self-regulation of the Civil Service, which operates within the most ill-defined prerogative framework, has become a weakness now that the service is so fragmented into agencies. There is a serious conflict of loyalties, and no clear principles of openness and accountability. The traditional immunity of the Crown enables the executive to avoid the effect of statutes in circumstances where it would be clearly for the public benefit for it to be bound by them. Increasingly it uses its power of contract to provide services, but in such a way as to make both political and legal accountability more difficult. The extent of its liability in tort, despite the provisions of the Crown Proceedings Act 1947, is far from clear, and has not been made any clearer by recent decisions of the courts, especially in relation to both breaches of statutory duty and negligence. Although, starting with the *GCHQ* case, the courts have shown a growing willingness to review the exercise of prerogative powers, they are hampered by the inherent uncertainty of their scope and by the lack of any clear principles by which to define them.

Our experience of the executive's use of prerogative powers makes a strong case for the adoption of a written constitution with a charter of rights. It is possible that a consequence of the incorporation of the European Convention on Human Rights will be to persuade the people of this country of the benefits of having a more clearly defined structure within which the process of government can take place. However, an exhaustive definition of executive powers would be impossible and, indeed, undesirable. Any attempt to define the scope of executive powers would risk either the rules being ignored and the law being brought into contempt, or an excessive legalism resulting in paralysis of the process of government. The conferment on the executive in the IPPR constitution of 'the rights, powers and capacities of a person of full age and capacity', together with specific powers in the fields of defence and foreign policy, within a framework of fundamental rights, probably strikes the right balance. Article 1 of the constitution emphasizes that it is 'the sole foundation for the exercise of executive, legislative and judicial power' and it excludes 'any law ... convention or constitutional practice [which is] inconsistent with this Constitution'. Given the extraordinary tenacity of prerogative powers, which might otherwise resurface in judgments of the Supreme Court, a specific exclusion would probably be the only effective means of ensuring their certain demise. All the existing prerogative powers are preserved by Article 14 of the Benn constitution, although they are transferred to the President, and may only be exercised with the consent of Parliament. The retention of the prerogative powers would continue much of the current uncertainty, although their exercise would be inhibited by the charter of rights which is incorporated in the Benn constitution.

Problems arising from the inability of the courts to undertake effective judicial review of the use of prerogative powers are exacerbated by the lack of political accountability. House of Commons rules exclude questions affecting a whole range of issues in the fields of defence, foreign policy and the use of the Civil Service. Select committees may be unable or unwilling to obtain the necessary information, and the current political organization of the House of Commons makes ministerial accountability largely ineffective. The reorganization of the Civil Service into the Next Steps agencies may have resulted in greater efficiency, but it has also served to confuse lines of accountability and responsibility. Decision-making at Council of Ministers level in the European Union operates as a function of foreign policy-making, when it should be incorporated as part of the legislative process at both European Parliament and Westminster levels. At present, there is a serious lack of representative involvement at all levels.

The scope of prerogative powers, and the lack of legal and political control and accountability, are clearly detrimental to civil citizenship. The very wide discretions enjoyed by the Crown as executive in relation to freedom of movement, passports, the maintenance of public order, freedom of expression for all citizens, including members of the armed forces and the Civil Service, and the culture of deference and secrecy within which they operate, all inhibit the proper exercise of civil rights and civil duties. The most fundamental rights are vulnerable to the whim of the smallest parliamentary majority. Political citizenship suffers as a result of the same culture and the same lack of accountability. A more open form of government should be accompanied by a greater participation by citizens at all levels of the decision-making process, both indirectly through their elected representatives, and directly through more formal consultation and discussion. This cannot be achieved by treating individuals as mere recipients of welfare or simply as consumers of services.

Citizenship can no longer be seen only in a national context. The globalization of the economy has diminished the powers of nation states to protect their own citizens, and has meant that social and economic citizenship rights will have to be protected, if at all, at a supranational level within the European Union. To achieve that, European Union citizenship will have to assume greater significance, both in providing a minimum floor of economic and social rights for all those who hold it, and in creating a greater sense of a European political identity. That process will involve a recognition of our moral obligation to non-citizens within the Union and our mutual interdependence upon all those outside it in the new world order.

Select Bibliography

BOOKS

Babington, A., *For the Sake of Example: Capital Courts Martial 1914–18* (Paladin, 1985).

Bagehot, W., *The English Constitution* (Fontana, 1963).

Barnett, A. (ed.), *Power and the Throne: The Monarchy Debate* (Vintage/Charter 88 1994).

Benn, T., *Out of the Wilderness, Diaries 1963–67* (Arrow Books, 1987).

Benn, T. and Hood, H., *Common Sense: A New Constitution for Britain* (Hutchinson, 1993).

Blackburn, R. (ed.), *Rights of Citizenship* (Mansell, 1993).

Blackstone, W., *Commentaries on the Laws of England* (Clarendon Press, 1767).

Bogdanor, V., *The Monarchy and the Constitution* (Clarendon Press, 1995).

Bonner, D., *Emergency Powers in Peacetime* (Sweet & Maxwell, 1985).

Buckle, G. (ed.), *Letters of Queen Victoria* (John Murray, 1926).

Cane, P., *An Introduction to Administrative Law* (Clarendon Press, 3rd edn, 1996).

Chitty, J., *Prerogatives of the Crown* (Butterworth, 1820).

Cripps, Y., *The Legal Implications of Disclosure in the Public Interest: An Analysis of Prohibitions and Protections with Particular Reference to Employers and Employees* (Sweet & Maxwell, 2nd edn, 1994).

Daintith, T. (ed.), *Implementing EC Law in the United Kingdom* (Wiley, 1995).

Daintith, T. (ed.), *Constitutional Implications of Executive Self-regulation: Comparative Experience* (ESRC/Institute of Advanced Legal Studies, 1996).

de Smith *Judicial Review of Administrative Action* (Evans J.M., ed.) (Stevens, 4th edn, 1980).

de Smith, *Constitutional and Administrative Law* (Street, H. and Brazier. R., eds) (Penguin, 5th edn, 1985).

Dicey, A.V., *Law and Public Opinion in England* (Macmillan, 2nd edn, 1914).

Dicey, A.V., *Law of the Constitution* (Macmillan, 9th edn, 1950).

Dummett, A. and Nicol, A., *Subjects, Citizens, Aliens and Others* (Weidenfeld and Nicholson, 1990).

Evans, J.M., *Immigration Law* (Sweet & Maxwell, 2nd edn, 1983).

Federal Trust, *European Citizenship 1999*, January 1996.

Ganz, G., *Quasi-legislation; Recent Developments in Secondary Legislation* (Sweet & Maxwell, 1987).

Gardner, J.P. (ed.), *Hallmarks of Citizenship* (Institute for Citizenship Studies and British Institute of International and Comparative Law, 1993).

Gordon Walker P., *The Cabinet* (Jonathan Cape, 1970).

Griffith, J.A.G., *The Politics of the Judiciary* (Fontana, 3rd edn, 1985).

Griffith, J.A.G., *Public Rights and Private Interests* (Academy of Legal Publications, 1991).

Harden, I. and Lewis, N., *The Noble Lie: The British Constitution and the Rule of Law* (Hutchinson, 1986).

Harlow, C., *Compensation and Government Torts* (Sweet & Maxwell 1982).

Harris, R., *Good and Faithful Servant* (Faber and Faber, 1990).

Hartley, T.C., *The Foundations of European Community Law* (Clarendon Press, 3rd edn, 1994)

Hennessy, P., *The Hidden Wiring: Unearthing the British Constitution* (Gollancz, 1995).

Hennessy, P., *Muddling Through* (Gollancz, 1996).

Heuston, R.F.V., *Essays in Constitutional Law* (Stevens, 2nd edn, 1964).

Hobbes, T., *Leviathan* (J.M. Dent/Everyman, 1914).

Holdsworth, W.S., *A History of English Law*, Vol. X (Sweet & Maxwell, 1938).

Holdsworth, W.S. (Goodhart, A.L. and Hanbury, H.G., eds), *Essays in Law and History* (Clarendon Press, 1946).

Hutton, W., *The State We're In* (Cape, 1995).

Institute for Public Policy Research, *A Written Constitution for the United Kingdom* (Mansell, 1993).

Jenkins, S., *Accountable to None: The Tory Nationalization of Britain* (Penguin, 1996).

Jennings, I,, *Parliamentary Reform* (Gollancz, 1934).

Jennings, I., *The Queen's Government* (Penguin, 1954).

Jennings, I., *Cabinet Government* (Cambridge University Press, 1959).

Jennings, I., *Parliament* (Cambridge University Press, 1970).

Jowell, J. and Oliver, D., *The Changing Constitution* (Clarendon Press, 3rd edn, 1994).

Judge, D., *The Parliamentary State* (Sage, 1993).

Keir, D.L., *The Constitutional History of Modern Britain 1485–1937* (Black, 1938).

Keir, D.L. and Lawson, F.H., *Cases in Constitutional Law* (Clarendon Press, 4th edn, 1954).

Kellner, P. and Lord Crowther-Hunt, *The Civil Servants* (Macdonald Futura, 1980).

Kenyon, J.P., *The Stuart Constitution 1603–1688* (Cambridge University Press, 1969).

Laird, D., *How the Queen Reigns* (Hodder and Stoughton, 1959).

Lafitte, F., *The Internment of Aliens* (Penguin, 1940).

Landa, M.J., *The Alien Problem and Its Remedy* (King, 1911).

Lee, S., *Judging Judges* (Faber, 1988).

Lively, J. and Lively, A., *Democracy in Britain* (Blackwell, 1994).

Locke, J., *Two Treatises of Government* (Laslett, P., ed.) (Cambridge University Press, 1967).

Lustgarten, L., *The Governance of the Police* (Sweet & Maxwell, 1986).

McAuslan, P. and McEldowney, J.F., *Law, Legitimacy and the Constitution* (Sweet & Maxwell, 1985).

McMillan, G., *Honours for Sale: The Strange Story of Maundy Gregory* (Richards Press, 1954).

McNair, Lord and Watts, A.D., *The Legal Effects of War* (Cambridge University Press, 4th edn, 1966).

Maitland, F.W., *The Constitutional History of England* (Cambridge University Press, 1909).

Marshall, T.H., *Citizenship and Social Class* (Cambridge University Press, 1950).

Martin, K., *The Crown and the Establishment* (Penguin, 1962).

Marwick, A., *British Society since 1945* (Penguin, 3rd edn, 1996).

May, T. Erskine, *Constitutional History of England 1760–1860*, Vols I and II (Longman, Green 1861).

Middlemas, K., *Edward VII* (Cardinal, 1975).

Munro, C.R., *Studies in Constitutional Law* (Butterworth, 1987).

Ogg, D., *England in the Reign of James II and William III* (Oxford University Press, 2nd edn, 1963).

O'Keeffe, D. and Twomey, P.M. (eds), *Legal Issues of the Maastricht Treaty* (Wiley Chancery Law, 1994).

Peaker, F., *British Citizenship: Its Rights and Duties* (Ralph Holland, 1906).

Pimlott, B., *The Queen* (HarperCollins, 1996).

Pinder, J., *European Community: The Building of a Union* (Oxford University Press, 1991).

Plender, R., *International Migration Law* (A.W. Sijthoff, 1972).

Plumb, J.H., *The Growth of Political Stability in England 1675-1725* (Macmillan, 1967).

Ponting, C., *The Right to Know: The Inside Story of the Belgrano Affair* (Sphere Books, 1985).

Prothero, G.W., *Select Statutes and Other Constitutional Documents 1558–1625* (Clarendon Press, 4th edn, 1913).

Public Concern at Work, *Whistleblowing, Fraud and the European Union* (1996).

Randle, M., *Civil Resistance* (Fontana, 1994).

Roberts-Wray, K., *Commonwealth and Colonial Law* (Stevens, 1966).

Robertson, G., *Freedom, the Individual and the Law* (Penguin, 6th edn, 1989).

Sampson, A., *Anatomy of Britain Today* (Hodder & Stoughton, 1965).

Selbourne, D., *The Principle of Duty* (Sinclair-Stevenson 1994).

Sharpe, R.J., *The Law of Habeas Corpus* (Clarendon Press, 1976).

Stammers, N., *Civil Liberties in Britain during the Second World War* (Croom Helm, 1983).

Stephens Commentaries on the Laws of England (4 vols) (Clarendon Press, 1880).

Taswell-Langmead, T.P. (Poole, A.L., ed.), *English Constitutional History* (Sweet & Maxwell, 9th edn, 1929).

Thompson, B., *Textbook on Constitutional and Administrative Law* (Blackstone, 1993).

Tolstoy, N., *Victims of Yalta* (Hodder and Stoughton, 1977).

Troup, E., *The Home Office* (Putnam's, 1925).

Vincenzi, C., *Law of the European Community* (Pitman, 1996).

Wade, H.W.R., *Constitutional Fundamentals* (Stevens, 1980).

Weatherill, S. and Beaumont, P., *EC Law* (Penguin, 2nd edn, 1995).

West, N., *MI5* (Triad Grafton Books, 1983).

Wright, P. and Greengrass, P., *Spycatcher* (Heinemann, 1987).

Young, T. and Kettle, M., *Incitement to Disaffection* (Cobden Trust, 1976).

ARTICLES

Ackner, Lord, 'The erosion of judicial independence', *New Law Journal*, 6 December 1996, 1789.

Arrowsmith, S., 'Judicial review and the contractual powers of public authorities', (1990) 106 LQR 277.

Bainham, J., 'The Children Act 1989: the future of wardship' [1990] Fam Law 270.

Bogdanor, V., 'Ministers, civil servants and the constitution: a revolution in Whitehall?', *Institute of Advanced Legal Studies Bulletin*, 15 October 1993, 10.

Boyle, A., 'Freedom of expression as a public interest in English law' [1982] PL 574.

Bridge, J.W., 'The case of the rugby football team and the high prerogative writ' (1972) 88 LQR 83.

Brougham, H., 'The alien laws of England' (1825) *Edinburgh Review*, April, 99.

Collier, J.G., 'Act of state as a defence against a British subject' (1968) 26 CLJ 102.

Cotter, P., 'Emergency detention in wartime' (1954) 6 *Stanford LR* 238.

Craies, W.F., 'The right of aliens to enter British territory' (1890) 6 LQR 27.

Cripps, Y., 'Disclosure in the public interest: the predicament of the public sector employee' [1983] PL 600.

Daintith, T., 'Regulation by contract: the new prerogative' (1979) *Current Legal Problems* 4.

Dicey, A.V., 'The development of administrative law in England' (1915) 31 LQR 148, 152.

Dunleavy, P. and Weir, S., 'Public wants the law set on MPs', *Observer*, 14 May 1995.

Eyal, J., 'Conspiracy of silence', *Guardian*, 28 November 1996.

Freedland, M., 'Government by contract and public law' [1994] PL 86.

Gardner, J.P., 'What lawyers mean by citizenship', in *Encouraging Citizenship: The Report on the Commission on Citizenship* (HMSO, 1990).

Goodhart, W., 'Lions under Downing Street: the judiciary in a written constitution', *Institute of Advanced Legal Studies Bulletin*, 9 October 1991, 5.

Griffith, J.A.G., 'Judicial decision-making' [1985] PL 564.

Grosz, S., 'Pergau be dammed!', *New Law Journal*, 9 December 1994.

Hale-Bellot, H., 'The detention of Napoleon Bonaparte' (1923) 39 LQR 170.

Hare, D., 'The new republic', *Guardian*, 7 January 1995.

Harris, B.V., 'The third source of authority for government action' (1992) 109 LQR 626.

Haycraft, T.W., 'Aliens legislation and the prerogative of the crown' (1897) 13 LQR 165.

Hencke, D., 'Royal finance: the bottom line', *Guardian*, 10 January 1995.

Heuston, R.F.V., '*Liversidge* v. *Anderson* in retrospect' (1970) 86 LQR 33.

Holme, R., 'Our crumbling constitution', *Guardian*, 14 November 1988.

Jacob, J. 'The debates behind the Crown Proceedings Act: Crown proceedings reform 1920–1947' [1992] PL 452.

Jacob, J., 'From privileged crown to interested public' [1993] PL 123.

Jaconelli, J., 'The Justice Report on Passports' (1975) 38 MLR 314.

Jenkins, S., 'School for control freaks', *The Times*, 25 October 1995.

Leigh, I., 'The Gulf War deportations and the courts' [1991] PL 331.

Lenaerts, K., 'Fundamental rights to be included in a Community catalogue', (1991) 16 *EL Rev* 367.

Lester, A., 'An agenda for real reform', *Observer*, 20 November 1994.

Loughlin, M., 'Courts and governance', SPTL Seminar, 23 January 1993.

Lustgarten, L., 'The Security Services Act 1989' (1989) 52 MLR 80.

Lyon, A., 'Negligence and the field of battle', *New Law Journal*, 17 January 1997.

Mackenzie, J., 'Courts martial and human rights', *New Law Journal*, 19 January 1996, p. 48.

Mackenzie, J., 'The army and the rule of law', *New Law Journal*, 10 May 1996.

Mancini, G.F., 'The making of a constitution for Europe' (1989) 26 CML Rev 595.

Mitchell, J.D.B., 'The royal prerogative in modern Scots law' [1957] PL 304.

Mitchell, J.D.B., 'Causes and effects of the absence of a system of public law' [1965] PL 95.

Riddell, P., 'MPs have much to learn from Nolan and Scott', *The Times*, 22 March 1996.

Riddell, P., 'Cabinets codes and the courts', *The Times*, 13 May 1996.

Scarman, Lord, 'Declaration of the rights of Britons', *Guardian*, 14 November 1988.

Scarman, Lord, 'A Bill of Rights could become the conscience of the nation', *Independent*, 9 June 1989.

Sedley, S., 'The sound of silence: constitutional law without a constitution' (1994) 110 LQR 270.

Shawcross, W., 'The mysterious monarch', *The Sunday Times*, 14 April 1996.

Steketee, M., 'Whatever happened to the republic?', *Australian*, 7 September 1996.

Stent, R., 'The internment of Her Majesty's loyal enemy aliens' (1981) 9 *Oral History* 24.

Stephens, P., 'Seductive words: Tony Blair's vision of constitutional reform', *Financial Times*, 2 February 1996.

Szyszczak, E., 'Making Europe more relevant to its citizens: effective judicial process', (1996) 21 EL Rev. 351.

Thornberry, C., 'Dr Soblen and the alien law of the United Kingdom' (1963) 12 ICLQ 414.

Tomkins, A., 'A right to mislead Parliament?' (1996) 16 *Legal Studies* 63.

Vickers, L., 'Whistleblowing and freedom of speech in the NHS', *New Law Journal*, 18 August 1995, p. 1257.

Vincenzi, C., 'Aliens and the judicial review of immigration law' [1985] PL 93.

Vincenzi, C., 'Extra-statutory ministerial discretion in immigration law' [1992] PL 300.

Vincenzi, C., 'European citizenship and free movement rights in the United Kingdom' [1995] PL 259.

Wade, H.W.R., 'The rule of law only just upheld' (1992) 108 LQR 173.

Wade, H.W.R., 'The Crown – old platitudes and new heresies', *New Law Journal*, 18 September 1992.

Walker, C., 'Review of the prerogative: the remaining issues' [1987] PL 62.

Walker, P., 'What's wrong with irrationality?' [1995] PL 556.

Woodhouse, D. 'Ministerial responsibility: something old, something new', [1997] PL 262.

Zellick, G., 'To whom do civil servants owe loyalty?', *New Law Journal*, 12 October 1990.

REPORTS

Report of the Committee on the Political Activities of Civil Servants, Cmd 7718, 1949.

Report of the Public Accounts Committee (Session 1981–1982) HC 339.

Fourth Report from the House of Commons Defence Committee (1985–86).

Seventh Report from the Treasury and Civil Service Committee, Vol. II (1985–86) HC 92.

Fourth Report from the Select Committee on Procedure: The Scrutiny of European Legislation (1988–89) HC 622.

Second Report from the Select Committee on Procedure: The Working of the Select Committee System (1988–89) HC 19.

Seventh Report from the Treasury and Civil Service Committee: The Next Steps Initiative (1990–91) HC 496.

First Report from the Select Committee on Procedure: Review of the European Standing Committees (1991–92) HC 31.

Questions of Procedure for Ministers (1992).

Report of the Royal Trustees 1993, The Times, 13 July 1996.

Administrative Law: Judicial Review and Statutory Appeals, Law Com. No. 226, HC 669 (26 October 1994).

Sir Richard Scott, V-C, *Report of the Inquiry into Export of Defence Equipment and Dual-use Goods to Iraq and Related Prosecutions*, HC 115, 1996.

Rights Brought Home: The Human Rights Bill CM 3782, October 1997.

Index

Abolition of Feudal Tenures Act
(1660), 241
Act of Settlement (1700), 16, 92,
191, 252
acts of state, 148, 161–3
Adeane, Sir Michael, 73, 74
Albert, Prince Regent, 65, 314
Alexandra, Princess, 80
Alice, Princess, 80
Alien Labour Act, 98
Aliens Act (1793), 122–3
Aliens Act (1905), 90, 103, 147
Aliens Order (1953), 149
Aliens Restriction Act (1914), 100,
133, 134, 147
Aliens Restriction Order (1914),
147
Allason, Rupert, 221
Allied Forces Act (1940), 125, 148
Amekrane (Moroccan airforce
officer), 150
American Declaration of
Independence (1776), 18
American War of Independence, 250
Andrew, HRH The Duke of York,
80, 82
Anne, Queen, 25, 76, 250
Anne, The Princess Royal, 80, 82
Aristotle, 280
armed forces *see under* national

defence and the security
services
Armed Forces Act (1966), 115
Armed Forces Act (1996), 118
Armstrong, Sir Robert: *Note of
Guidance on the Duties and
Responsibilities of Civil Servants
in Relation to Ministers*, 183
Army Act (1955), 118
Army (Rules of Procedure 1976),
118
Arrowsmith, Susan, 217
'Articles of War', 120
Ascension Island, 247
Asquith, Herbert, Earl of Oxford
and Asquith, 71, 122
Assent Act (1967), 25
Association Agreement with
Turkey, 160
Asylum and Immigration Act
(1996), 107, 161, 289
Asylum and Immigration Appeals
Act (1993), 106, 107,
149–50, 155, 161
asylum applications, 150–51, 274
Atiyah, P.S., 251
Atkin, Lord, 9, 107, 132, 193
Atkinson, Lord, 53–4, 98, 99
Attlee, Clement, Earl, 72, 73, 75,
170